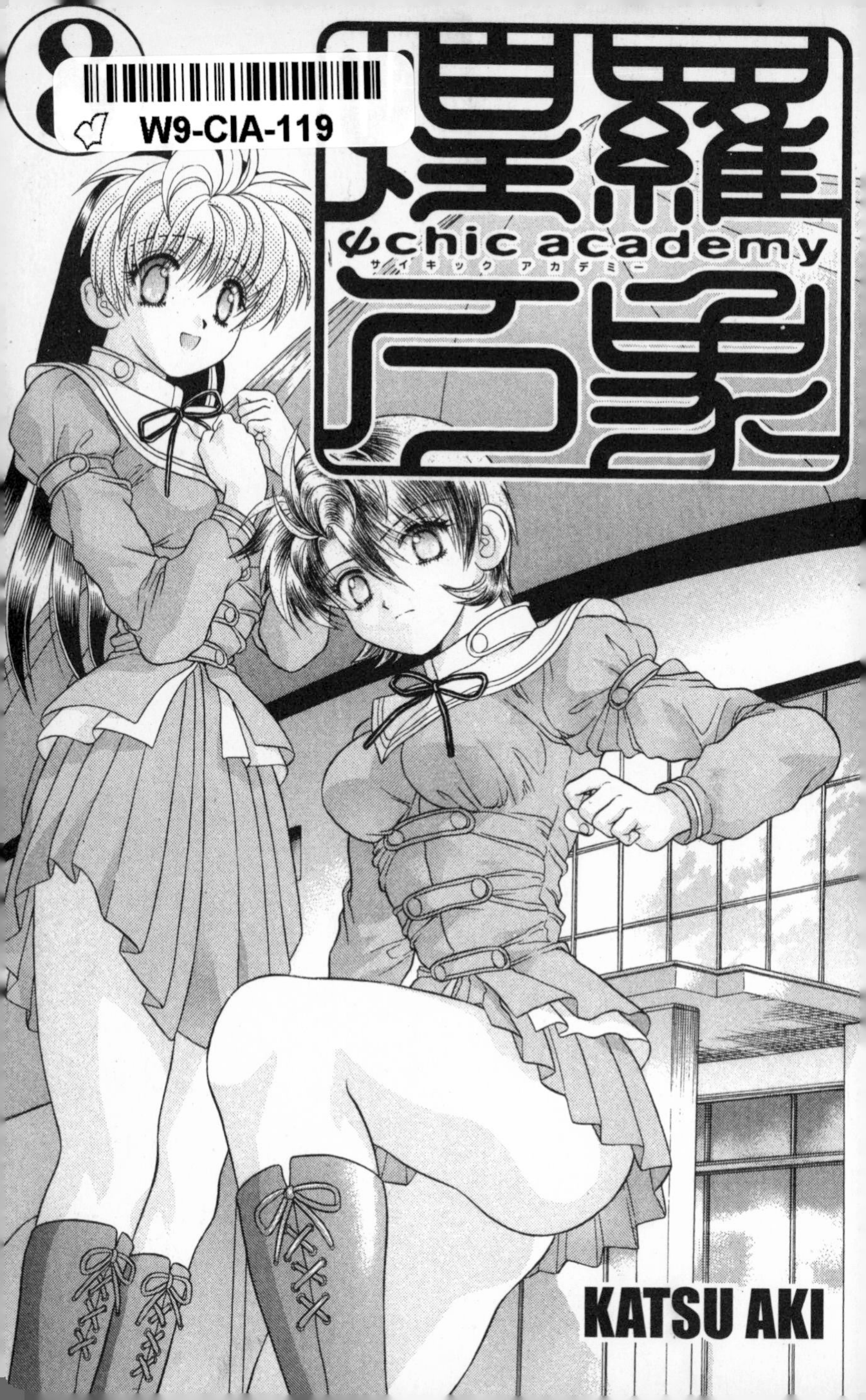
8
煌羅
ψchic academy
サイキックアカデミー
万象
KATSU AKI

PSYCHIC ACADEMY

VOLUME 8

By
Katsu Aki

TOKYOPOP®

HAMBURG // LONDON // LOS ANGELES // TOKYO

Psychic Academy Vol. 8
Created by Katsu Aki

Translation - Yuki N. Johnson
English Adaptation - Nathan Johnson
Copy Editors - Peter Ahlstrom and Aaron Sparrow
Retouch and Lettering - Lucas Rivera
Production Artist - Jason Milligan
Cover Design - Seth Cable

Editor - Aaron Suhr
Digital Imaging Manager - Chris Buford
Pre-Press Manager - Antonio DePietro
Production Managers - Jennifer Miller and Mutsumi Miyazaki
Art Director - Matt Alford
Managing Editor - Jill Freshney
VP of Production - Ron Klamert
Editor-in-Chief - Mike Kiley
President and C.O.O. - John Parker
Publisher and C.E.O. - Stuart Levy

A  TOKYOPOP® Manga

TOKYOPOP Inc.
5900 Wilshire Blvd. Suite 2000
Los Angeles, CA 90036

E-mail: info@TOKYOPOP.com
Come visit us online at www.TOKYOPOP.com

ISBN: 1-59532-427-5

First TOKYOPOP printing: June 2005
10 9 8 7 6 5 4 3 2 1
Printed in the USA

Story Thus Far...

PSYCHIC ACADEMY

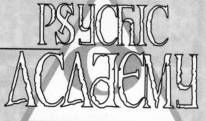

Zerodyme Kyupura Pa Azalraku Vairu Rua Darogu (a.k.a. Zero) stopped the evil demon lord with his incredible psychic ability, thereby saving the world from destruction and garnering the honorable and highly imaginative title "The Vanquisher of the Dark Overlord." Now he has accepted a position as teacher at Psychic Academy, a school for gifted psychokinetic youngsters who have demonstrated incredible raw psychic powers and desire to learn how to hone their abilities. Among the student body is young Ai Shiomi, Zero's little brother, a somewhat meek boy who, despite his parents' prodding and his fraternal reputation, feels that his limited skills hardly warrant enrollment at the prestigious academy. However, everyone else is convinced that he, too, is destined for greatness—a lot of pressure for a boy just entering adolescence.

A kiss here, a touch there and secrets everywhere! A secluded motel is the perfect setting for a steamy romance between Ai and Orina ... or so they thought! Loving affection begins to simmer between Ai and Orina, until Ai senses Mew's cries for help in her fight against Tokimitsu. When he rushes to Mew's aid—leaving Orina in the dust—could Ai turn out to be the boy Mew has been looking for all her life?

CONTENTS

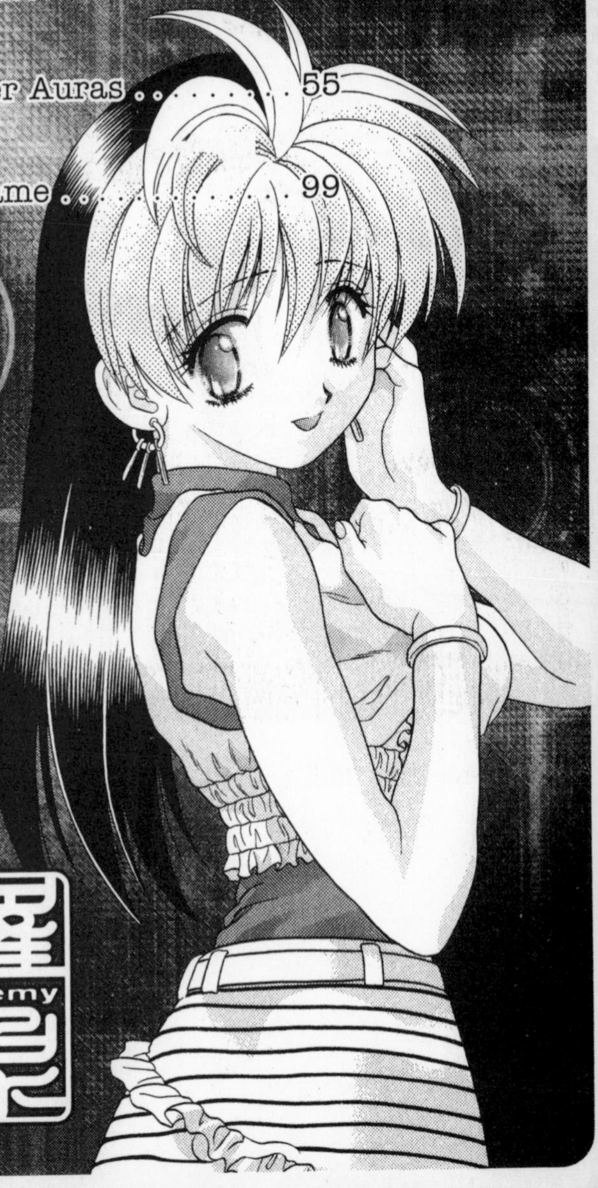

煌羅万象
ψchic academy

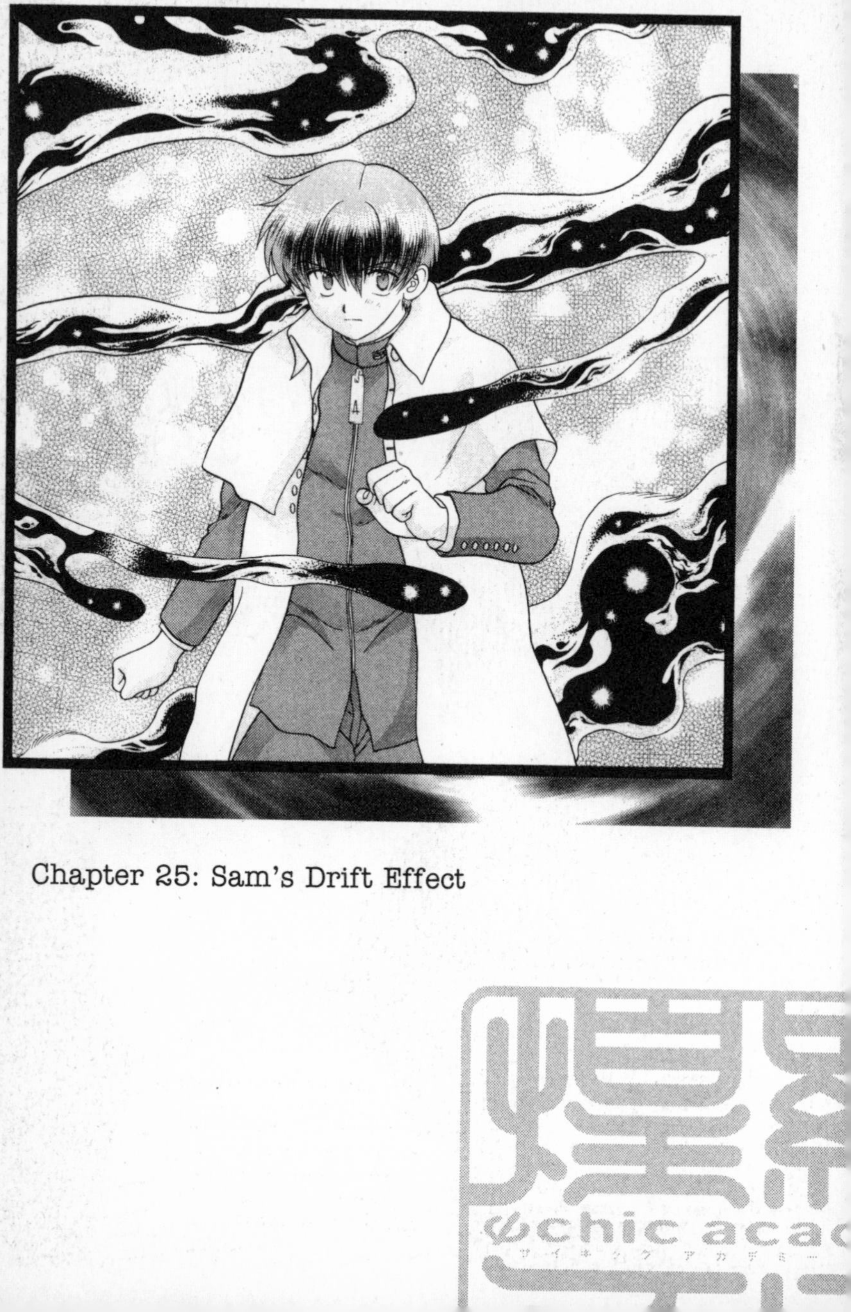

Chapter 25: Sam's Drift Effect

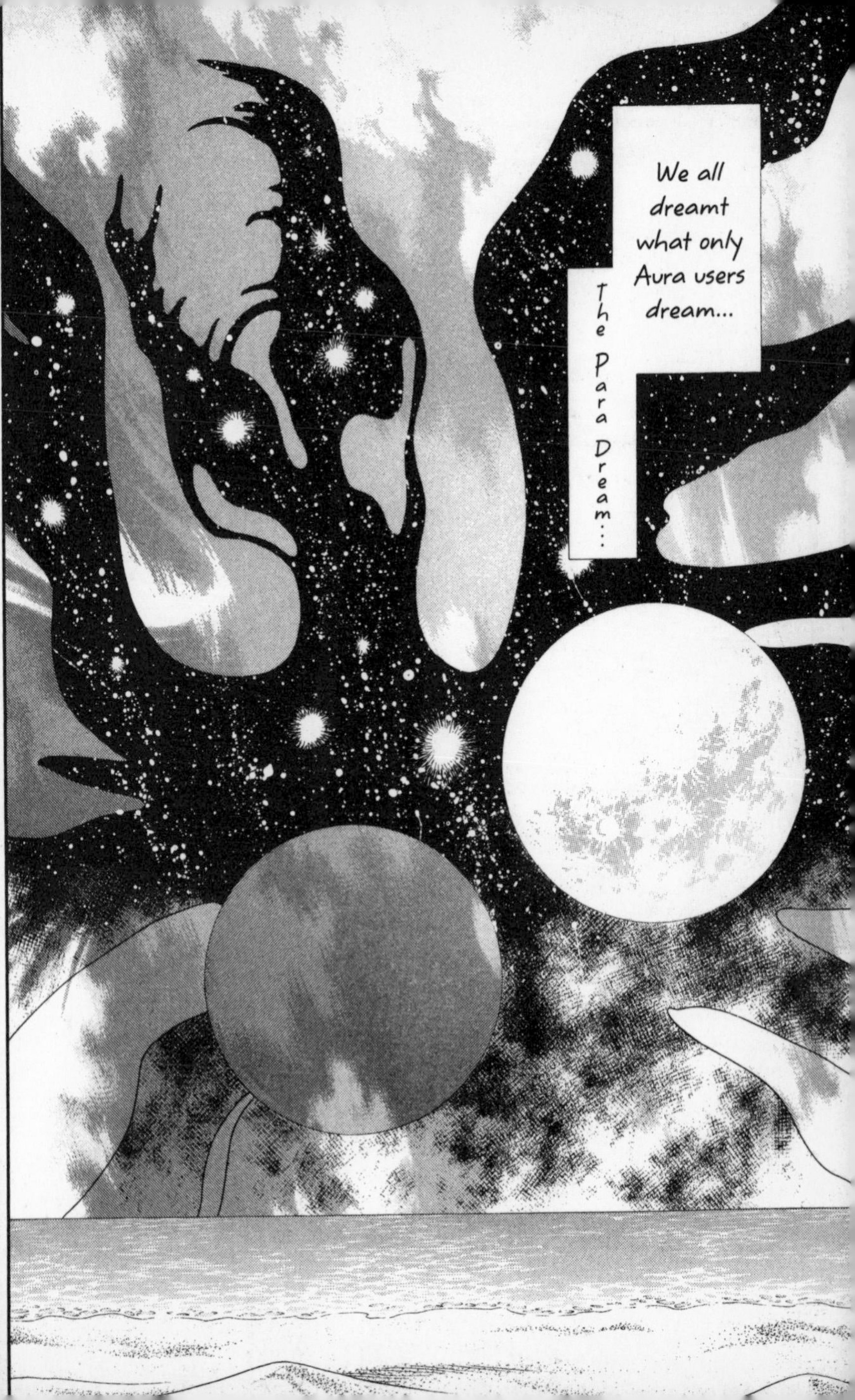
We all dreamt what only Aura users dream...
The Para Dream...

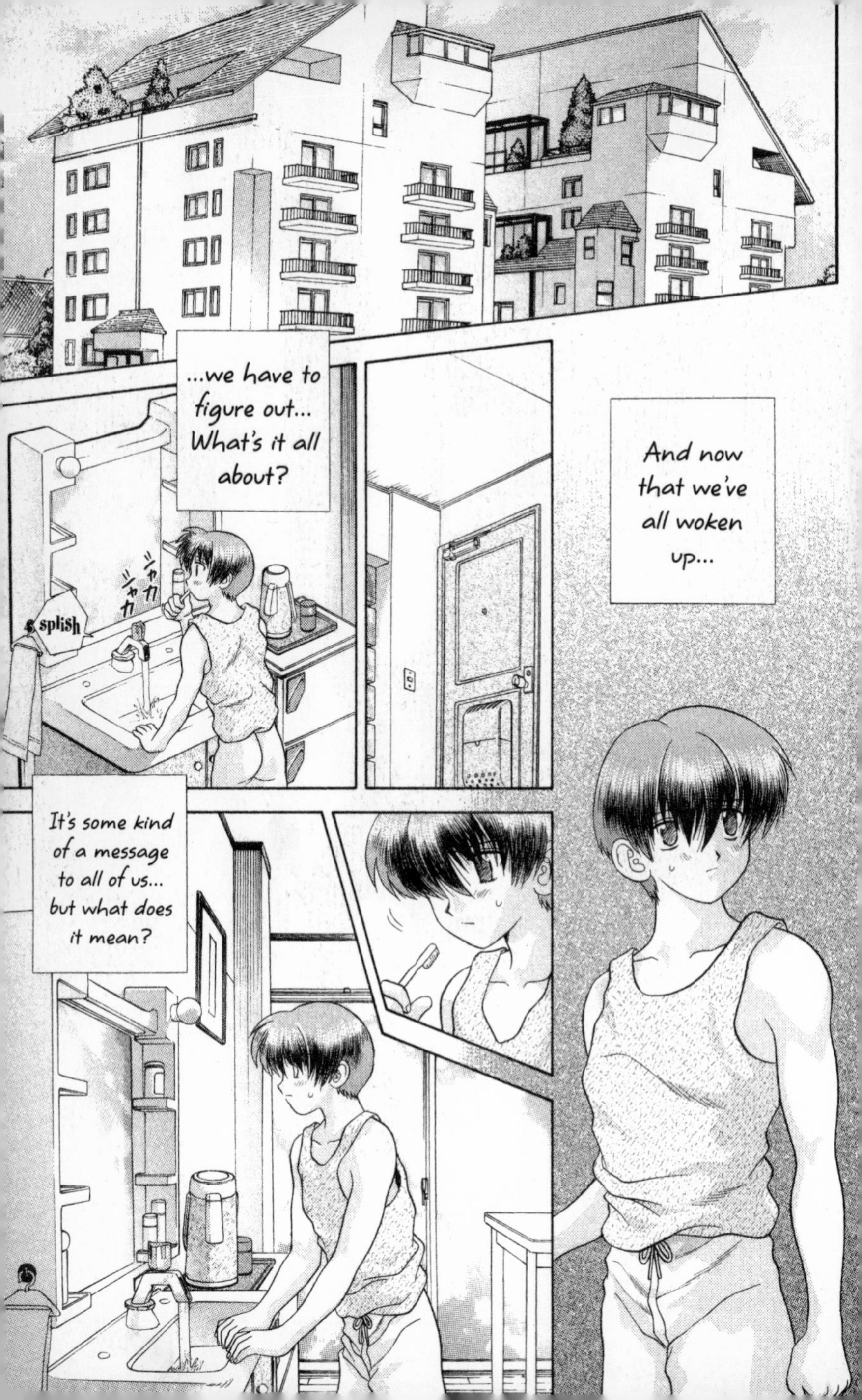
And now that we've all woken up...
...we have to figure out... What's it all about?
シャカ
シャカ
splish
It's some kind of a message to all of us... but what does it mean?

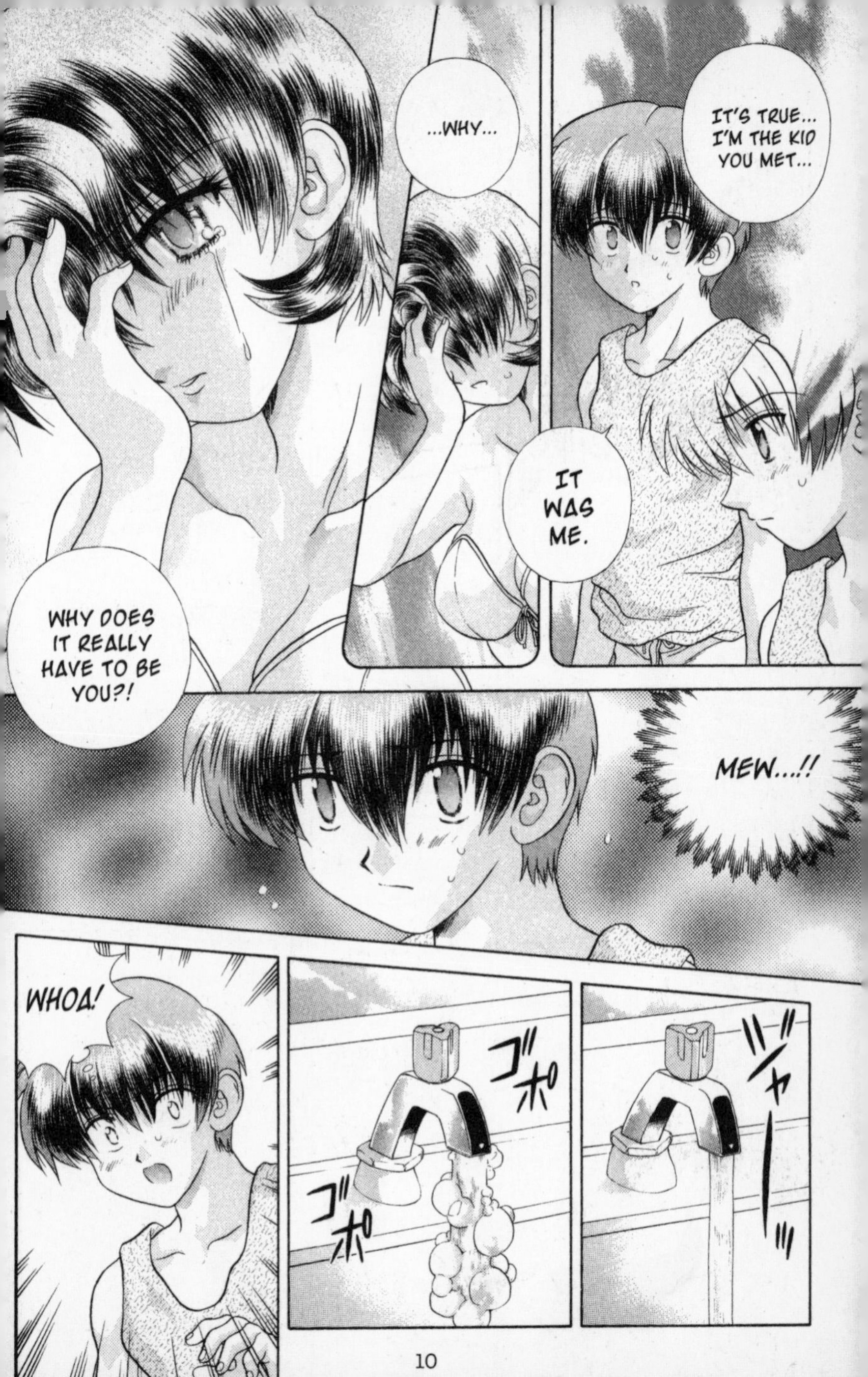
IT'S TRUE... I'M THE KID YOU MET...
IT WAS ME.
...WHY...
WHY DOES IT REALLY HAVE TO BE YOU?!
MEW...!!
ジャー
ゴポ
ゴポ
WHOA!

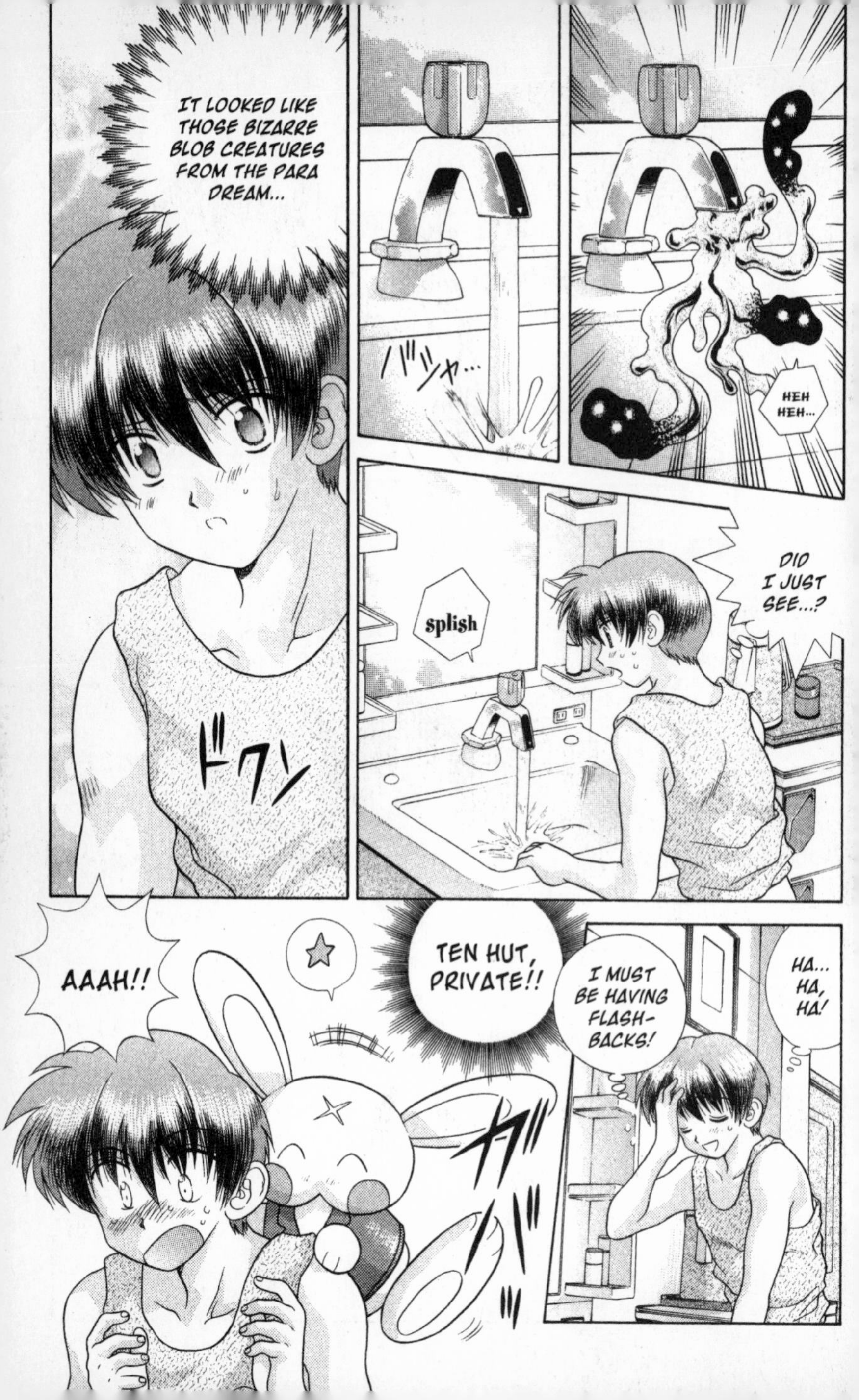
HEH HEH...
バシャ...
DID I JUST SEE...?
splish
IT LOOKED LIKE THOSE BIZARRE BLOB CREATURES FROM THE PARA DREAM...
ドクン
HA... HA, HA!
I MUST BE HAVING FLASH-BACKS!
TEN HUT, PRIVATE!!
AAAH!!

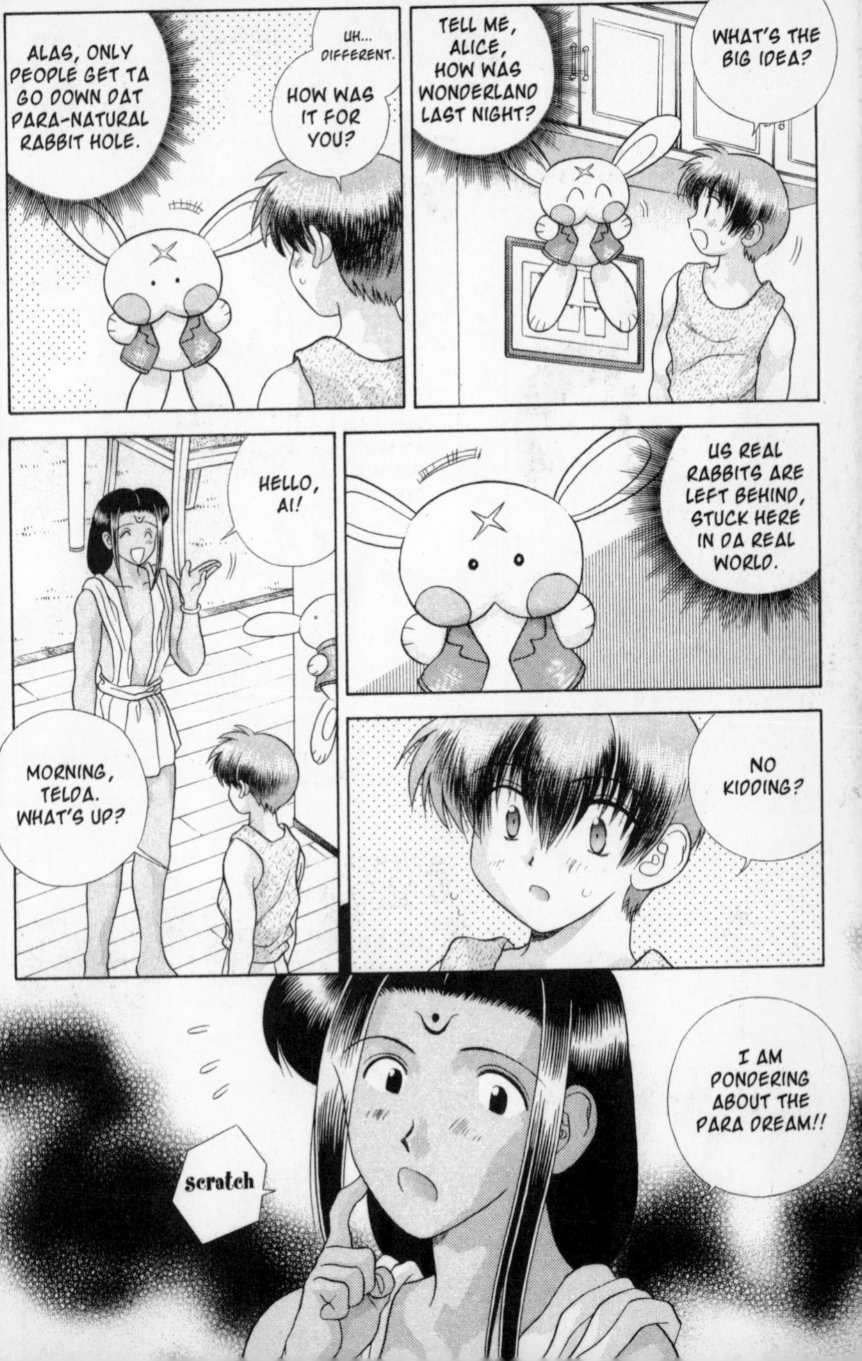
WHAT'S THE BIG IDEA?
TELL ME, ALICE, HOW WAS WONDERLAND LAST NIGHT?
UH... DIFFERENT.
HOW WAS IT FOR YOU?
ALAS, ONLY PEOPLE GET TA GO DOWN DAT PARA-NATURAL RABBIT HOLE.
US REAL RABBITS ARE LEFT BEHIND, STUCK HERE IN DA REAL WORLD.
NO KIDDING?
HELLO, AI!
MORNING, TELDA. WHAT'S UP?
I AM PONDERING ABOUT THE PARA DREAM!!
scratch

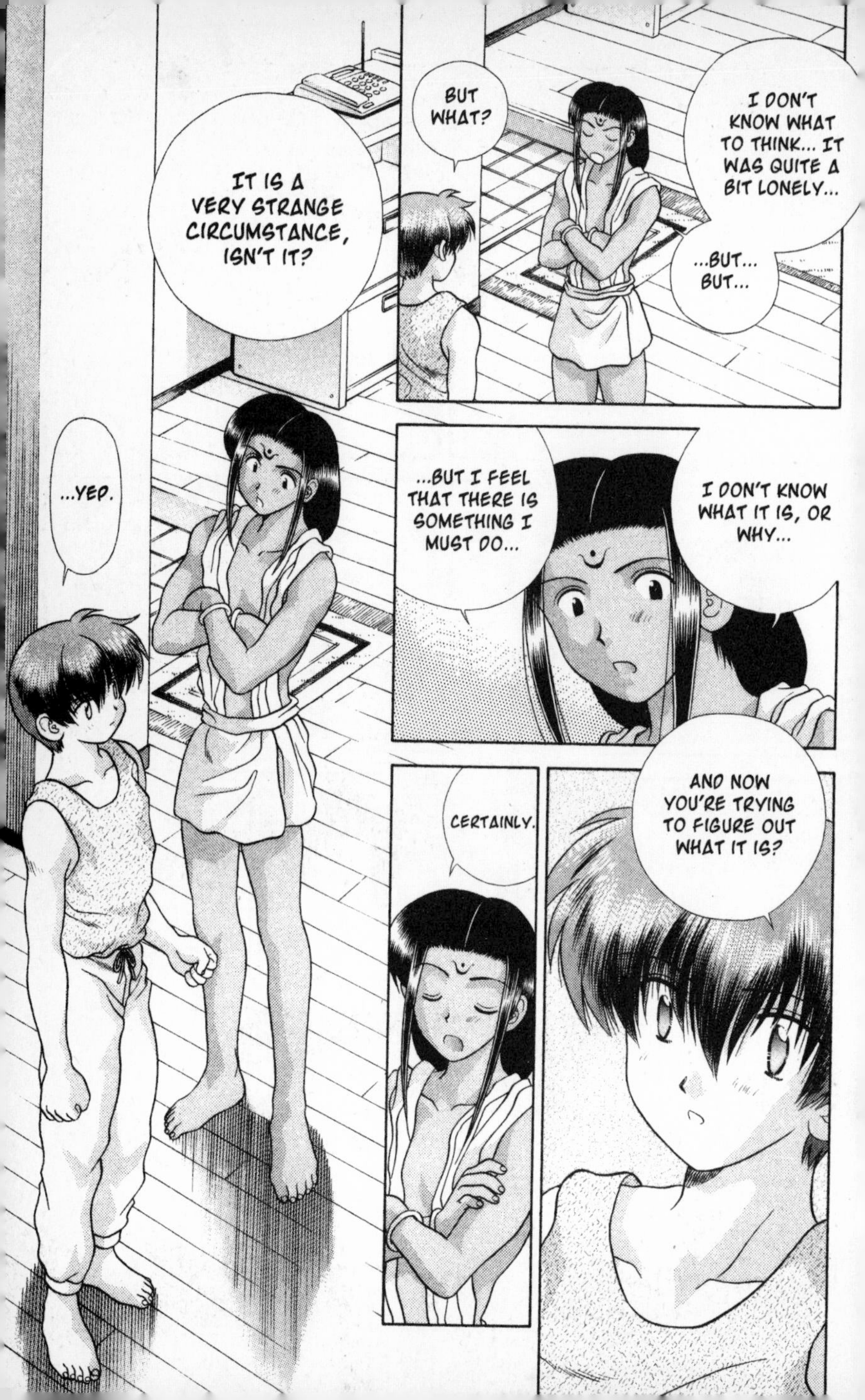
I DON'T KNOW WHAT TO THINK... IT WAS QUITE A BIT LONELY...
...BUT... BUT...
BUT WHAT?
I DON'T KNOW WHAT IT IS, OR WHY...
...BUT I FEEL THAT THERE IS SOMETHING I MUST DO...
AND NOW YOU'RE TRYING TO FIGURE OUT WHAT IT IS?
CERTAINLY.
IT IS A VERY STRANGE CIRCUMSTANCE, ISN'T IT?
...YEP.

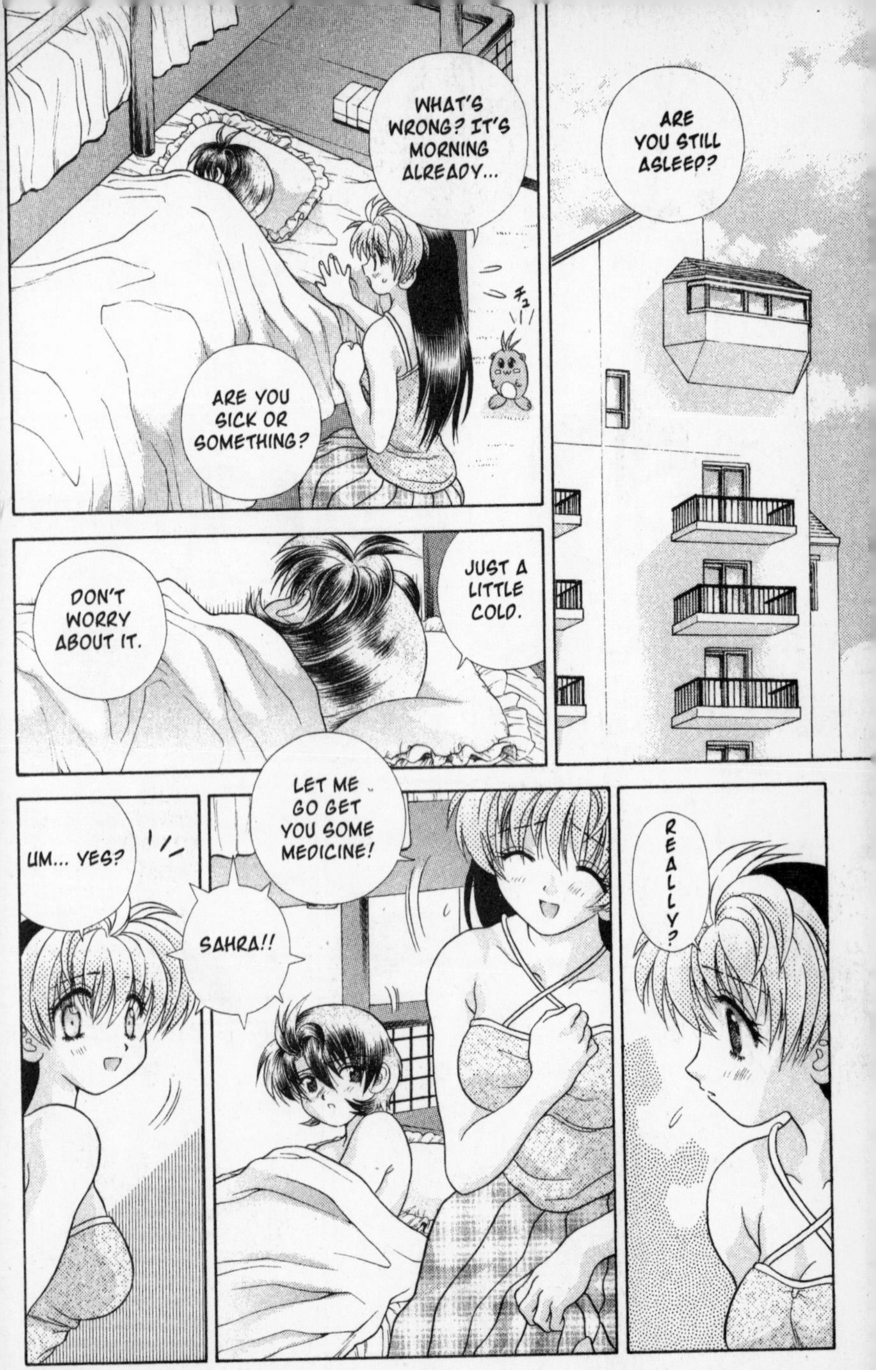
ARE YOU STILL ASLEEP?
WHAT'S WRONG? IT'S MORNING ALREADY...
チュ
ARE YOU SICK OR SOMETHING?
JUST A LITTLE COLD.
DON'T WORRY ABOUT IT.
REALLY?
LET ME GO GET YOU SOME MEDICINE!
SAHRA!!
UM... YES?

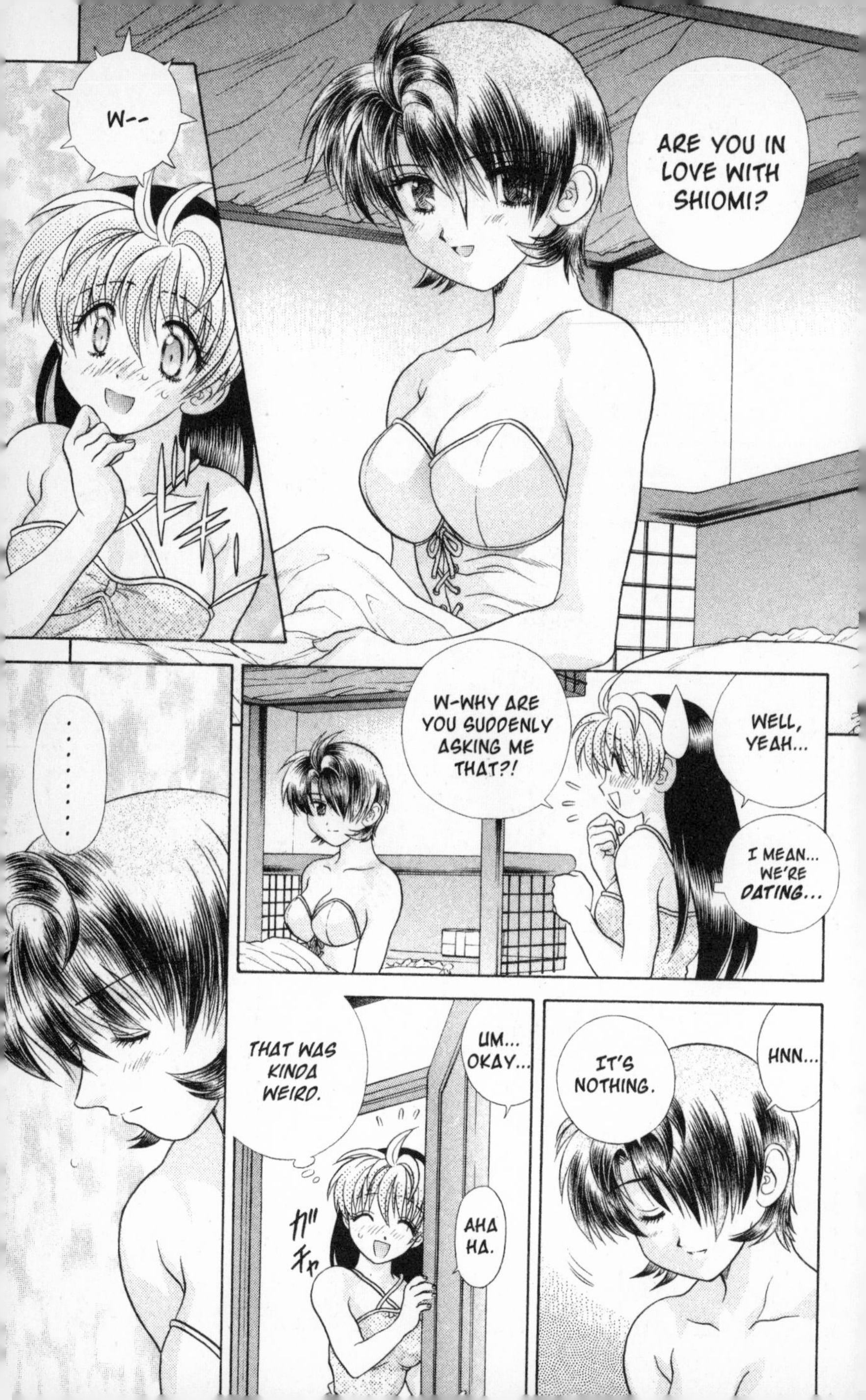
ARE YOU IN LOVE WITH SHIOMI?
W--
ドキ
WELL, YEAH...
I MEAN... WE'RE DATING...
W-WHY ARE YOU SUDDENLY ASKING ME THAT?!
......
HNN...
IT'S NOTHING.
UM... OKAY...
THAT WAS KINDA WEIRD.
AHA HA.
ガチャ

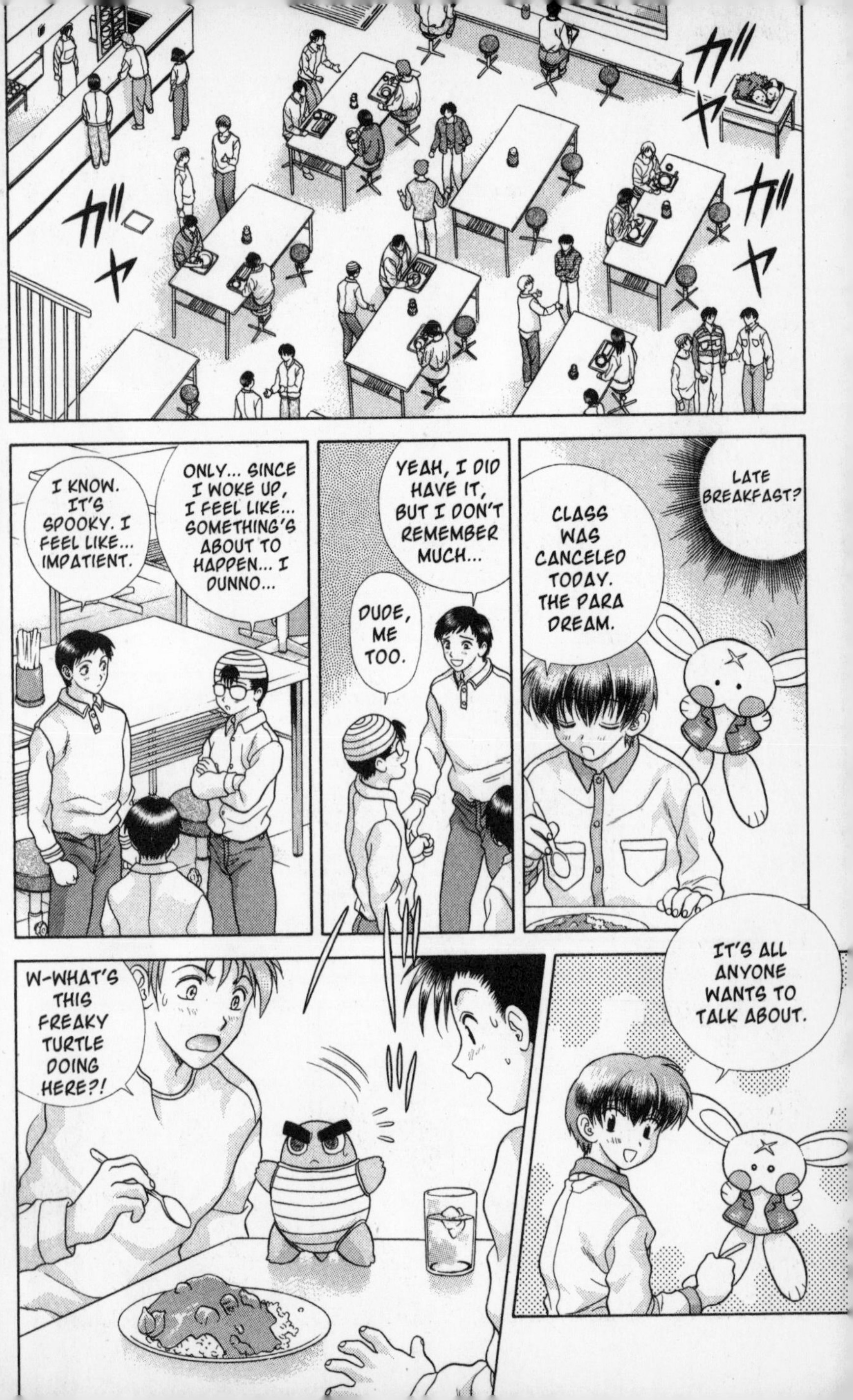
ガヤ
ガヤ
ガヤ
LATE BREAKFAST?
CLASS WAS CANCELED TODAY. THE PARA DREAM.
YEAH, I DID HAVE IT, BUT I DON'T REMEMBER MUCH...
DUDE, ME TOO.
ONLY... SINCE I WOKE UP, I FEEL LIKE... SOMETHING'S ABOUT TO HAPPEN... I DUNNO...
I KNOW. IT'S SPOOKY. I FEEL LIKE... IMPATIENT.
IT'S ALL ANYONE WANTS TO TALK ABOUT.
W-WHAT'S THIS FREAKY TURTLE DOING HERE?!

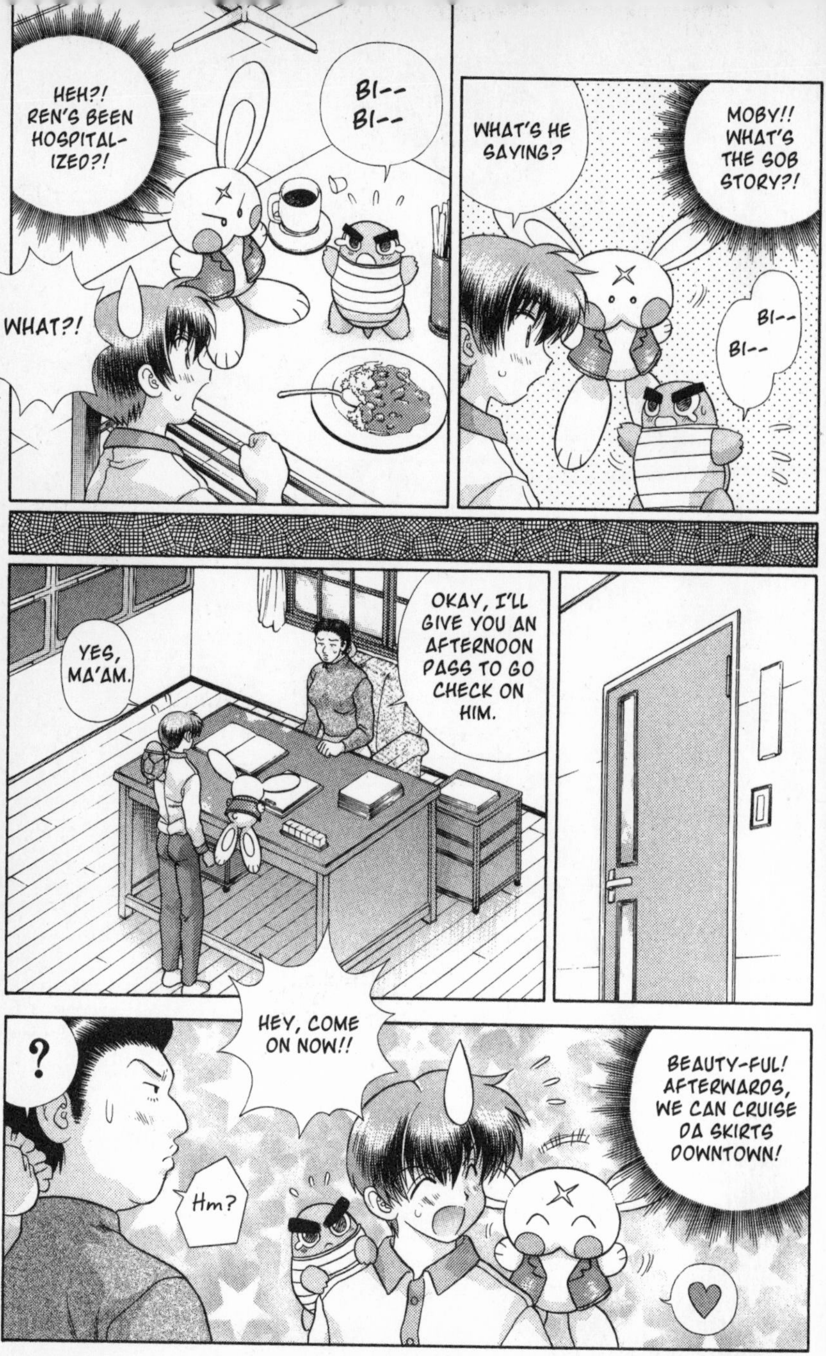

HEH?! REN'S BEEN HOSPITAL-IZED?!
BI-- BI--
WHAT?!
WHAT'S HE SAYING?
MOBY!! WHAT'S THE SOB STORY?!
BI-- BI--
YES, MA'AM.
OKAY, I'LL GIVE YOU AN AFTERNOON PASS TO GO CHECK ON HIM.
?
HEY, COME ON NOW!!
Hm?
BEAUTY-FUL! AFTERWARDS, WE CAN CRUISE DA SKIRTS DOWNTOWN!

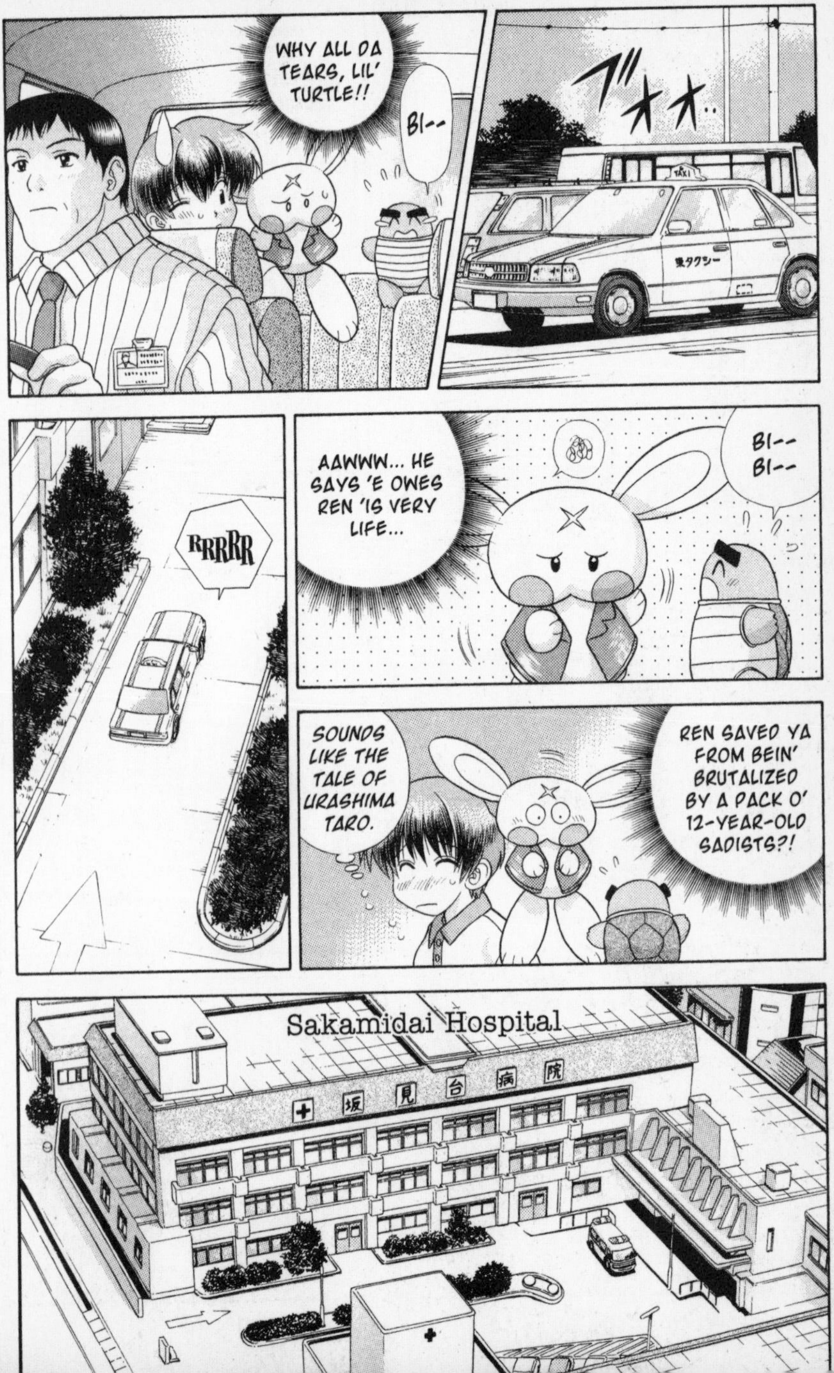
ブォォ..
TAXI
東タクシー
WHY ALL DA TEARS, LIL' TURTLE!!
BI--
BI-- BI--
AAWWW... HE SAYS 'E OWES REN 'IS VERY LIFE...
RRRRR
REN SAVED YA FROM BEIN' BRUTALIZED BY A PACK O' 12-YEAR-OLD SADISTS?!
SOUNDS LIKE THE TALE OF URASHIMA TARO.
Sakamidai Hospital
坂見台病院

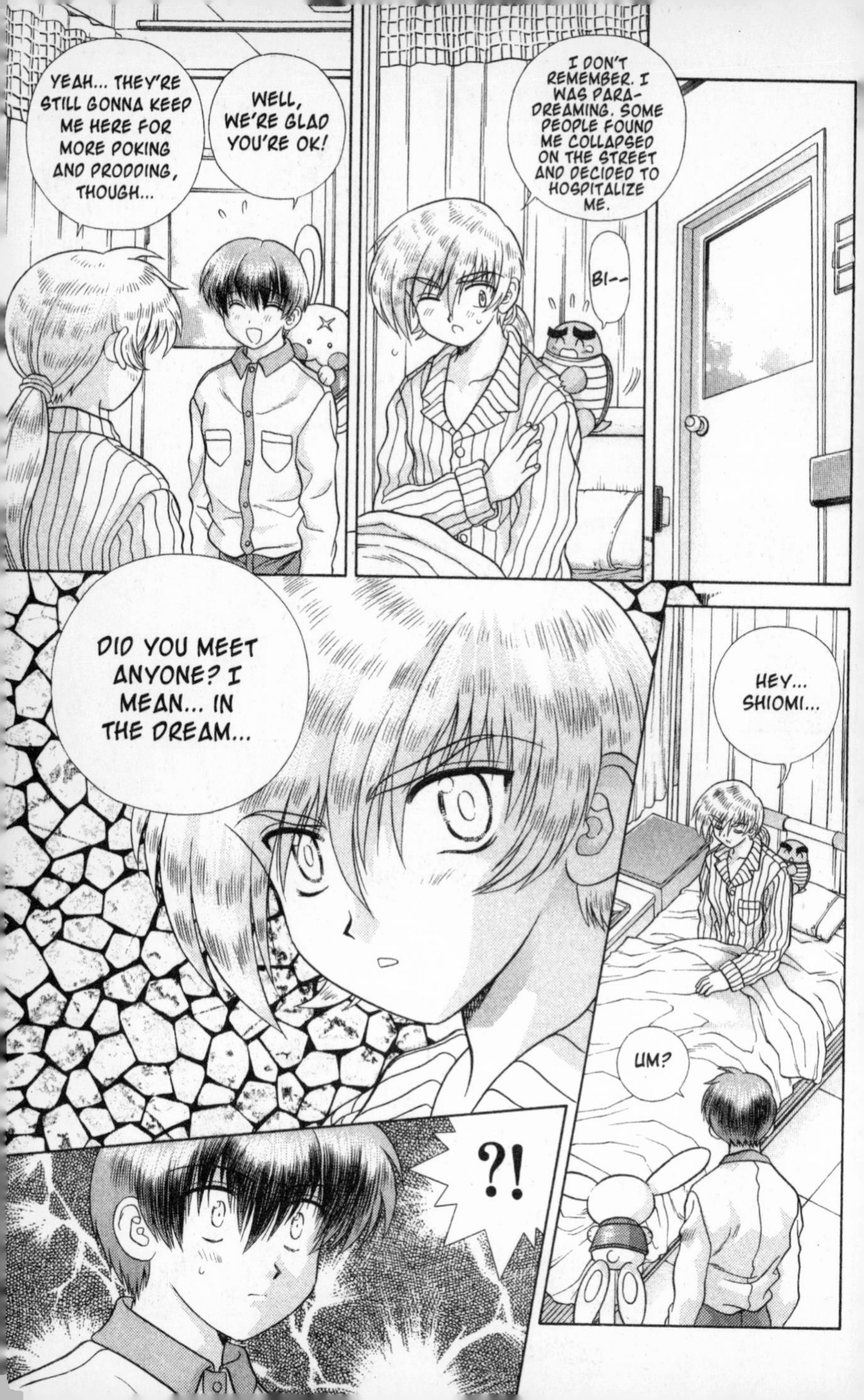
I DON'T REMEMBER. I WAS PARA-DREAMING. SOME PEOPLE FOUND ME COLLAPSED ON THE STREET AND DECIDED TO HOSPITALIZE ME.
BI--
WELL, WE'RE GLAD YOU'RE OK!
YEAH... THEY'RE STILL GONNA KEEP ME HERE FOR MORE POKING AND PRODDING, THOUGH...
HEY... SHIOMI...
UM?
DID YOU MEET ANYONE? I MEAN... IN THE DREAM...
?!

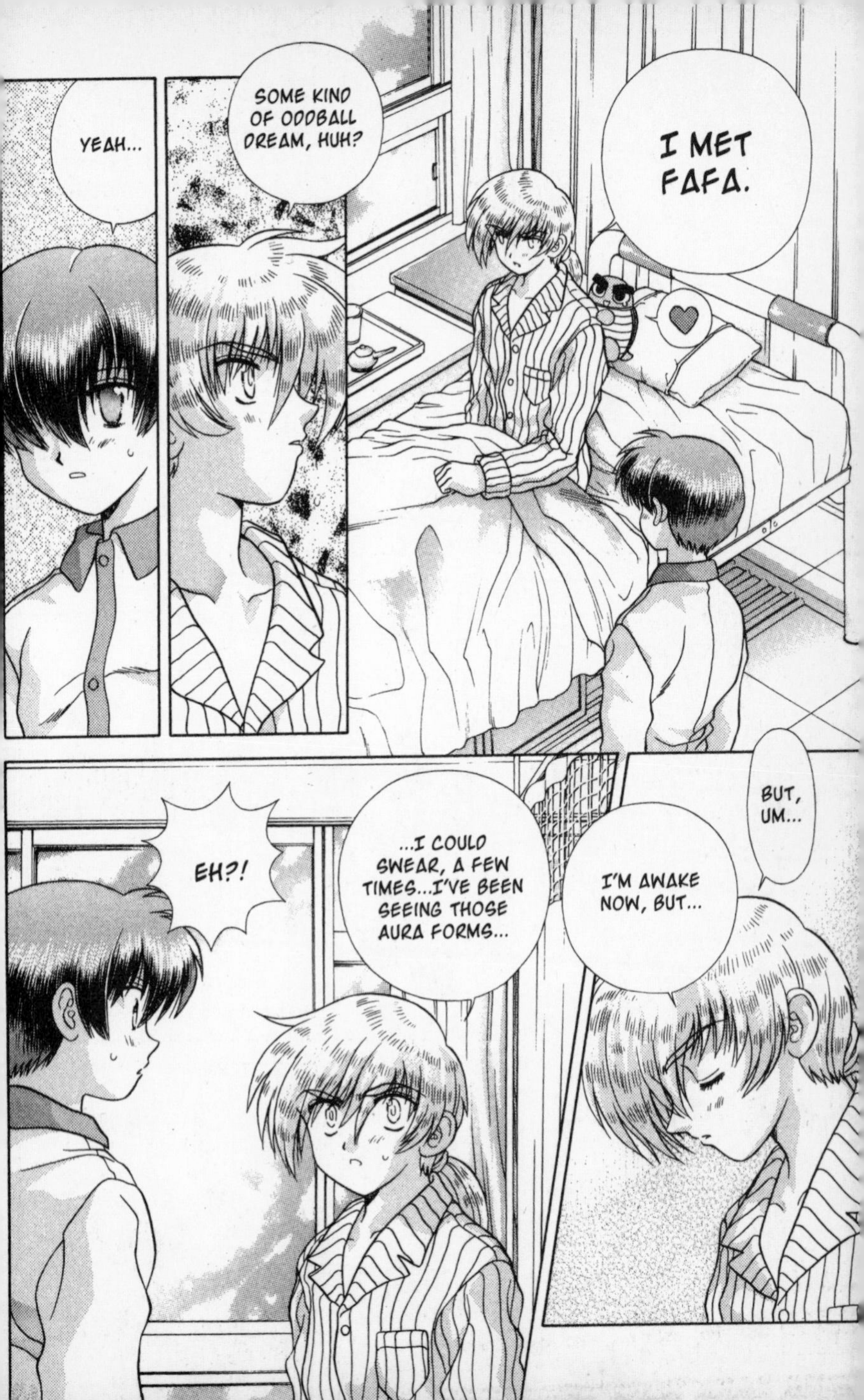
I MET FAFA.
SOME KIND OF ODDBALL DREAM, HUH?
YEAH...
BUT, UM...
I'M AWAKE NOW, BUT...
...I COULD SWEAR, A FEW TIMES...I'VE BEEN SEEING THOSE AURA FORMS...
EH?!

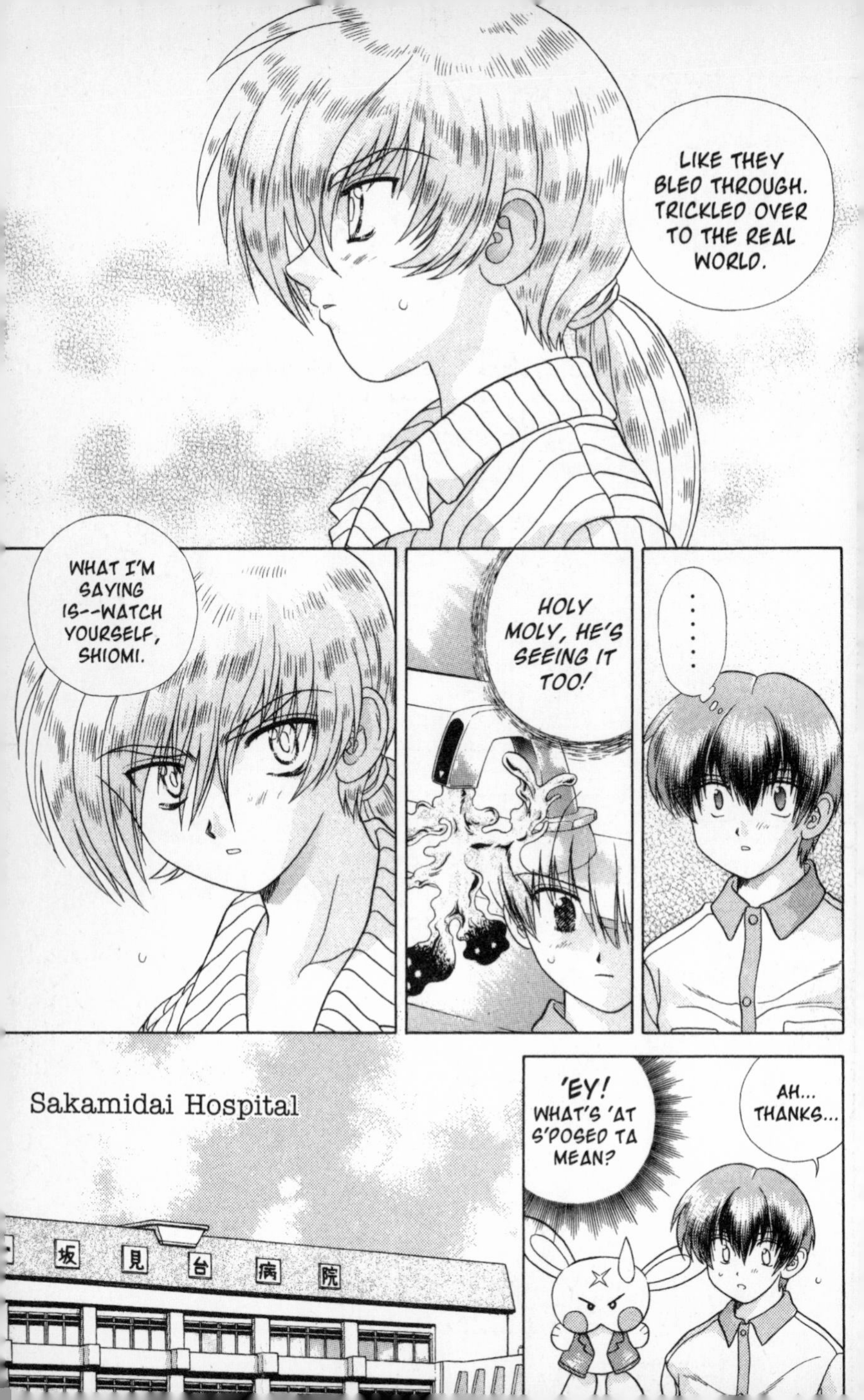
LIKE THEY BLED THROUGH. TRICKLED OVER TO THE REAL WORLD.
......
HOLY MOLY, HE'S SEEING IT TOO!
WHAT I'M SAYING IS--WATCH YOURSELF, SHIOMI.
AH... THANKS...
'EY! WHAT'S 'AT S'POSED TA MEAN?
Sakamidai Hospital
坂見台病院

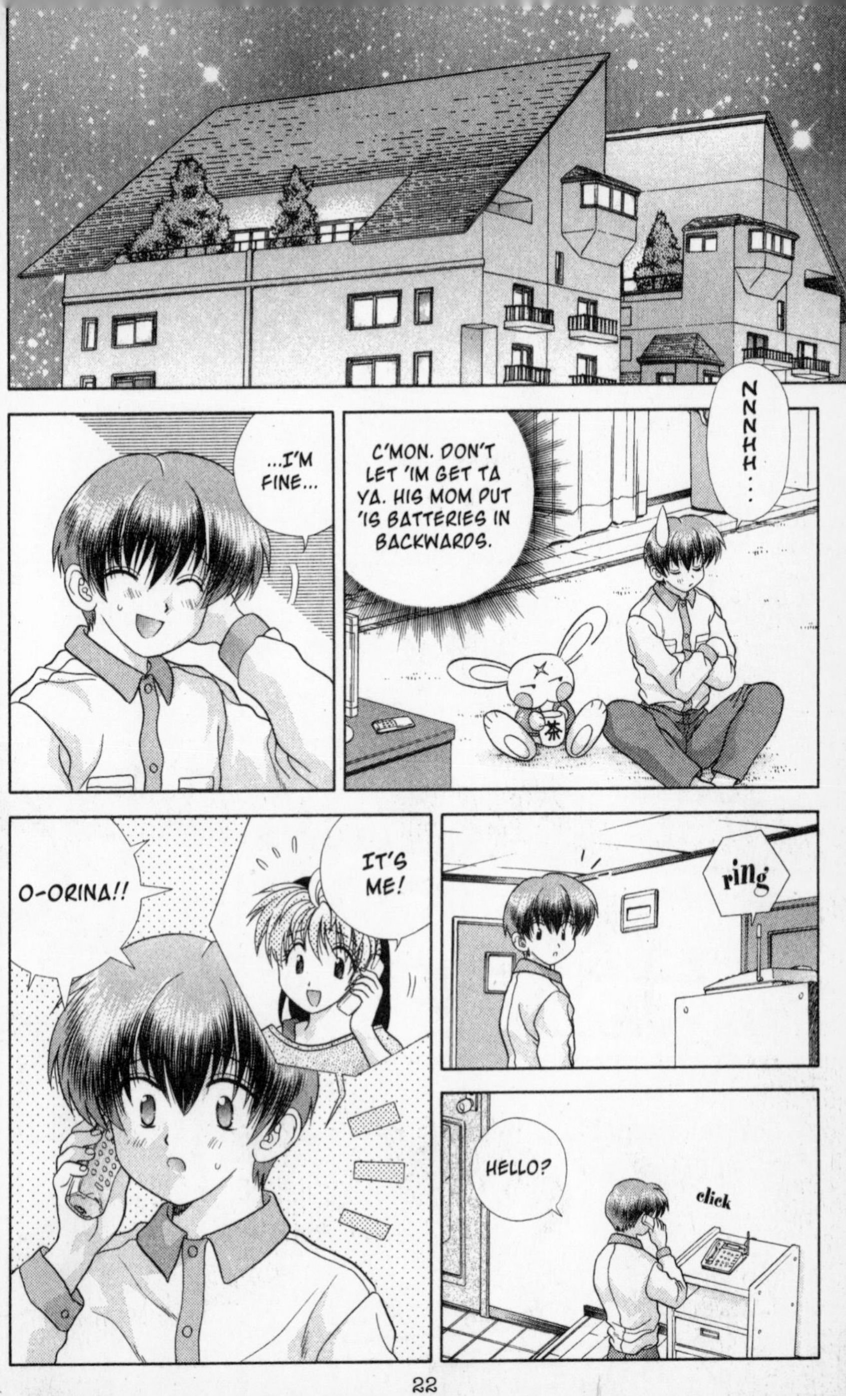
NNNHH...
C'MON. DON'T LET 'IM GET TA YA. HIS MOM PUT 'IS BATTERIES IN BACKWARDS.
...I'M FINE...
ring
HELLO?
click
IT'S ME!
O-ORINA!!

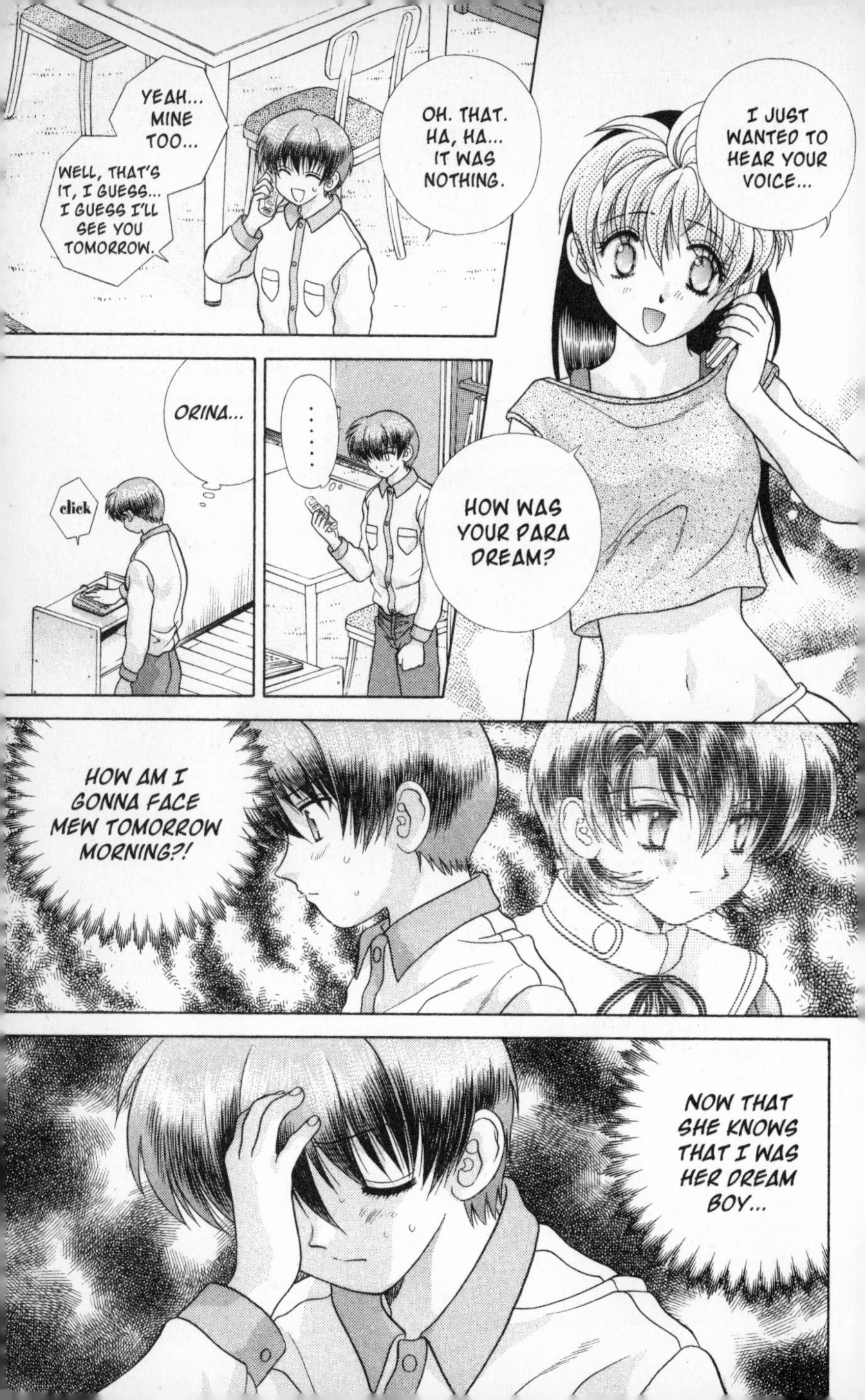
HOW WAS YOUR PARA DREAM?
OH. THAT. HA, HA... IT WAS NOTHING.
I JUST WANTED TO HEAR YOUR VOICE...
YEAH... MINE TOO...
WELL, THAT'S IT, I GUESS... I GUESS I'LL SEE YOU TOMORROW.
......
ORINA...
click
HOW AM I GONNA FACE MEW TOMORROW MORNING?!
NOW THAT SHE KNOWS THAT I WAS HER DREAM BOY...

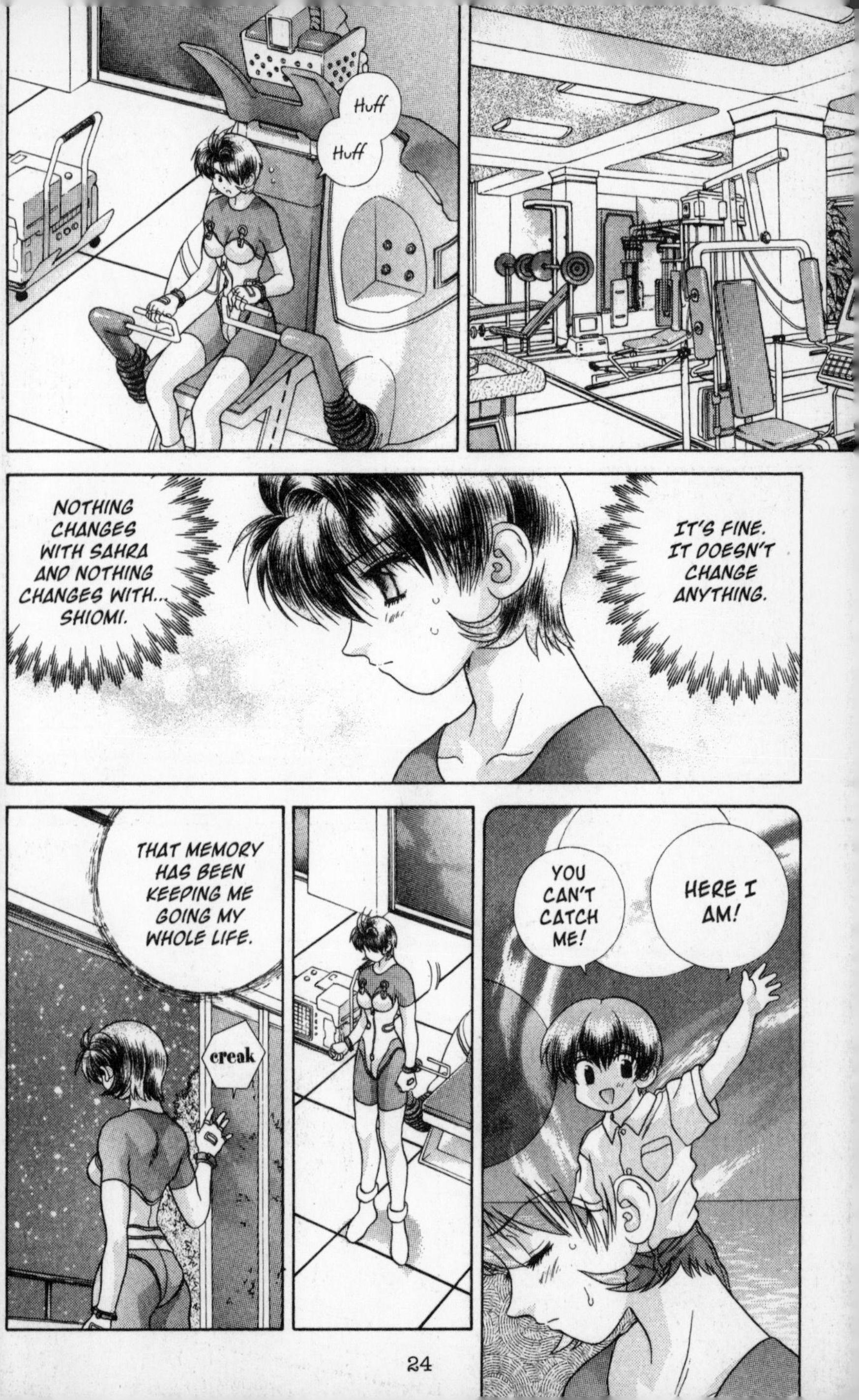
Huff
Huff
NOTHING CHANGES WITH SAHRA AND NOTHING CHANGES WITH... SHIOMI.
IT'S FINE. IT DOESN'T CHANGE ANYTHING.
THAT MEMORY HAS BEEN KEEPING ME GOING MY WHOLE LIFE.
creak
HERE I AM!
YOU CAN'T CATCH ME!

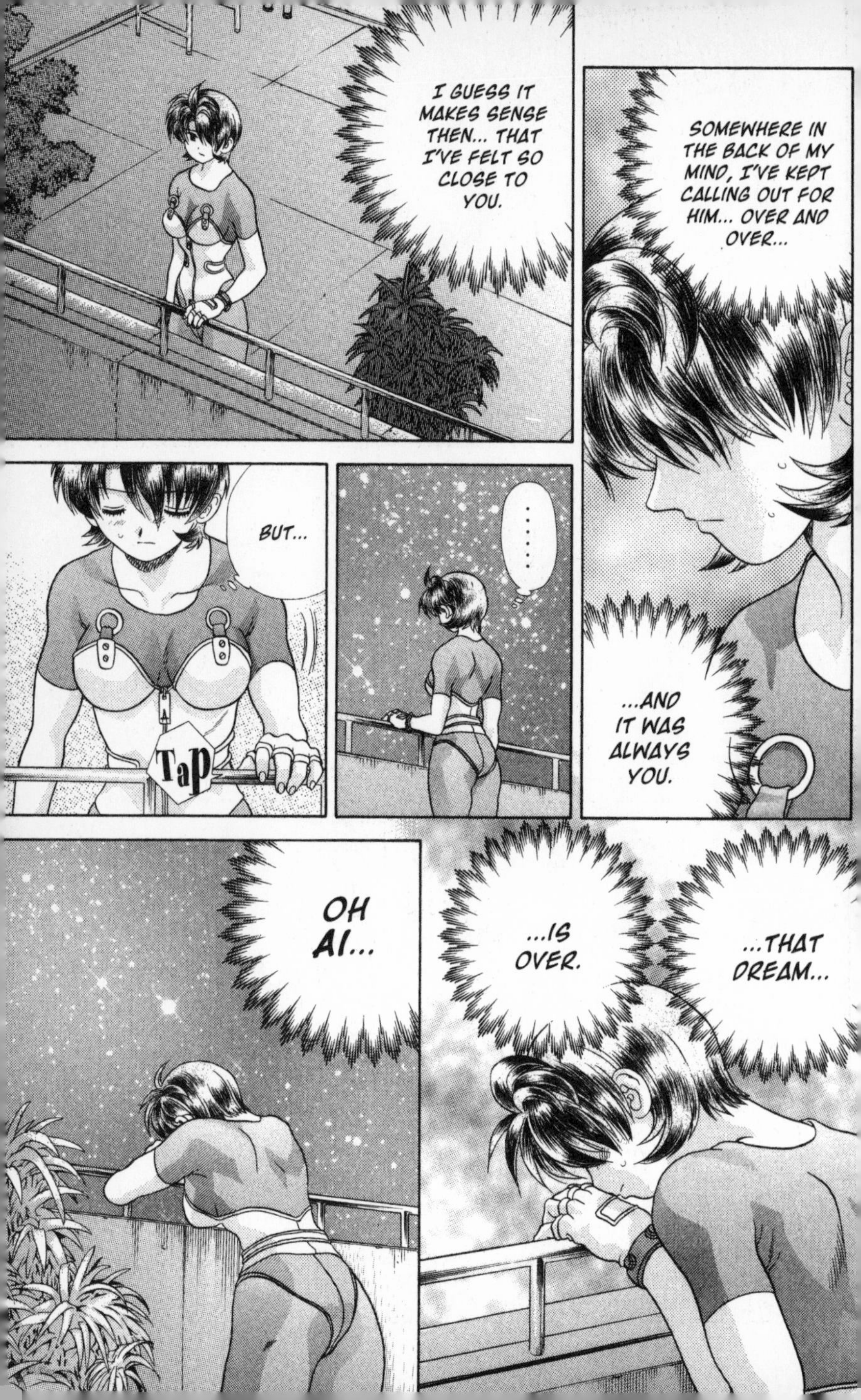
I GUESS IT MAKES SENSE THEN... THAT I'VE FELT SO CLOSE TO YOU.
SOMEWHERE IN THE BACK OF MY MIND, I'VE KEPT CALLING OUT FOR HIM... OVER AND OVER...
...AND IT WAS ALWAYS YOU.
......
BUT...
Tap
...THAT DREAM...
...IS OVER.
OH AI...

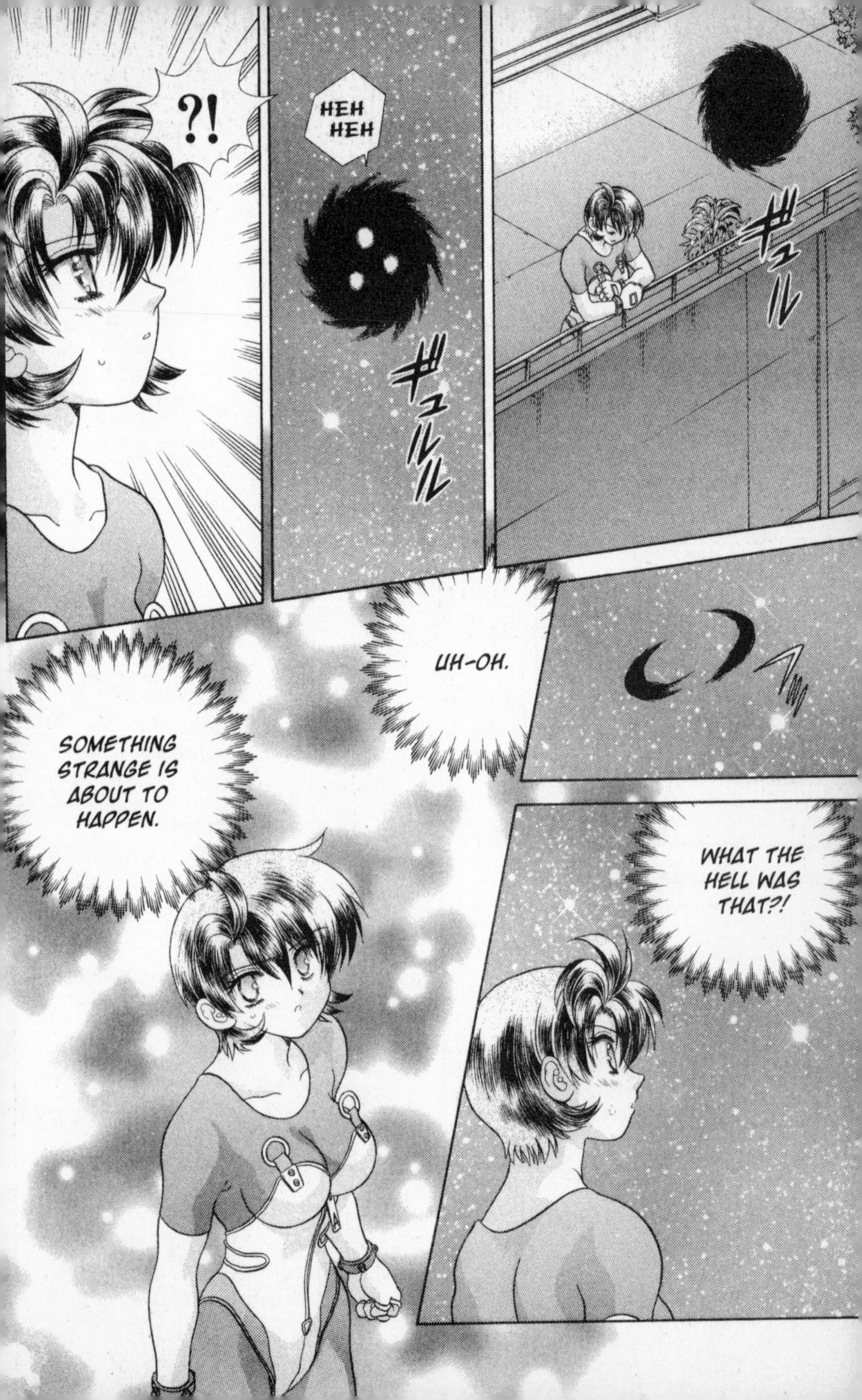
ギュル
HEH HEH
ギュルル
?!
UH-OH.
WHAT THE HELL WAS THAT?!
SOMETHING STRANGE IS ABOUT TO HAPPEN.

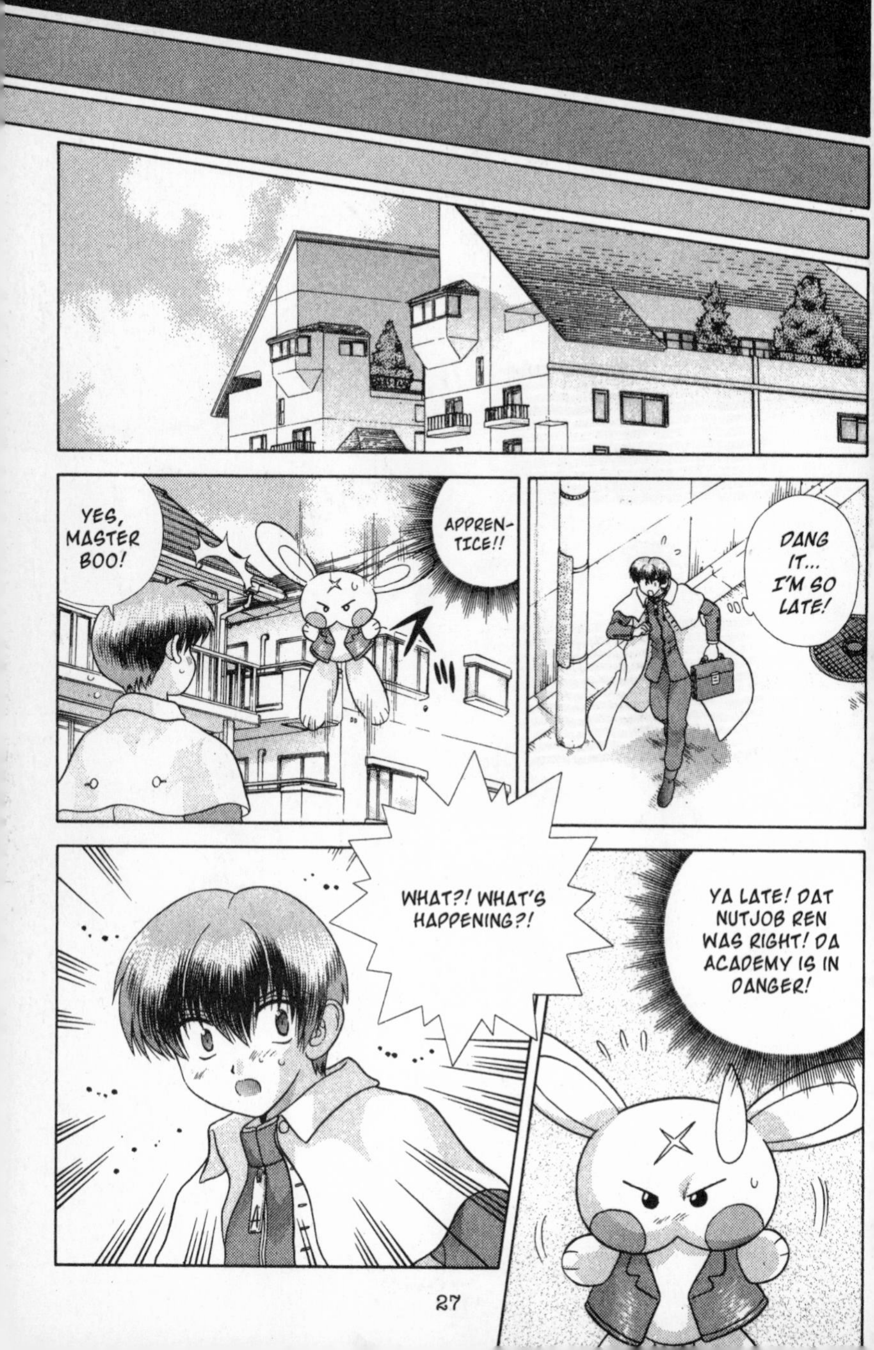
DANG IT... I'M SO LATE!
APPRENTICE!!
YES, MASTER BOO!
WHAT?! WHAT'S HAPPENING?!
YA LATE! DAT NUTJOB REN WAS RIGHT! DA ACADEMY IS IN DANGER!

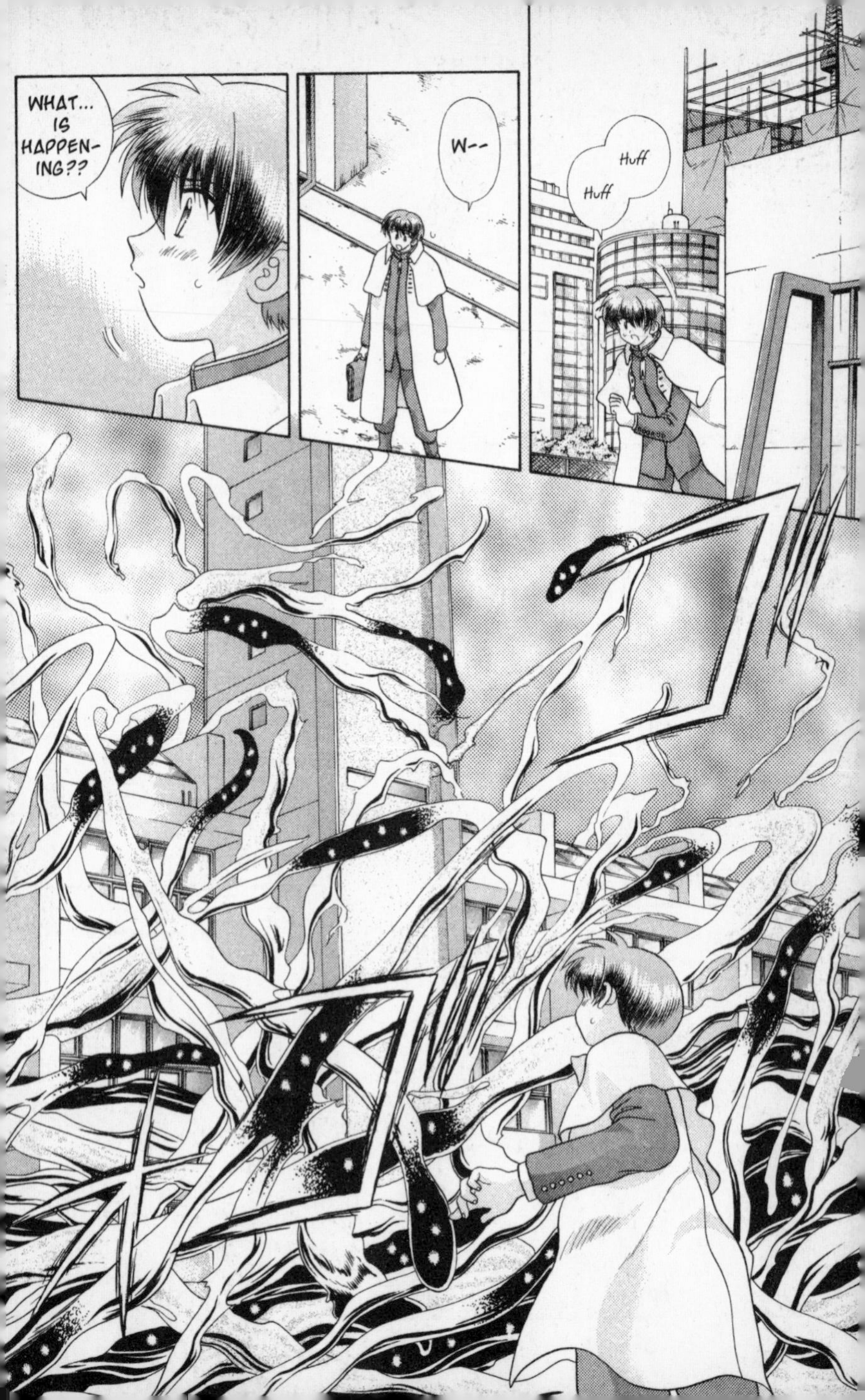

WHAT... IS HAPPENING??
W--
Huff
Huff

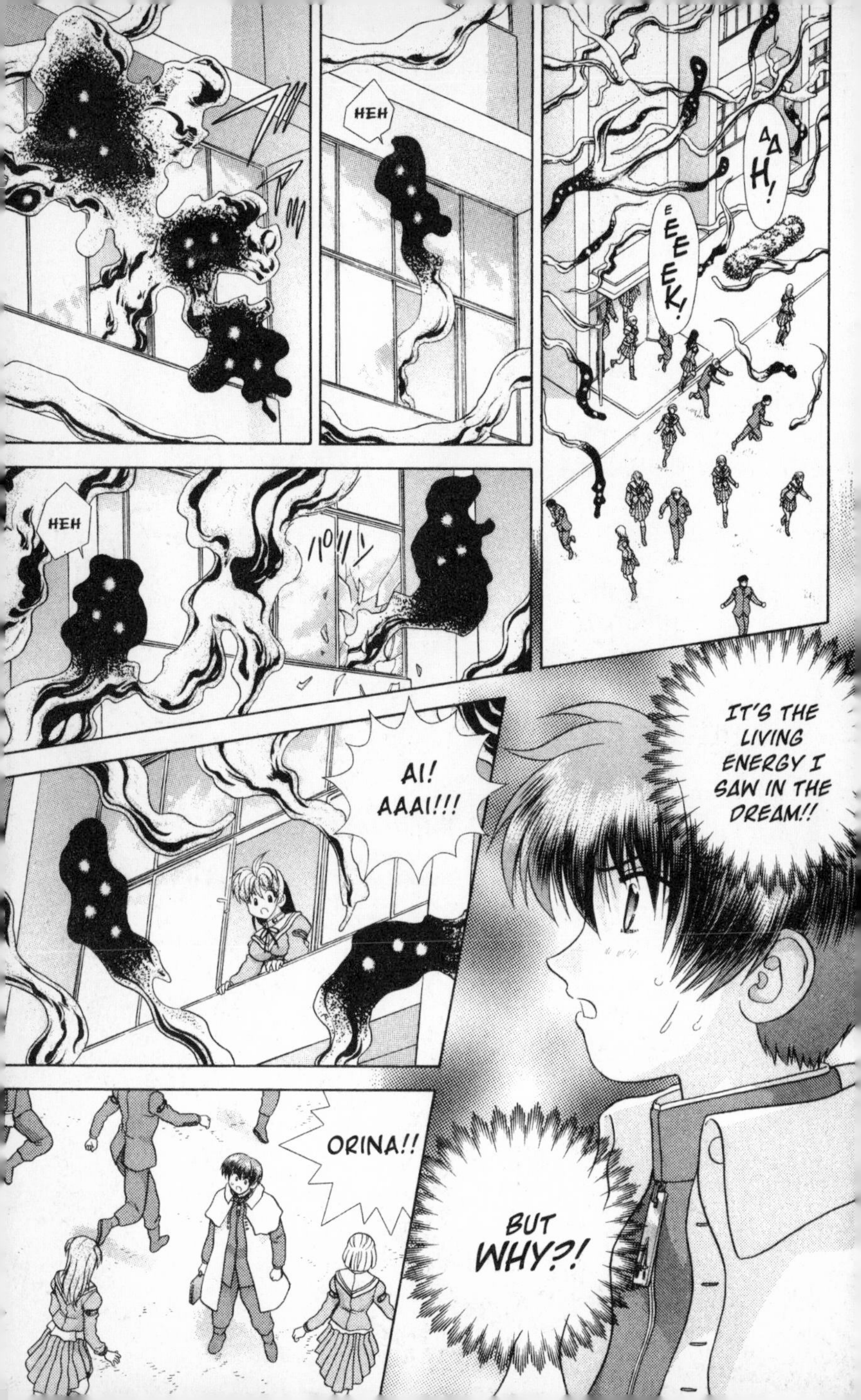

AAH!
EEEEK!
HEH
HEH
AI! AAAI!!!
IT'S THE LIVING ENERGY I SAW IN THE DREAM!!
ORINA!!
BUT WHY?!

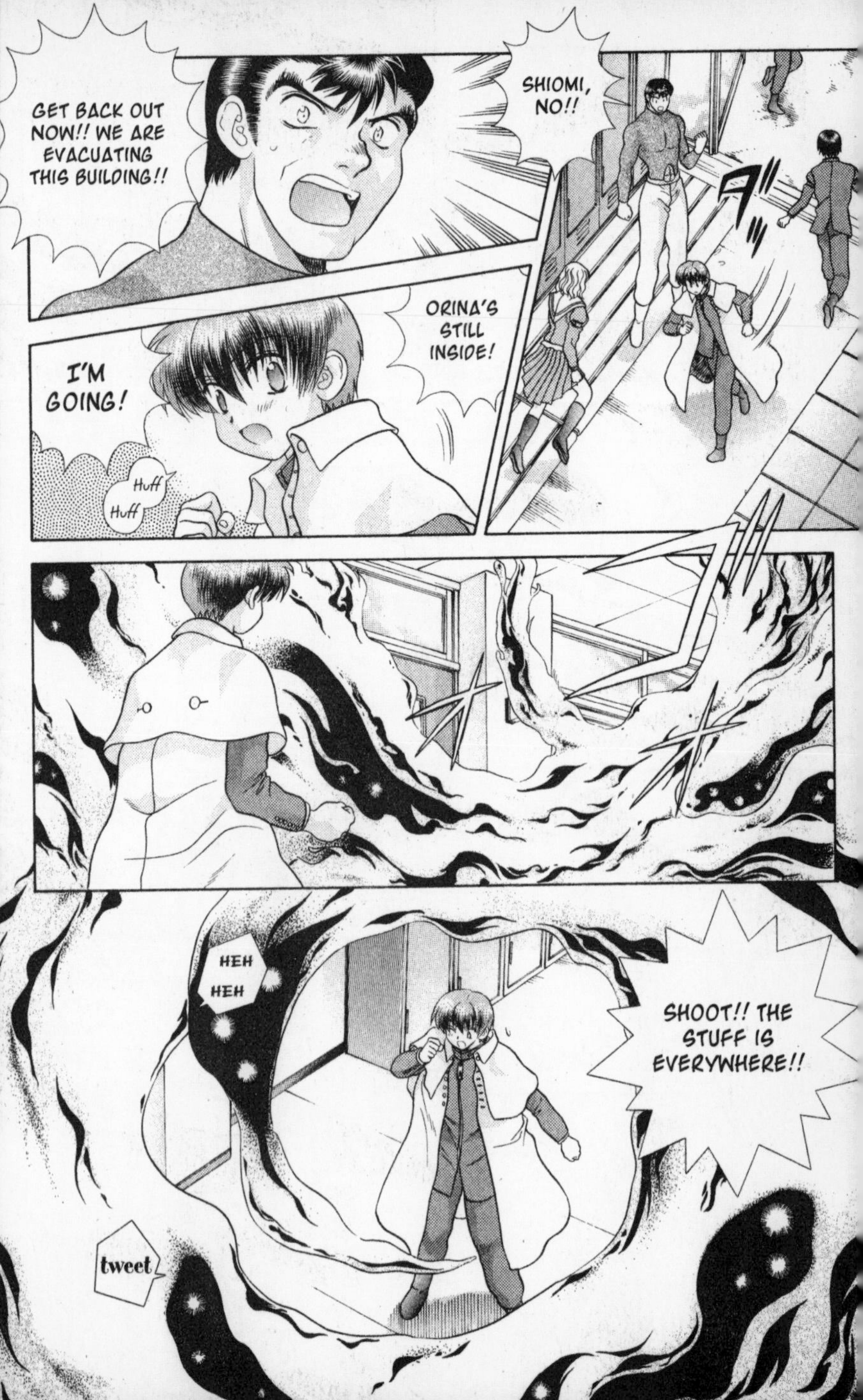
SHIOMI, NO!!
GET BACK OUT NOW!! WE ARE EVACUATING THIS BUILDING!!
ORINA'S STILL INSIDE!
I'M GOING!
Huff Huff
SHOOT!! THE STUFF IS EVERYWHERE!!
HEH HEH
tweet

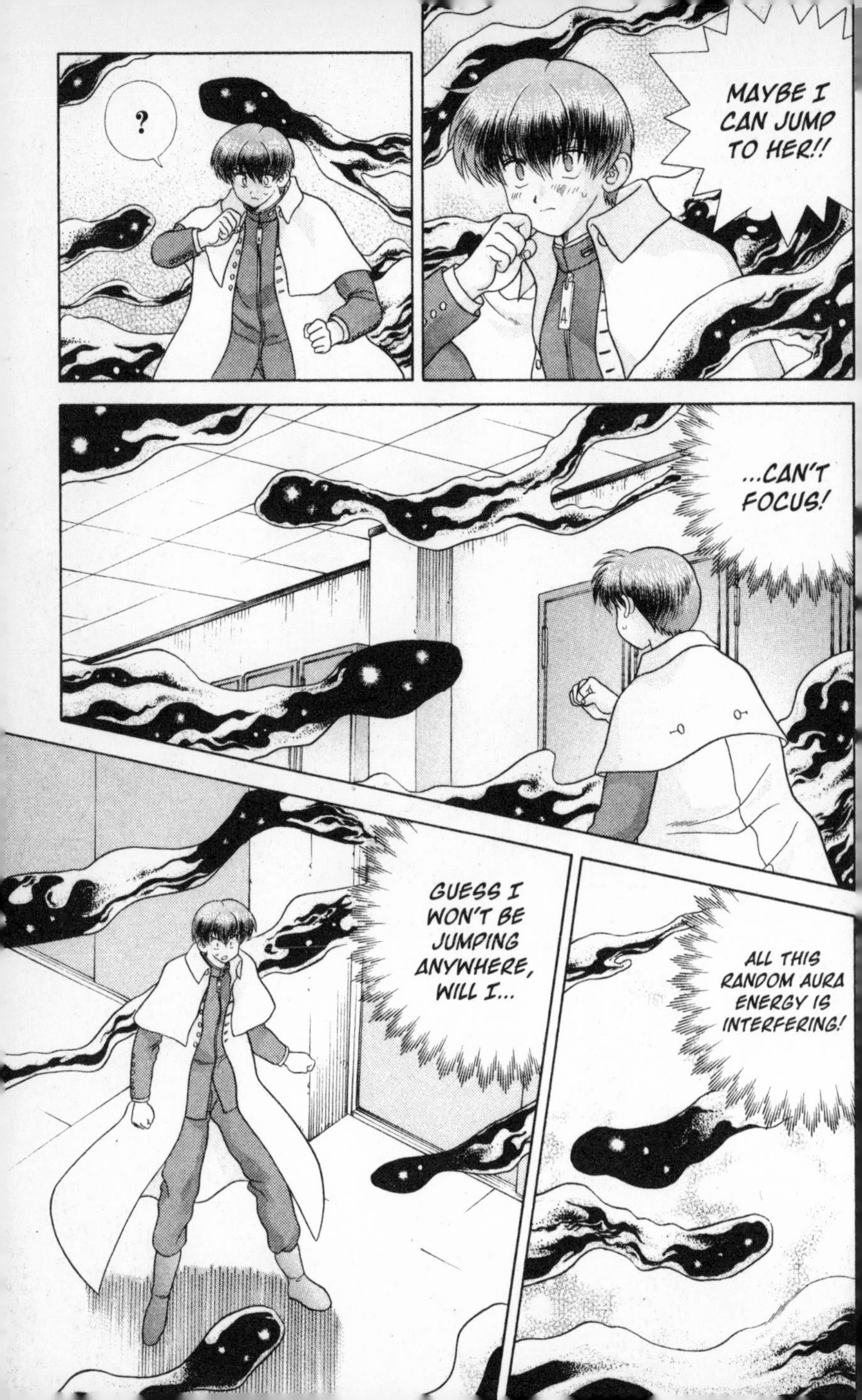
?
MAYBE I CAN JUMP TO HER!!
...CAN'T FOCUS!
ALL THIS RANDOM AURA ENERGY IS INTERFERING!
GUESS I WON'T BE JUMPING ANYWHERE, WILL I...

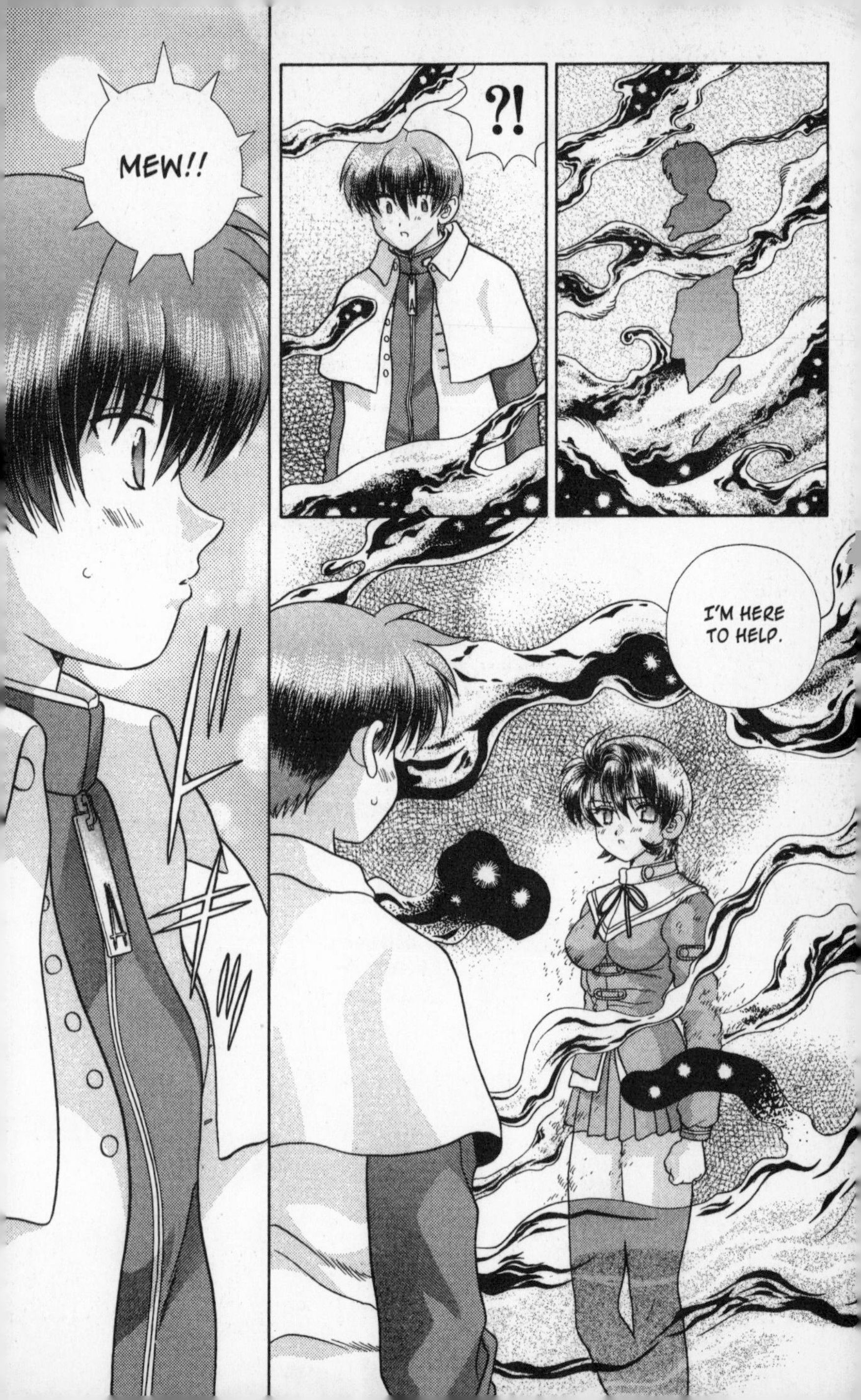
?!
I'M HERE TO HELP.
MEW!!

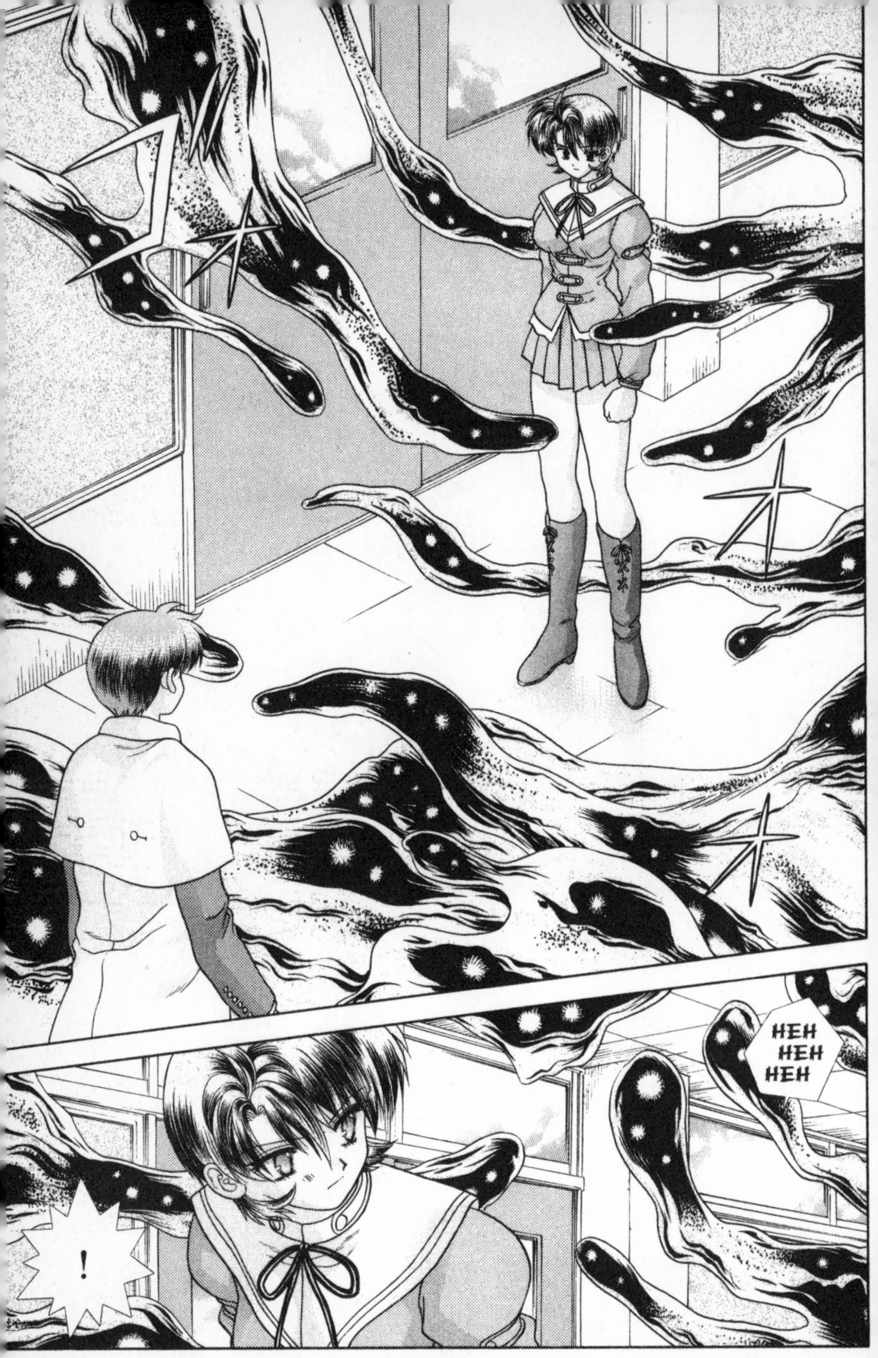
HEH
HEH
HEH
!

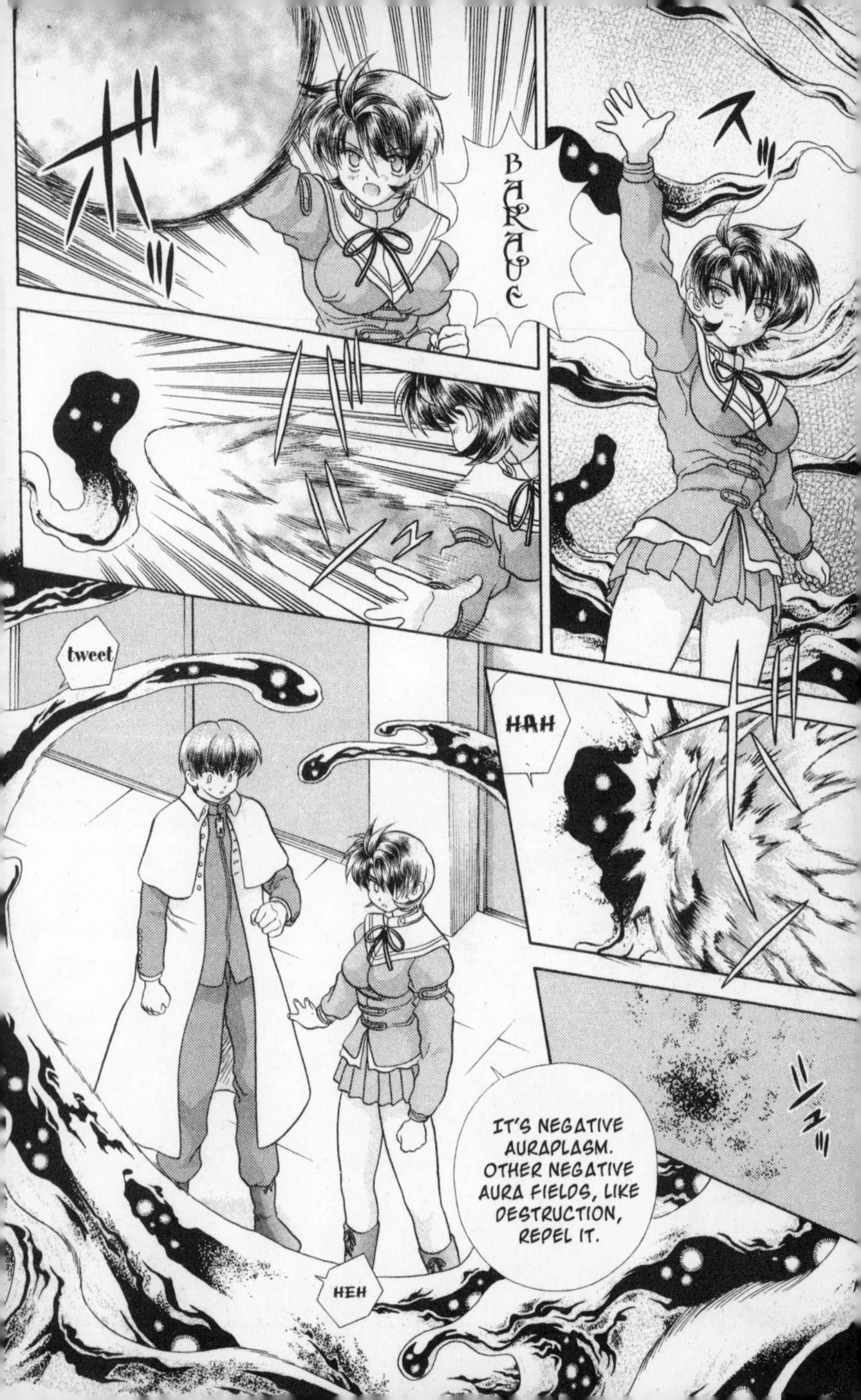

BARAGUE
tweet
HAH
IT'S NEGATIVE AURAPLASM. OTHER NEGATIVE AURA FIELDS, LIKE DESTRUCTION, REPEL IT.
HEH

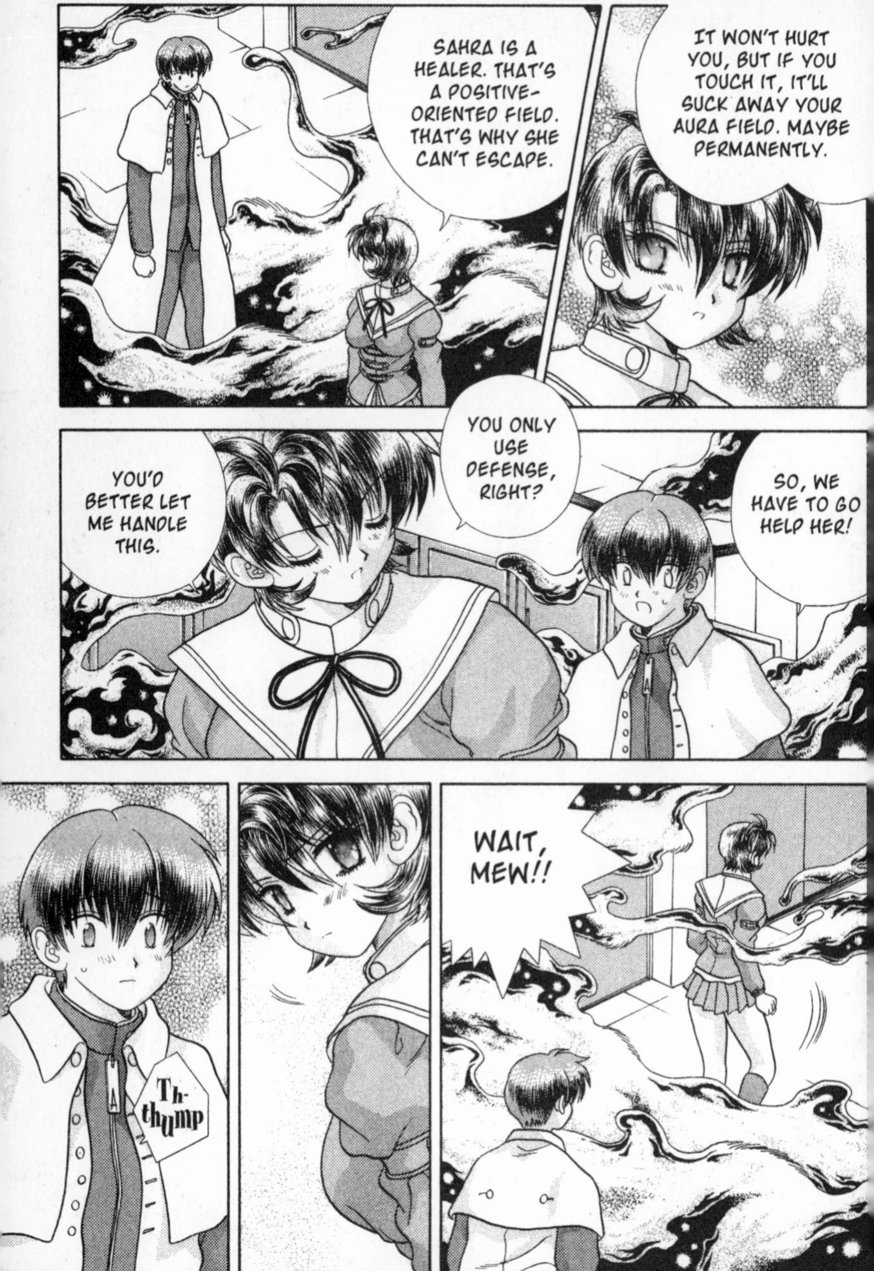
IT WON'T HURT YOU, BUT IF YOU TOUCH IT, IT'LL SUCK AWAY YOUR AURA FIELD. MAYBE PERMANENTLY.
SAHRA IS A HEALER. THAT'S A POSITIVE-ORIENTED FIELD. THAT'S WHY SHE CAN'T ESCAPE.
SO, WE HAVE TO GO HELP HER!
YOU ONLY USE DEFENSE, RIGHT?
YOU'D BETTER LET ME HANDLE THIS.
WAIT, MEW!!
Th-thump

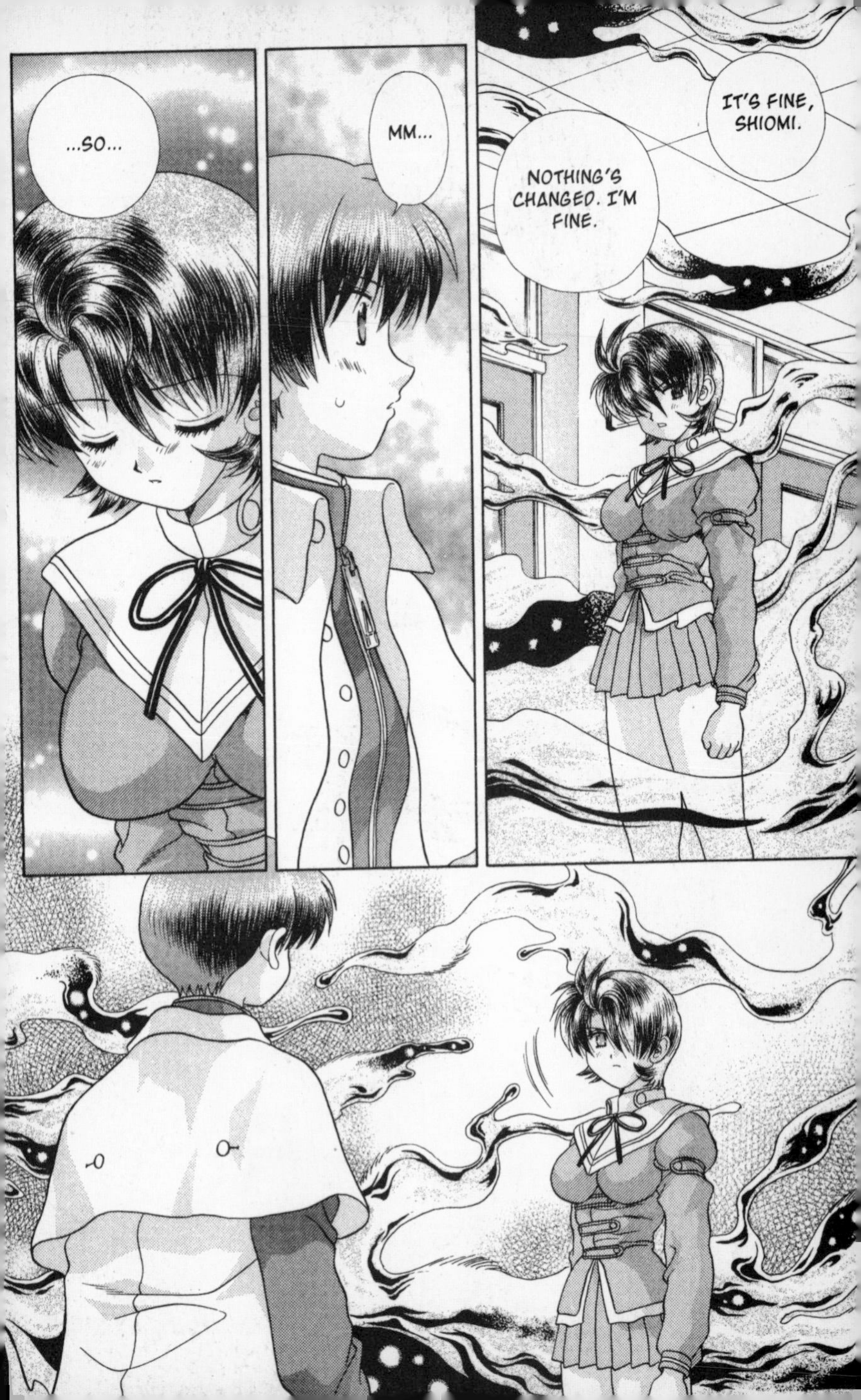

IT'S FINE, SHIOMI.
NOTHING'S CHANGED. I'M FINE.
MM...
...SO...

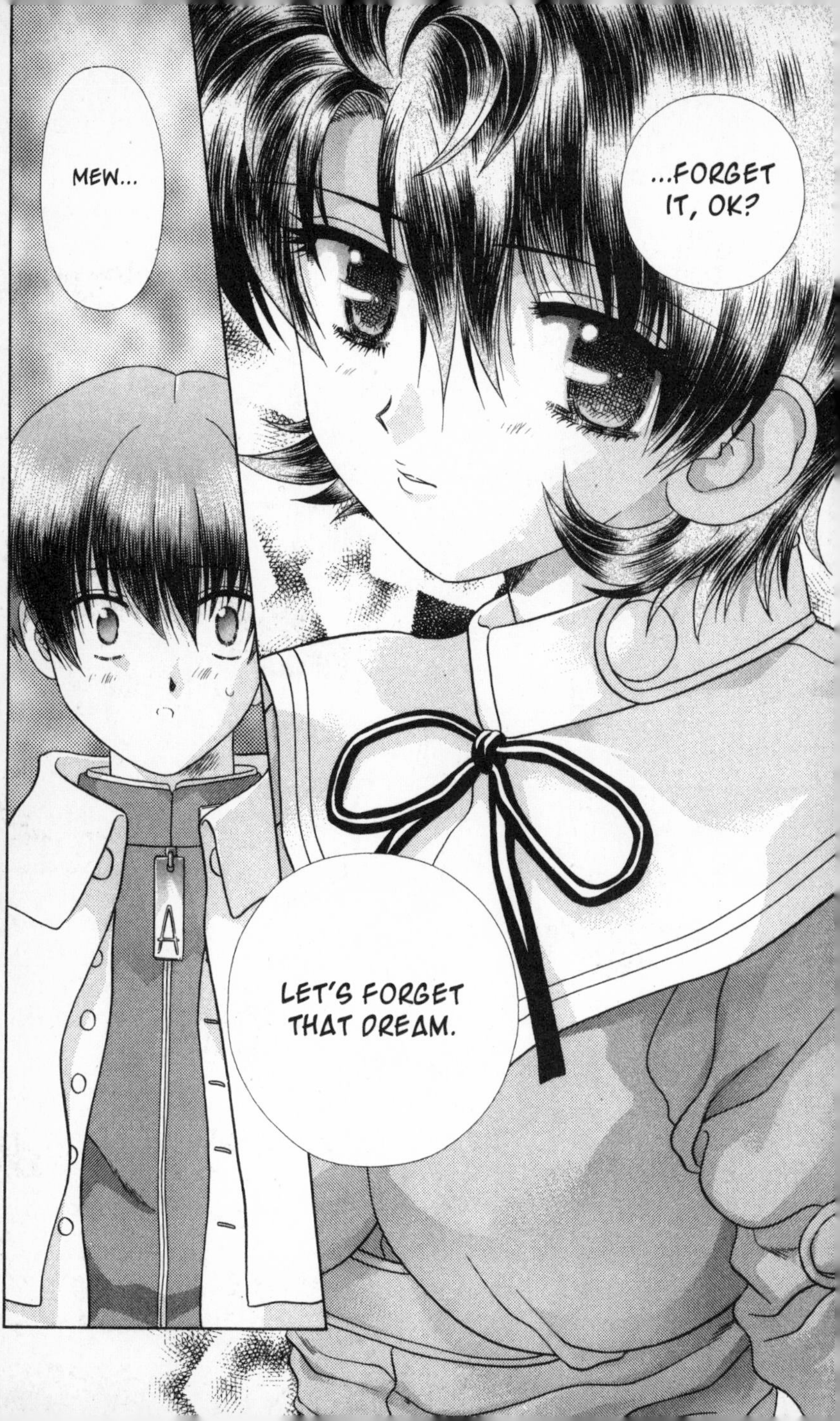

...FORGET IT, OK?
MEW...
LET'S FORGET THAT DREAM.

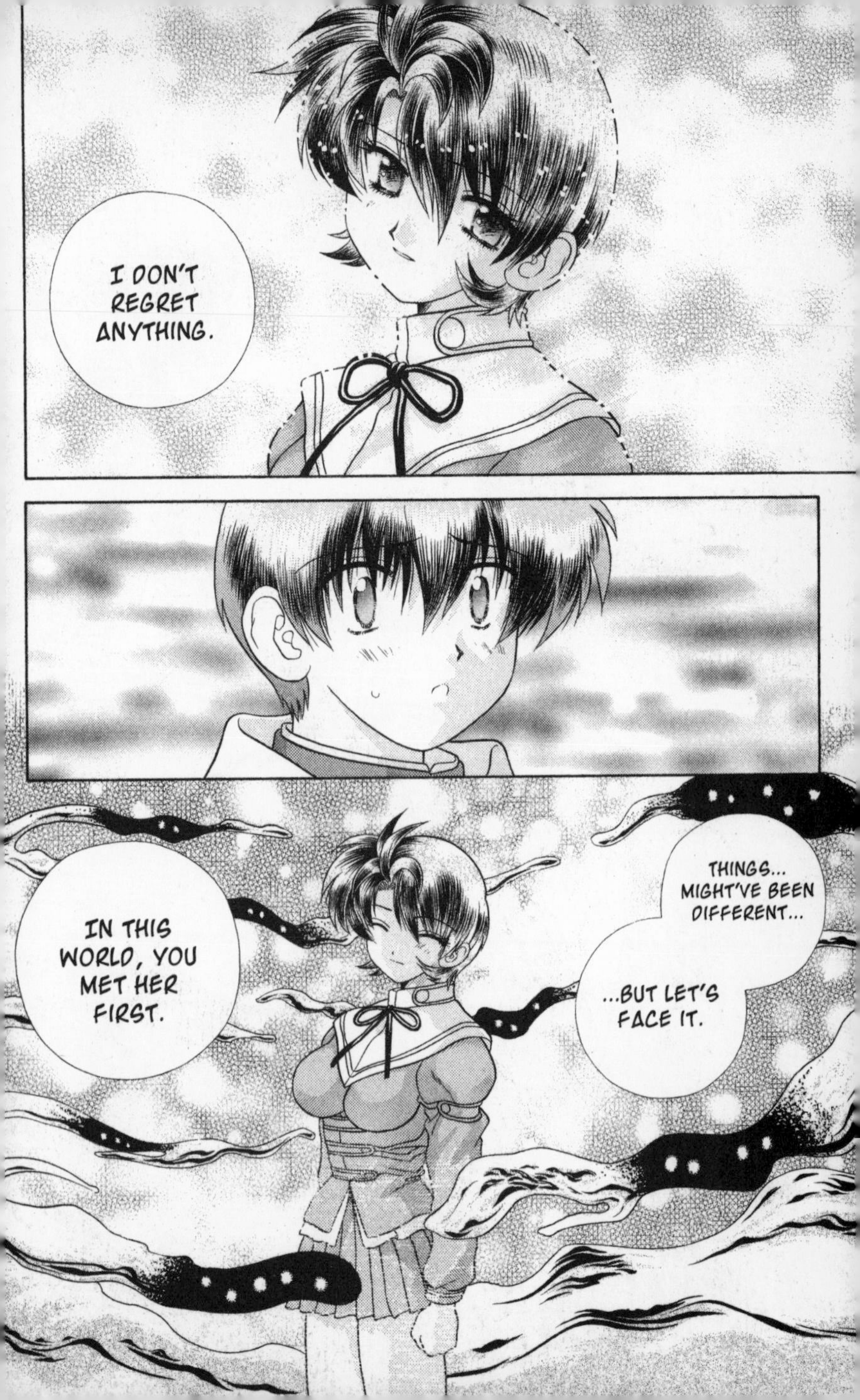
I DON'T REGRET ANYTHING.
THINGS... MIGHT'VE BEEN DIFFERENT...
...BUT LET'S FACE IT.
IN THIS WORLD, YOU MET HER FIRST.

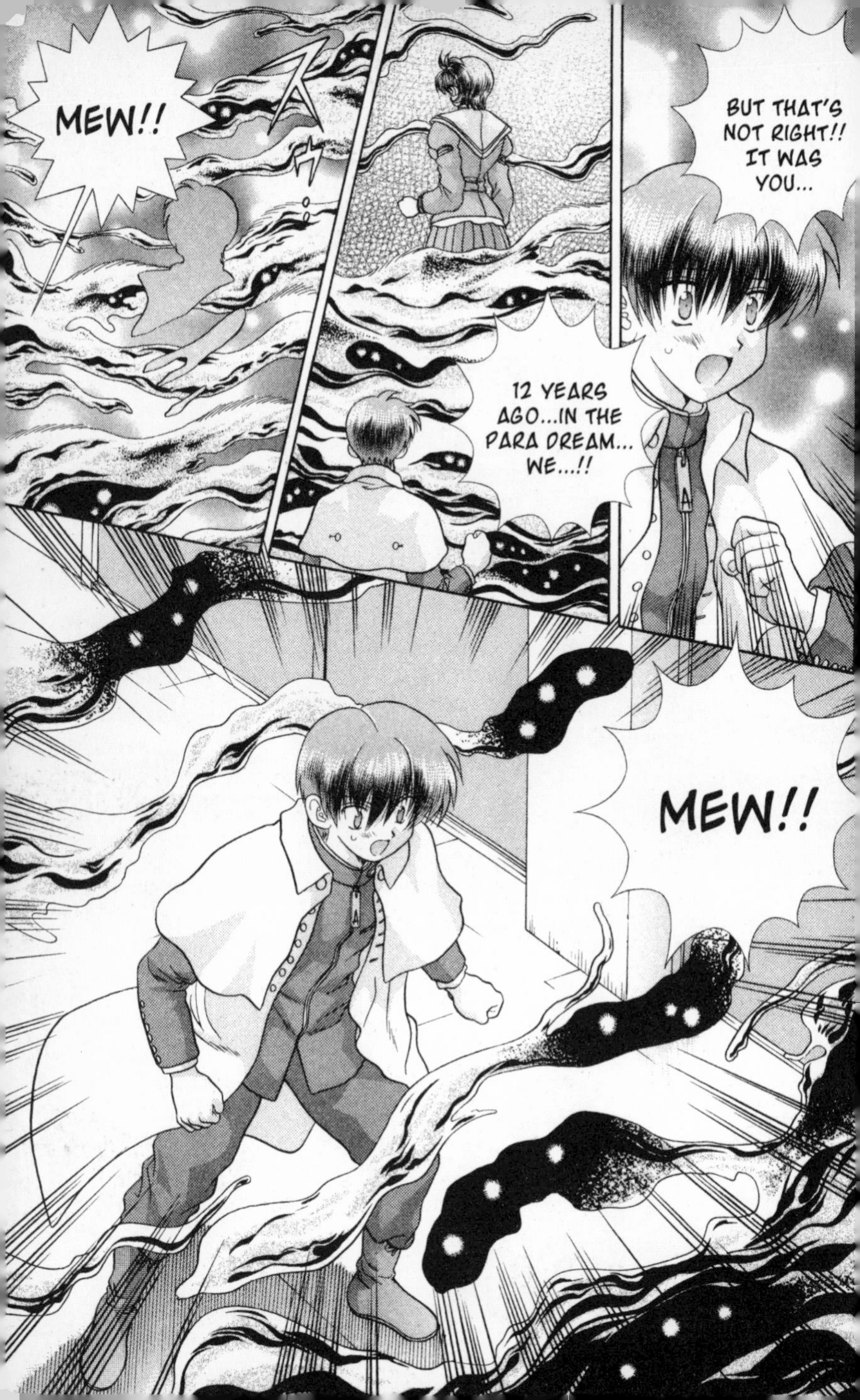
BUT THAT'S NOT RIGHT!! IT WAS YOU...
12 YEARS AGO...IN THE PARA DREAM... WE...!!
MEW!!
MEW!!

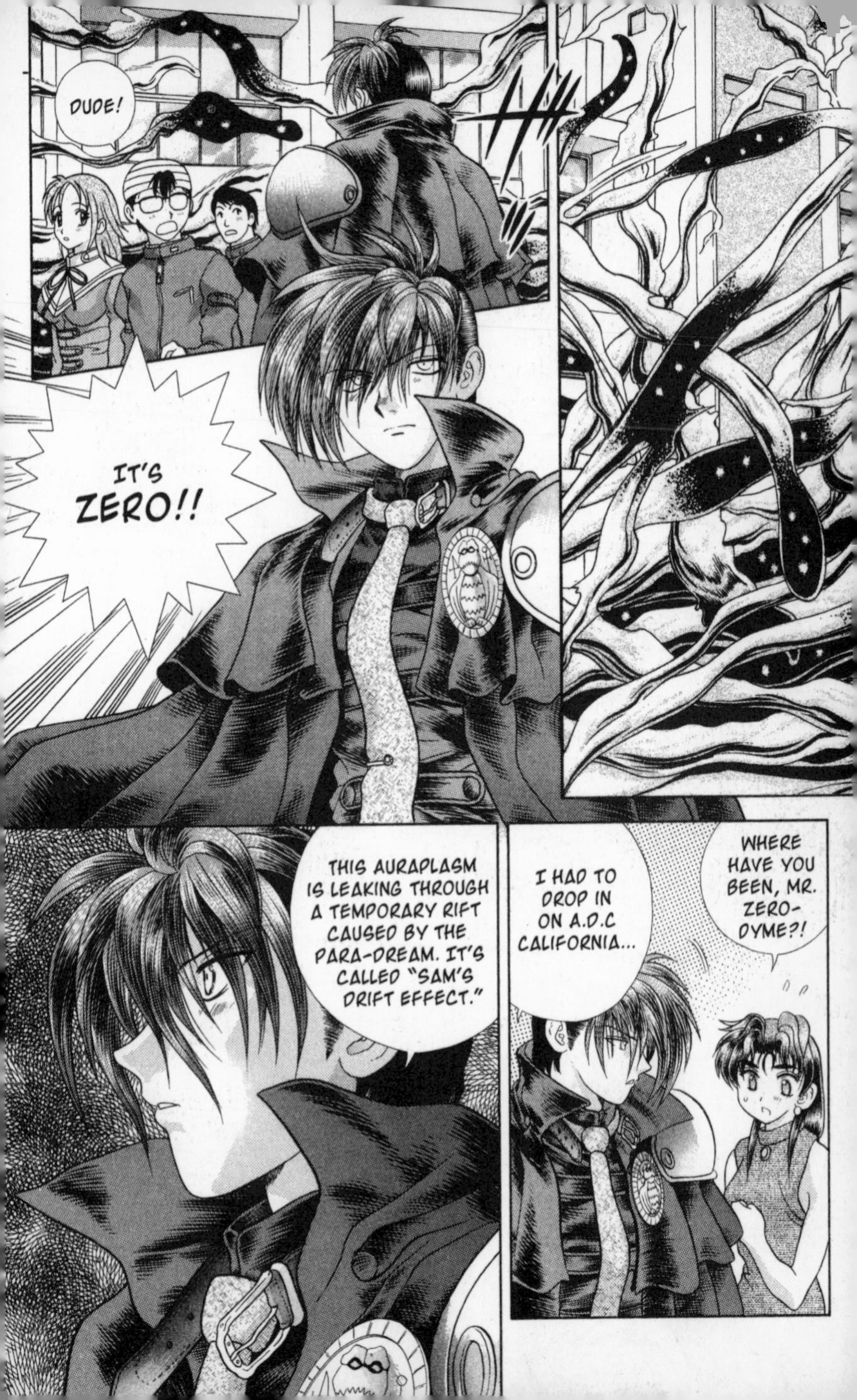
DUDE!
IT'S ZERO!!
WHERE HAVE YOU BEEN, MR. ZERO-DYME?!
I HAD TO DROP IN ON A.D.C CALIFORNIA...
THIS AURAPLASM IS LEAKING THROUGH A TEMPORARY RIFT CAUSED BY THE PARA-DREAM. IT'S CALLED "SAM'S DRIFT EFFECT."

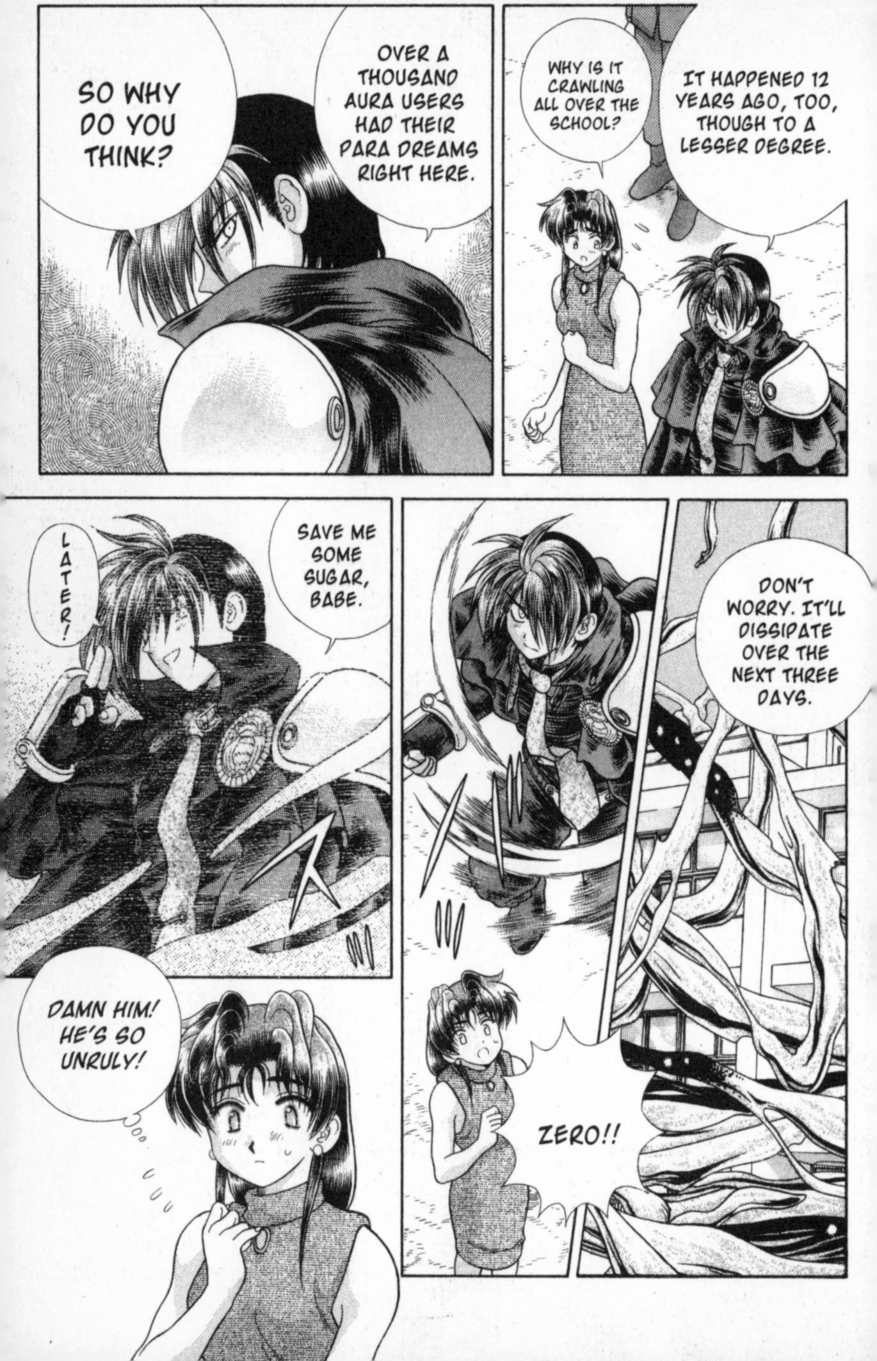

WHY IS IT CRAWLING ALL OVER THE SCHOOL?
IT HAPPENED 12 YEARS AGO, TOO, THOUGH TO A LESSER DEGREE.
OVER A THOUSAND AURA USERS HAD THEIR PARA DREAMS RIGHT HERE.
SO WHY DO YOU THINK?
DON'T WORRY. IT'LL DISSIPATE OVER THE NEXT THREE DAYS.
SAVE ME SOME SUGAR, BABE.
LATER!
ZERO!!
DAMN HIM! HE'S SO UNRULY!

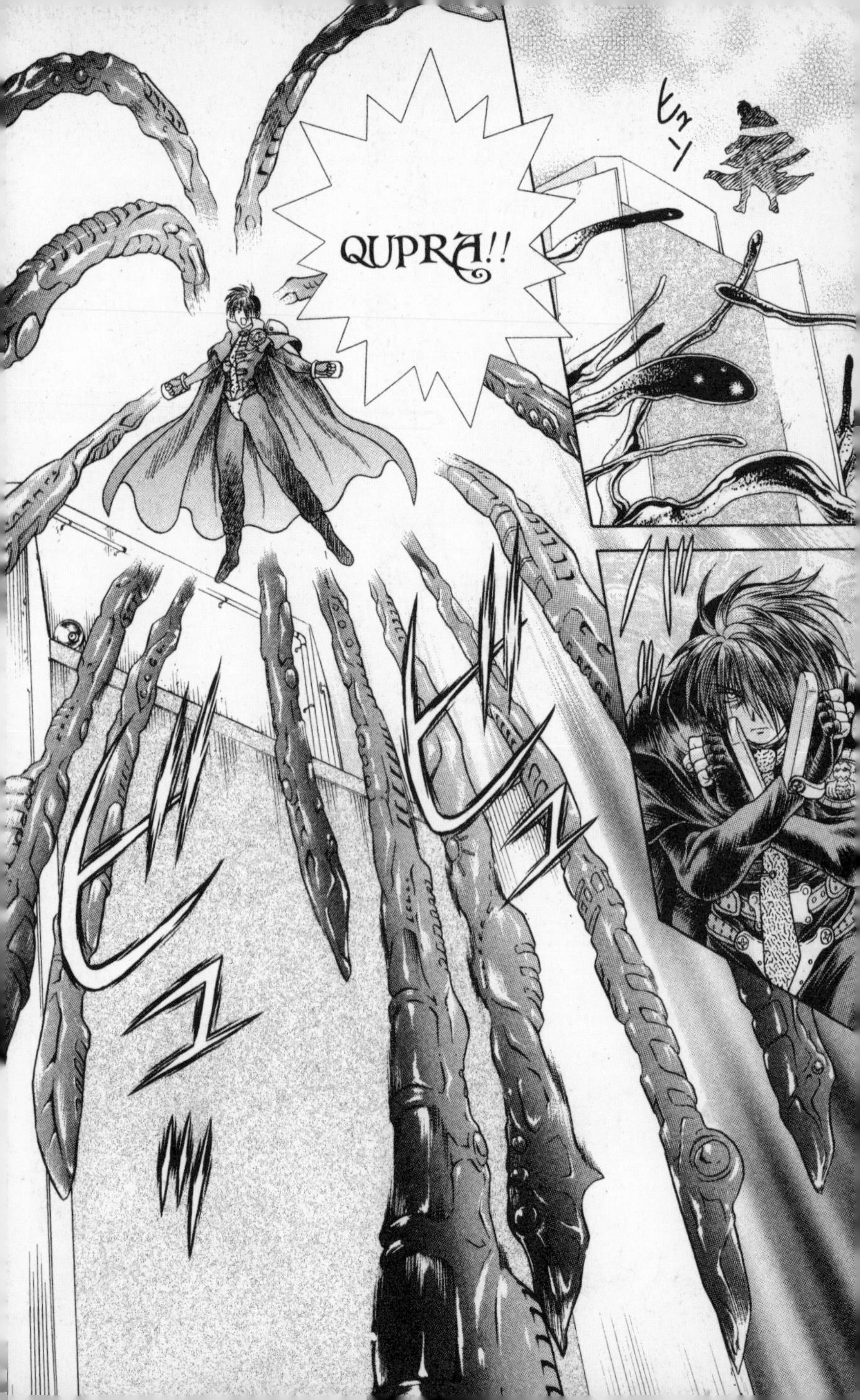
QUPRA!!

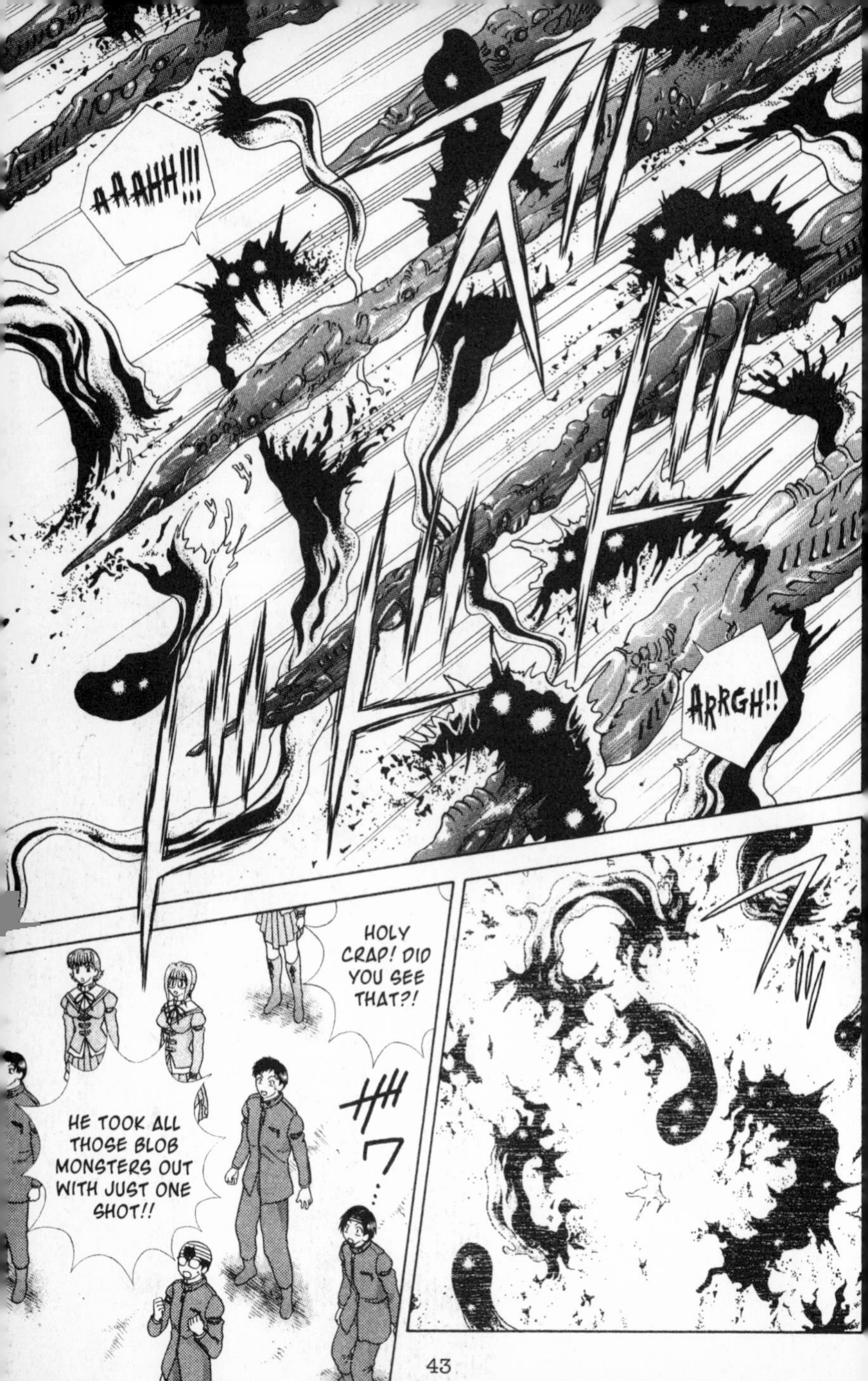
AAAHH!!!
ARRGH!!
HOLY CRAP! DID YOU SEE THAT?!
HE TOOK ALL THOSE BLOB MONSTERS OUT WITH JUST ONE SHOT!!

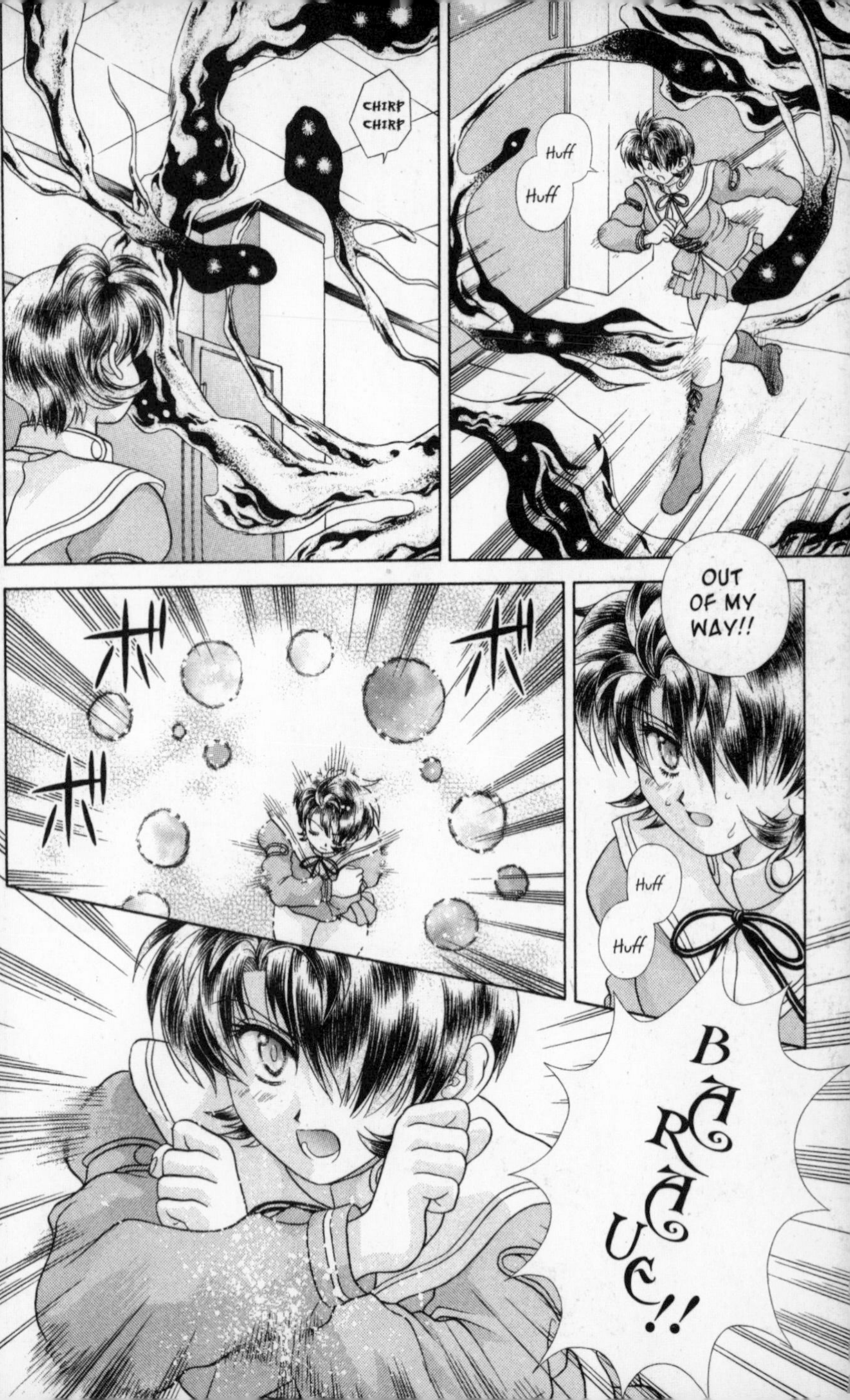
Huff
Huff
CHIRP CHIRP
OUT OF MY WAY!!
Huff
Huff
ボ
ボ
ボ
BARACUC!!

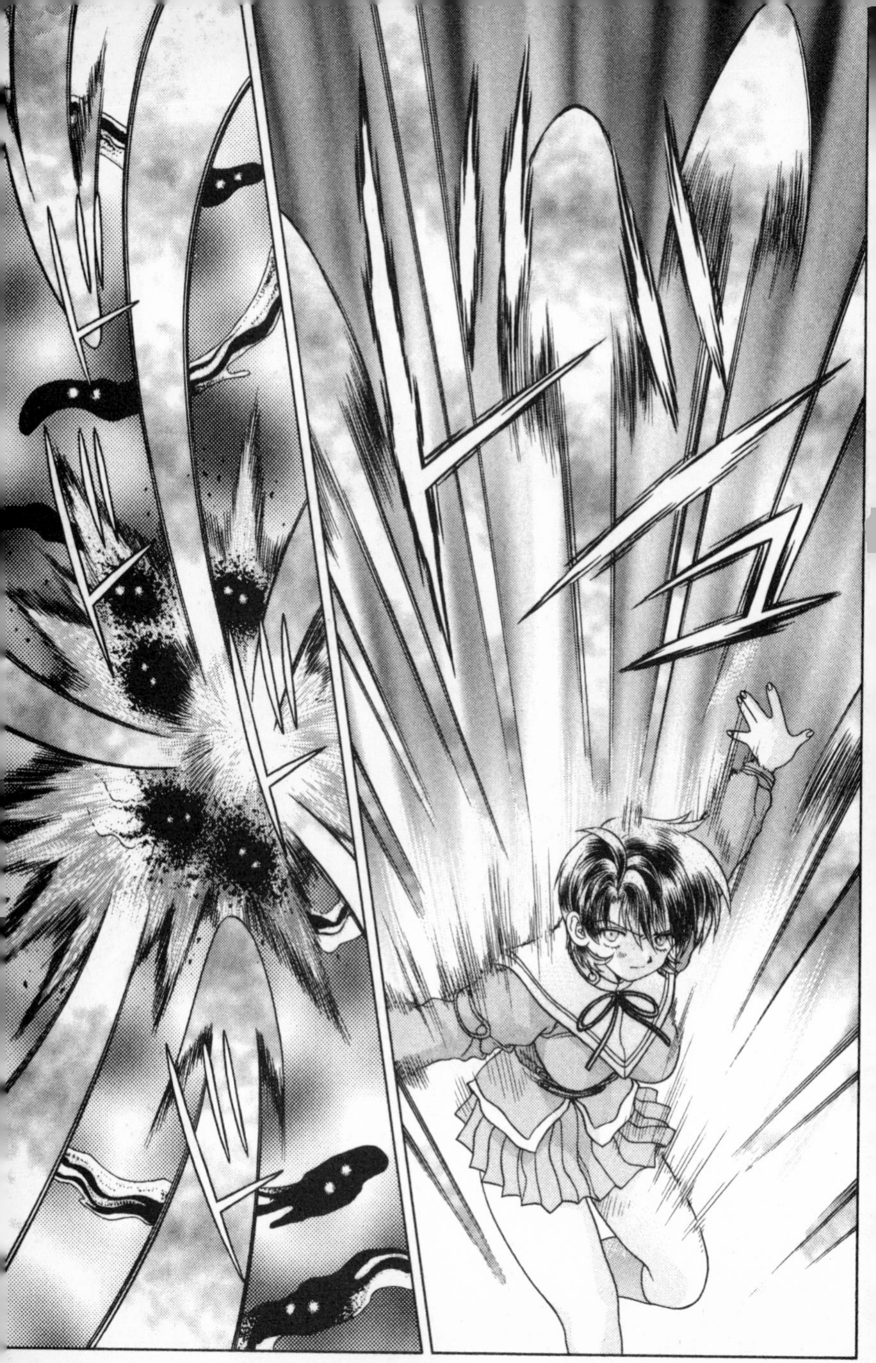

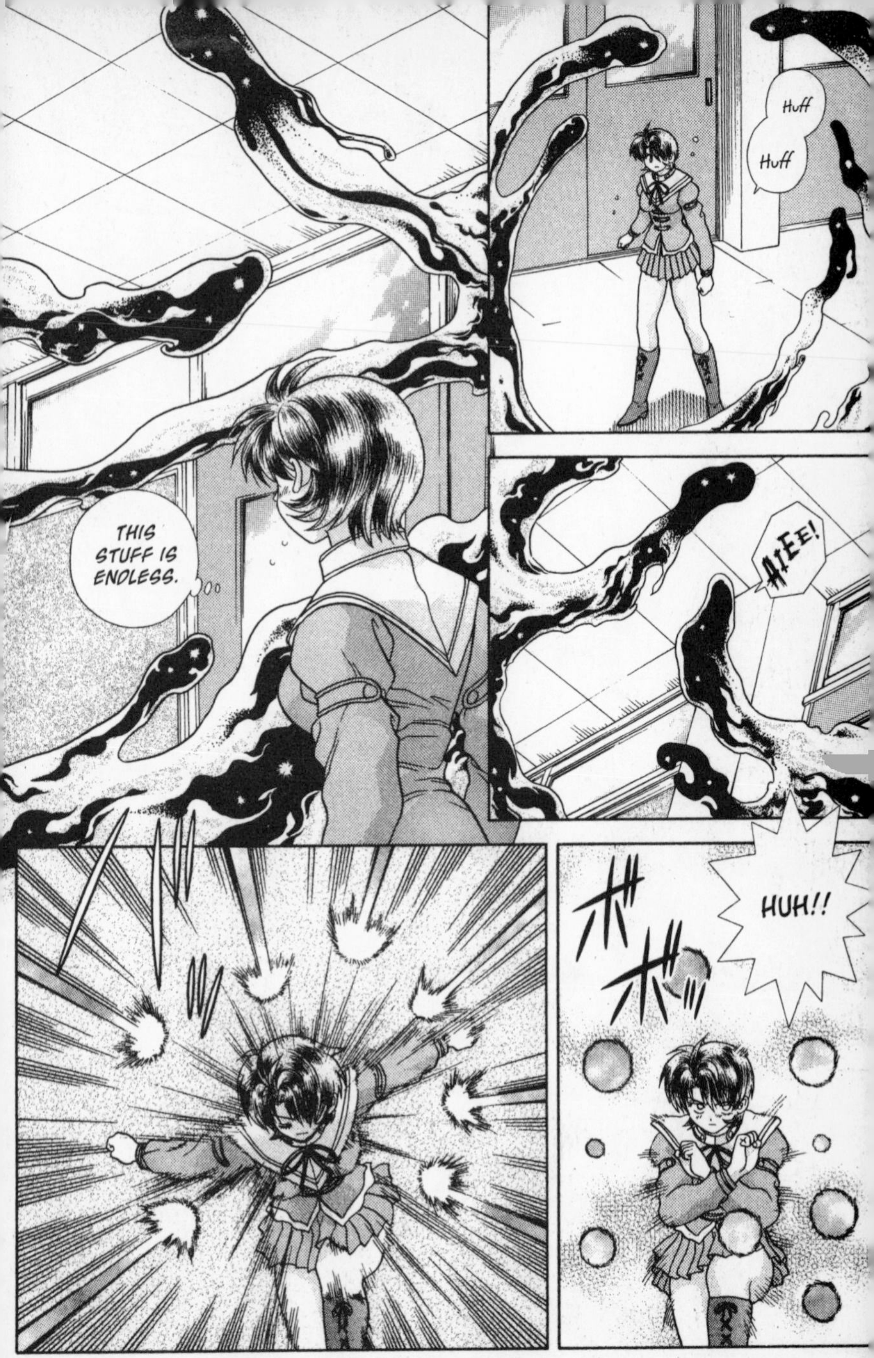

Huff
Huff
AIEEE!
THIS STUFF IS ENDLESS.
HUH!!

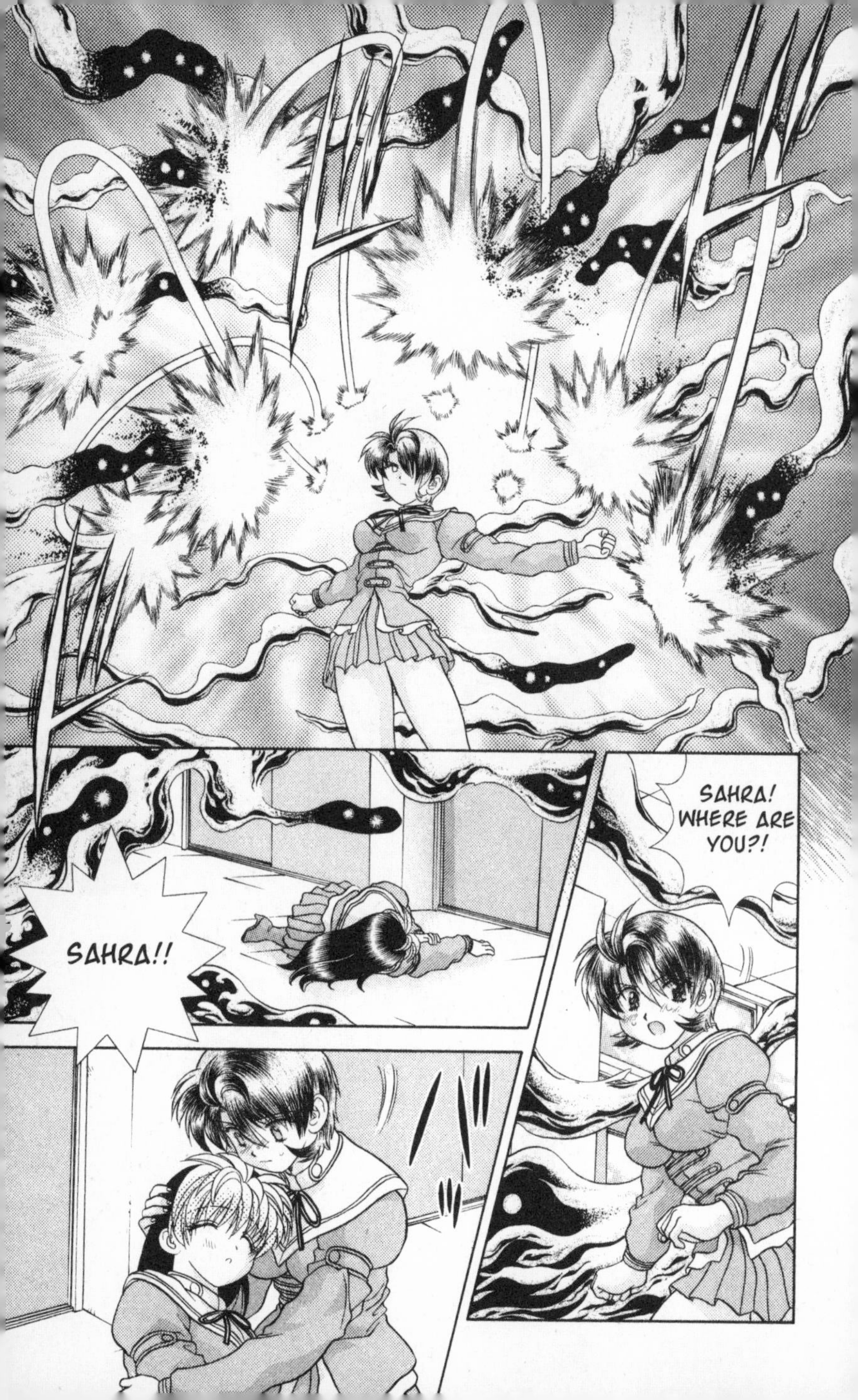
SAHRA! WHERE ARE YOU?!
SAHRA!!

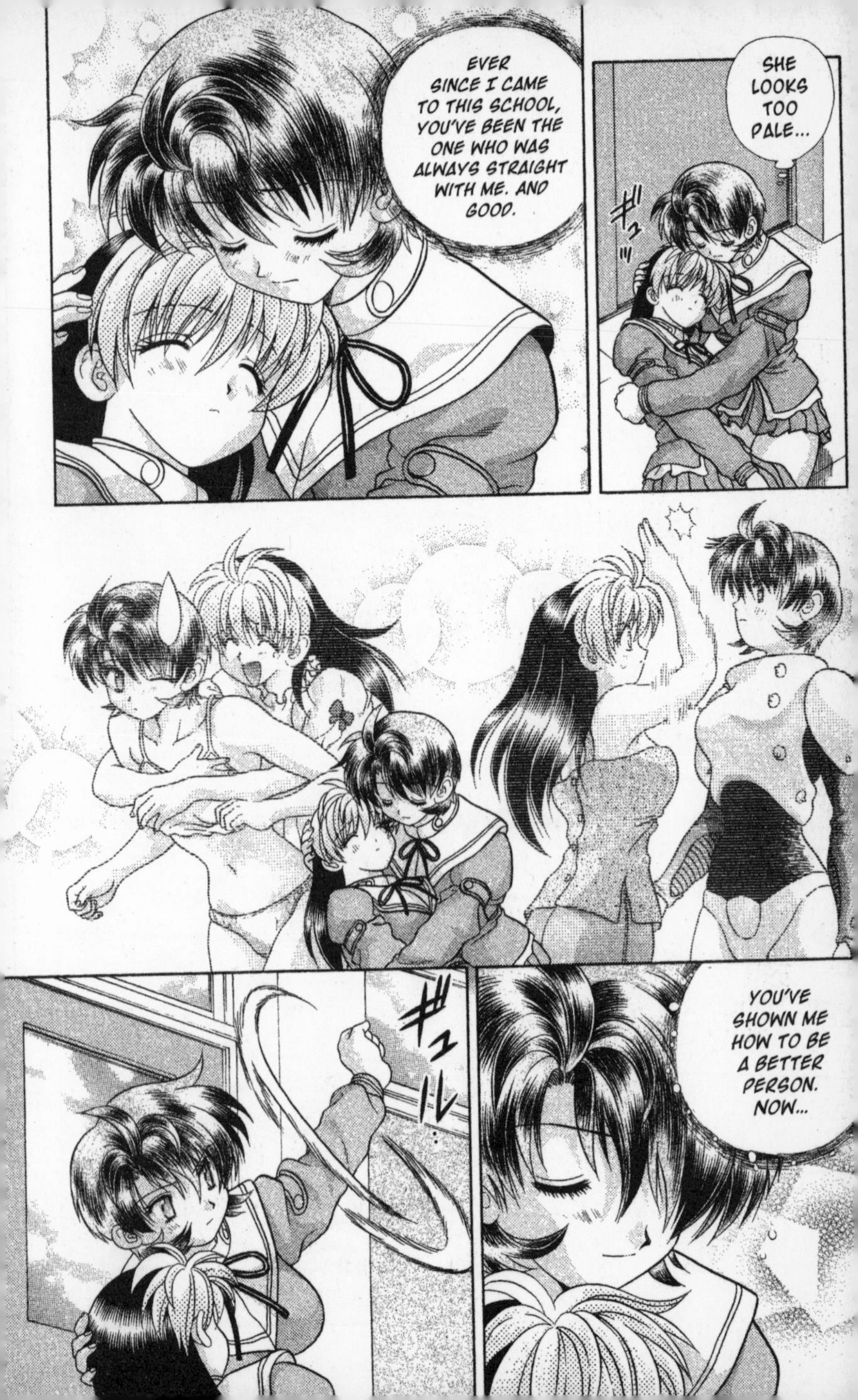
SHE LOOKS TOO PALE...
ギュッ
EVER SINCE I CAME TO THIS SCHOOL, YOU'VE BEEN THE ONE WHO WAS ALWAYS STRAIGHT WITH ME. AND GOOD.
YOU'VE SHOWN ME HOW TO BE A BETTER PERSON. NOW...
ギュル

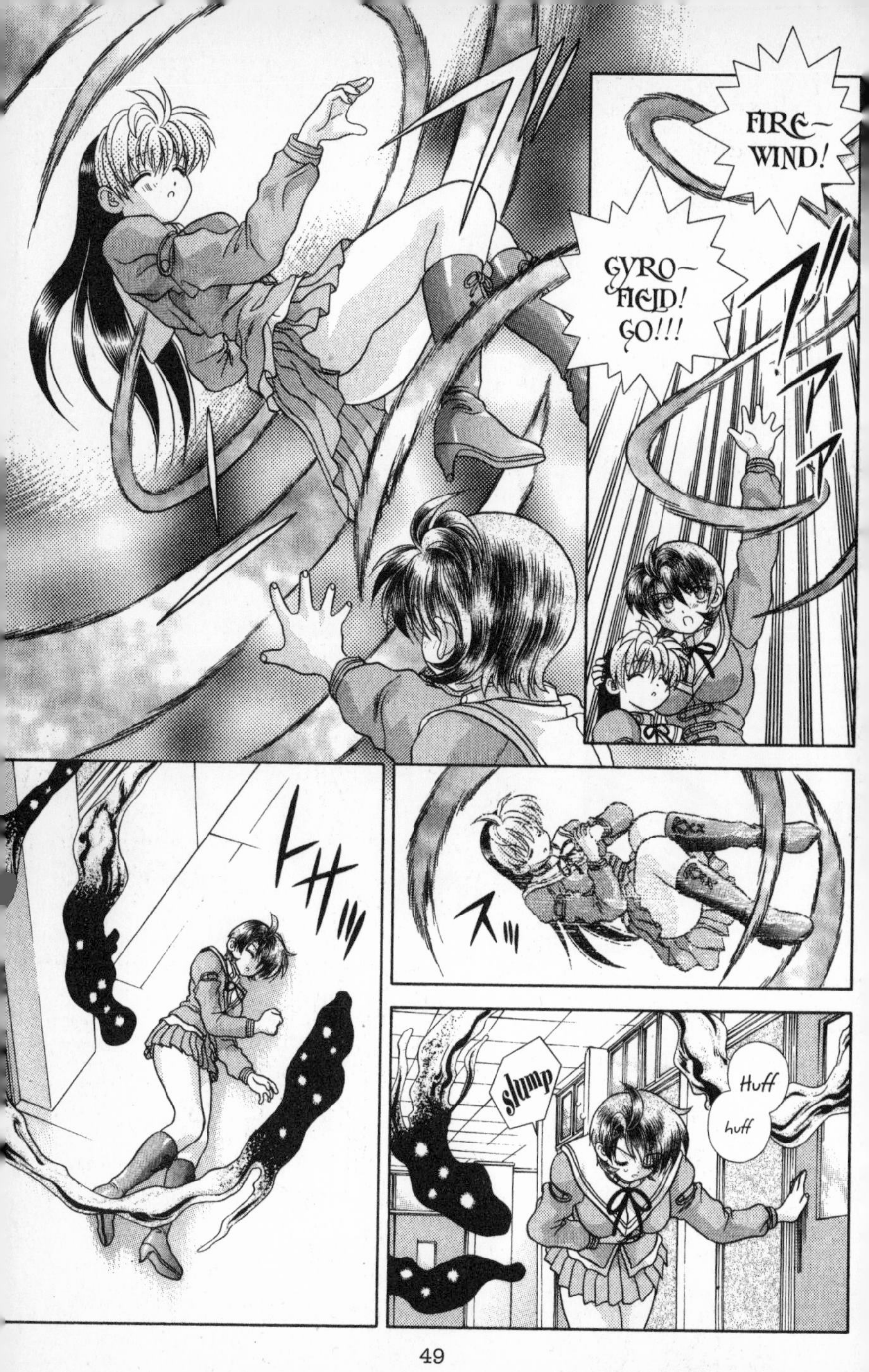
FIRE-WIND!
GYRO-FIELD! GO!!!
slump
Huff
huff

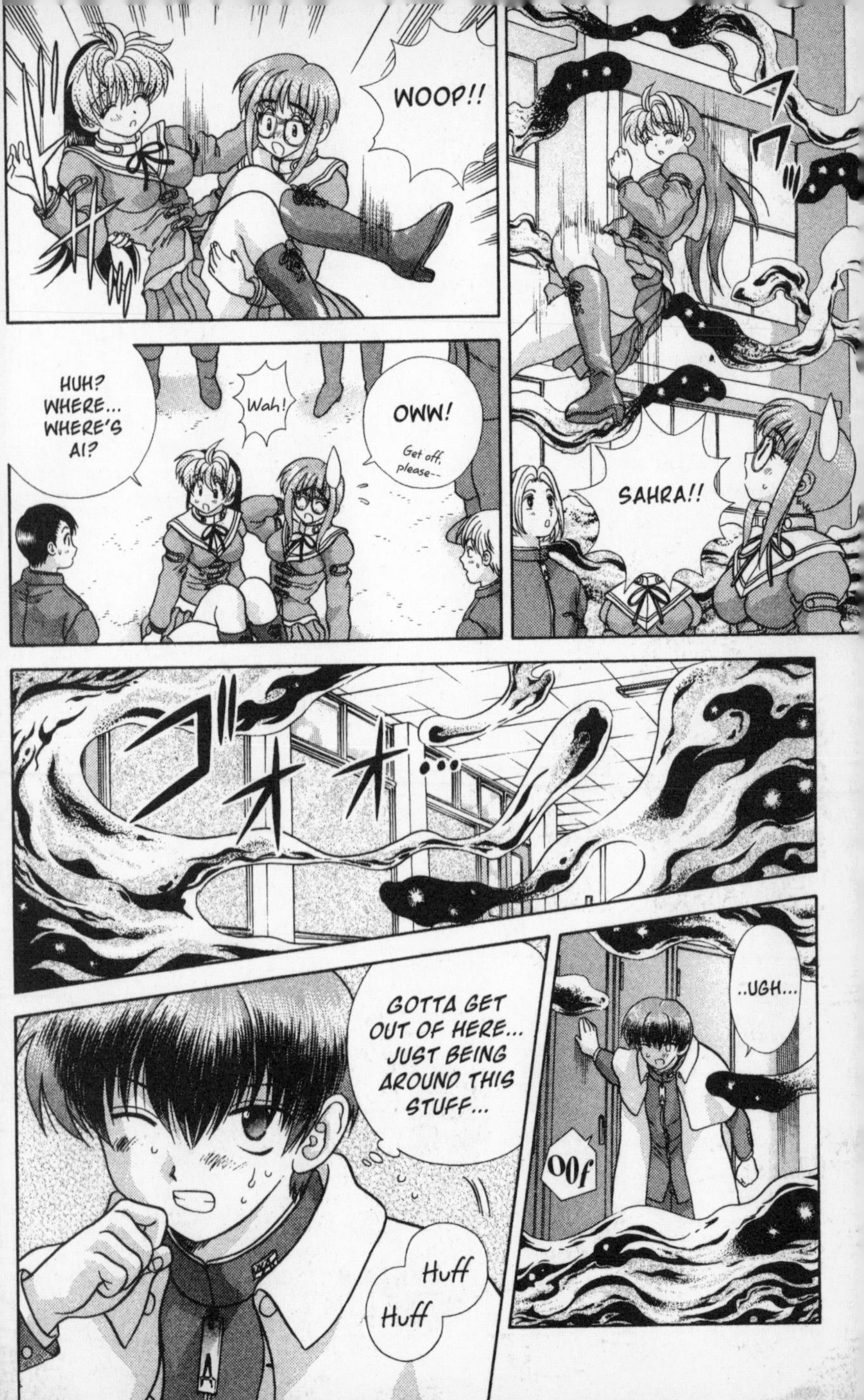
WOOP!!
SAHRA!!
OWW!
Get off, please--
Wah!
HUH? WHERE... WHERE'S AI?
..UGH...
OOf
GOTTA GET OUT OF HERE... JUST BEING AROUND THIS STUFF...
Huff
Huff

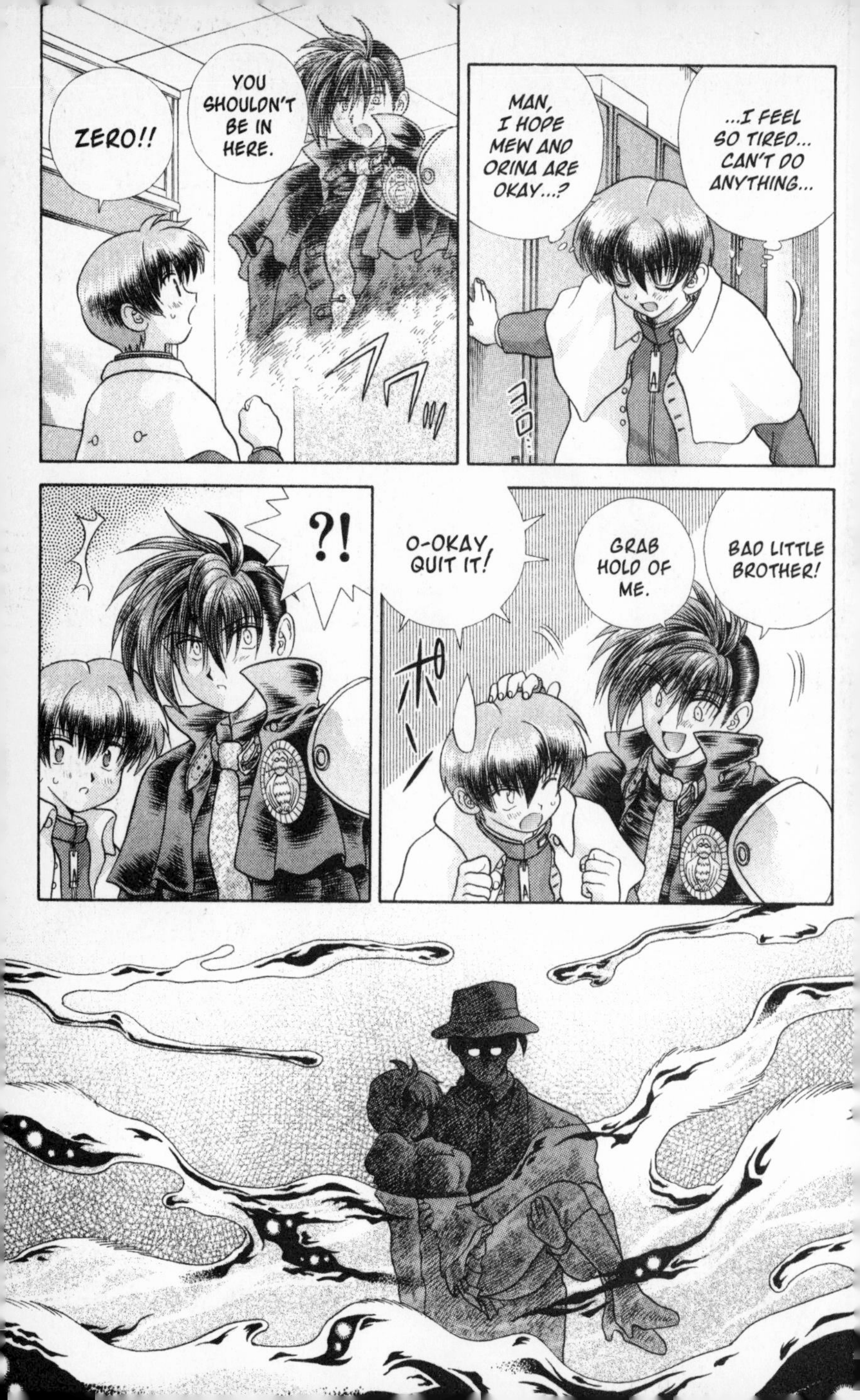
...I FEEL SO TIRED... CAN'T DO ANYTHING...
MAN, I HOPE MEW AND ORINA ARE OKAY...?
YOU SHOULDN'T BE IN HERE.
ZERO!!
BAD LITTLE BROTHER!
GRAB HOLD OF ME.
O-OKAY QUIT IT!
?!

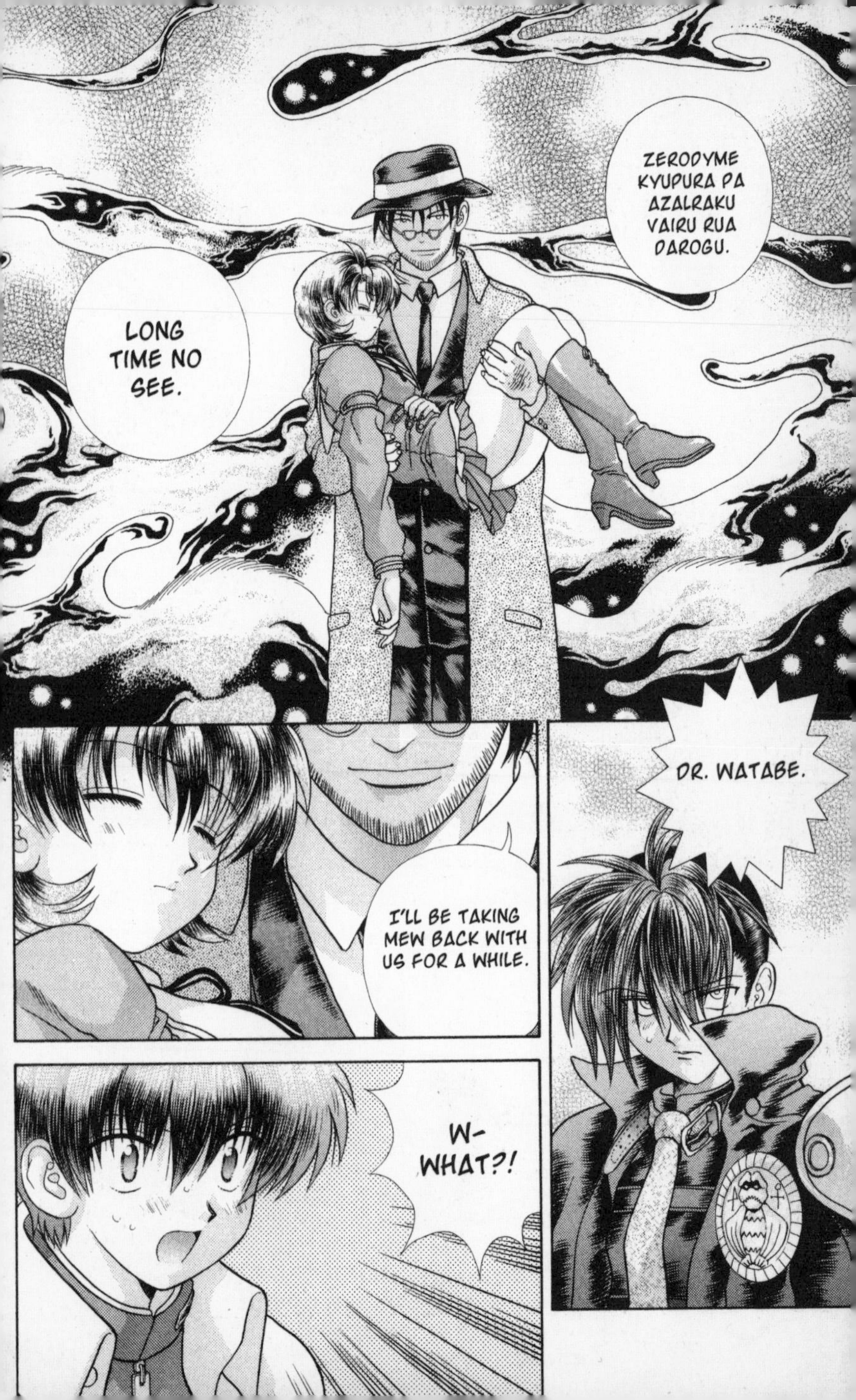
ZERODYME KYUPURA PA AZALRAKU VAIRU RUA DAROGU.
LONG TIME NO SEE.
DR. WATABE.
I'LL BE TAKING MEW BACK WITH US FOR A WHILE.
W- WHAT?!

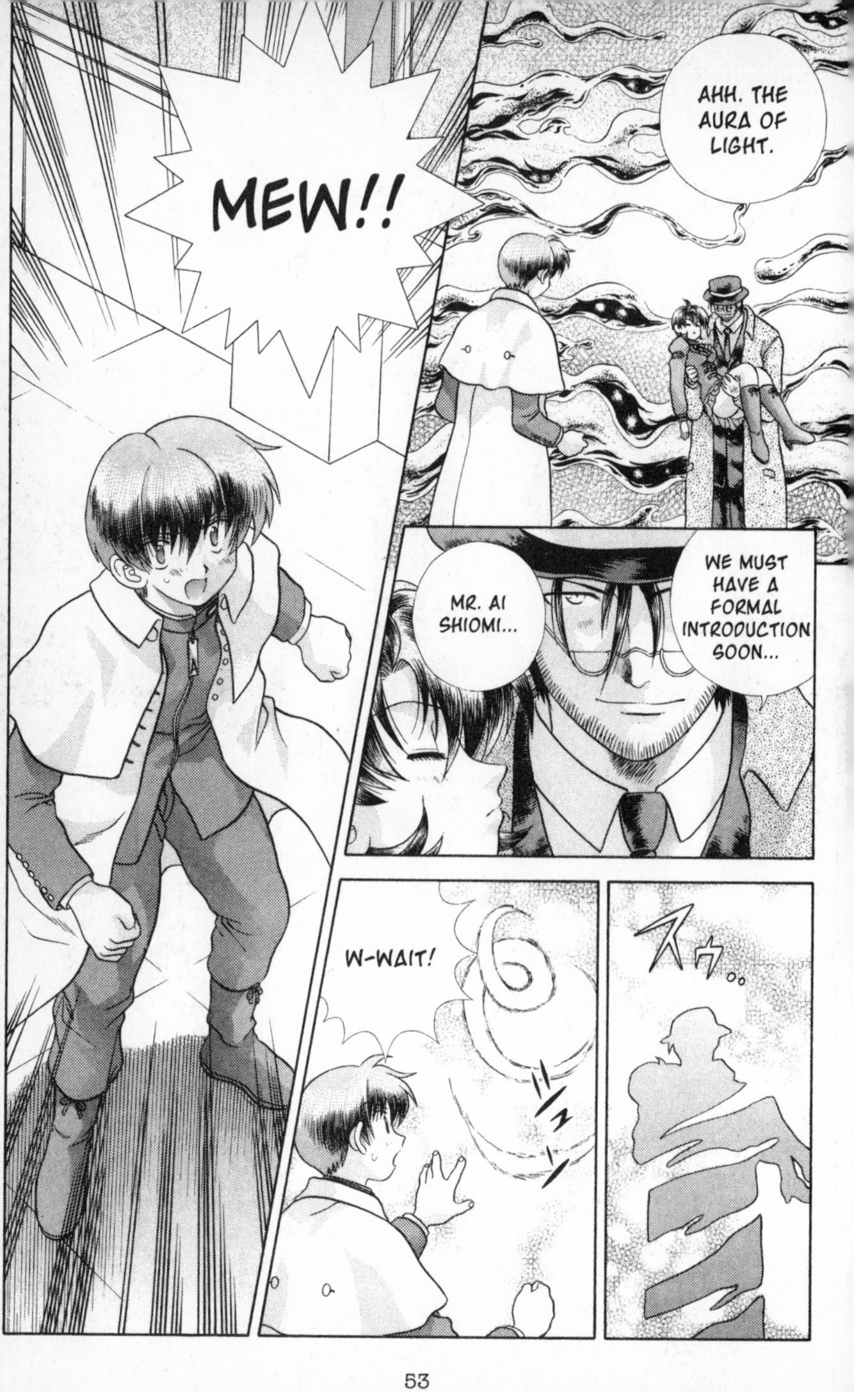
AHH. THE AURA OF LIGHT.
WE MUST HAVE A FORMAL INTRODUCTION SOON...
MR. AI SHIOMI...
スウ..
W-WAIT!
MEW!!

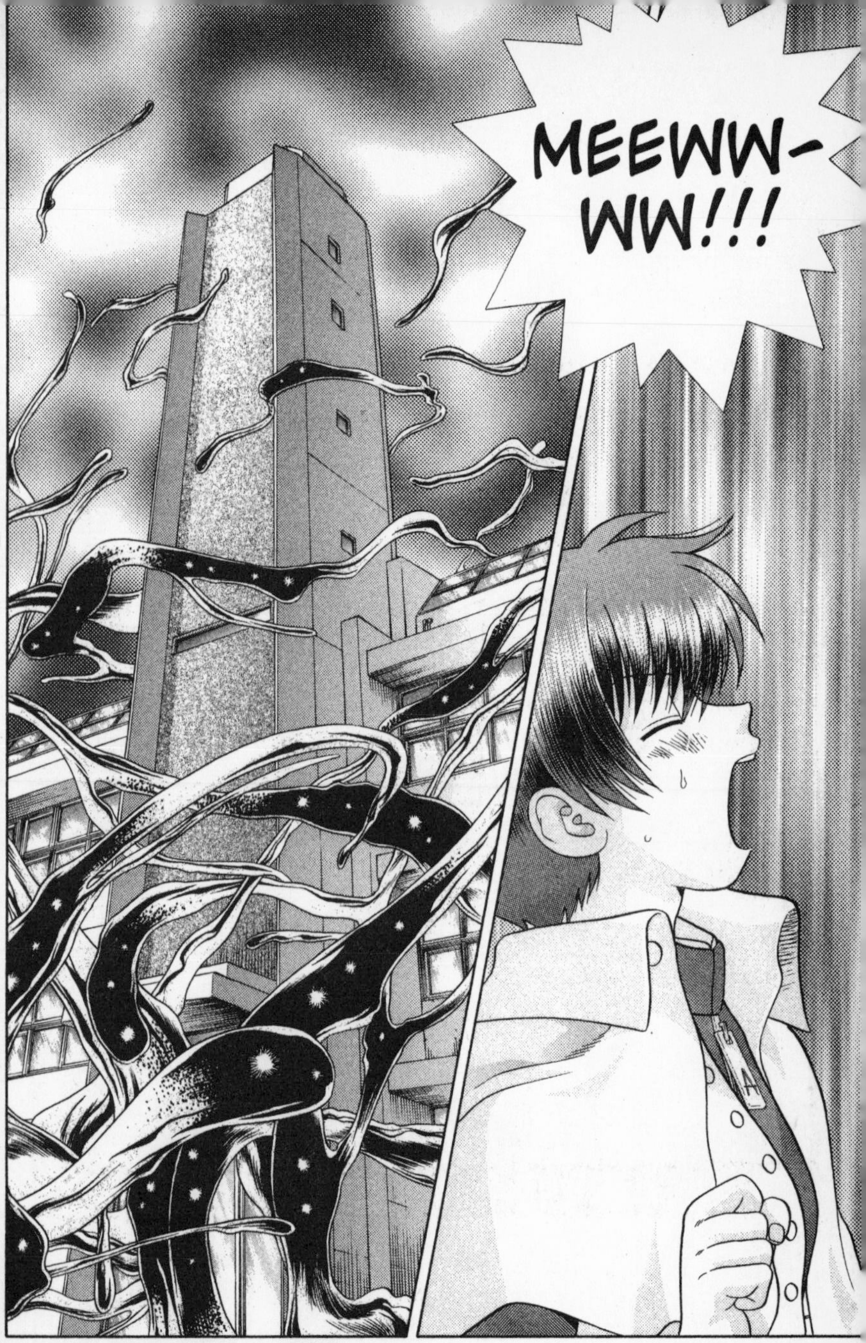
MEEWW-
WW!!!

Sam's Drift Effect END

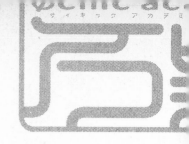

Chapter 26: Watabe's Better Auras

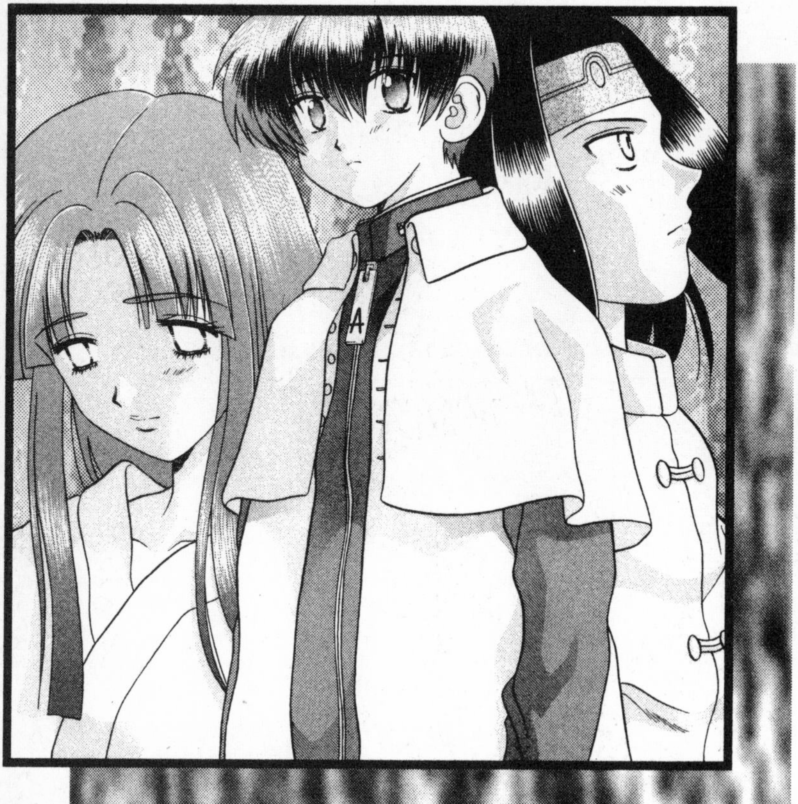

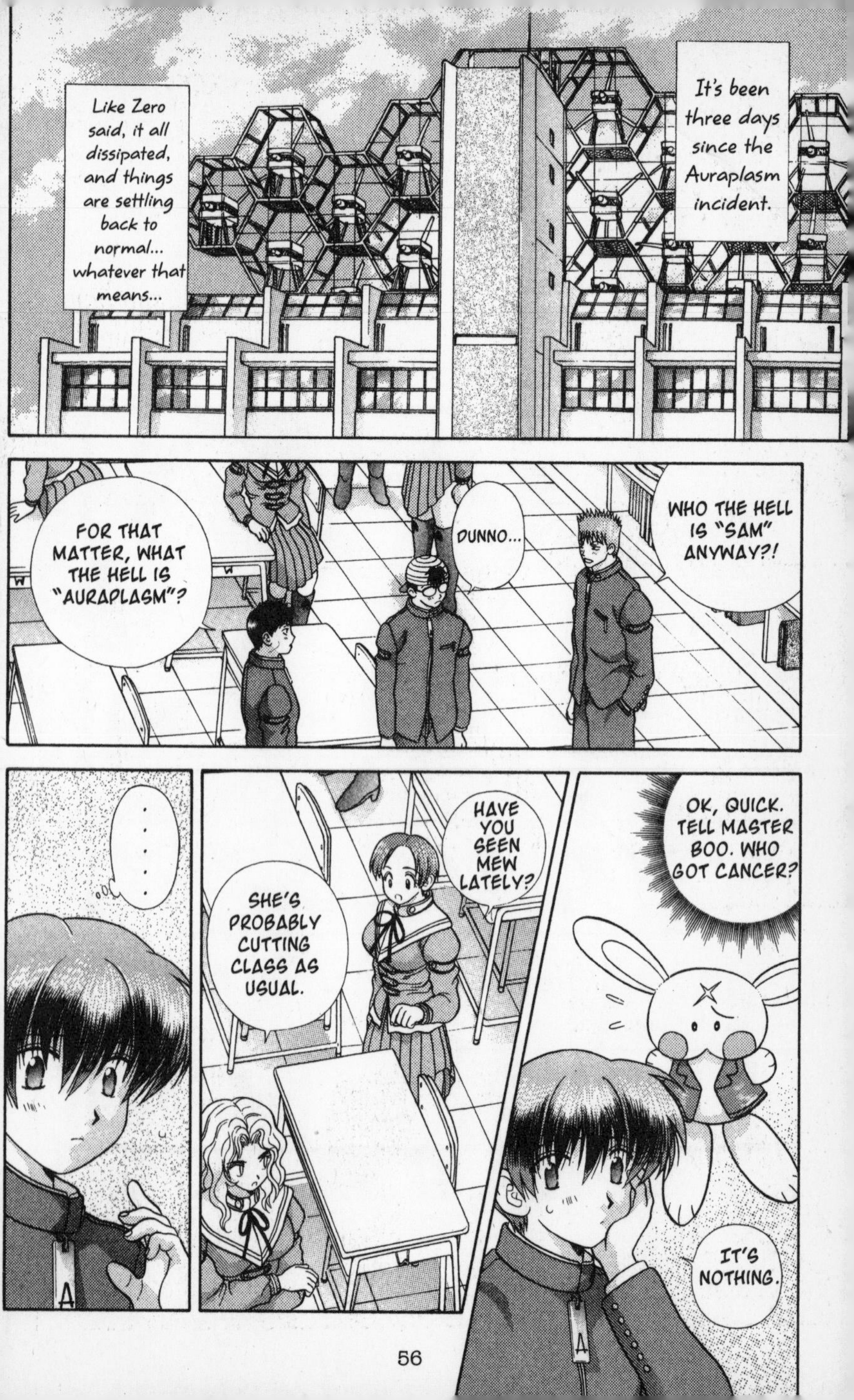
It's been three days since the Auraplasm incident.
Like Zero said, it all dissipated, and things are settling back to normal... whatever that means...
WHO THE HELL IS "SAM" ANYWAY?!
DUNNO...
FOR THAT MATTER, WHAT THE HELL IS "AURAPLASM"?
OK, QUICK. TELL MASTER BOO. WHO GOT CANCER?
IT'S NOTHING.
HAVE YOU SEEN MEW LATELY?
SHE'S PROBABLY CUTTING CLASS AS USUAL.
......

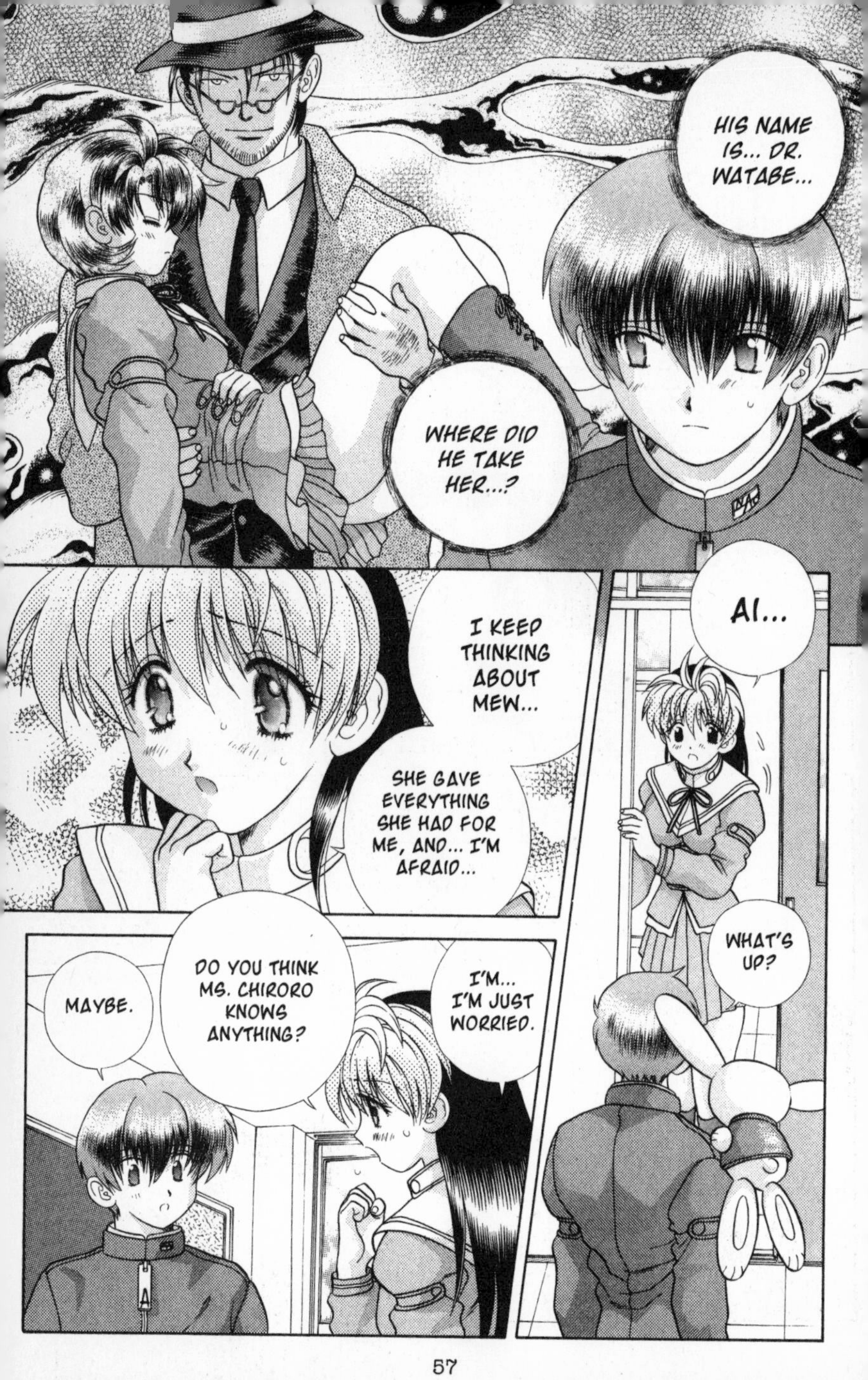
HIS NAME IS... DR. WATABE...
WHERE DID HE TAKE HER...?
AI...
WHAT'S UP?
I KEEP THINKING ABOUT MEW...
SHE GAVE EVERYTHING SHE HAD FOR ME, AND... I'M AFRAID...
I'M... I'M JUST WORRIED.
DO YOU THINK MS. CHIRORO KNOWS ANYTHING?
MAYBE.

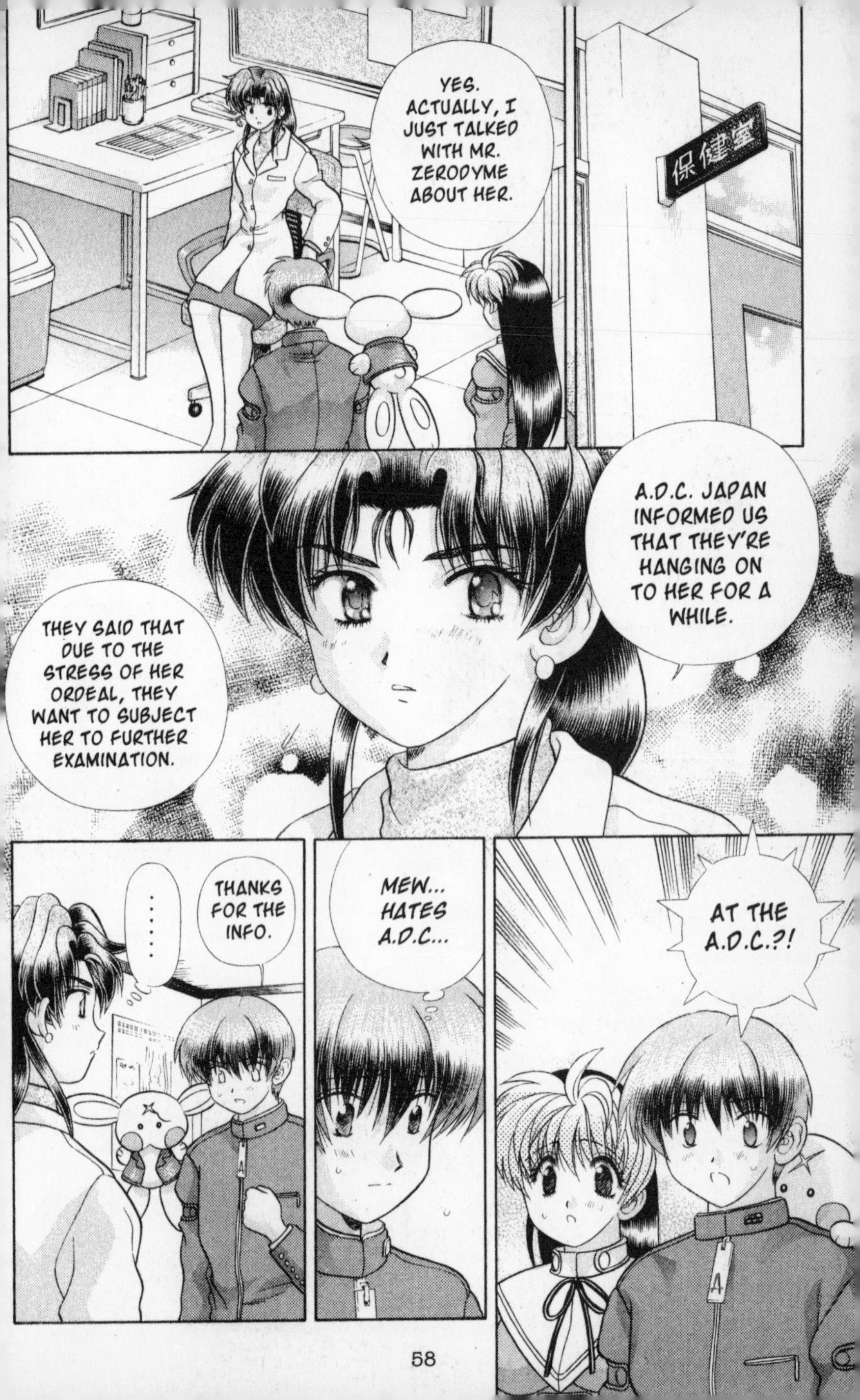
保健室
YES. ACTUALLY, I JUST TALKED WITH MR. ZERODYME ABOUT HER.
A.D.C. JAPAN INFORMED US THAT THEY'RE HANGING ON TO HER FOR A WHILE.
THEY SAID THAT DUE TO THE STRESS OF HER ORDEAL, THEY WANT TO SUBJECT HER TO FURTHER EXAMINATION.
AT THE A.D.C.?!
MEW... HATES A.D.C...
THANKS FOR THE INFO.
......

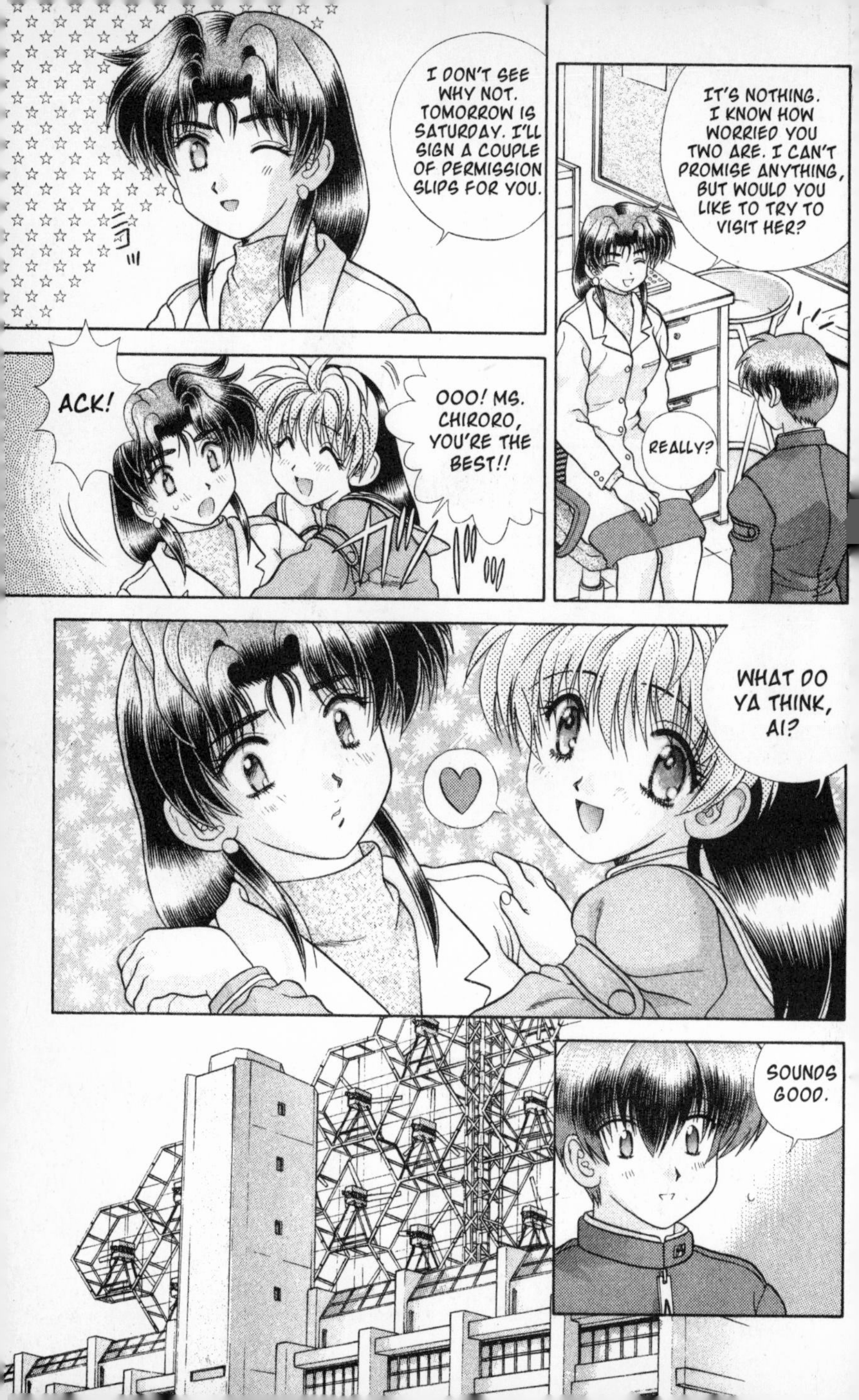
IT'S NOTHING. I KNOW HOW WORRIED YOU TWO ARE. I CAN'T PROMISE ANYTHING, BUT WOULD YOU LIKE TO TRY TO VISIT HER?
REALLY?
I DON'T SEE WHY NOT. TOMORROW IS SATURDAY. I'LL SIGN A COUPLE OF PERMISSION SLIPS FOR YOU.
OOO! MS. CHIRORO, YOU'RE THE BEST!!
ACK!
WHAT DO YA THINK, AI?
SOUNDS GOOD.

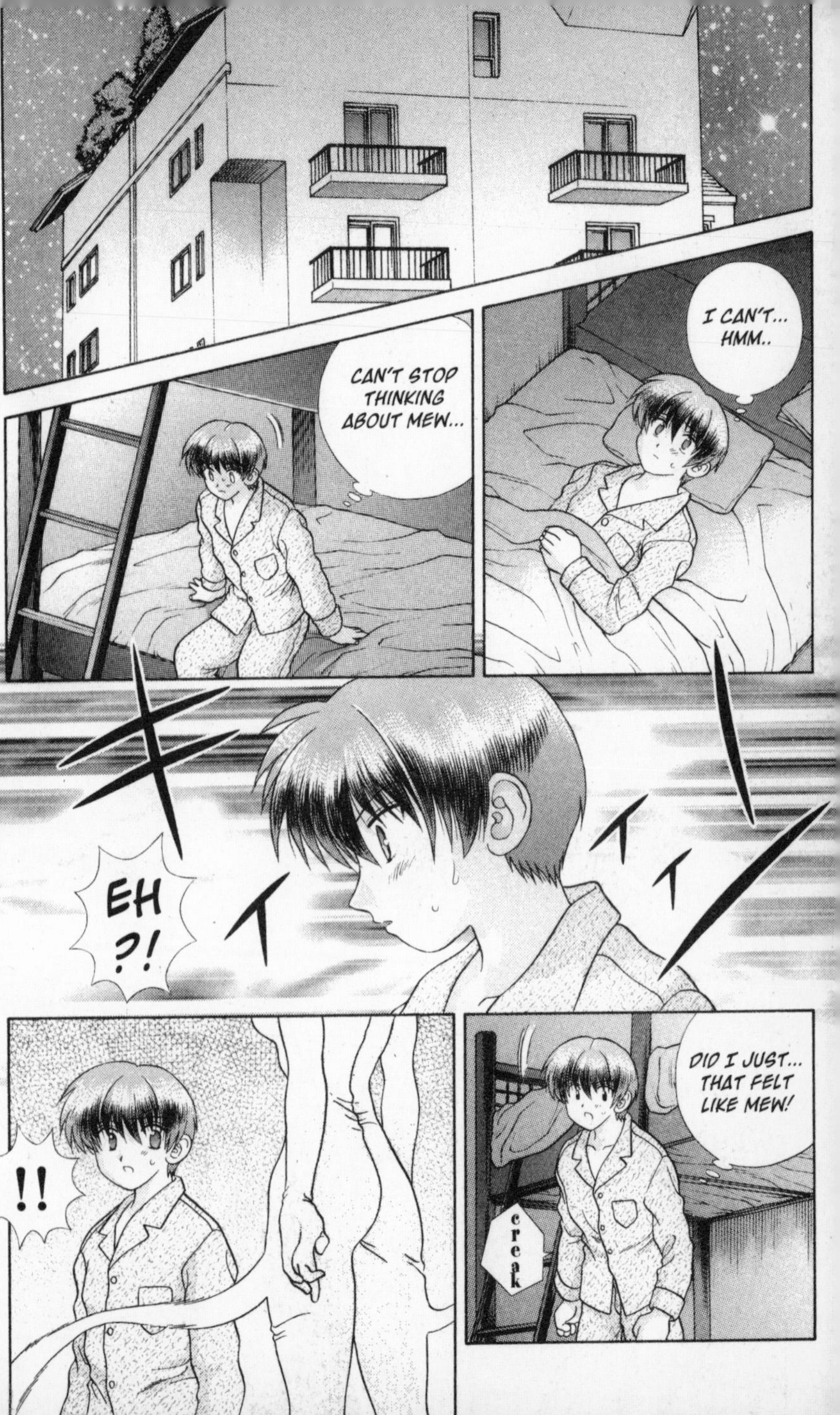
I CAN'T... HMM..
CAN'T STOP THINKING ABOUT MEW...
EH ?!
DID I JUST... THAT FELT LIKE MEW!
creak
!!

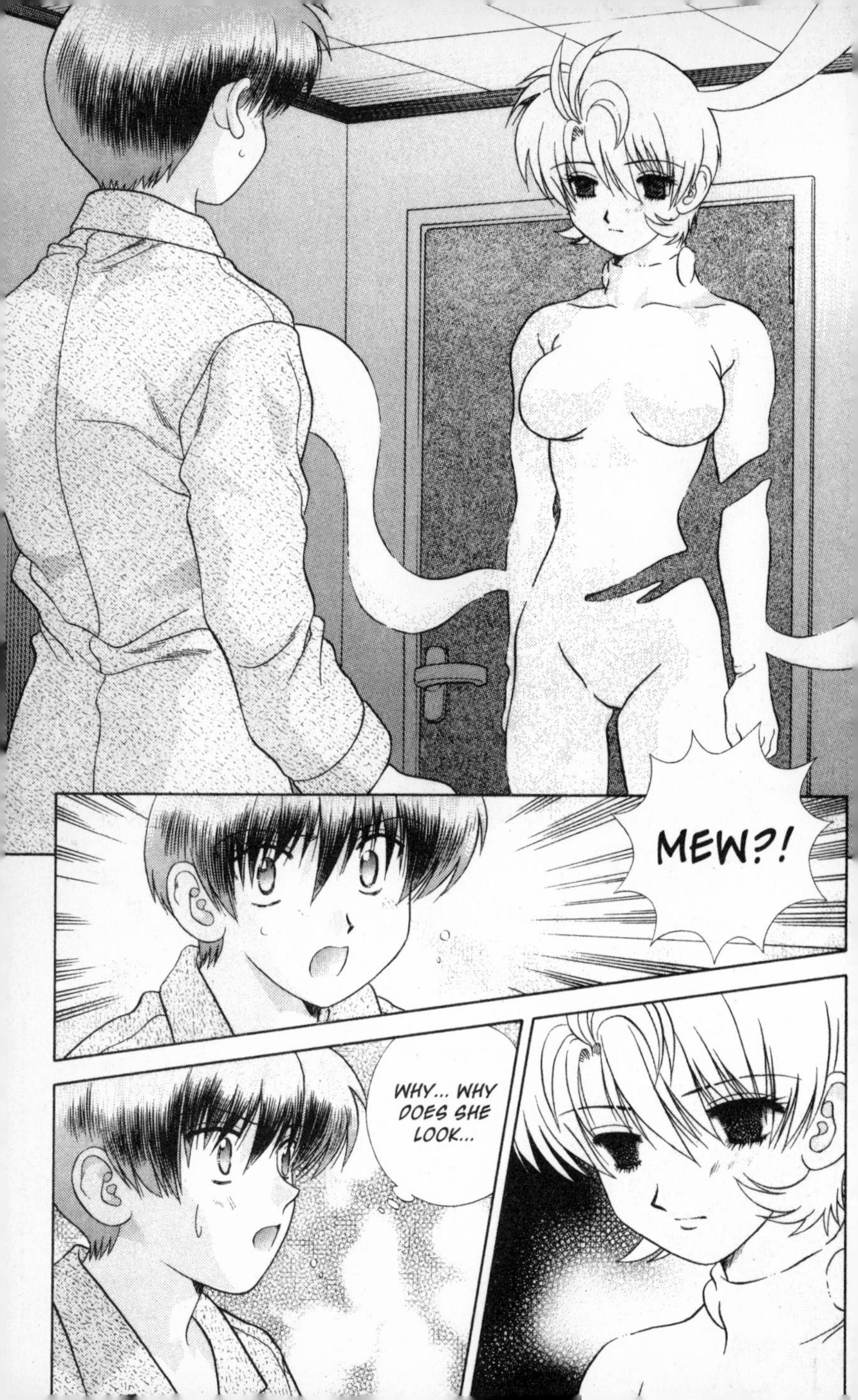
MEW?!
WHY... WHY DOES SHE LOOK...

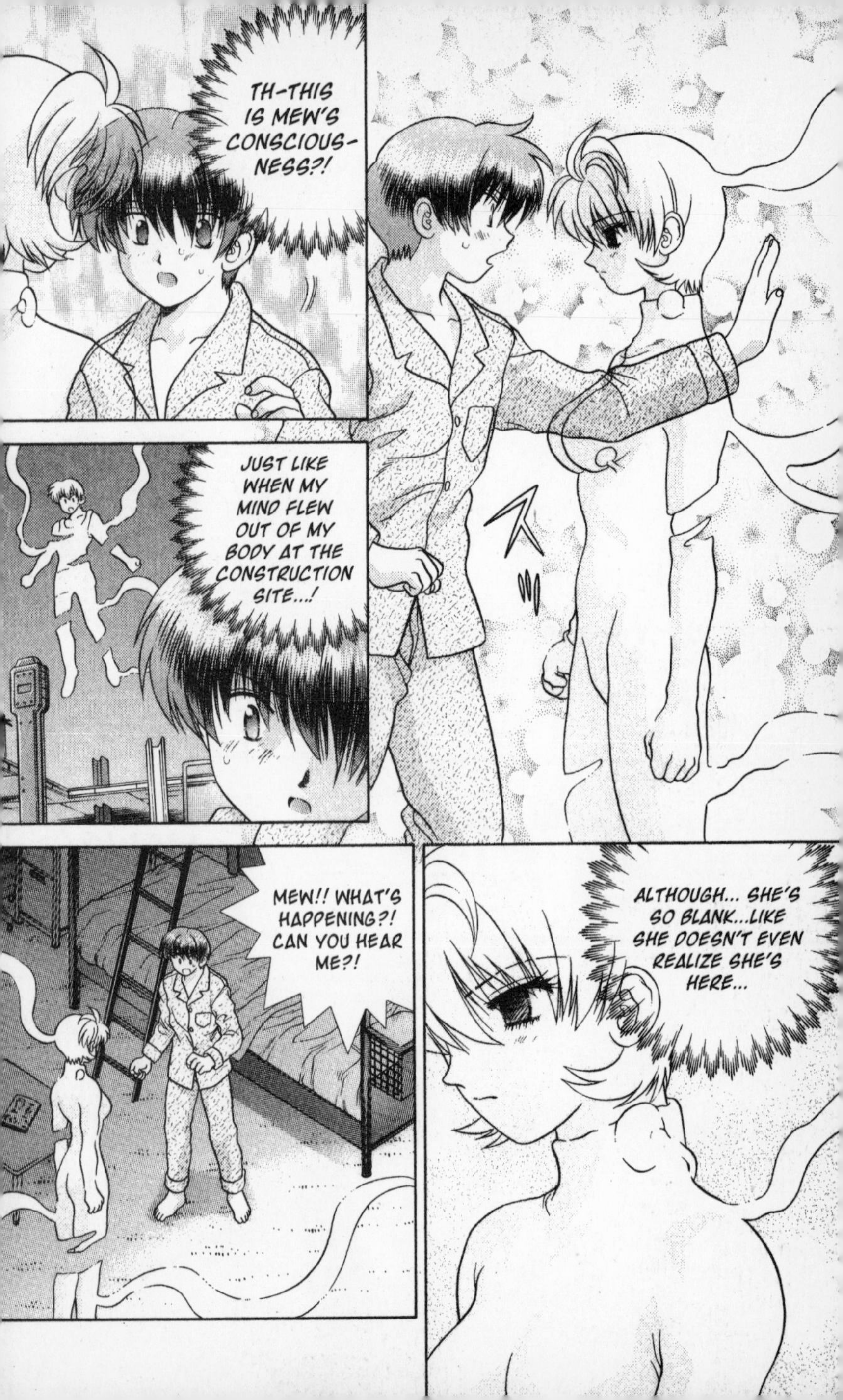
ス
TH-THIS IS MEW'S CONSCIOUS-NESS?!
JUST LIKE WHEN MY MIND FLEW OUT OF MY BODY AT THE CONSTRUCTION SITE...!
ALTHOUGH... SHE'S SO BLANK...LIKE SHE DOESN'T EVEN REALIZE SHE'S HERE...
MEW!! WHAT'S HAPPENING?! CAN YOU HEAR ME?!

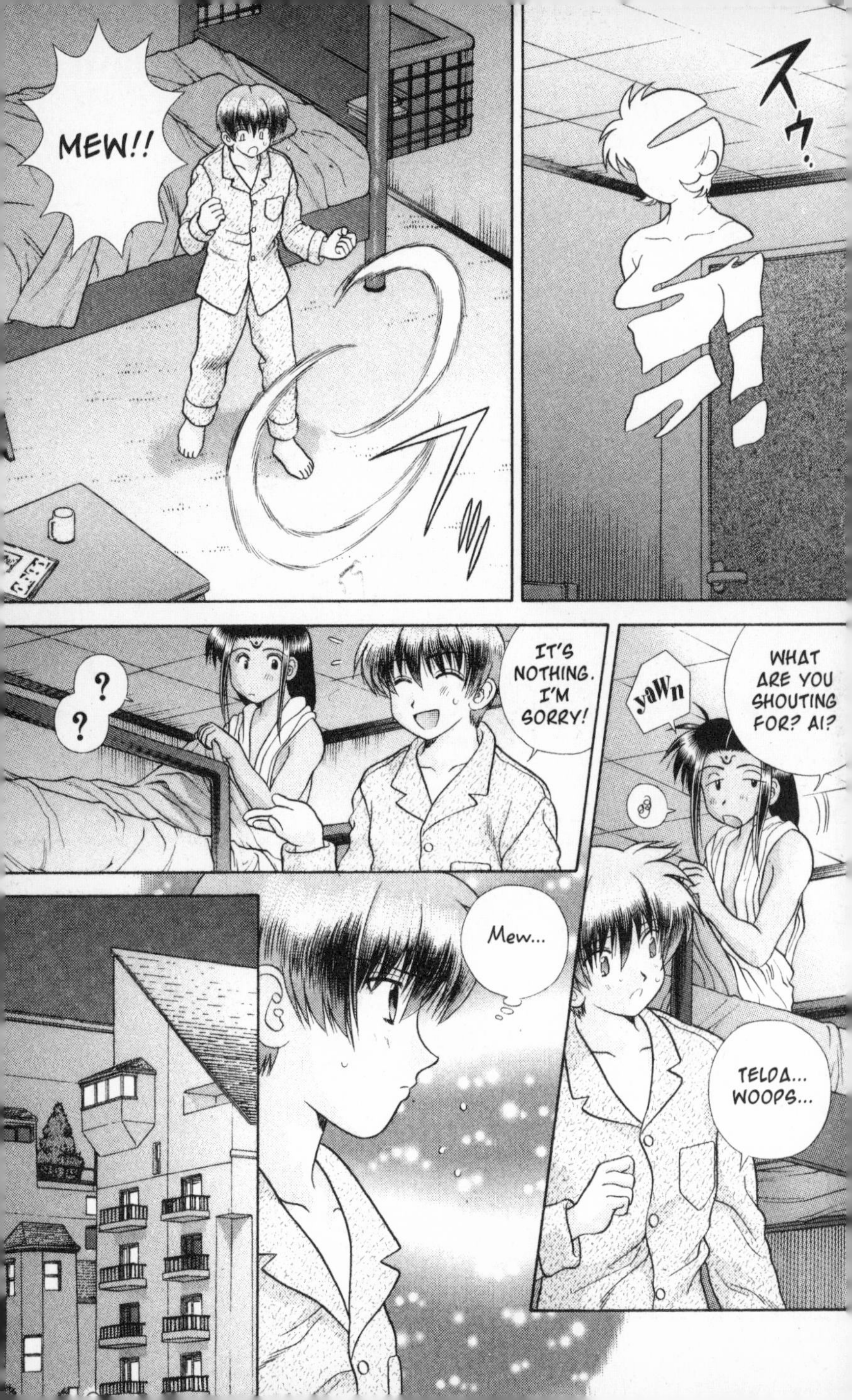

スゥ..
MEW!!
yaWn
WHAT ARE YOU SHOUTING FOR? AI?
? ?
IT'S NOTHING. I'M SORRY!
TELDA... WOOPS...
Mew...

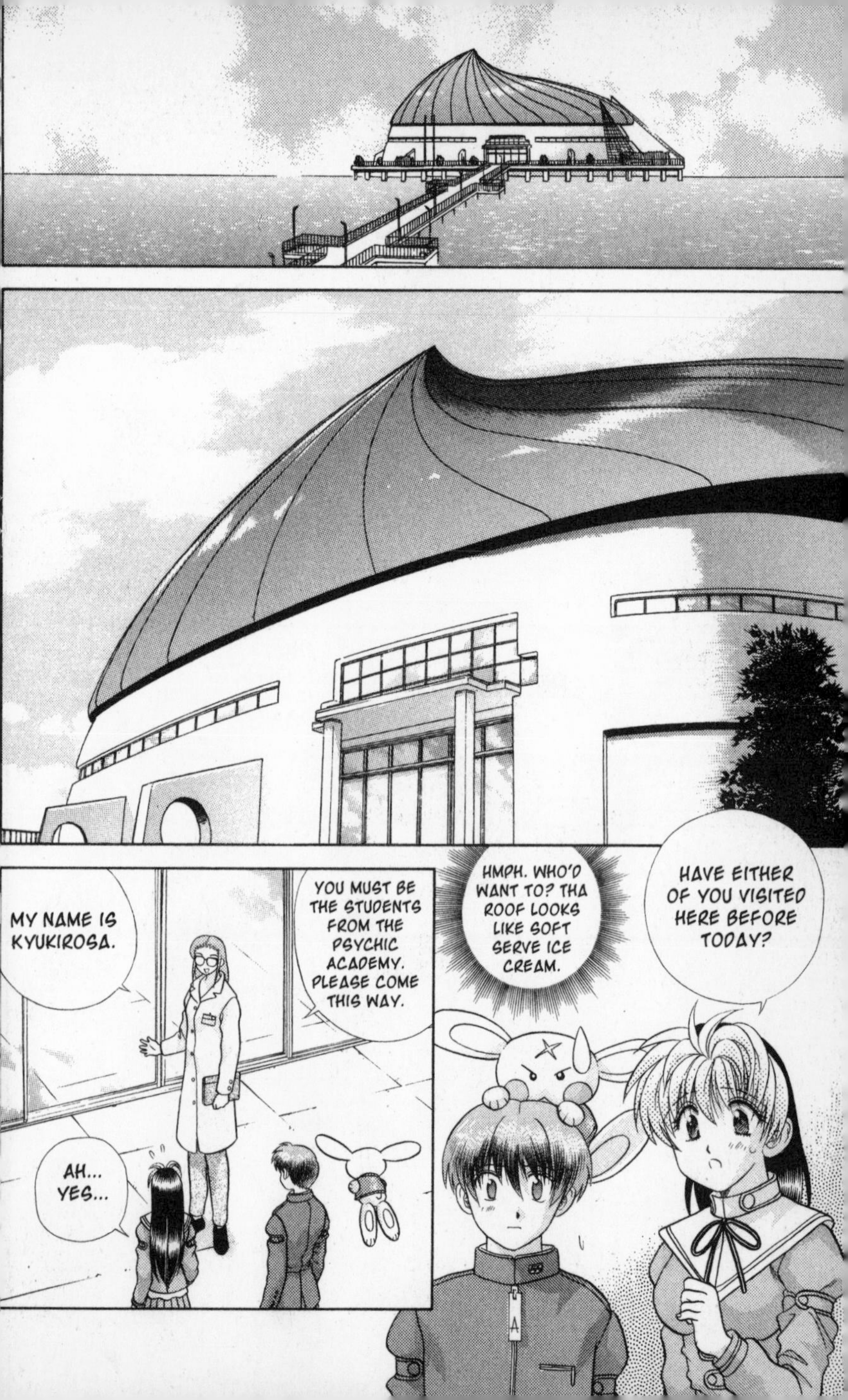
HAVE EITHER OF YOU VISITED HERE BEFORE TODAY?
HMPH. WHO'D WANT TO? THA ROOF LOOKS LIKE SOFT SERVE ICE CREAM.
YOU MUST BE THE STUDENTS FROM THE PSYCHIC ACADEMY. PLEASE COME THIS WAY.
MY NAME IS KYUKIROSA.
AH... YES...

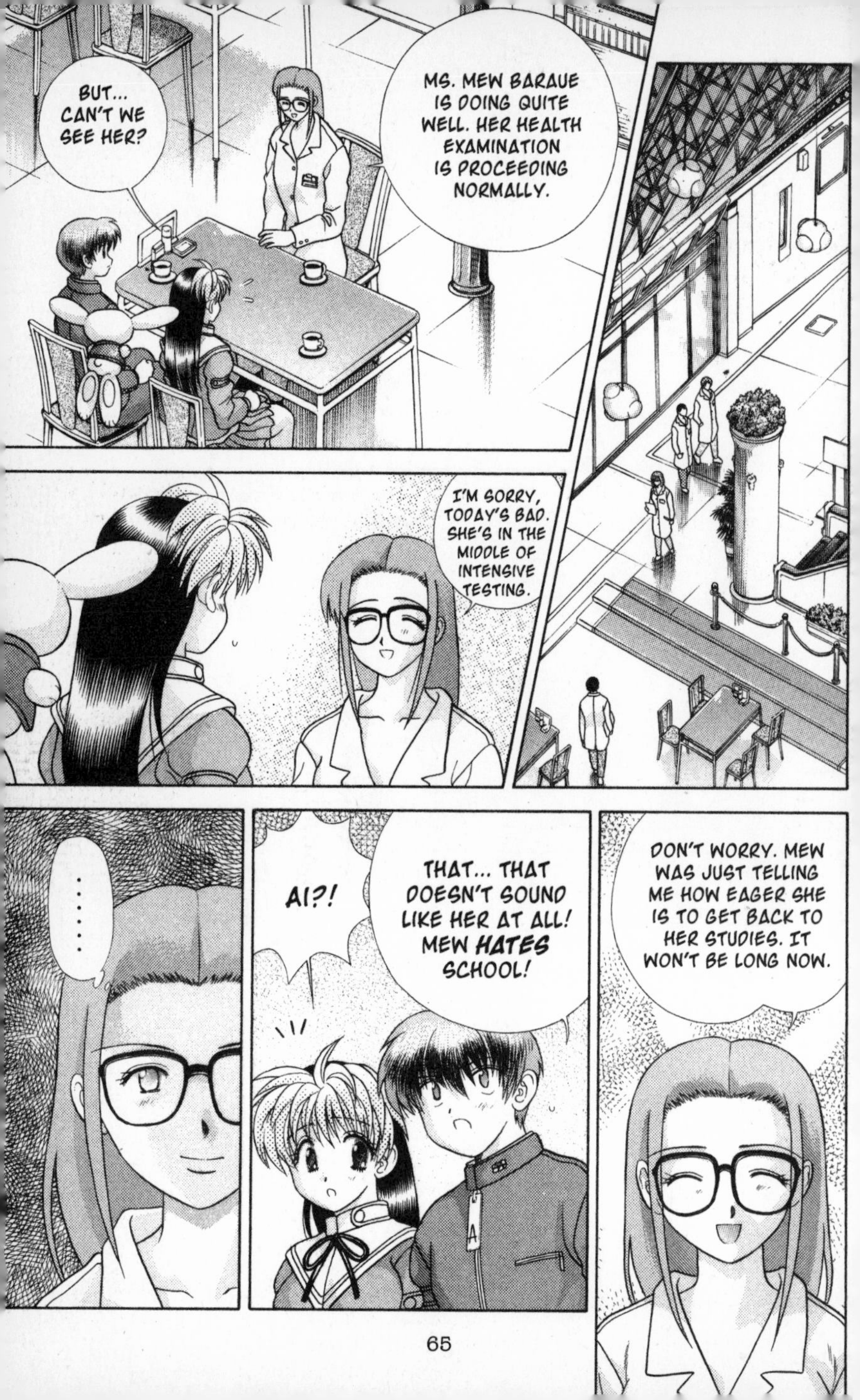
MS. MEW BARAUE IS DOING QUITE WELL. HER HEALTH EXAMINATION IS PROCEEDING NORMALLY.
BUT... CAN'T WE SEE HER?
I'M SORRY, TODAY'S BAD. SHE'S IN THE MIDDLE OF INTENSIVE TESTING.
DON'T WORRY. MEW WAS JUST TELLING ME HOW EAGER SHE IS TO GET BACK TO HER STUDIES. IT WON'T BE LONG NOW.
THAT... THAT DOESN'T SOUND LIKE HER AT ALL! MEW **HATES** SCHOOL!
AI?!
......

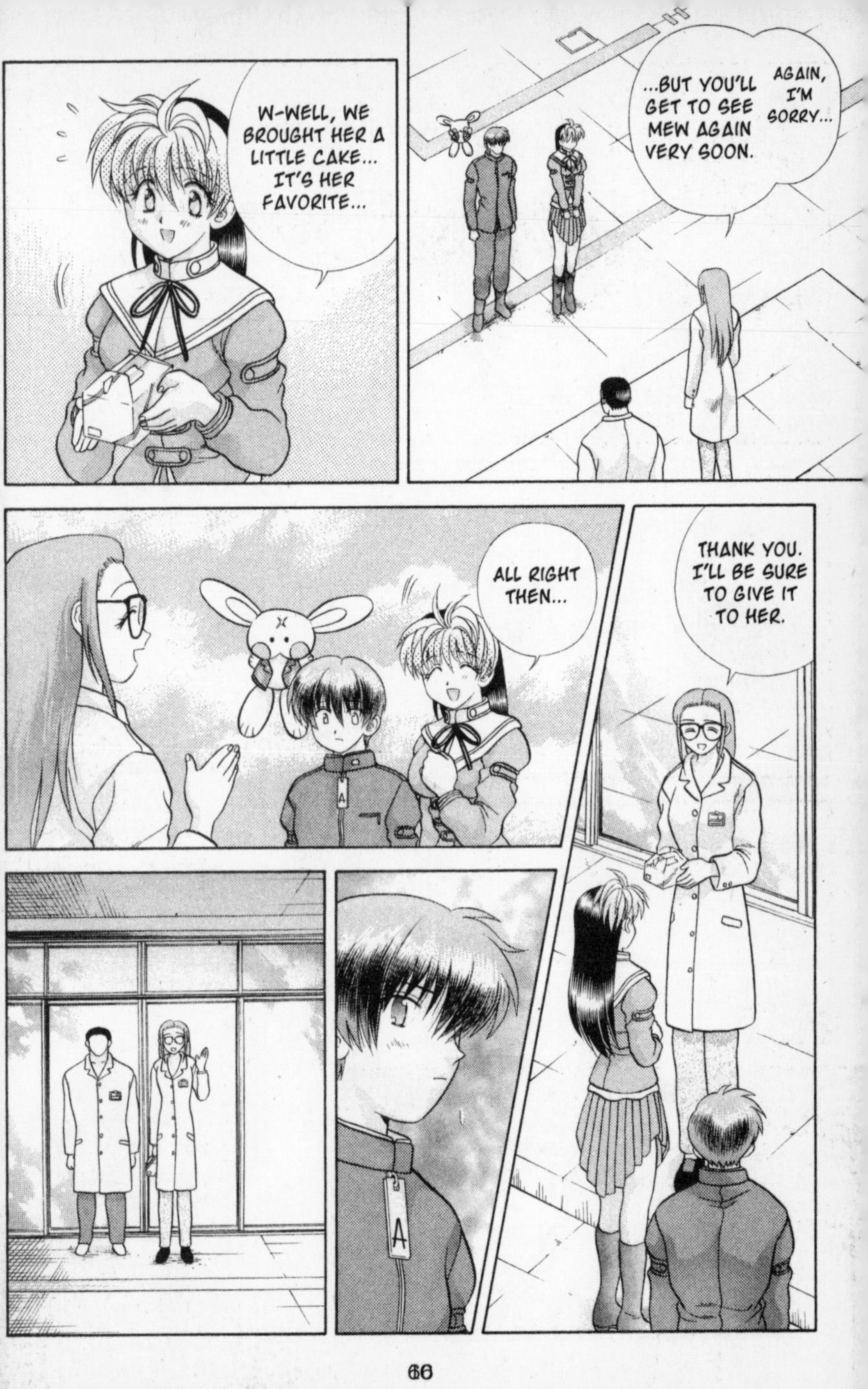
AGAIN, I'M SORRY...
...BUT YOU'LL GET TO SEE MEW AGAIN VERY SOON.
W-WELL, WE BROUGHT HER A LITTLE CAKE... IT'S HER FAVORITE...
THANK YOU. I'LL BE SURE TO GIVE IT TO HER.
ALL RIGHT THEN...
A
A

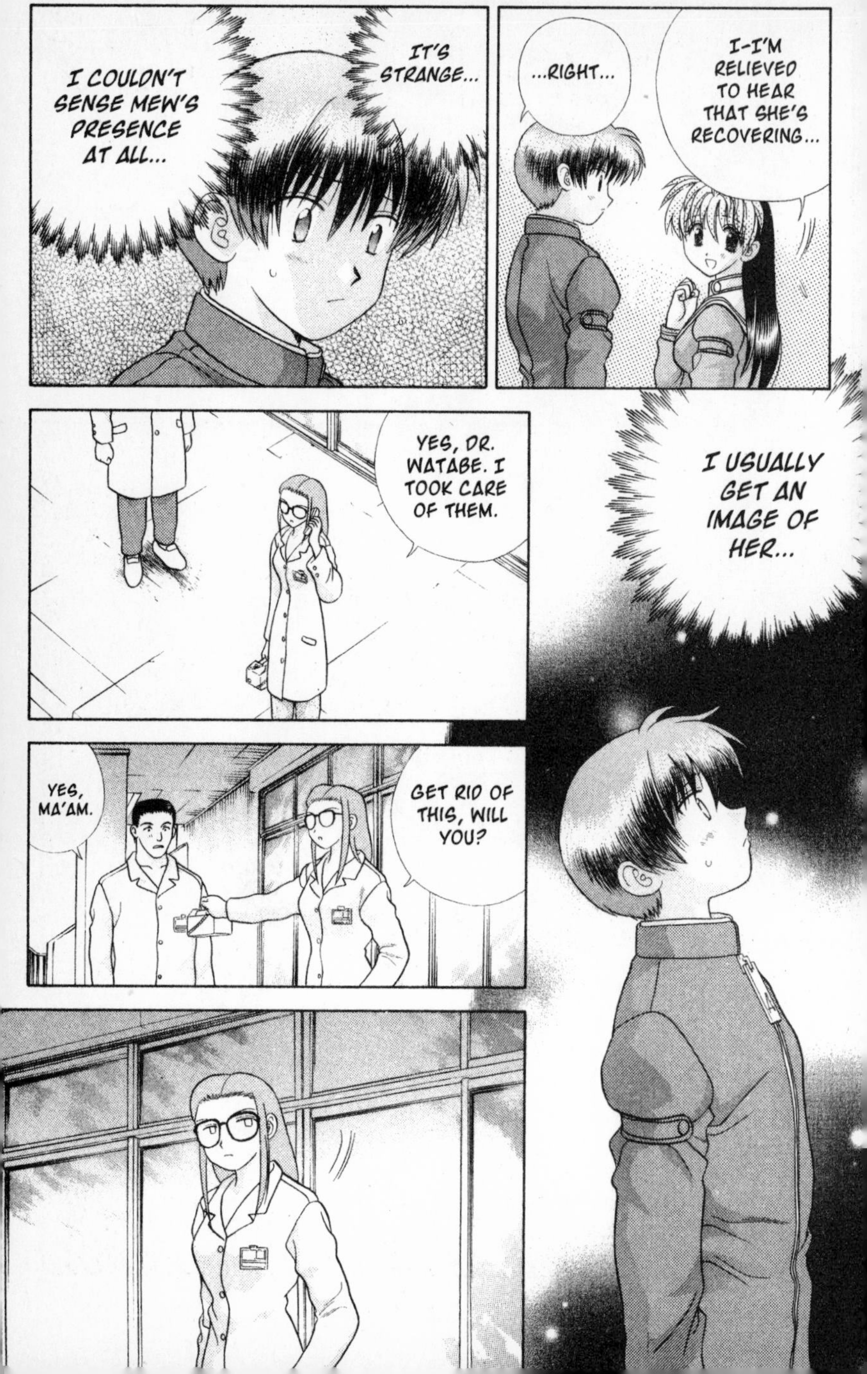
I-I'M RELIEVED TO HEAR THAT SHE'S RECOVERING...
...RIGHT...
IT'S STRANGE...
I COULDN'T SENSE MEW'S PRESENCE AT ALL...
I USUALLY GET AN IMAGE OF HER...
YES, DR. WATABE. I TOOK CARE OF THEM.
GET RID OF THIS, WILL YOU?
YES, MA'AM.

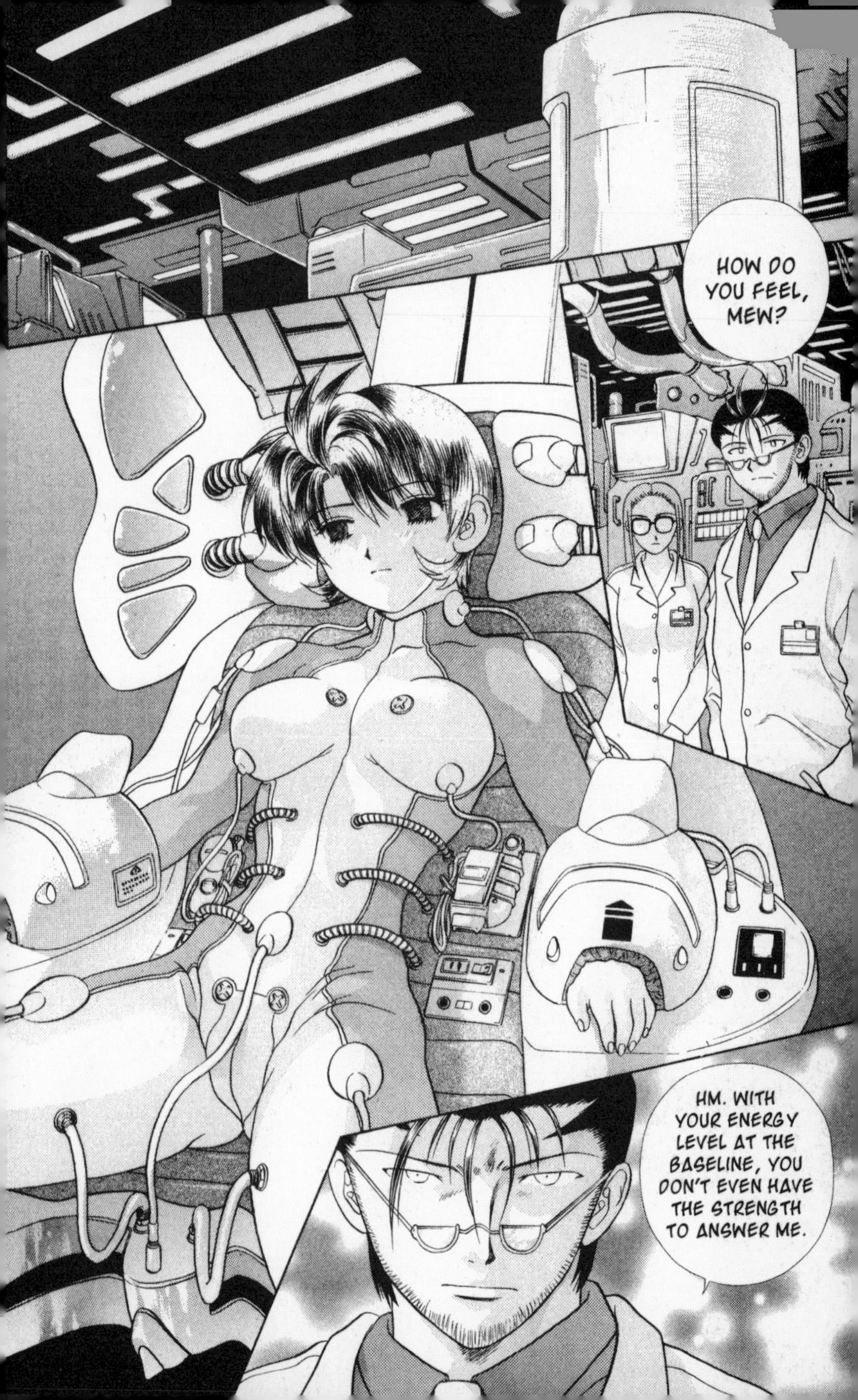
HOW DO YOU FEEL, MEW?
HM. WITH YOUR ENERGY LEVEL AT THE BASELINE, YOU DON'T EVEN HAVE THE STRENGTH TO ANSWER ME.

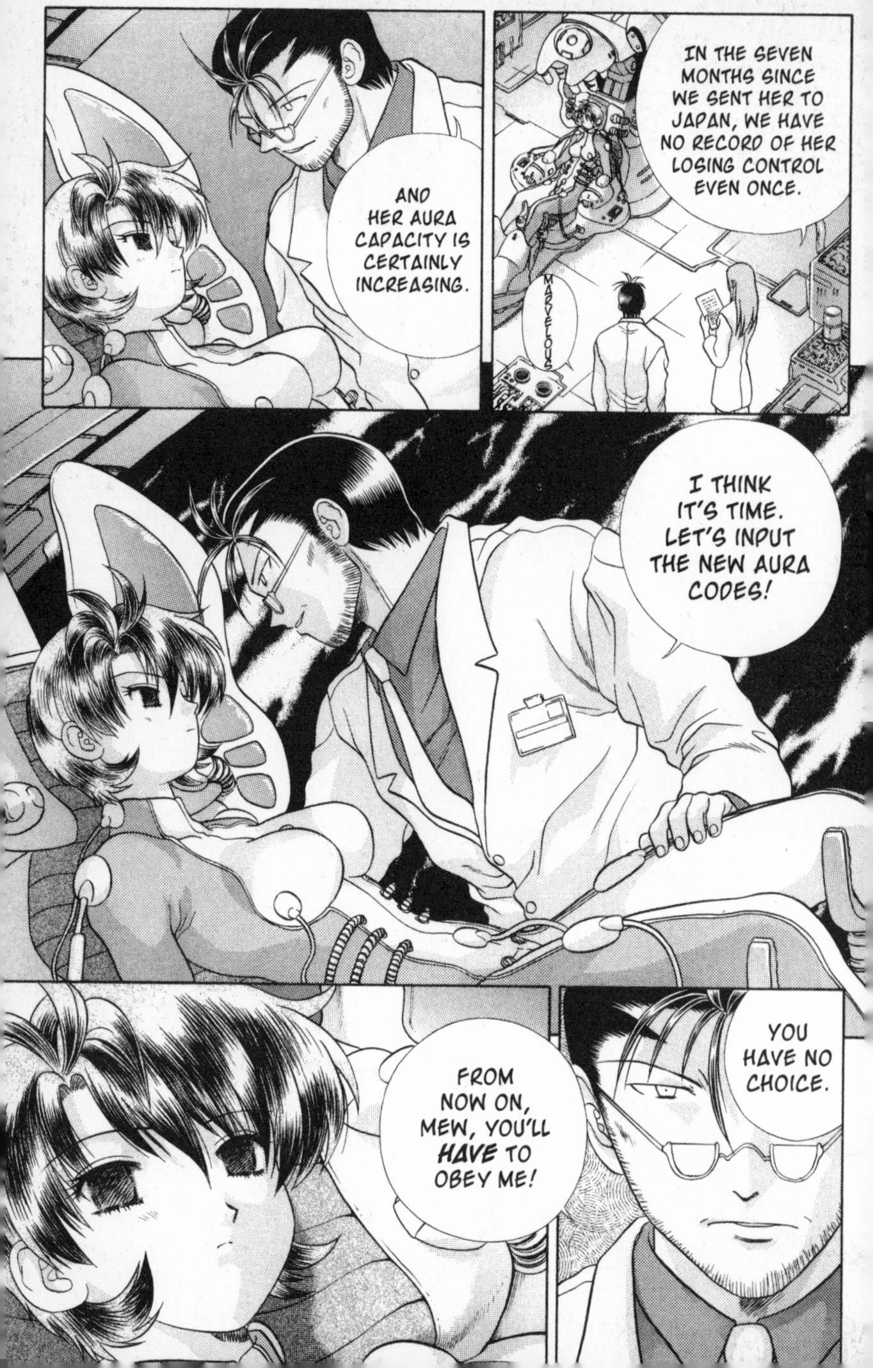
IN THE SEVEN MONTHS SINCE WE SENT HER TO JAPAN, WE HAVE NO RECORD OF HER LOSING CONTROL EVEN ONCE.
MARVELOUS
AND HER AURA CAPACITY IS CERTAINLY INCREASING.
I THINK IT'S TIME. LET'S INPUT THE NEW AURA CODES!
YOU HAVE NO CHOICE.
FROM NOW ON, MEW, YOU'LL *HAVE* TO OBEY ME!

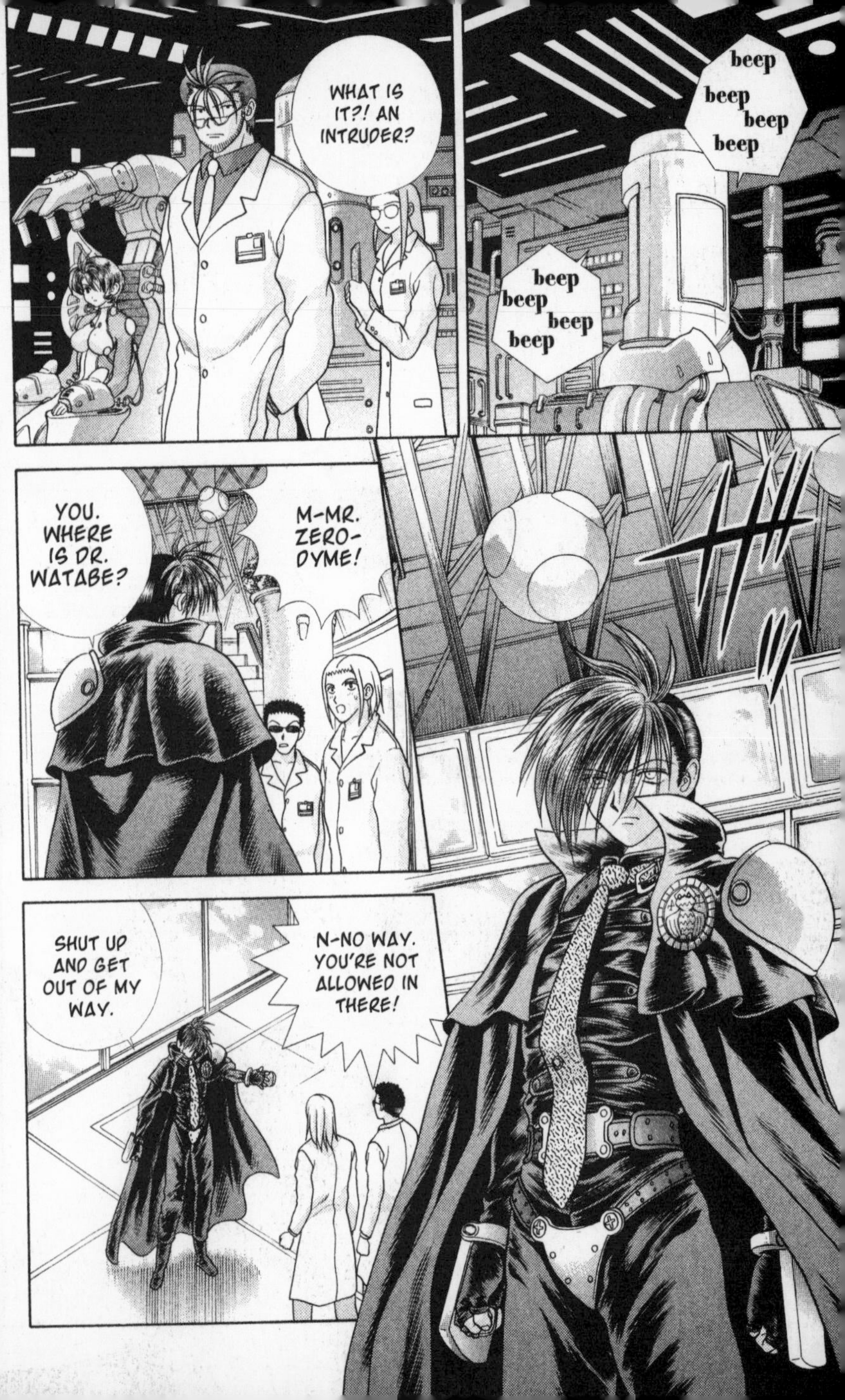
beep
beep
beep
beep
beep
beep
beep
beep
WHAT IS IT?! AN INTRUDER?
M-MR. ZERO-DYME!
YOU. WHERE IS DR. WATABE?
N-NO WAY. YOU'RE NOT ALLOWED IN THERE!
SHUT UP AND GET OUT OF MY WAY.

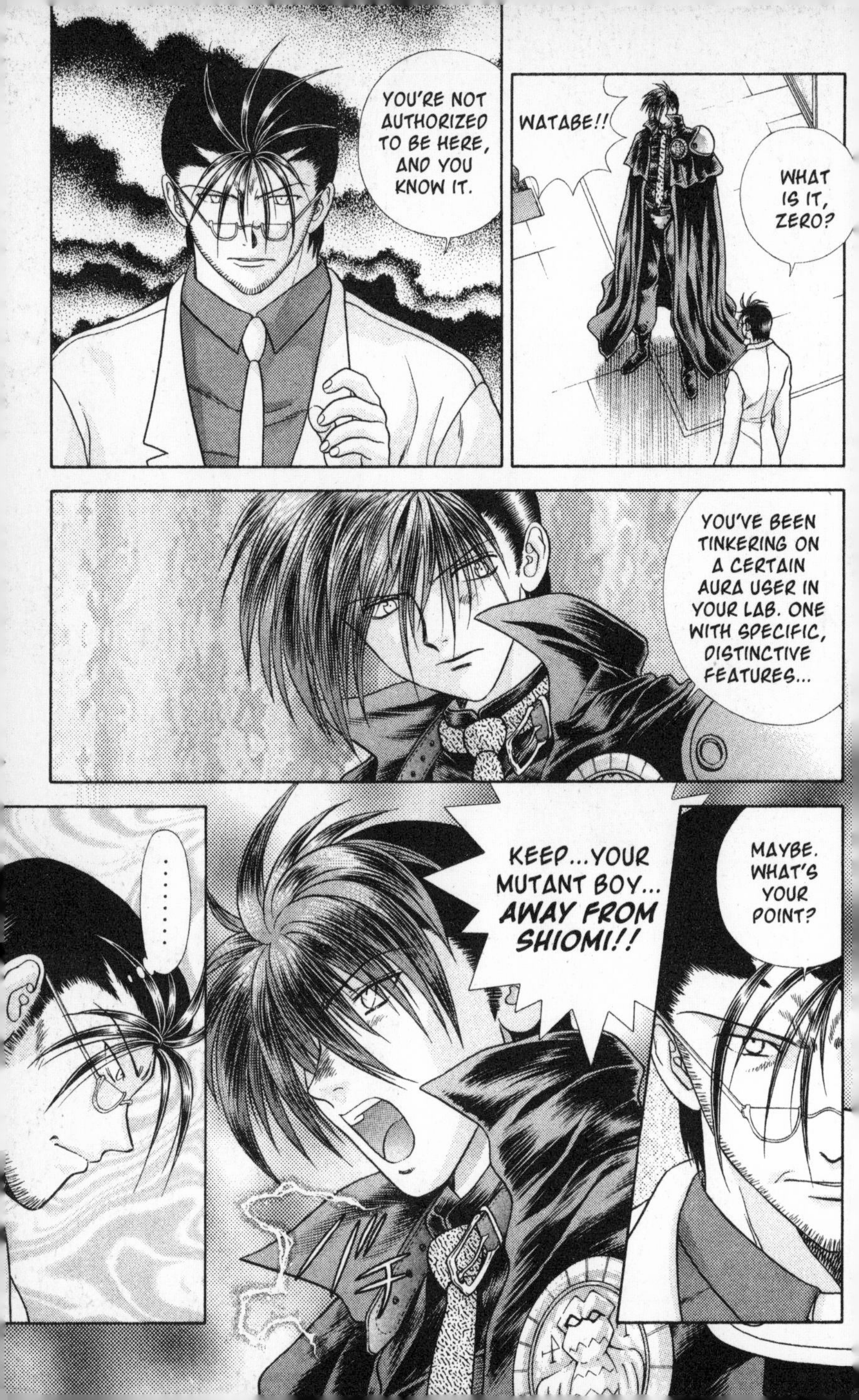
WATABE!!
WHAT IS IT, ZERO?
YOU'RE NOT AUTHORIZED TO BE HERE, AND YOU KNOW IT.
YOU'VE BEEN TINKERING ON A CERTAIN AURA USER IN YOUR LAB. ONE WITH SPECIFIC, DISTINCTIVE FEATURES...
MAYBE. WHAT'S YOUR POINT?
KEEP...YOUR MUTANT BOY... AWAY FROM SHIOMI!!
......

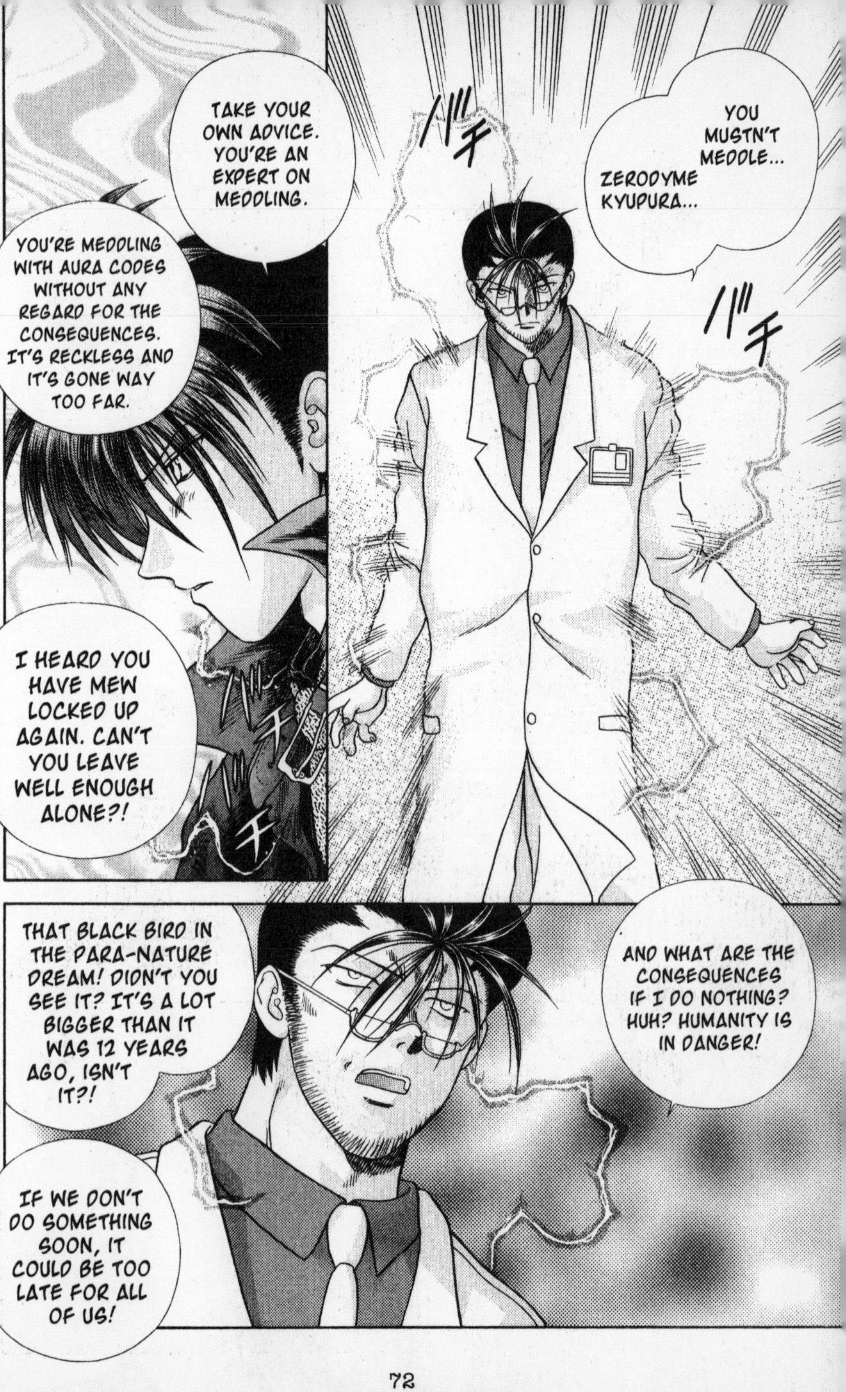
YOU MUSTN'T MEDDLE... ZERODYME KYUPURA...
バチ
バチ
TAKE YOUR OWN ADVICE. YOU'RE AN EXPERT ON MEDDLING.
YOU'RE MEDDLING WITH AURA CODES WITHOUT ANY REGARD FOR THE CONSEQUENCES. IT'S RECKLESS AND IT'S GONE WAY TOO FAR.
I HEARD YOU HAVE MEW LOCKED UP AGAIN. CAN'T YOU LEAVE WELL ENOUGH ALONE?!
AND WHAT ARE THE CONSEQUENCES IF I DO NOTHING? HUH? HUMANITY IS IN DANGER!
THAT BLACK BIRD IN THE PARA-NATURE DREAM! DIDN'T YOU SEE IT? IT'S A LOT BIGGER THAN IT WAS 12 YEARS AGO, ISN'T IT?!
IF WE DON'T DO SOMETHING SOON, IT COULD BE TOO LATE FOR ALL OF US!

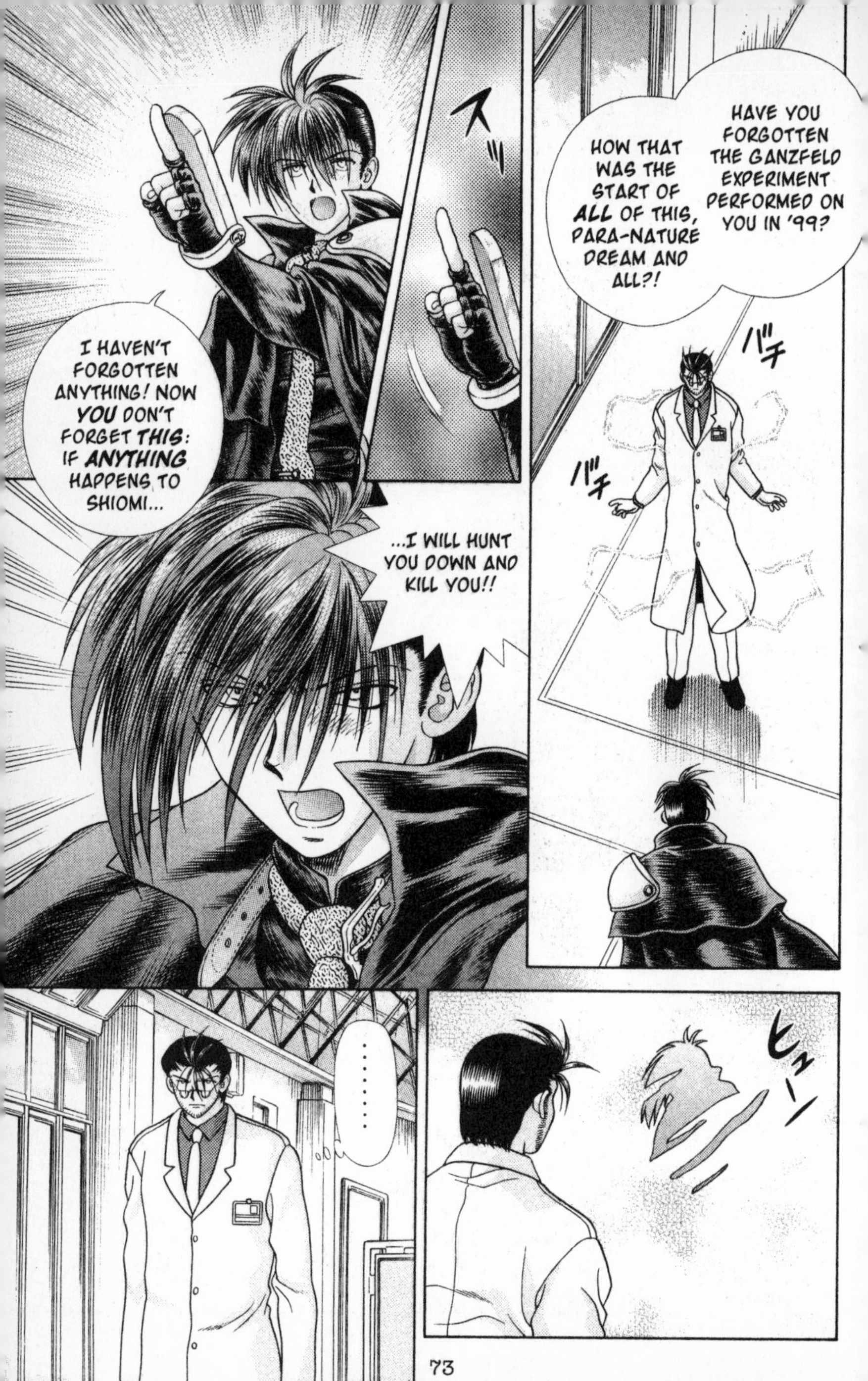
HAVE YOU FORGOTTEN THE GANZFELD EXPERIMENT PERFORMED ON YOU IN '99?
HOW THAT WAS THE START OF ALL OF THIS, PARA-NATURE DREAM AND ALL?!
I HAVEN'T FORGOTTEN ANYTHING! NOW YOU DON'T FORGET THIS: IF ANYTHING HAPPENS TO SHIOMI...
...I WILL HUNT YOU DOWN AND KILL YOU!!
......

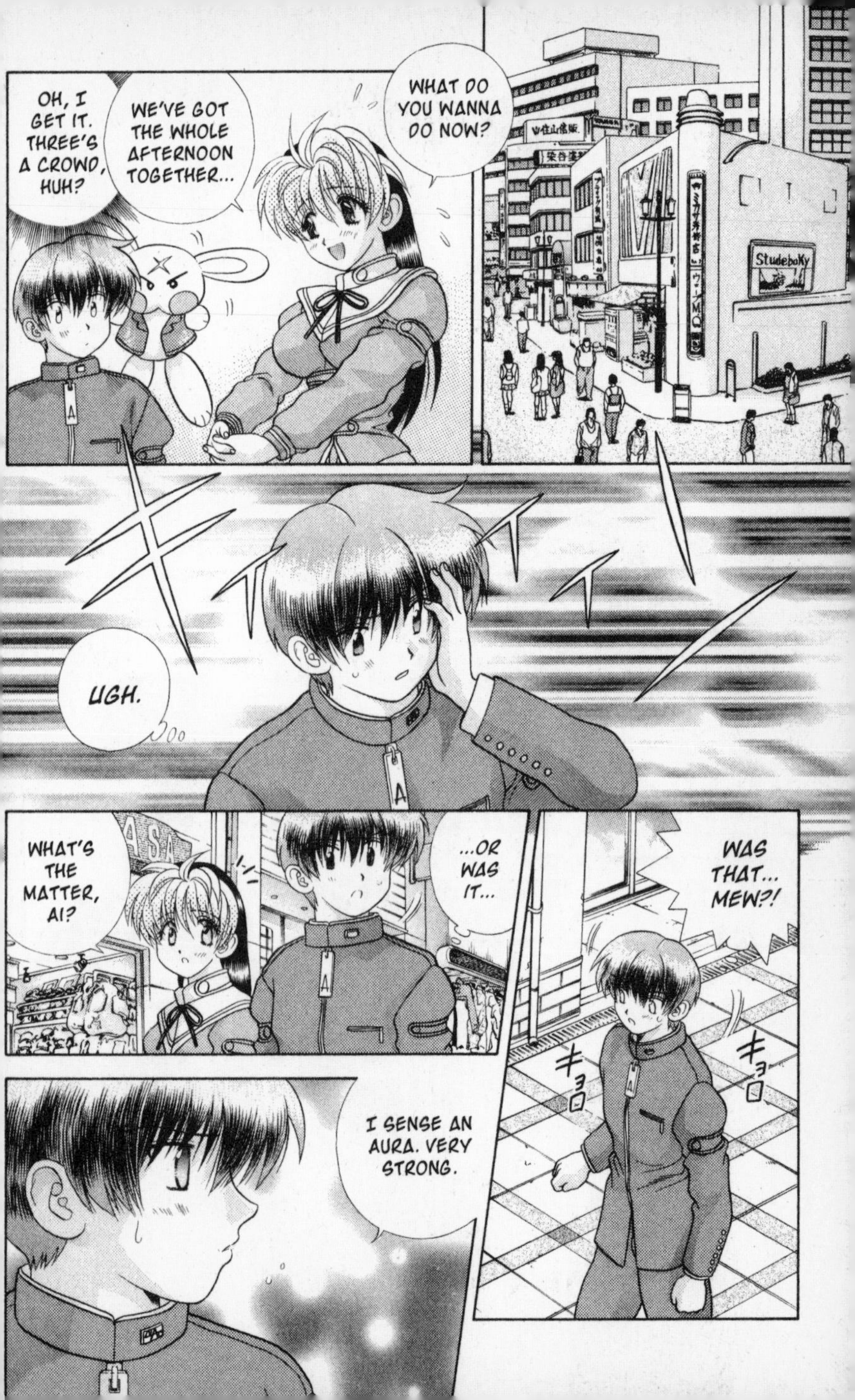
WHAT DO YOU WANNA DO NOW?
WE'VE GOT THE WHOLE AFTERNOON TOGETHER...
OH, I GET IT. THREE'S A CROWD, HUH?
UGH.
WAS THAT... MEW?!
キョロ
キョロ
...OR WAS IT...
WHAT'S THE MATTER, AI?
I SENSE AN AURA. VERY STRONG.

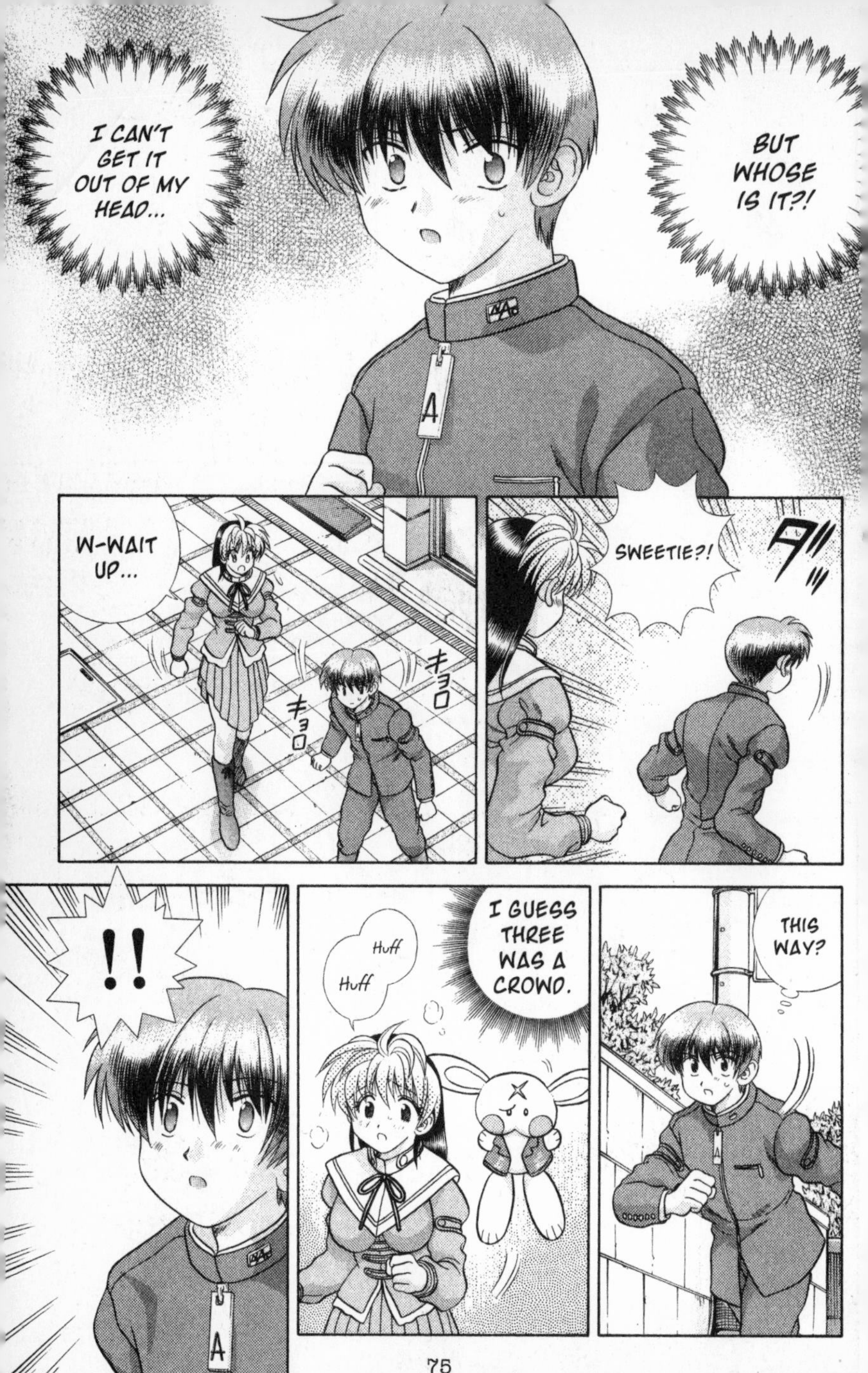
BUT WHOSE IS IT?!
I CAN'T GET IT OUT OF MY HEAD...
SWEETIE?!
W-WAIT UP...
キョロ
キョロ
THIS WAY?
I GUESS THREE WAS A CROWD.
Huff
Huff
!!

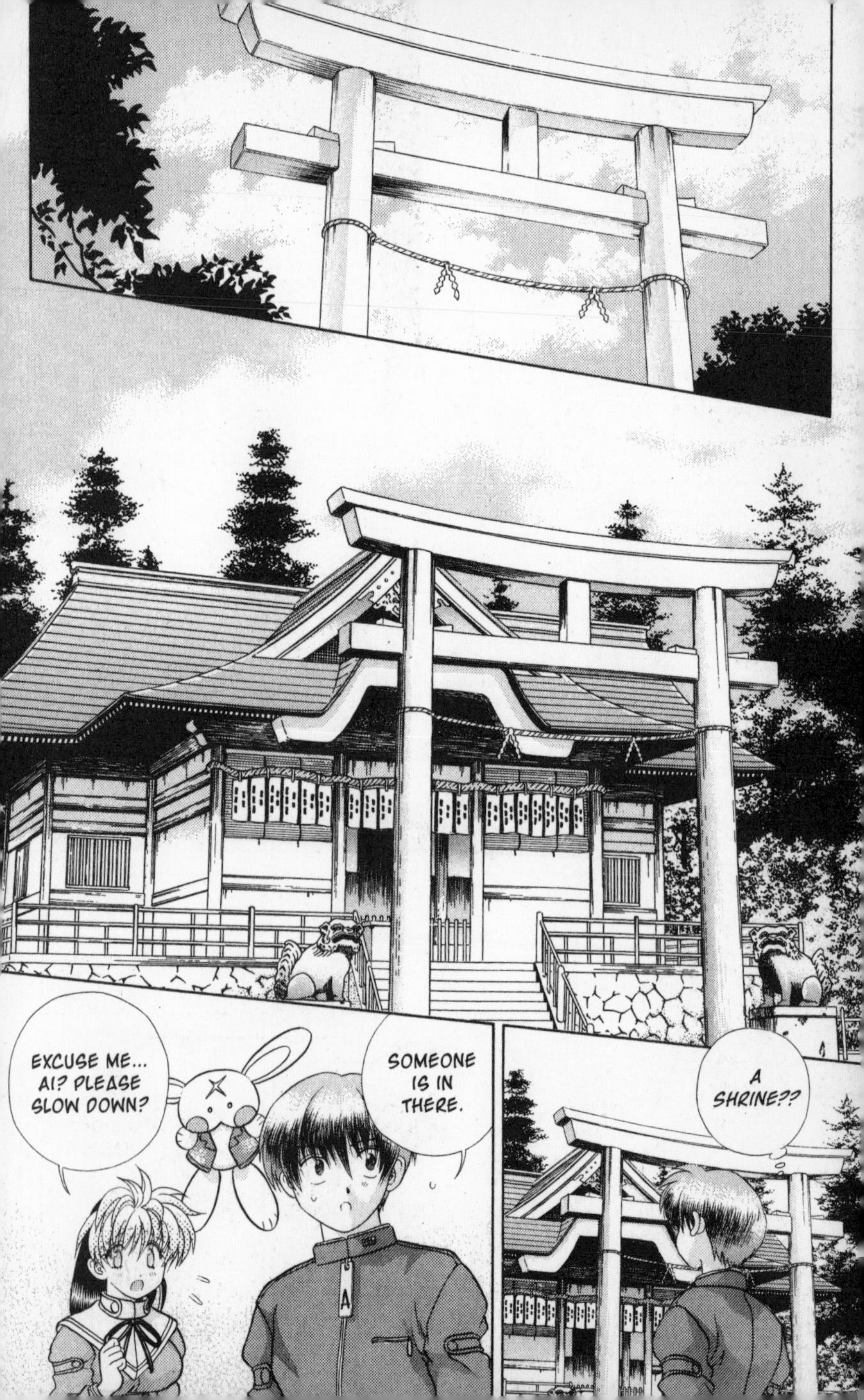
A SHRINE??
SOMEONE IS IN THERE.
EXCUSE ME... AI? PLEASE SLOW DOWN?

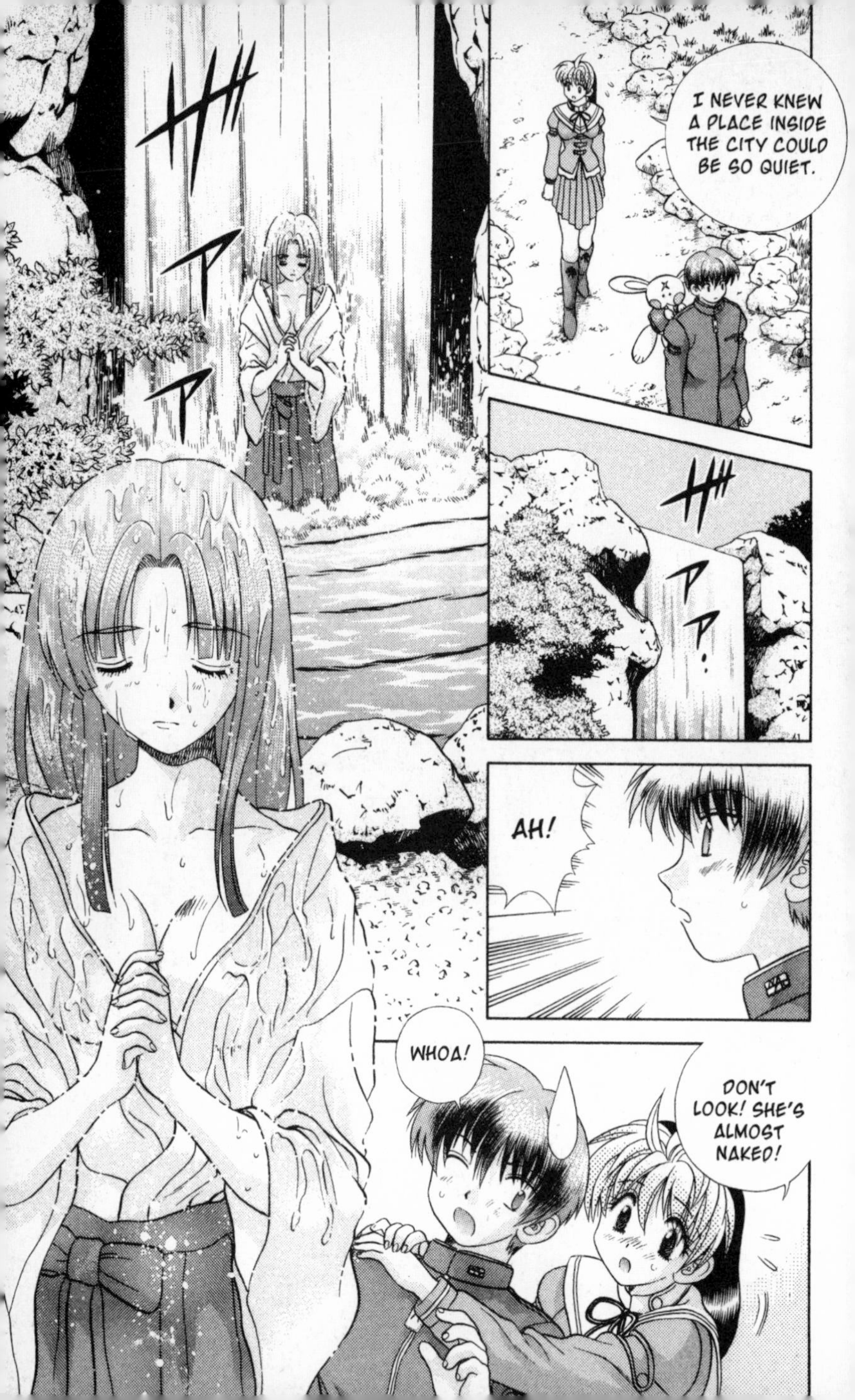
I NEVER KNEW A PLACE INSIDE THE CITY COULD BE SO QUIET.
AH!
DON'T LOOK! SHE'S ALMOST NAKED!
WHOA!

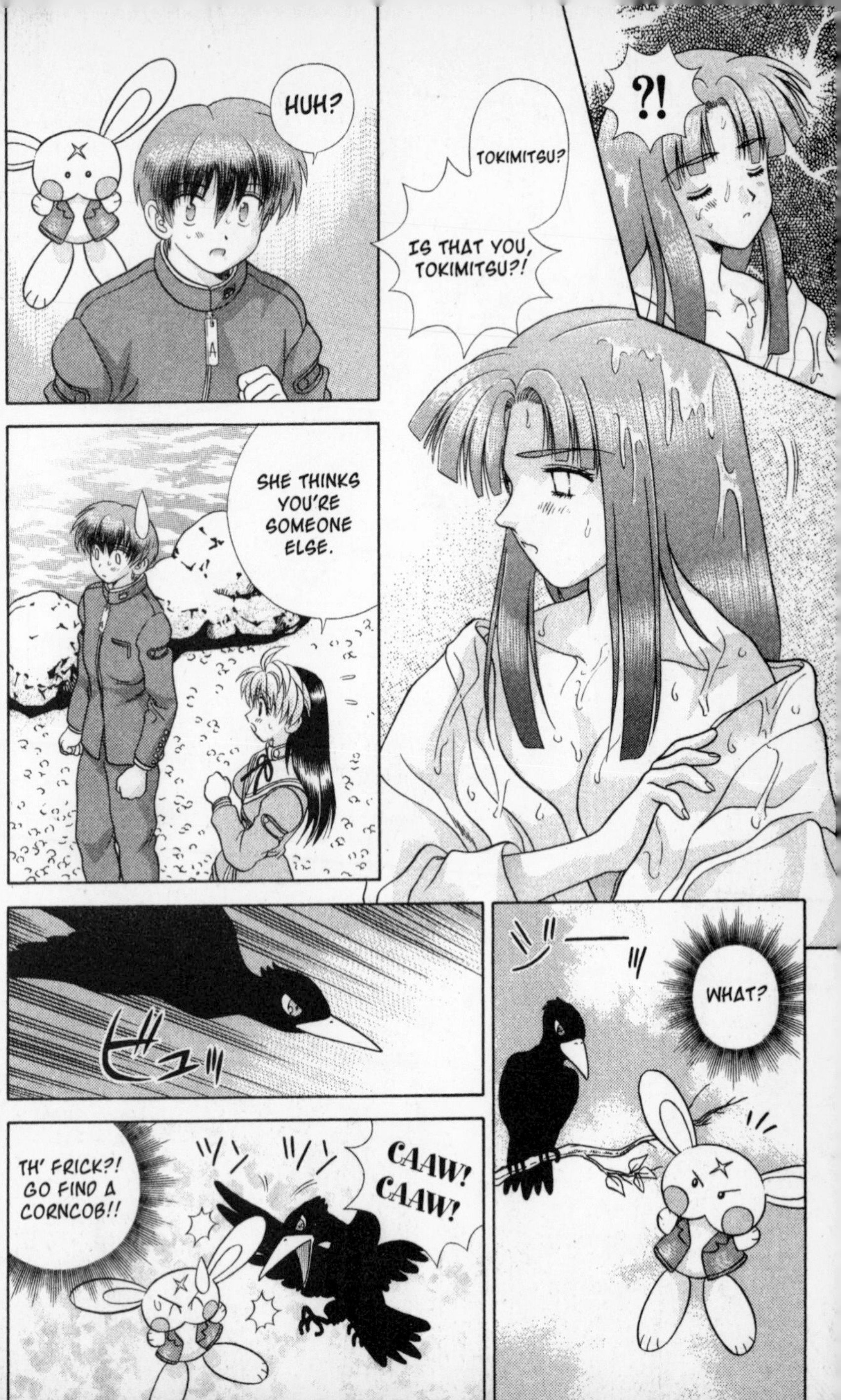
?!
TOKIMITSU?
IS THAT YOU, TOKIMITSU?!
HUH?
SHE THINKS YOU'RE SOMEONE ELSE.
WHAT?
CAAW! CAAW!
TH' FRICK?! GO FIND A CORNCOB!!

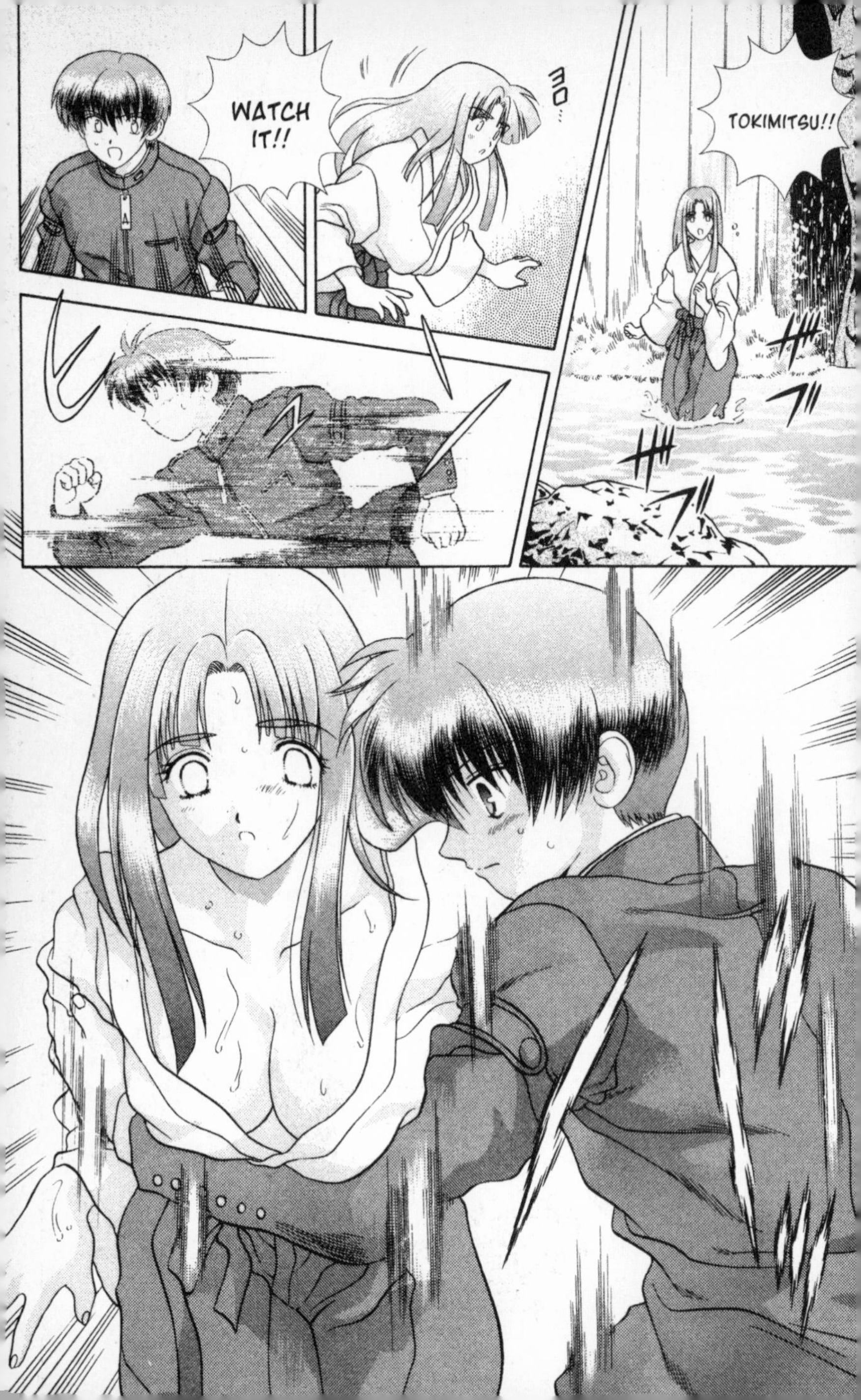

TOKIMITSU!!
WATCH IT!!

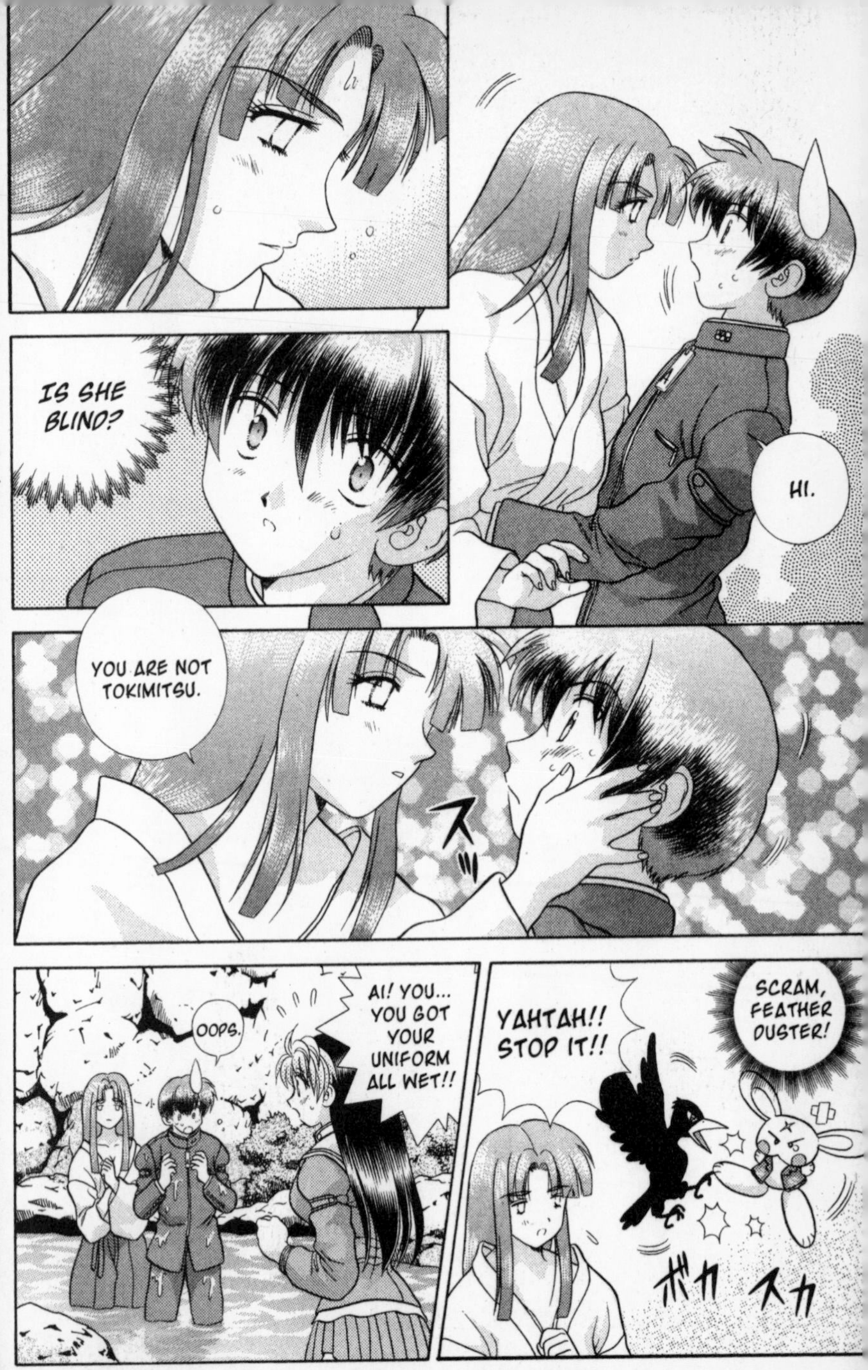
HI.
IS SHE BLIND?
YOU ARE NOT TOKIMITSU.
ス
SCRAM, FEATHER DUSTER!
YAHTAH!! STOP IT!!
ボカ スカ
AI! YOU... YOU GOT YOUR UNIFORM ALL WET!!
OOPS.

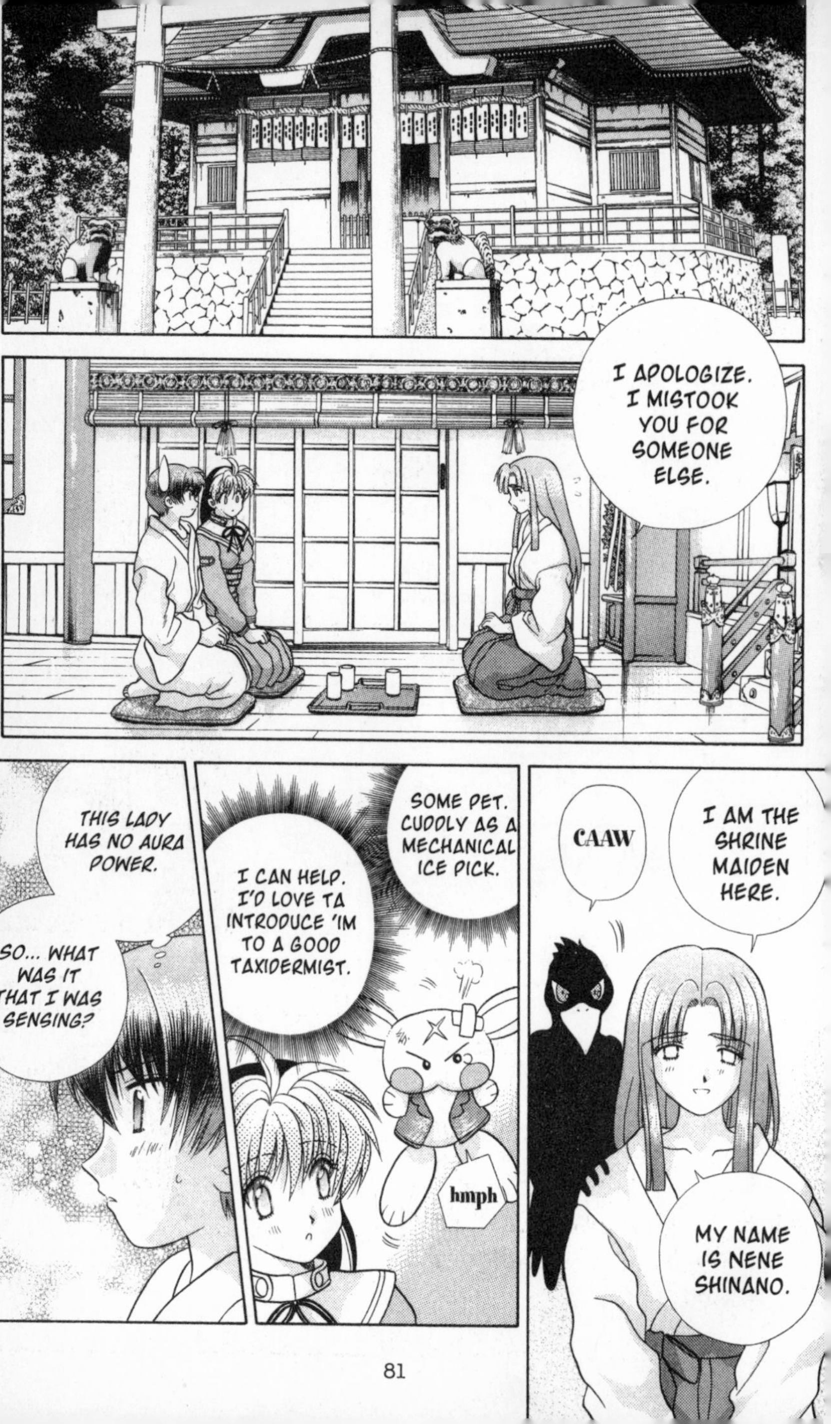
I APOLOGIZE. I MISTOOK YOU FOR SOMEONE ELSE.
I AM THE SHRINE MAIDEN HERE.
CAAW
MY NAME IS NENE SHINANO.
SOME PET. CUDDLY AS A MECHANICAL ICE PICK.
I CAN HELP. I'D LOVE TA INTRODUCE 'IM TO A GOOD TAXIDERMIST.
hmph
THIS LADY HAS NO AURA POWER.
SO... WHAT WAS IT THAT I WAS SENSING?

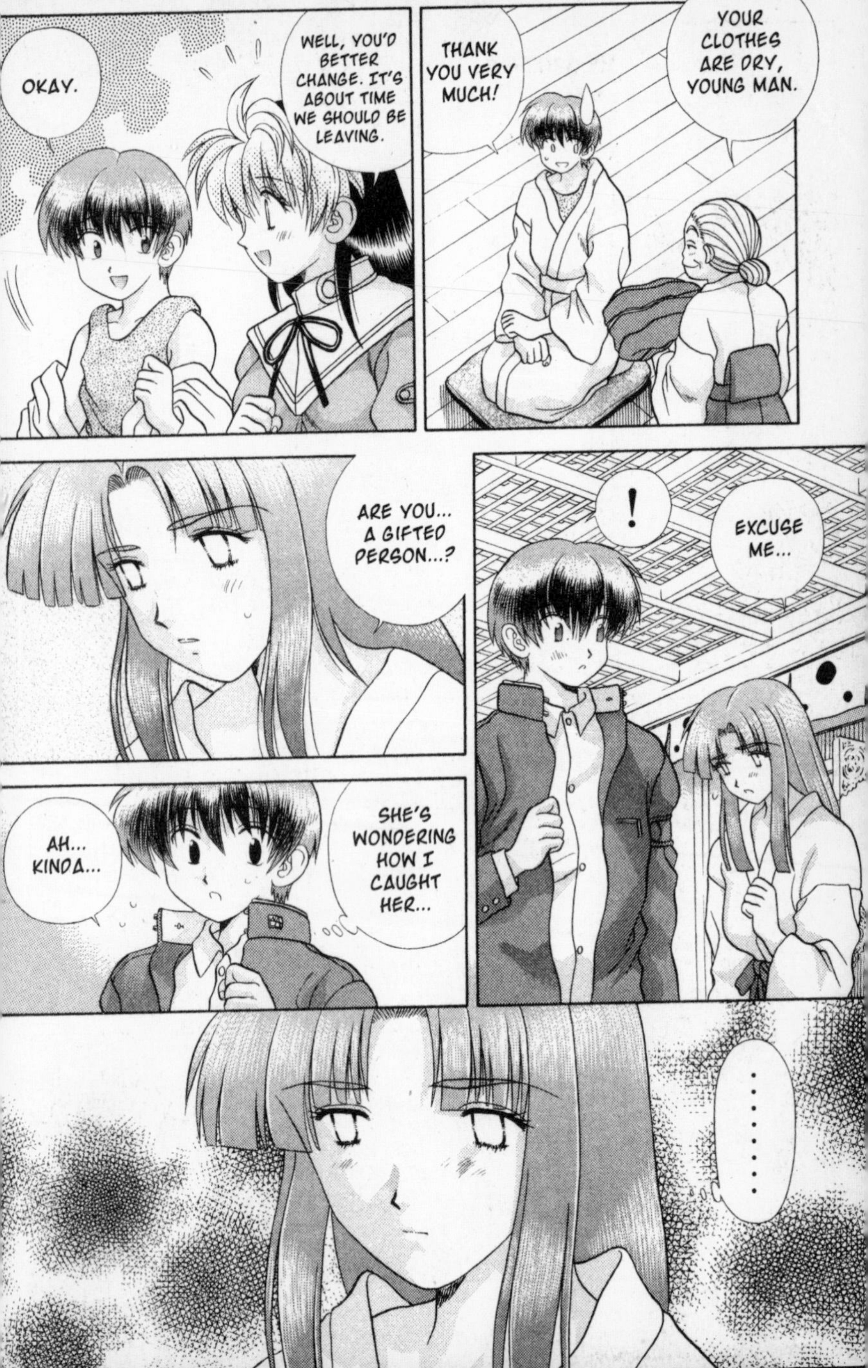
YOUR CLOTHES ARE DRY, YOUNG MAN.
THANK YOU VERY MUCH!
WELL, YOU'D BETTER CHANGE. IT'S ABOUT TIME WE SHOULD BE LEAVING.
OKAY.
EXCUSE ME...
!
ARE YOU... A GIFTED PERSON...?
SHE'S WONDERING HOW I CAUGHT HER...
AH... KINDA...
....

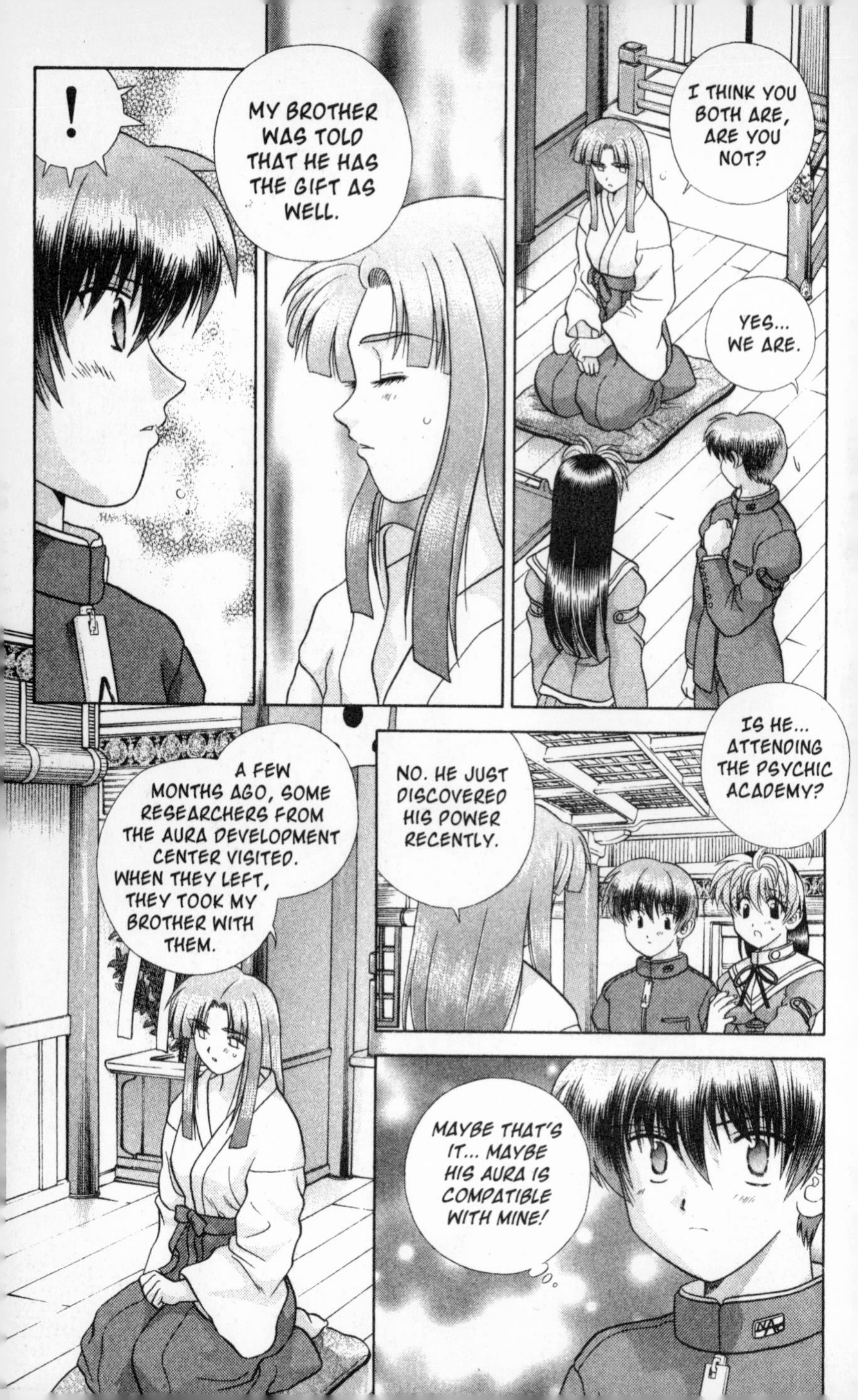
I THINK YOU BOTH ARE, ARE YOU NOT?
YES... WE ARE.
MY BROTHER WAS TOLD THAT HE HAS THE GIFT AS WELL.
!
IS HE... ATTENDING THE PSYCHIC ACADEMY?
NO. HE JUST DISCOVERED HIS POWER RECENTLY.
A FEW MONTHS AGO, SOME RESEARCHERS FROM THE AURA DEVELOPMENT CENTER VISITED. WHEN THEY LEFT, THEY TOOK MY BROTHER WITH THEM.
MAYBE THAT'S IT... MAYBE HIS AURA IS COMPATIBLE WITH MINE!

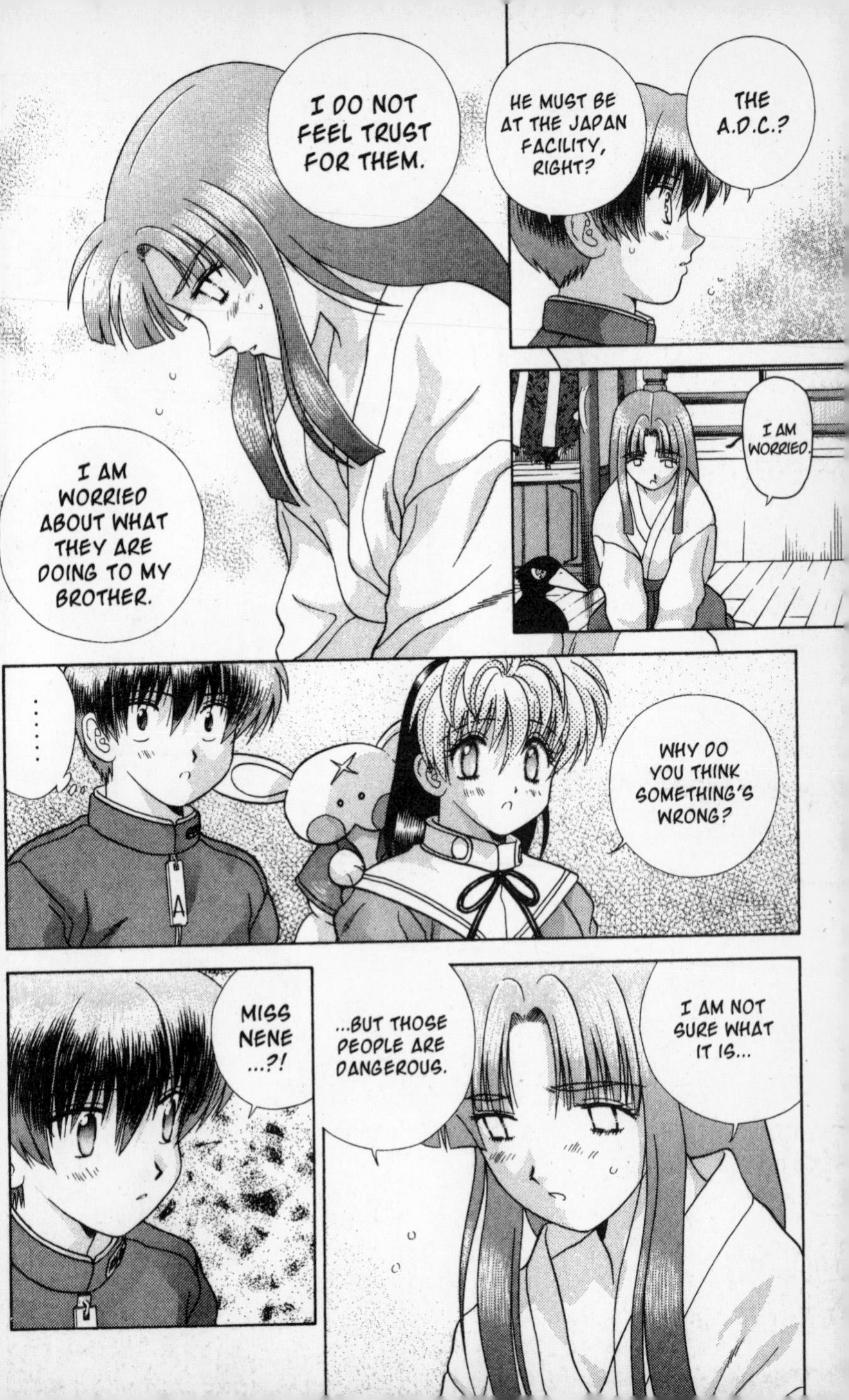
THE A.D.C.?
HE MUST BE AT THE JAPAN FACILITY, RIGHT?
I DO NOT FEEL TRUST FOR THEM.
I AM WORRIED.
I AM WORRIED ABOUT WHAT THEY ARE DOING TO MY BROTHER.
WHY DO YOU THINK SOMETHING'S WRONG?
......
I AM NOT SURE WHAT IT IS...
...BUT THOSE PEOPLE ARE DANGEROUS.
MISS NENE ...?!

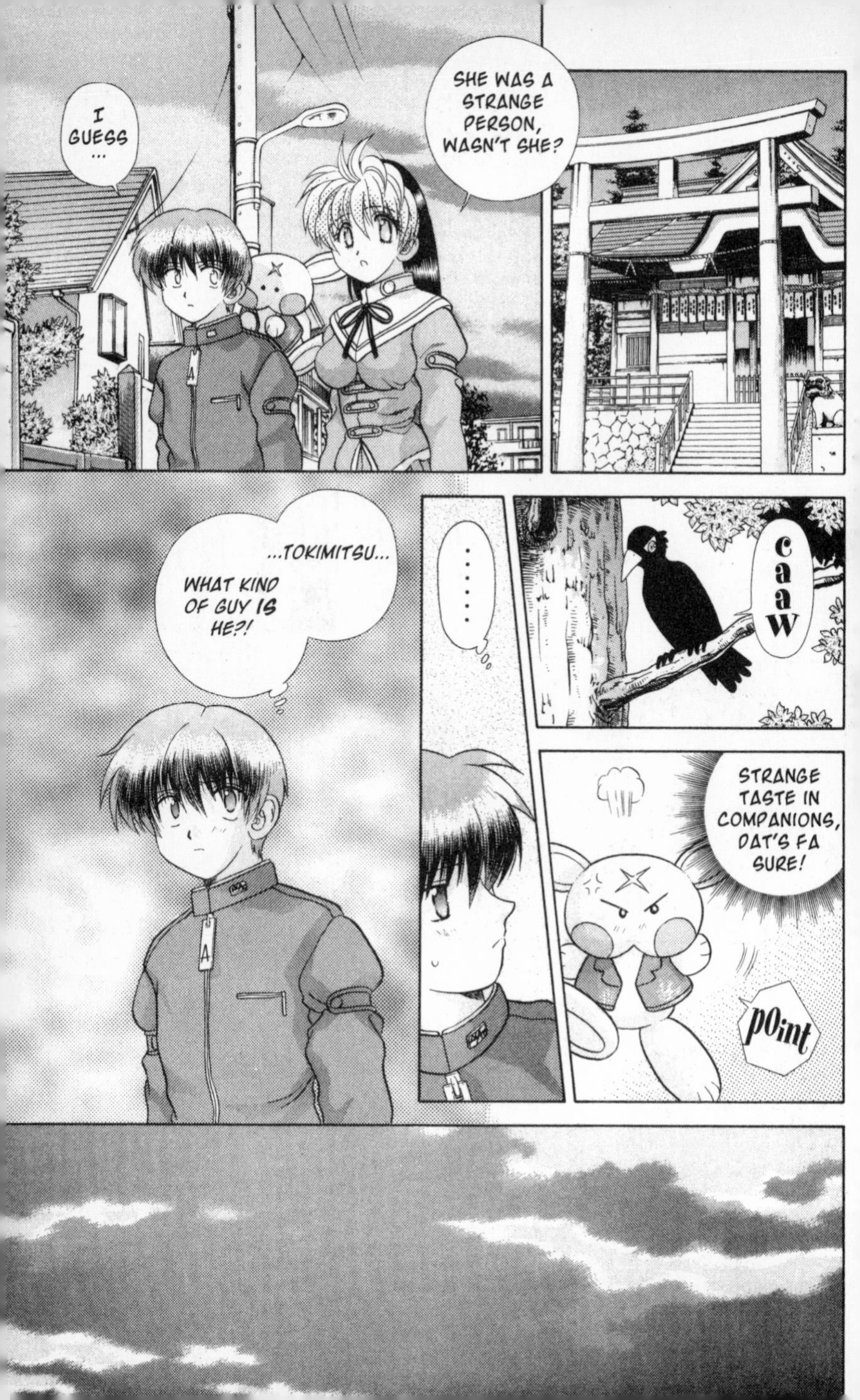

SHE WAS A STRANGE PERSON, WASN'T SHE?
I GUESS ...
caaw
......
...TOKIMITSU... WHAT KIND OF GUY IS HE?!
STRANGE TASTE IN COMPANIONS, DAT'S FA SURE!
p0int

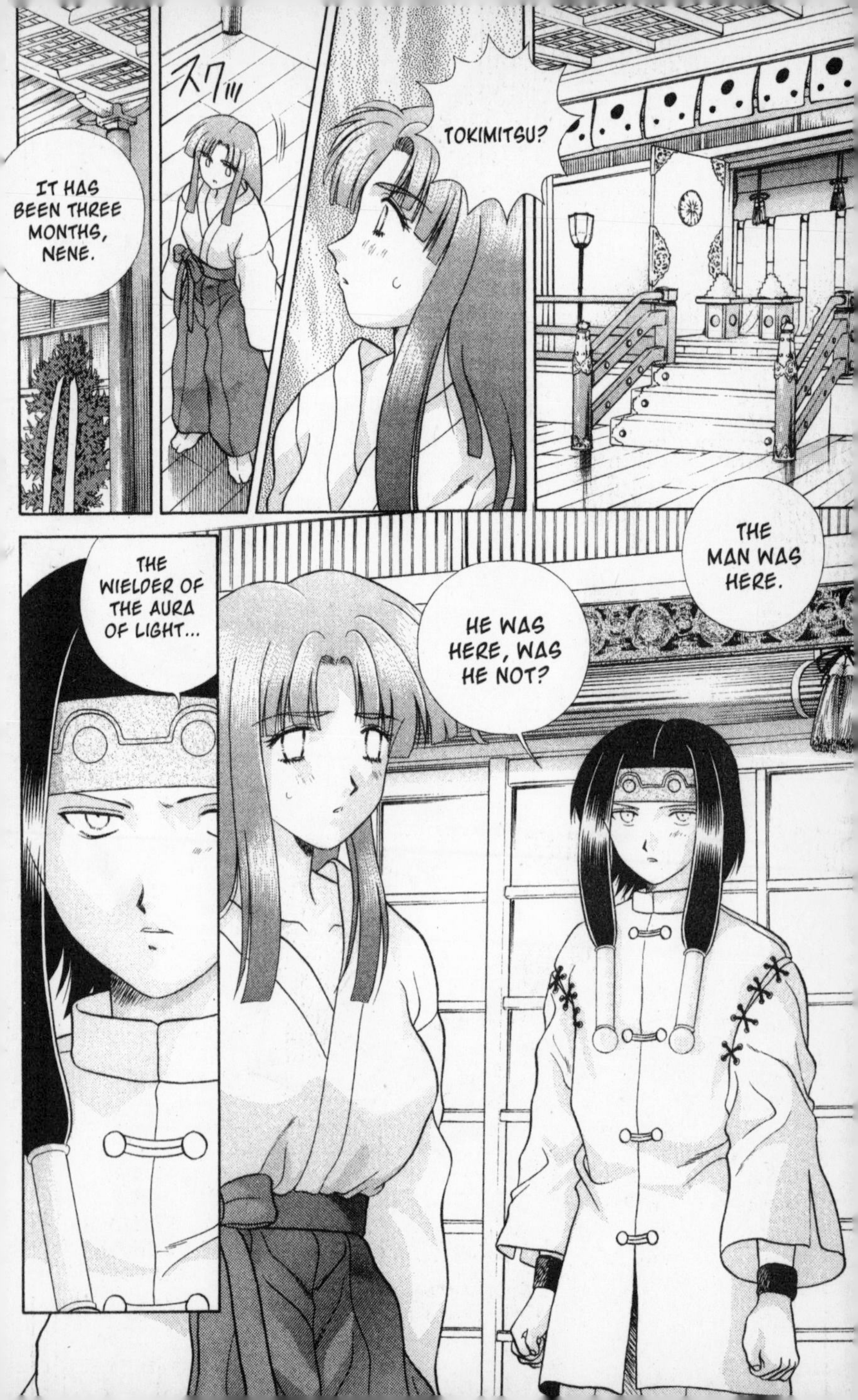
TOKIMITSU?
スワ
IT HAS BEEN THREE MONTHS, NENE.
THE MAN WAS HERE.
HE WAS HERE, WAS HE NOT?
THE WIELDER OF THE AURA OF LIGHT...

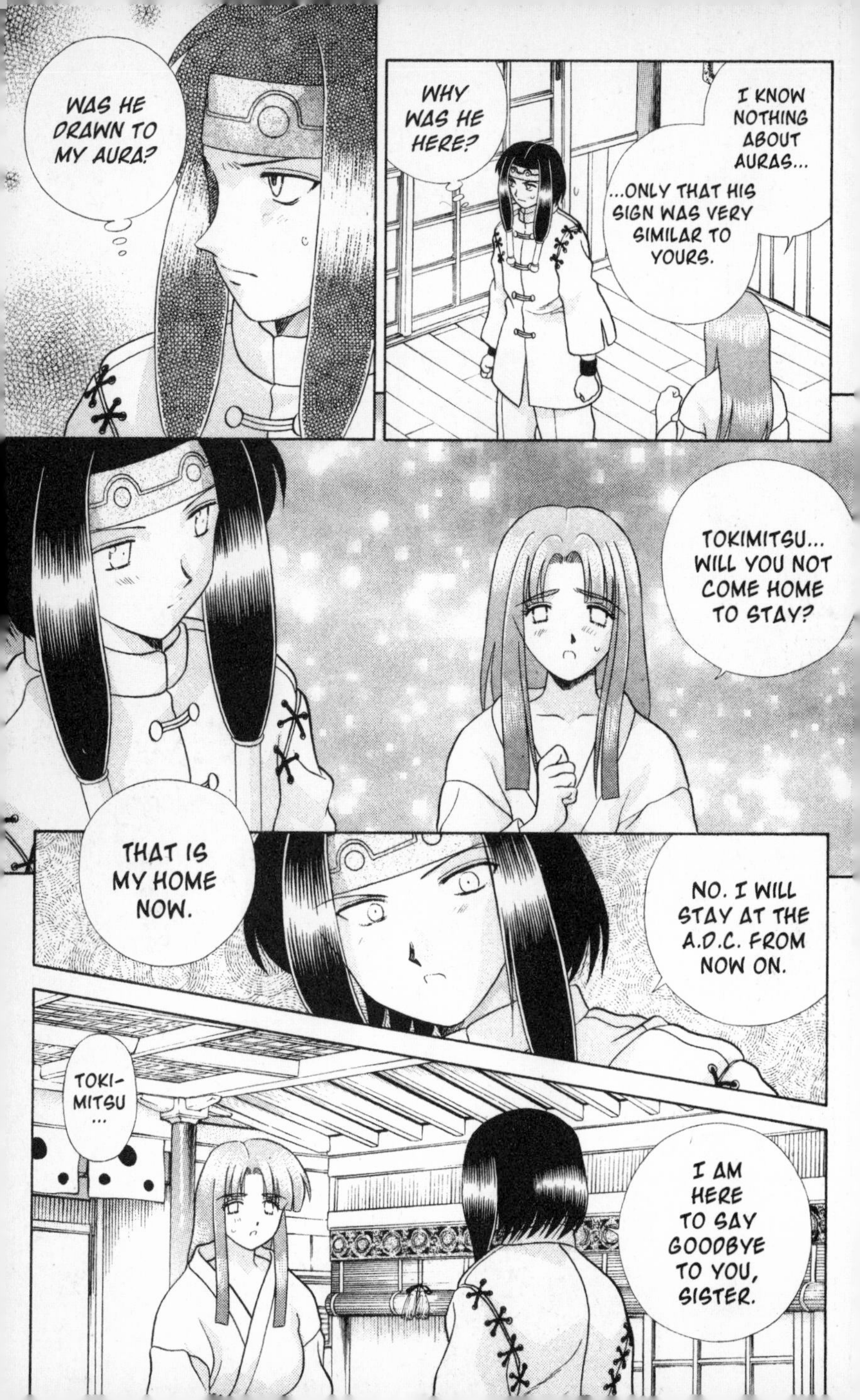
I KNOW NOTHING ABOUT AURAS...
...ONLY THAT HIS SIGN WAS VERY SIMILAR TO YOURS.
WHY WAS HE HERE?
WAS HE DRAWN TO MY AURA?
TOKIMITSU... WILL YOU NOT COME HOME TO STAY?
NO. I WILL STAY AT THE A.D.C. FROM NOW ON.
THAT IS MY HOME NOW.
I AM HERE TO SAY GOODBYE TO YOU, SISTER.
TOKI-MITSU ...

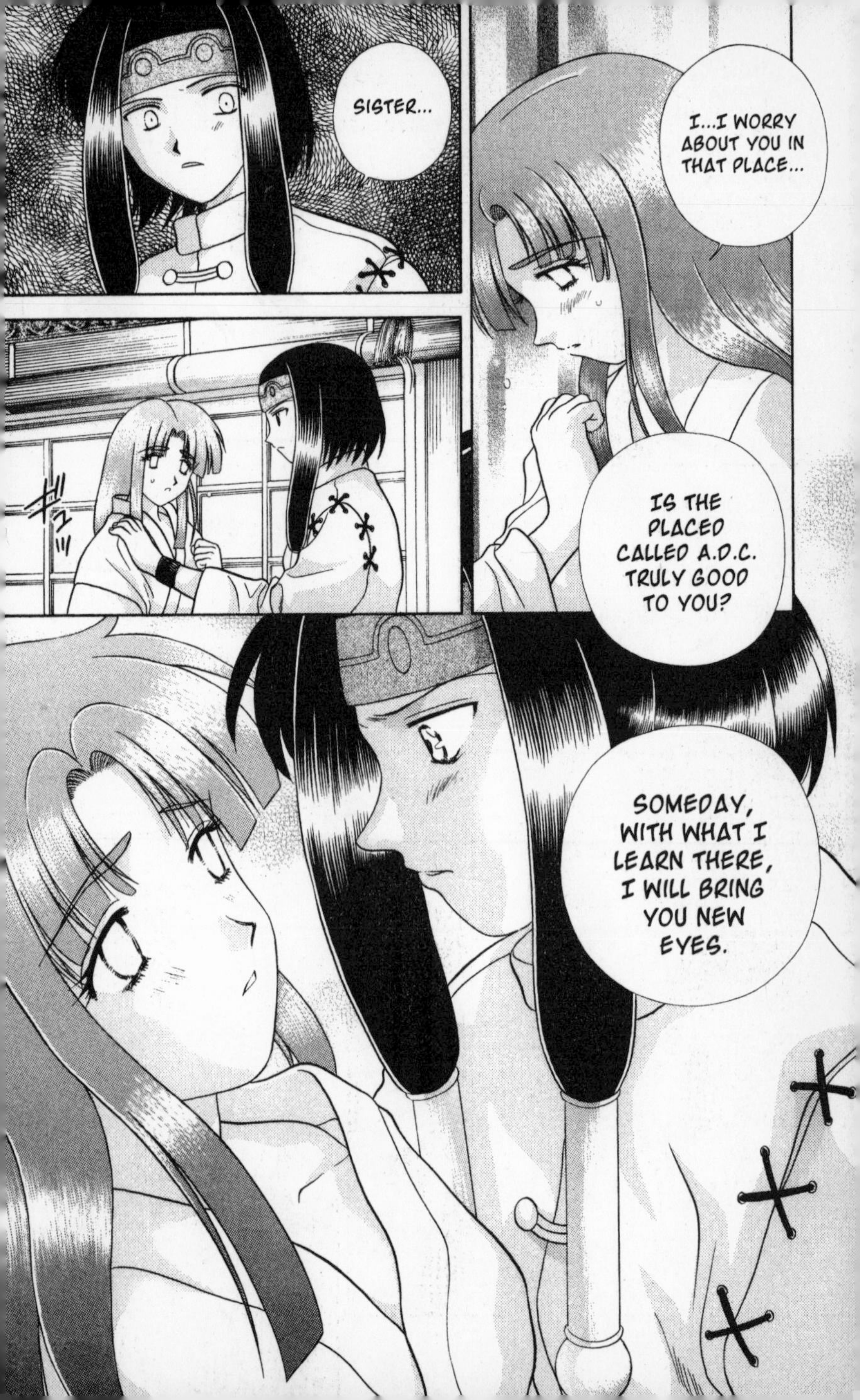
I...I WORRY ABOUT YOU IN THAT PLACE...
IS THE PLACED CALLED A.D.C. TRULY GOOD TO YOU?
SISTER...
ギュッ
SOMEDAY, WITH WHAT I LEARN THERE, I WILL BRING YOU NEW EYES.

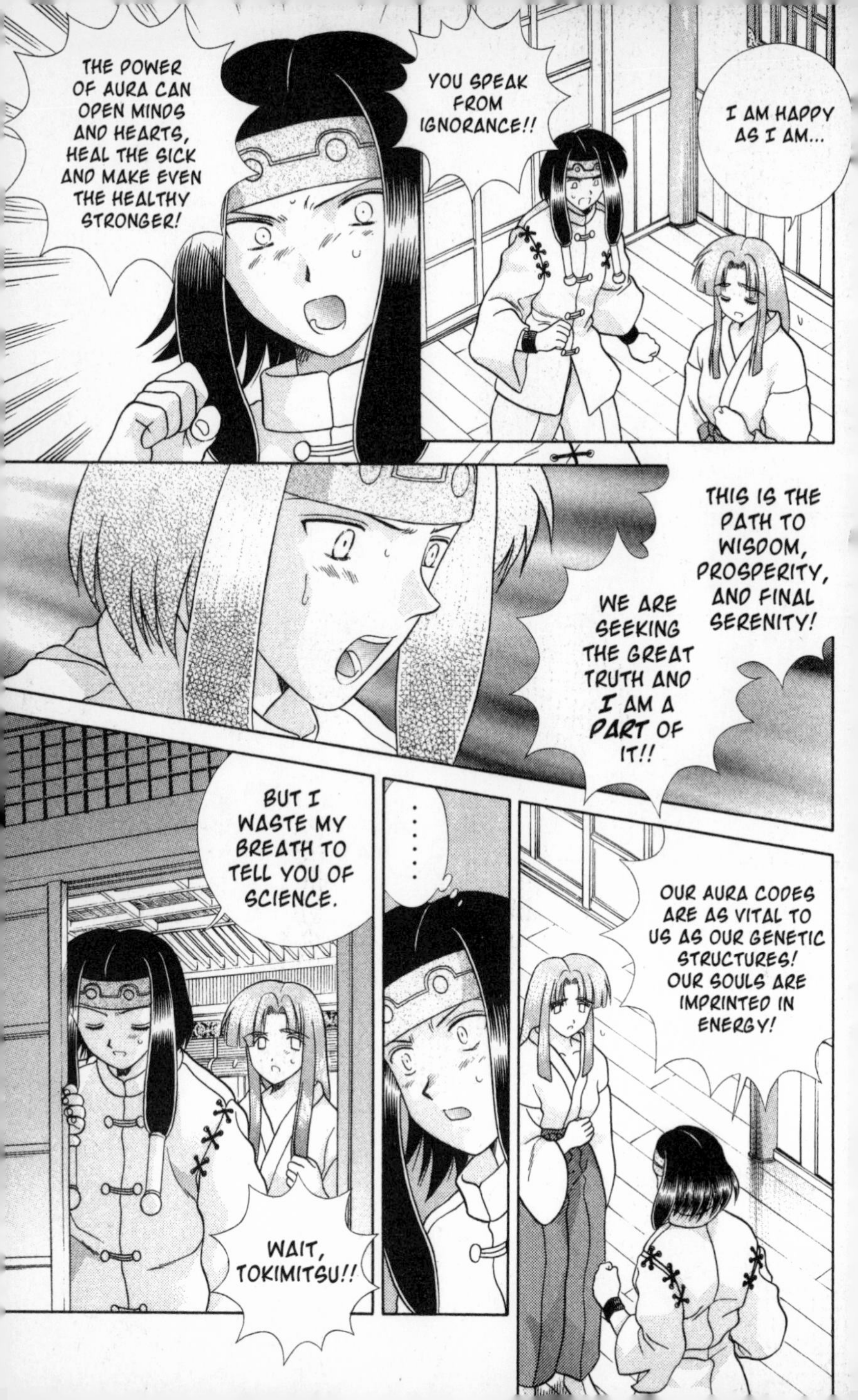
I AM HAPPY AS I AM...
YOU SPEAK FROM IGNORANCE!!
THE POWER OF AURA CAN OPEN MINDS AND HEARTS, HEAL THE SICK AND MAKE EVEN THE HEALTHY STRONGER!
WE ARE SEEKING THE GREAT TRUTH AND I AM A PART OF IT!!
THIS IS THE PATH TO WISDOM, PROSPERITY, AND FINAL SERENITY!
OUR AURA CODES ARE AS VITAL TO US AS OUR GENETIC STRUCTURES! OUR SOULS ARE IMPRINTED IN ENERGY!
......
BUT I WASTE MY BREATH TO TELL YOU OF SCIENCE.
WAIT, TOKIMITSU!!

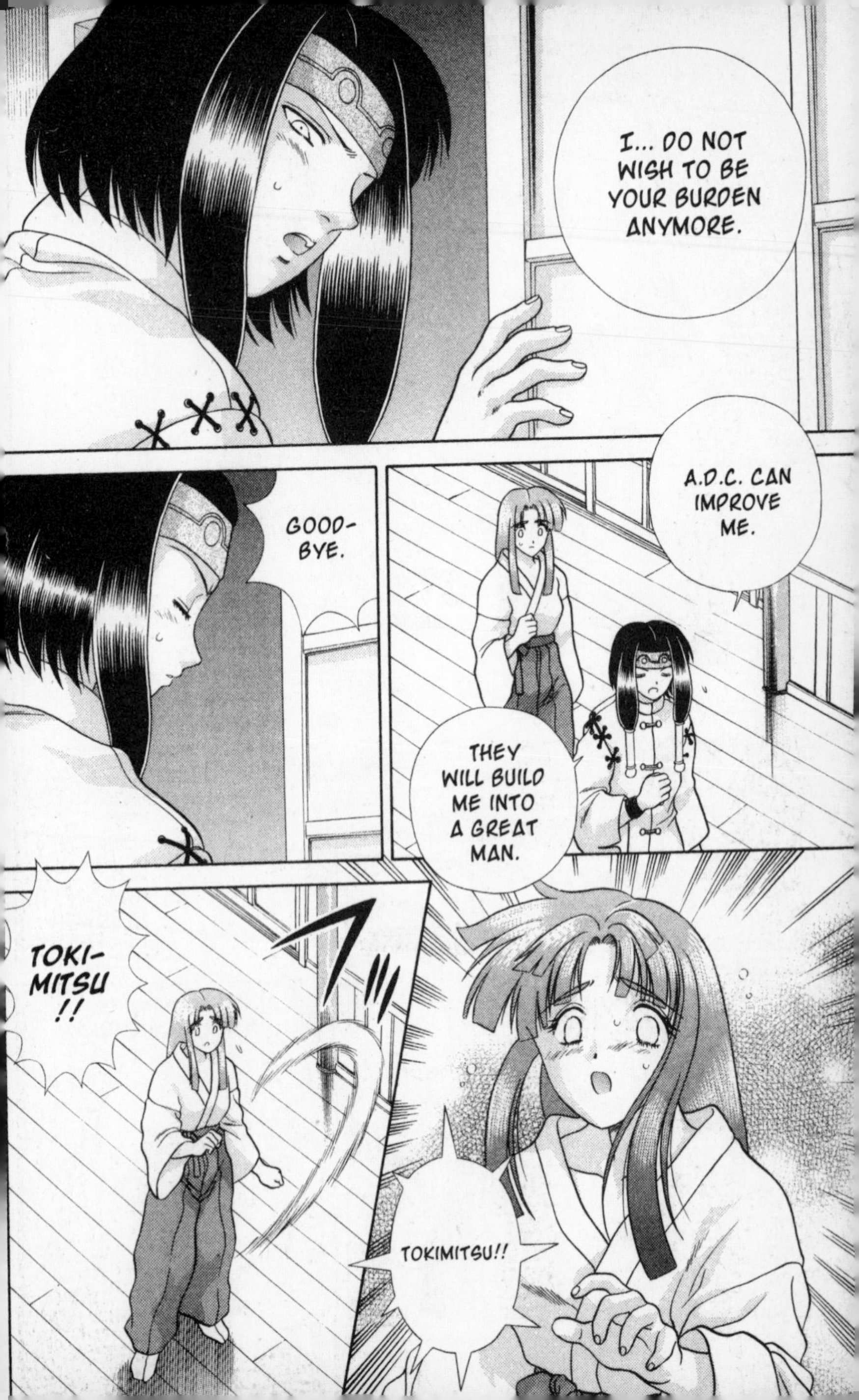
I... DO NOT WISH TO BE YOUR BURDEN ANYMORE.
A.D.C. CAN IMPROVE ME.
THEY WILL BUILD ME INTO A GREAT MAN.
GOOD-BYE.
TOKIMITSU!!
TOKI-MITSU!!

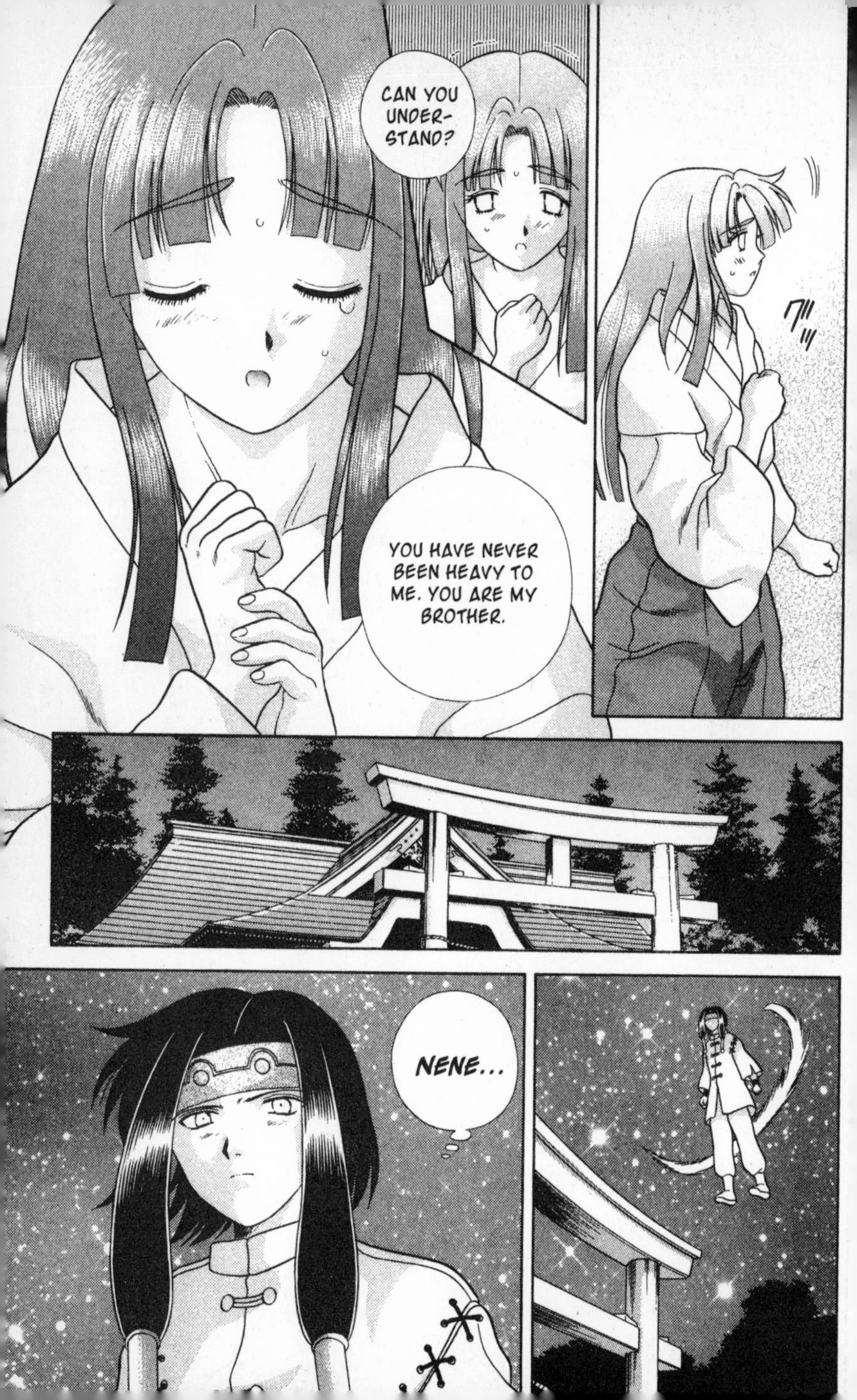
CAN YOU UNDER-STAND?
YOU HAVE NEVER BEEN HEAVY TO ME. YOU ARE MY BROTHER.
NENE...

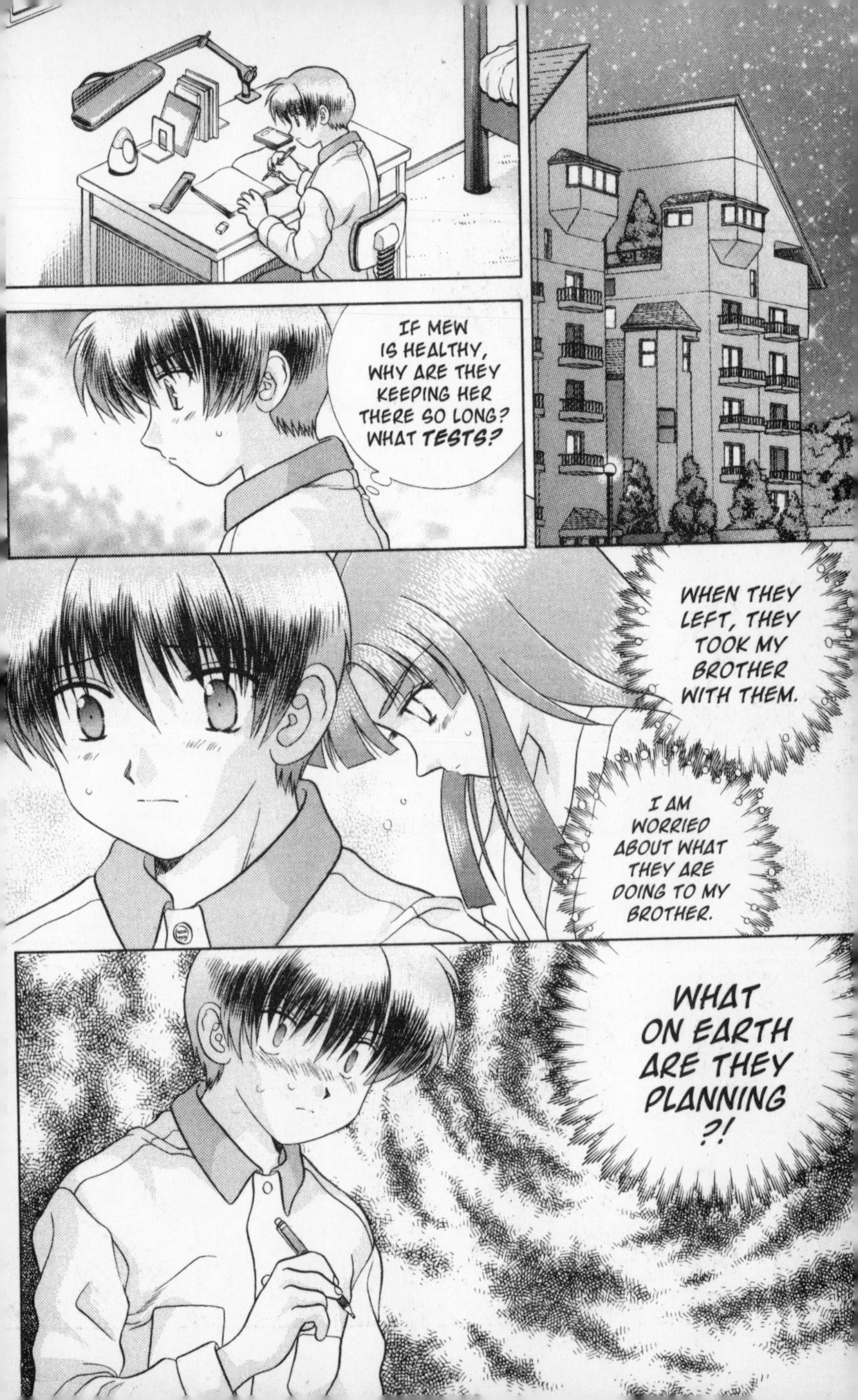
IF MEW IS HEALTHY, WHY ARE THEY KEEPING HER THERE SO LONG? WHAT TESTS?
WHEN THEY LEFT, THEY TOOK MY BROTHER WITH THEM.
I AM WORRIED ABOUT WHAT THEY ARE DOING TO MY BROTHER.
WHAT ON EARTH ARE THEY PLANNING ?!

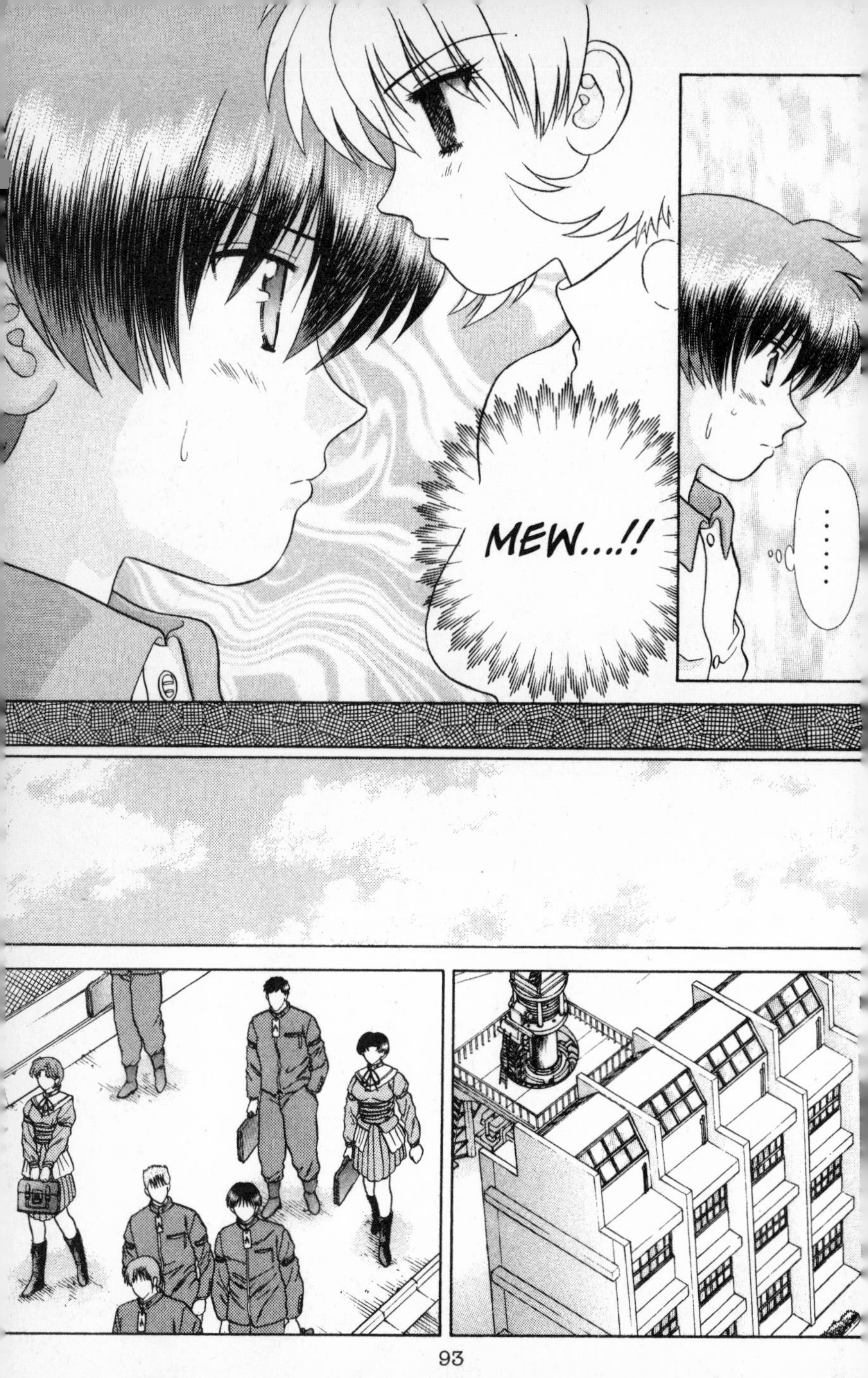
MEW...!!
......

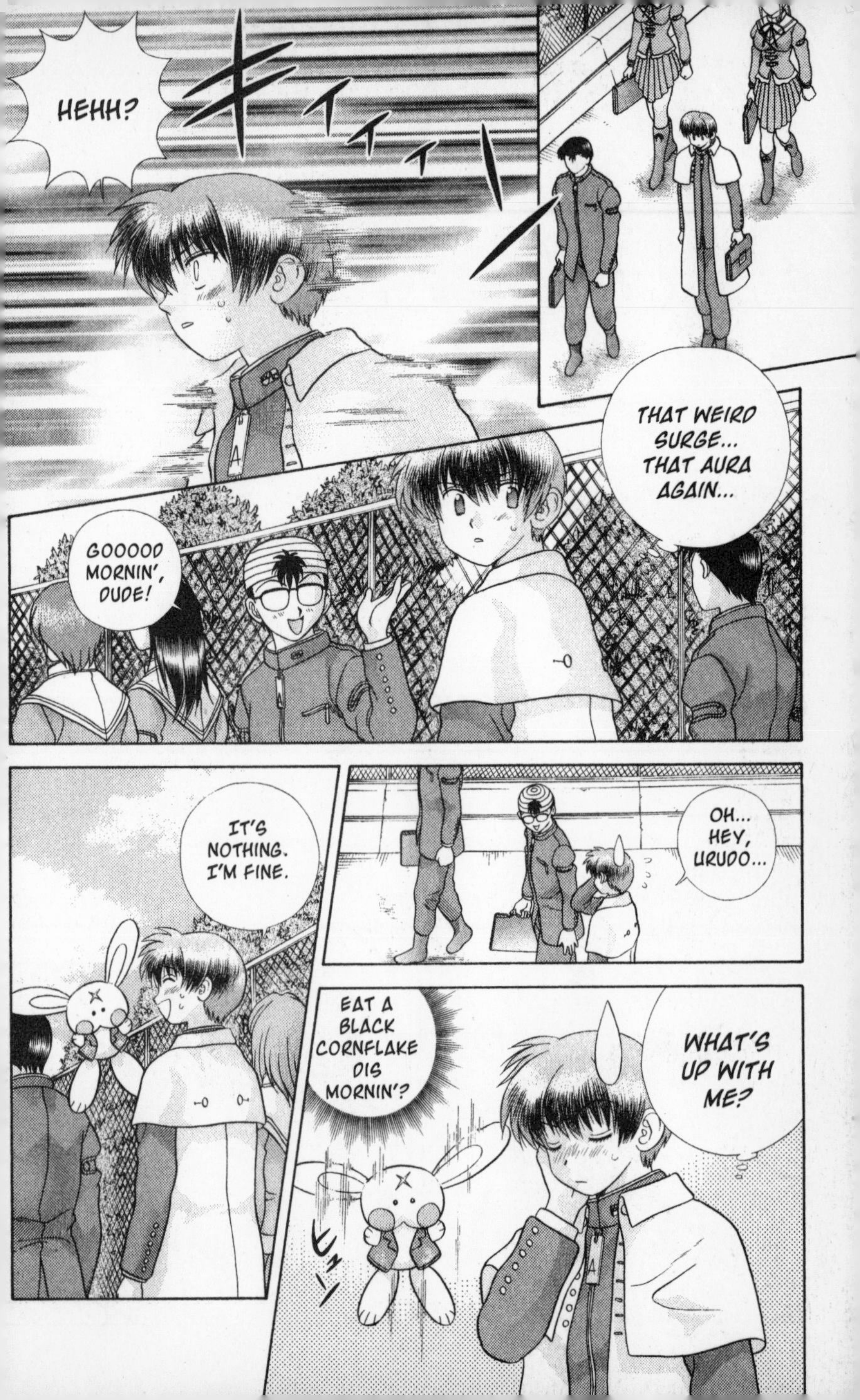
HEHH?
THAT WEIRD SURGE... THAT AURA AGAIN...
GOOOOD MORNIN', DUDE!
OH... HEY, URUDO...
IT'S NOTHING. I'M FINE.
WHAT'S UP WITH ME?
EAT A BLACK CORNFLAKE DIS MORNIN'?

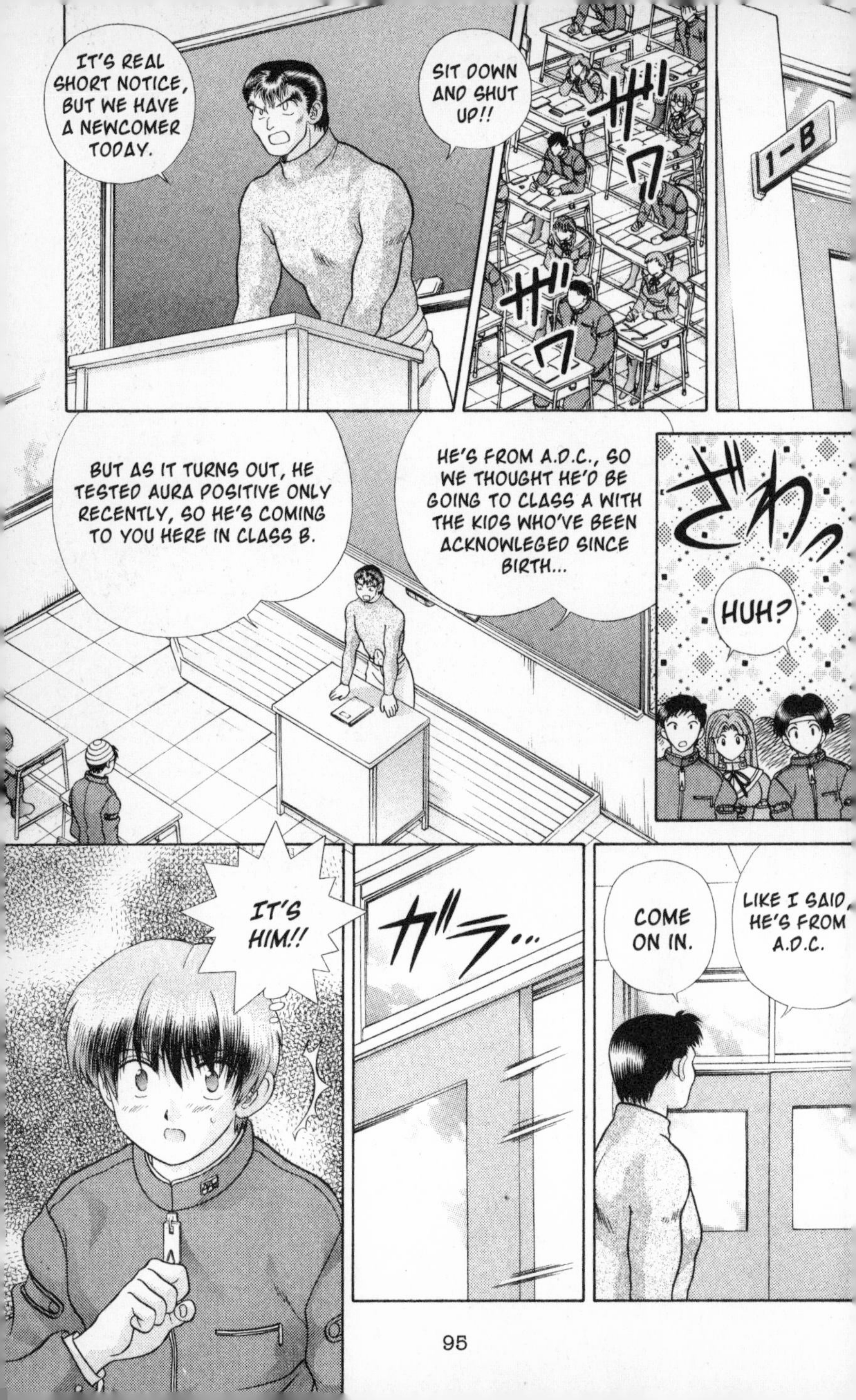
ザワ
ザワ
SIT DOWN AND SHUT UP!!
IT'S REAL SHORT NOTICE, BUT WE HAVE A NEWCOMER TODAY.
1-B
ざわっ
HUH?
HE'S FROM A.D.C., SO WE THOUGHT HE'D BE GOING TO CLASS A WITH THE KIDS WHO'VE BEEN ACKNOWLEGED SINCE BIRTH...
BUT AS IT TURNS OUT, HE TESTED AURA POSITIVE ONLY RECENTLY, SO HE'S COMING TO YOU HERE IN CLASS B.
LIKE I SAID, HE'S FROM A.D.C.
COME ON IN.
ガラ...
IT'S HIM!!

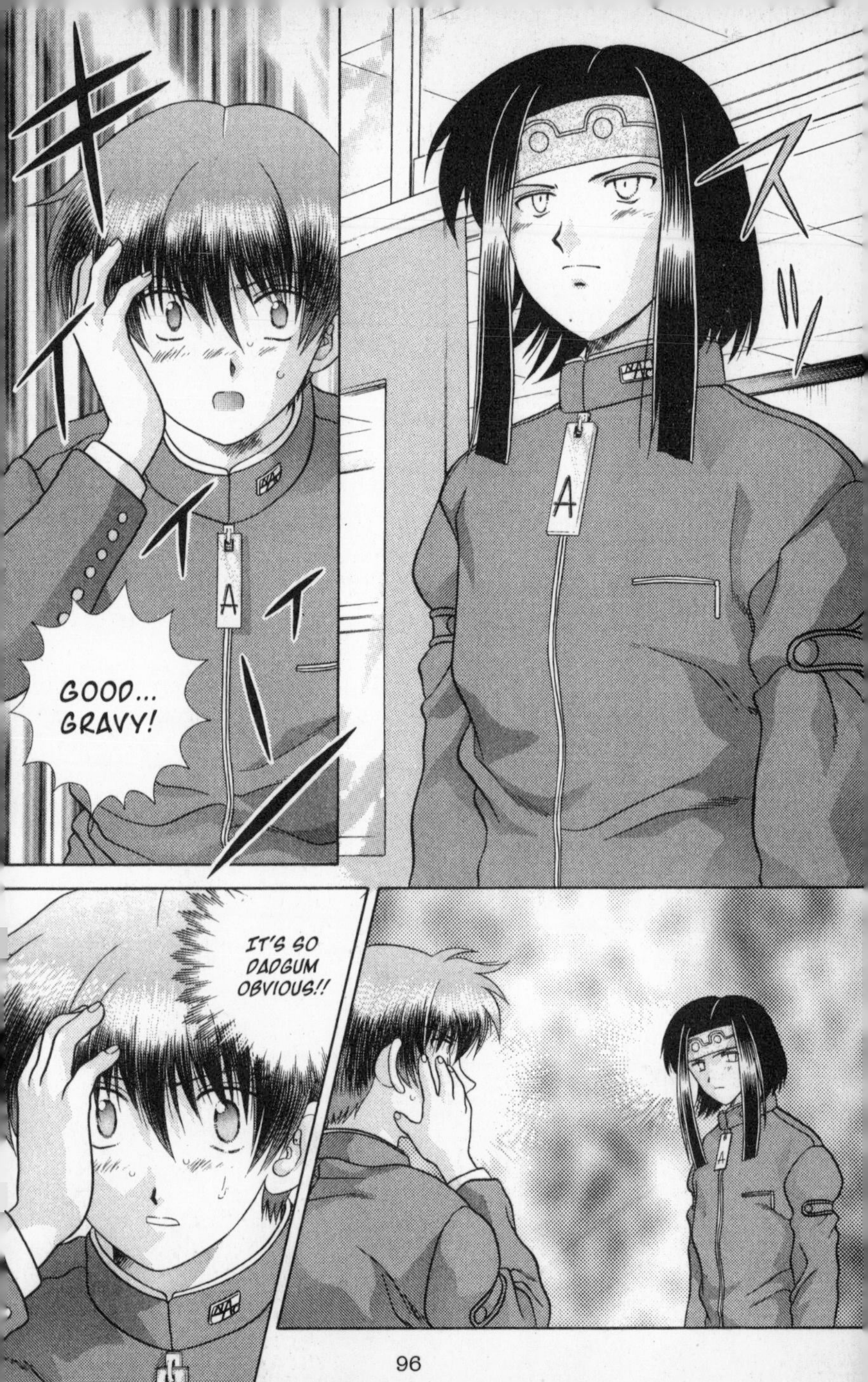
GOOD...
GRAVY!
IT'S SO
DADGUM
OBVIOUS!!

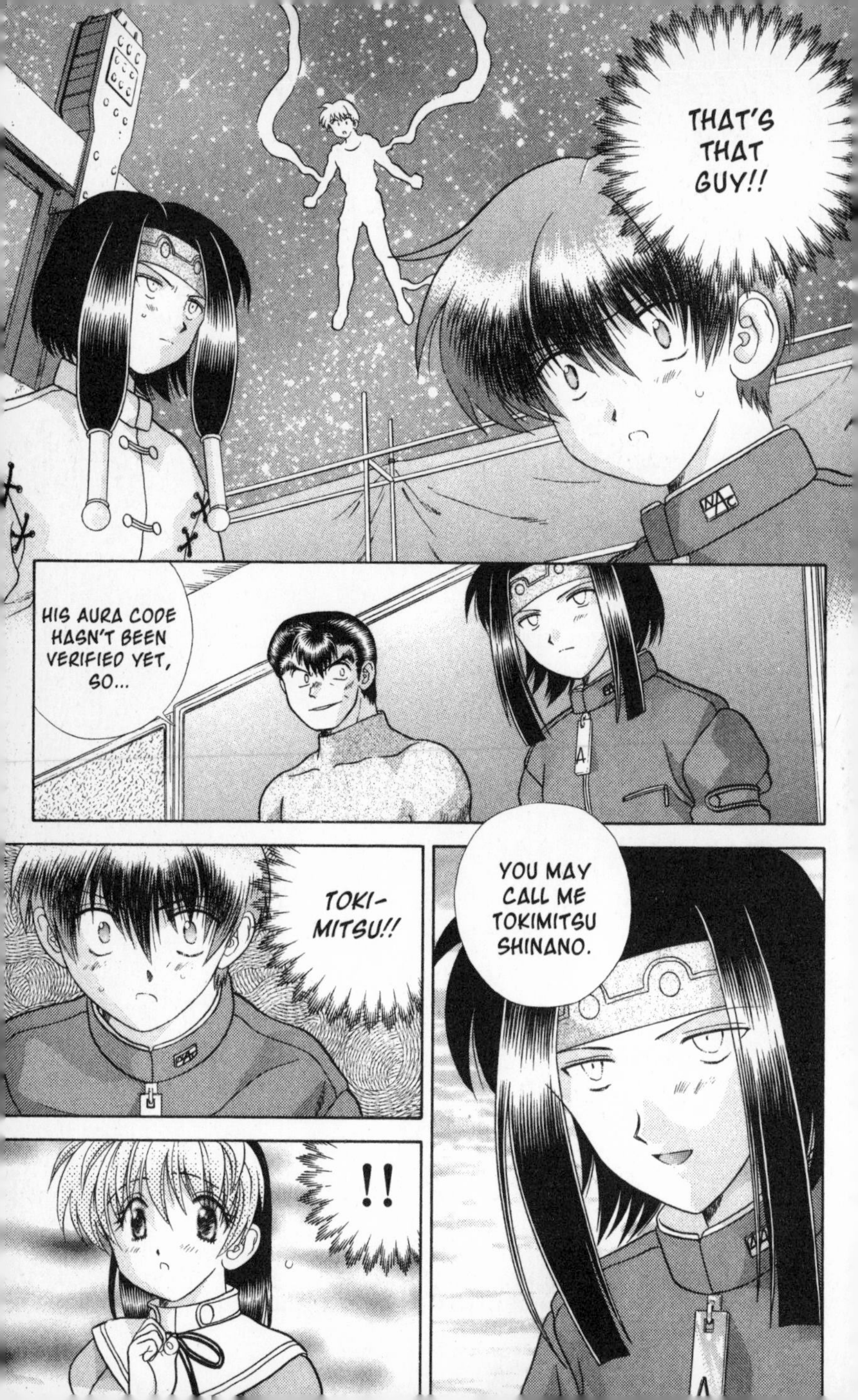
THAT'S THAT GUY!!
HIS AURA CODE HASN'T BEEN VERIFIED YET, SO...
YOU MAY CALL ME TOKIMITSU SHINANO.
TOKI-MITSU!!
!!

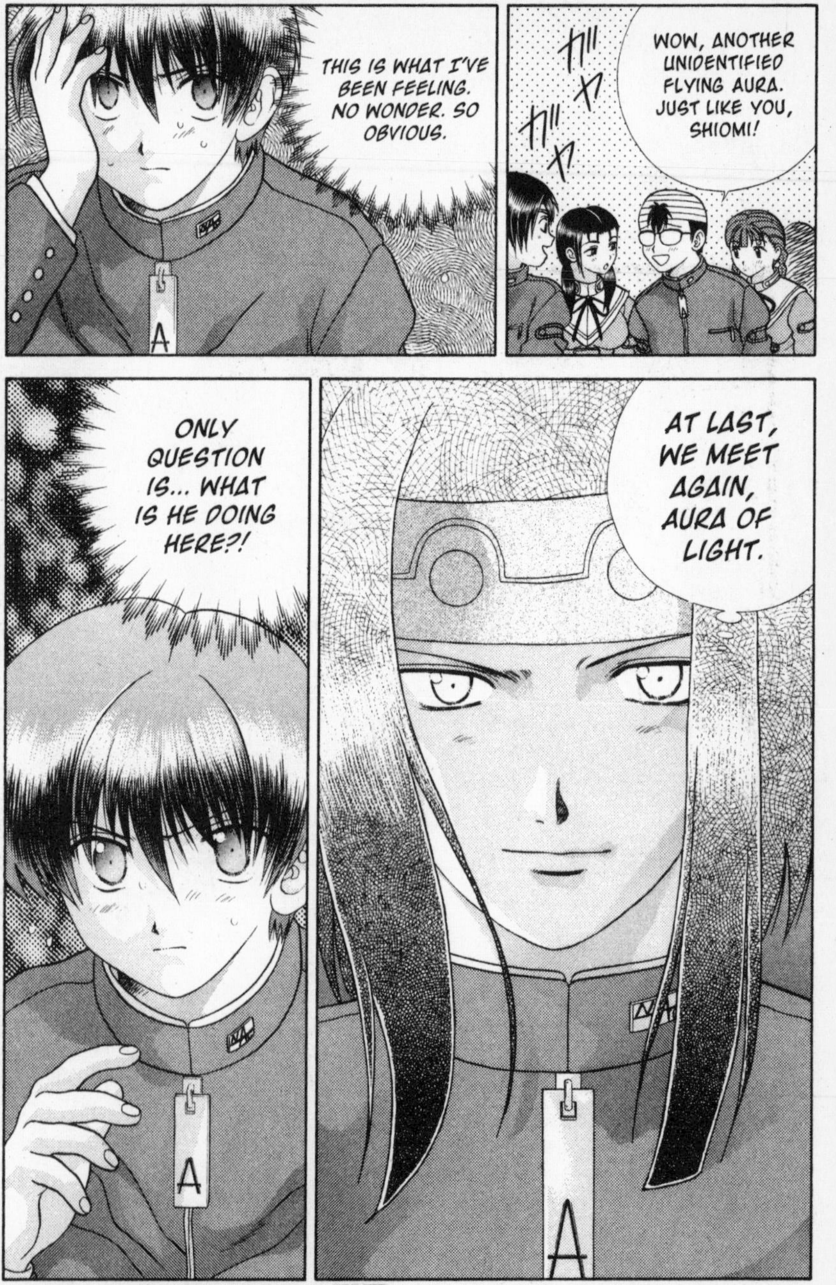
THIS IS WHAT I'VE BEEN FEELING. NO WONDER. SO OBVIOUS.
WOW, ANOTHER UNIDENTIFIED FLYING AURA. JUST LIKE YOU, SHIOMI!
ONLY QUESTION IS... WHAT IS HE DOING HERE?!
AT LAST, WE MEET AGAIN, AURA OF LIGHT.

Watabe's Better Auras END

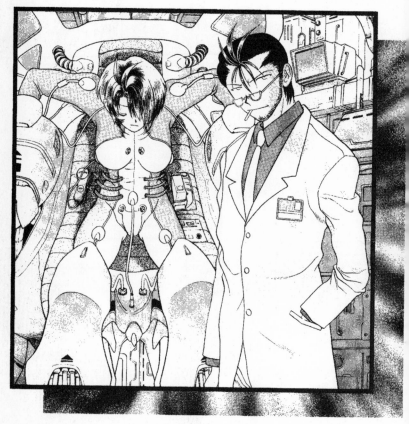

Chapter 27: Mew's New Name

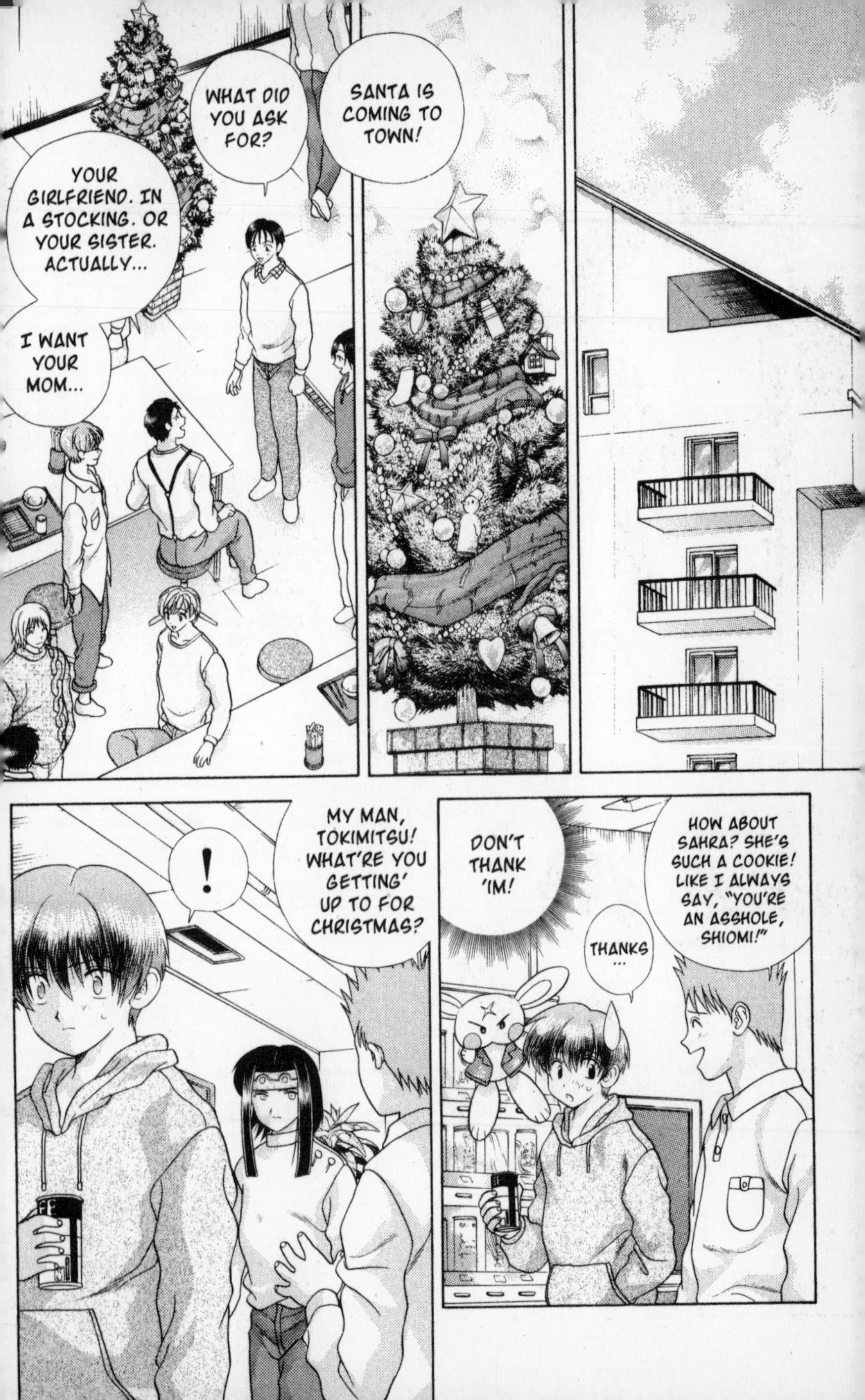
SANTA IS COMING TO TOWN!
WHAT DID YOU ASK FOR?
YOUR GIRLFRIEND. IN A STOCKING. OR YOUR SISTER. ACTUALLY...
I WANT YOUR MOM...
HOW ABOUT SAHRA? SHE'S SUCH A COOKIE! LIKE I ALWAYS SAY, "YOU'RE AN ASSHOLE, SHIOMI!"
THANKS...
DON'T THANK 'IM!
MY MAN, TOKIMITSU! WHAT'RE YOU GETTING' UP TO FOR CHRISTMAS?
!

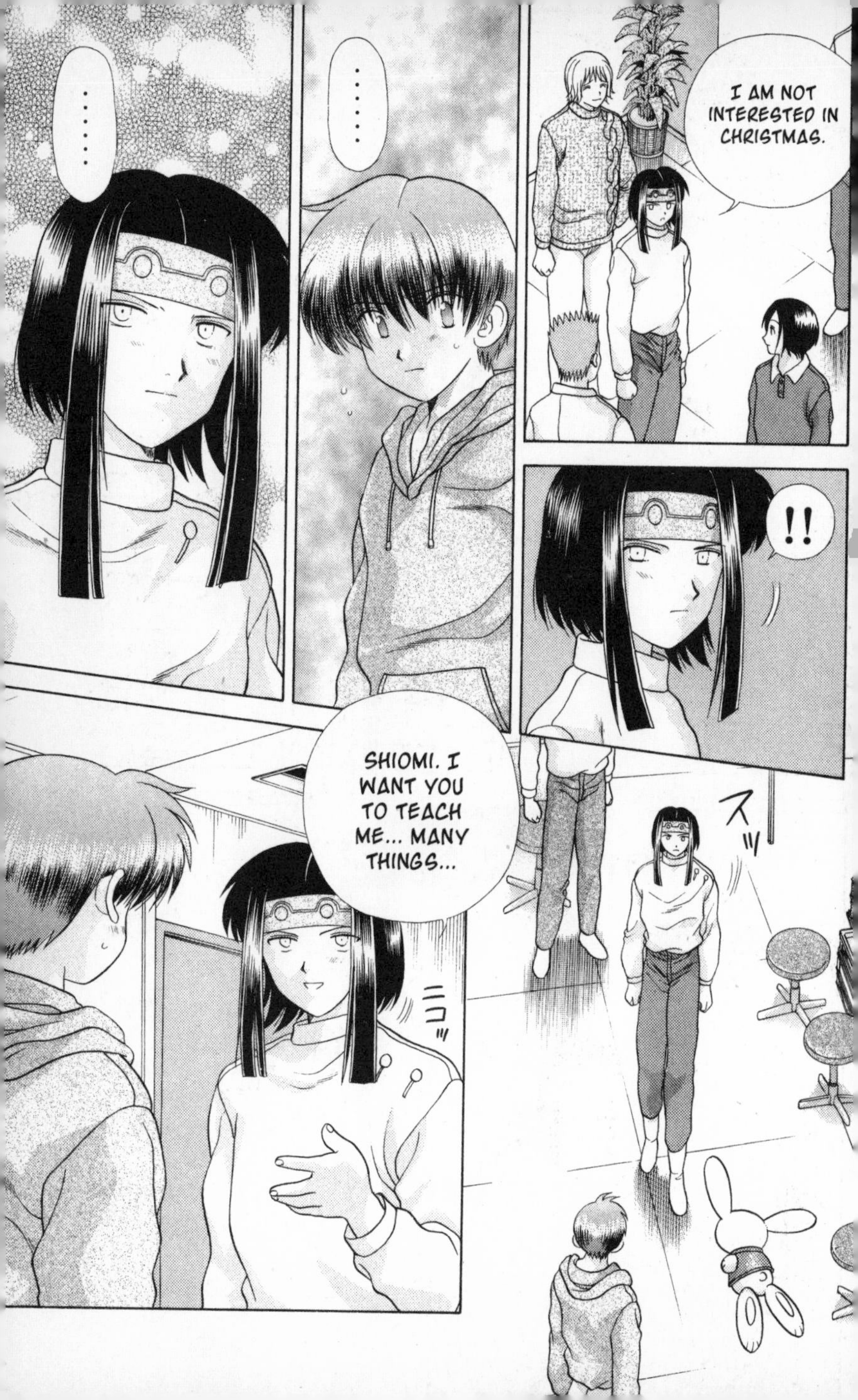
I AM NOT INTERESTED IN CHRISTMAS.
......
......
!!
スッ
SHIOMI. I WANT YOU TO TEACH ME... MANY THINGS...
ニコッ

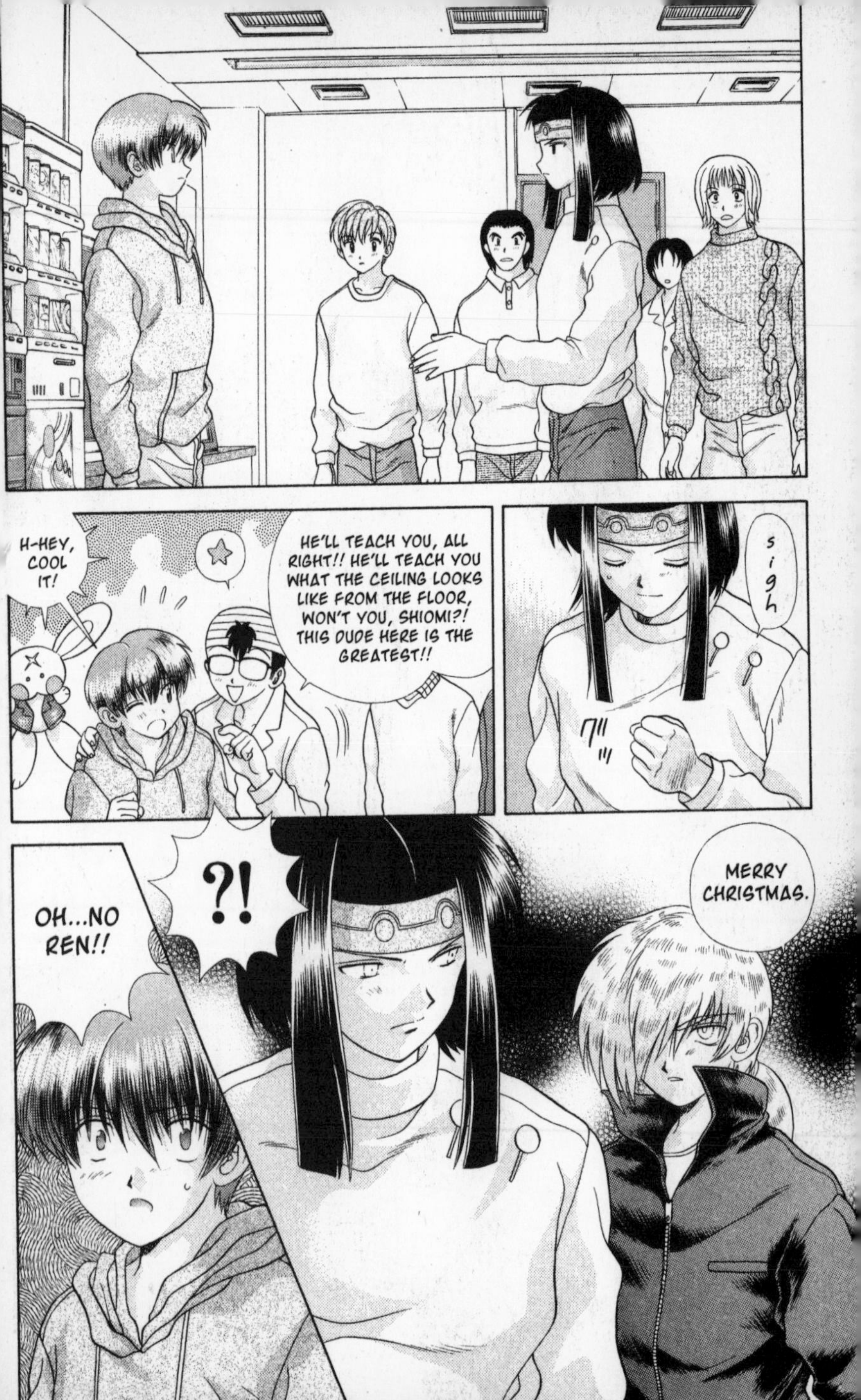
sigh
グッ
HE'LL TEACH YOU, ALL RIGHT!! HE'LL TEACH YOU WHAT THE CEILING LOOKS LIKE FROM THE FLOOR, WON'T YOU, SHIOMI?! THIS DUDE HERE IS THE GREATEST!!
H-HEY, COOL IT!
MERRY CHRISTMAS.
?!
OH...NO REN!!

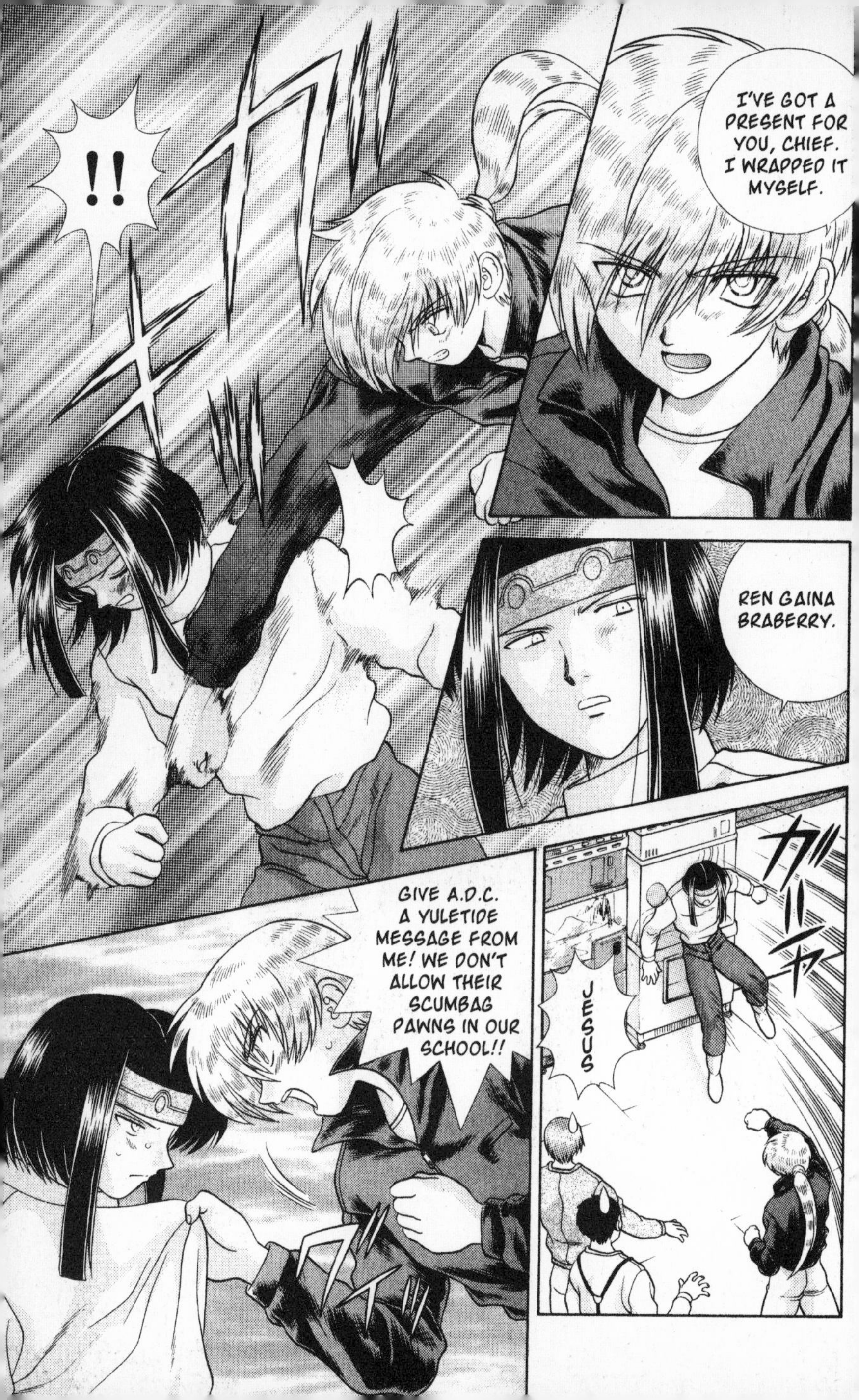
I'VE GOT A PRESENT FOR YOU, CHIEF. I WRAPPED IT MYSELF.
!!
REN GAINA BRABERRY.
JESUS
GIVE A.D.C. A YULETIDE MESSAGE FROM ME! WE DON'T ALLOW THEIR SCUMBAG PAWNS IN OUR SCHOOL!!

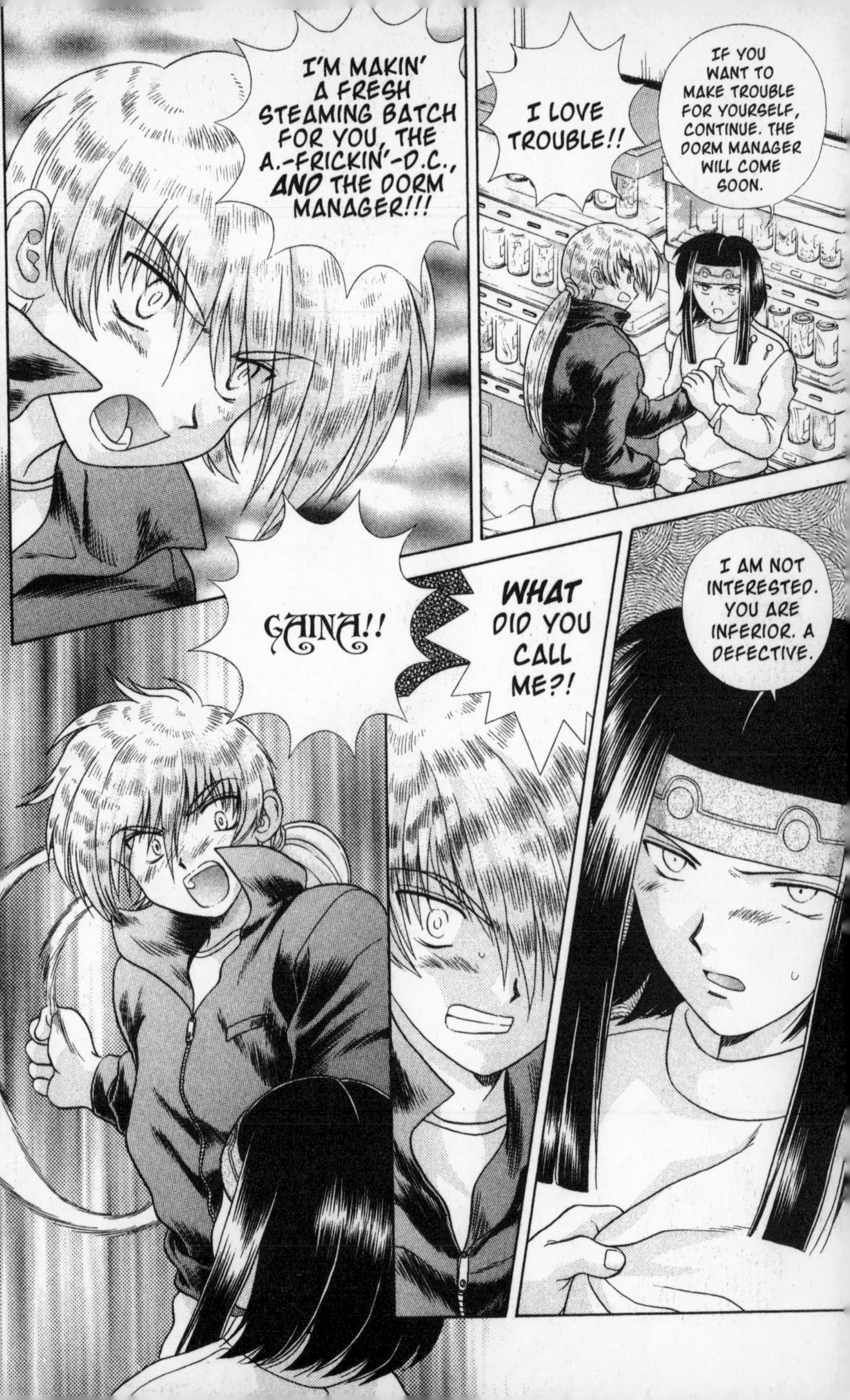
IF YOU WANT TO MAKE TROUBLE FOR YOURSELF, CONTINUE. THE DORM MANAGER WILL COME SOON.
I LOVE TROUBLE!!
I'M MAKIN' A FRESH STEAMING BATCH FOR YOU, THE A.-FRICKIN'-D.C., AND THE DORM MANAGER!!!
I AM NOT INTERESTED. YOU ARE INFERIOR. A DEFECTIVE.
WHAT DID YOU CALL ME?!
GAINA!!

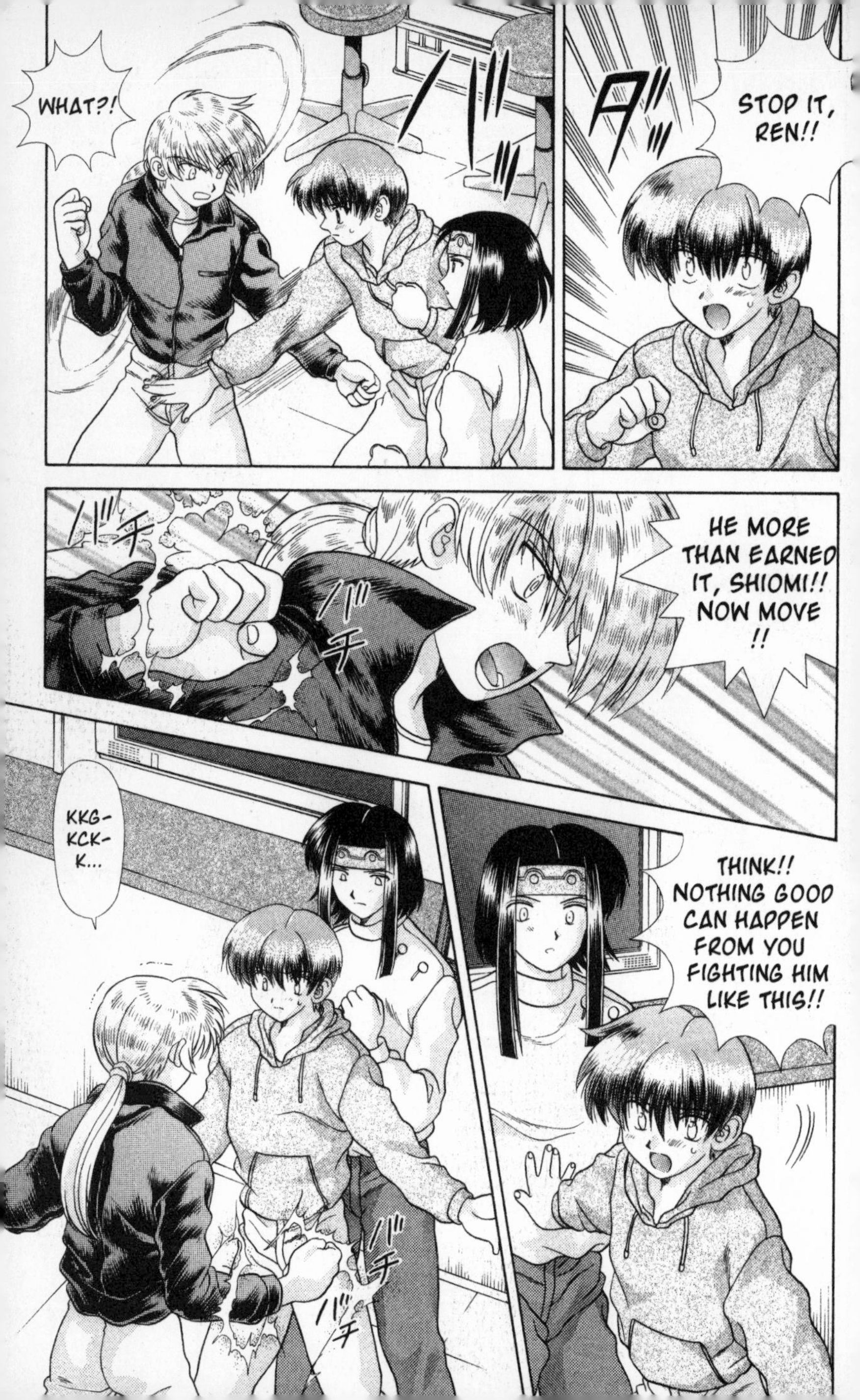
STOP IT, REN!!
WHAT?!
HE MORE THAN EARNED IT, SHIOMI!! NOW MOVE!!
THINK!! NOTHING GOOD CAN HAPPEN FROM YOU FIGHTING HIM LIKE THIS!!
KKG- KCK- K...

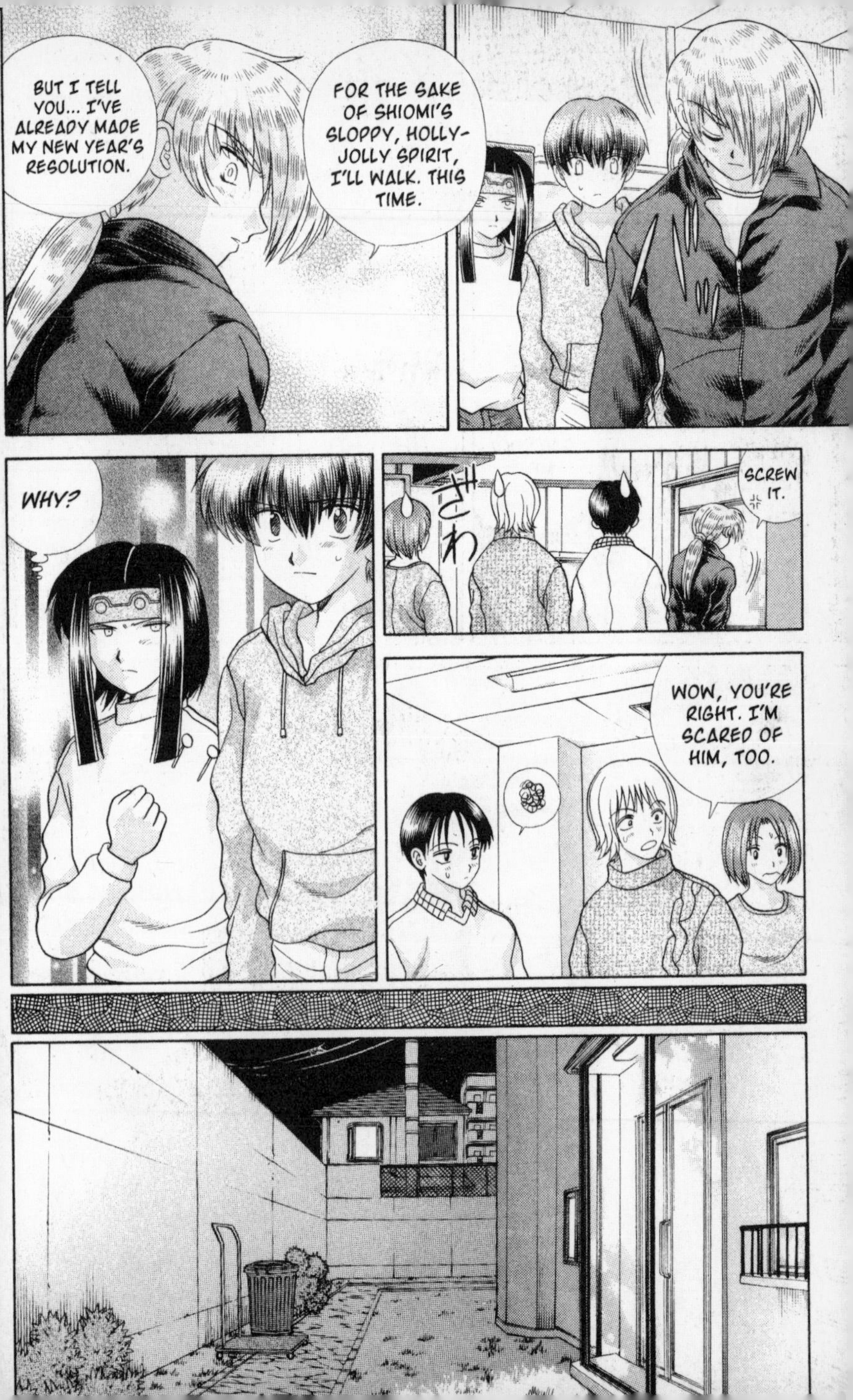
FOR THE SAKE OF SHIOMI'S SLOPPY, HOLLY-JOLLY SPIRIT, I'LL WALK. THIS TIME.
BUT I TELL YOU... I'VE ALREADY MADE MY NEW YEAR'S RESOLUTION.
SCREW IT.
ざわ
WHY?
WOW, YOU'RE RIGHT. I'M SCARED OF HIM, TOO.

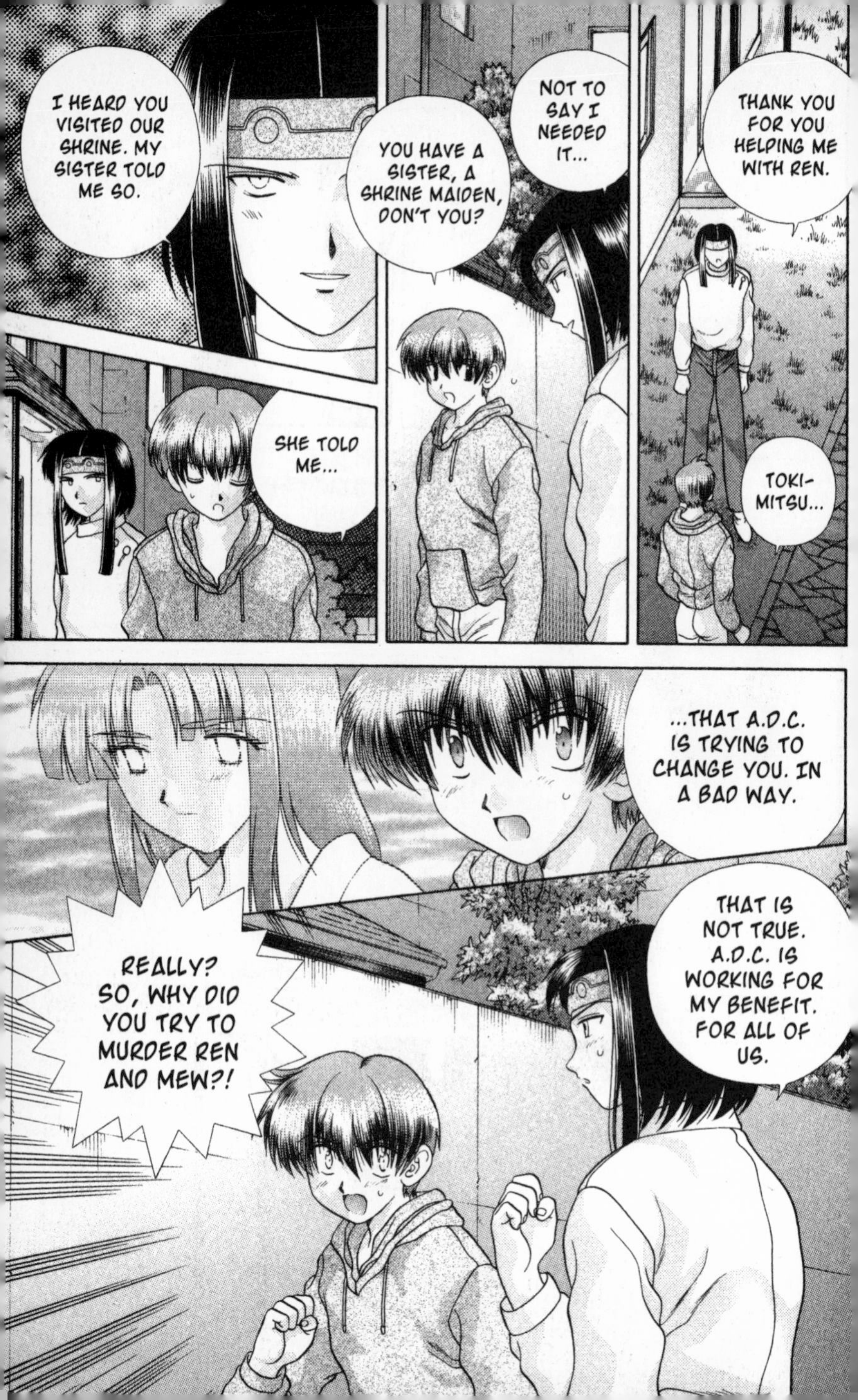
THANK YOU FOR YOU HELPING ME WITH REN.
TOKI-MITSU...
NOT TO SAY I NEEDED IT...
YOU HAVE A SISTER, A SHRINE MAIDEN, DON'T YOU?
I HEARD YOU VISITED OUR SHRINE. MY SISTER TOLD ME SO.
SHE TOLD ME...
...THAT A.D.C. IS TRYING TO CHANGE YOU. IN A BAD WAY.
THAT IS NOT TRUE. A.D.C. IS WORKING FOR MY BENEFIT. FOR ALL OF US.
REALLY? SO, WHY DID YOU TRY TO MURDER REN AND MEW?!

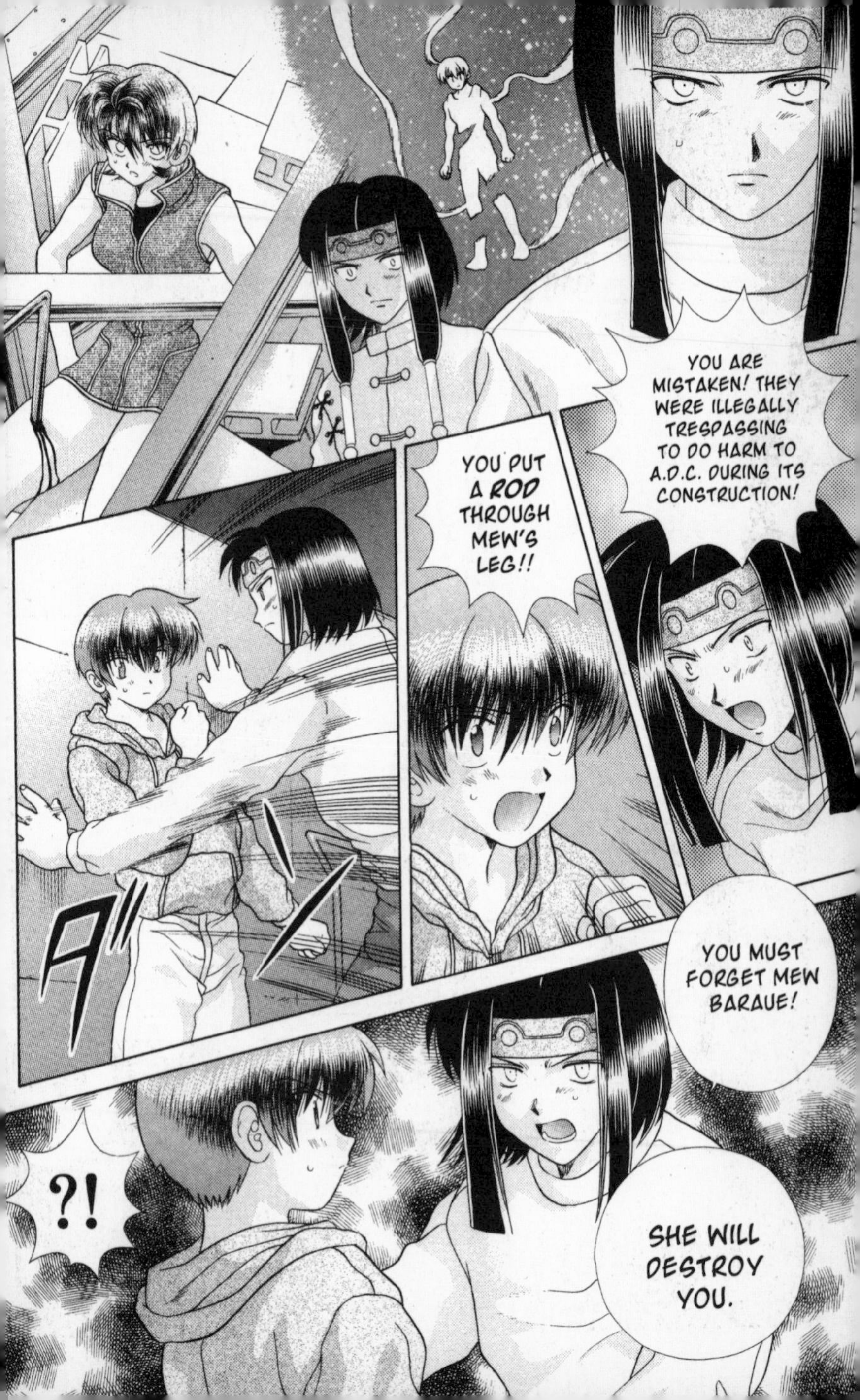
YOU PUT A ROD THROUGH MEW'S LEG!!
YOU ARE MISTAKEN! THEY WERE ILLEGALLY TRESPASSING TO DO HARM TO A.D.C. DURING ITS CONSTRUCTION!
YOU MUST FORGET MEW BARAUE!
SHE WILL DESTROY YOU.
?!

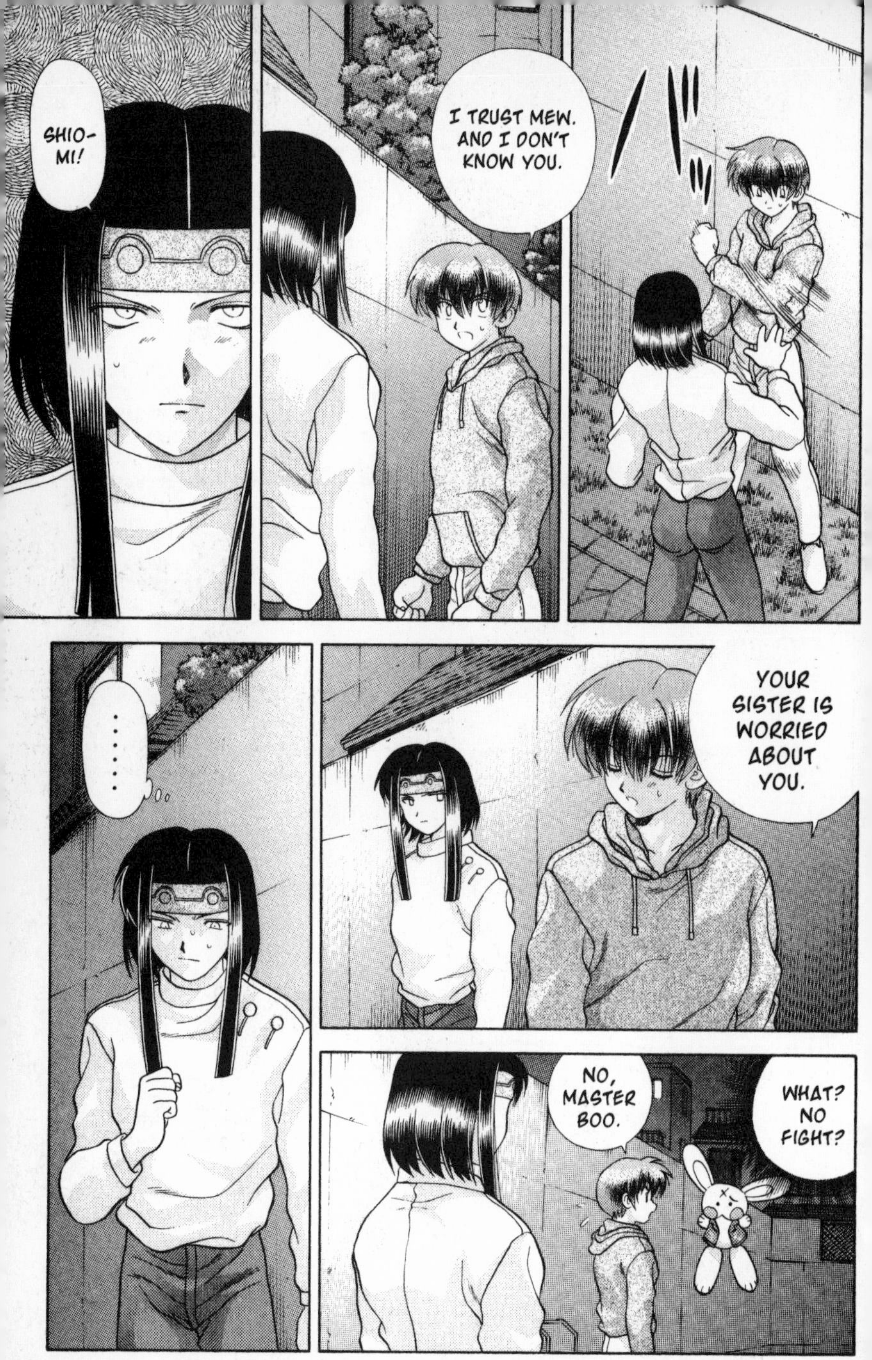
I TRUST MEW.
AND I DON'T
KNOW YOU.
SHIO-
MI!
YOUR
SISTER IS
WORRIED
ABOUT
YOU.
WHAT?
NO
FIGHT?
NO,
MASTER
BOO.
......

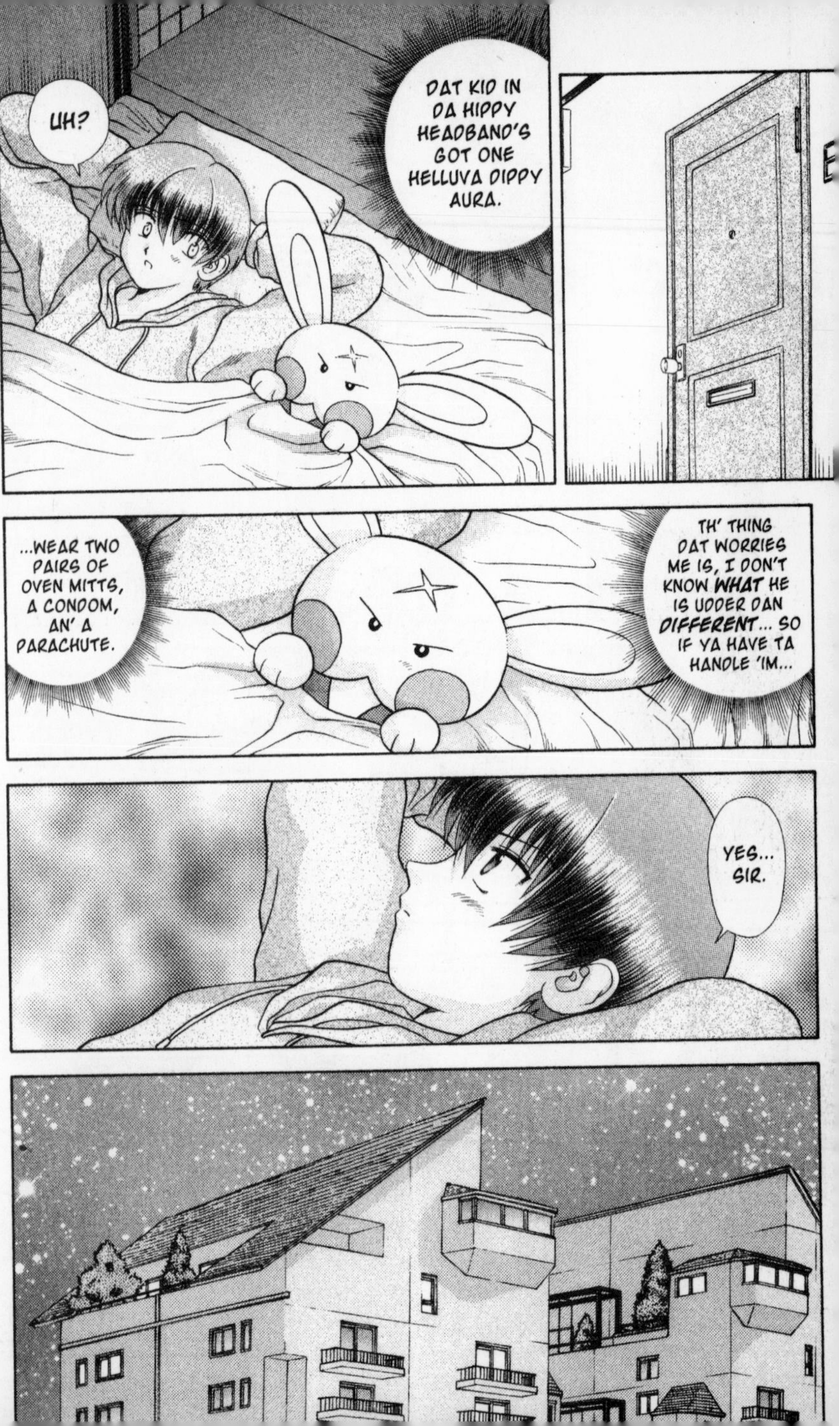
DAT KID IN DA HIPPY HEADBAND'S GOT ONE HELLUVA DIPPY AURA.
UH?
TH' THING DAT WORRIES ME IS, I DON'T KNOW WHAT HE IS UDDER DAN DIFFERENT... SO IF YA HAVE TA HANDLE 'IM...
...WEAR TWO PAIRS OF OVEN MITTS, A CONDOM, AN' A PARACHUTE.
YES... SIR.

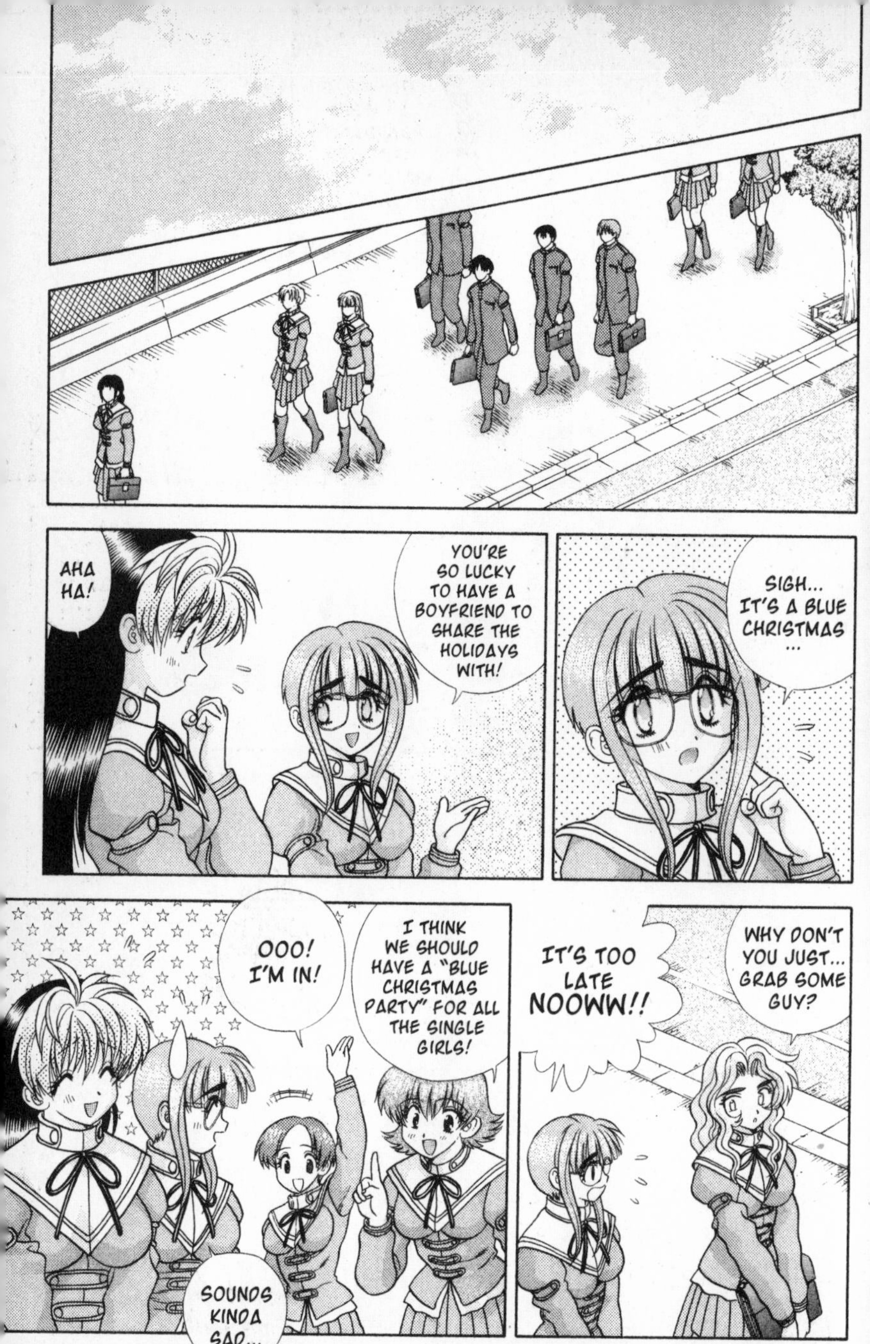
SIGH... IT'S A BLUE CHRISTMAS ...
YOU'RE SO LUCKY TO HAVE A BOYFRIEND TO SHARE THE HOLIDAYS WITH!
AHA HA!
WHY DON'T YOU JUST... GRAB SOME GUY?
IT'S TOO LATE NOOWW!!
I THINK WE SHOULD HAVE A "BLUE CHRISTMAS PARTY" FOR ALL THE SINGLE GIRLS!
OOO! I'M IN!
SOUNDS KINDA SAD...

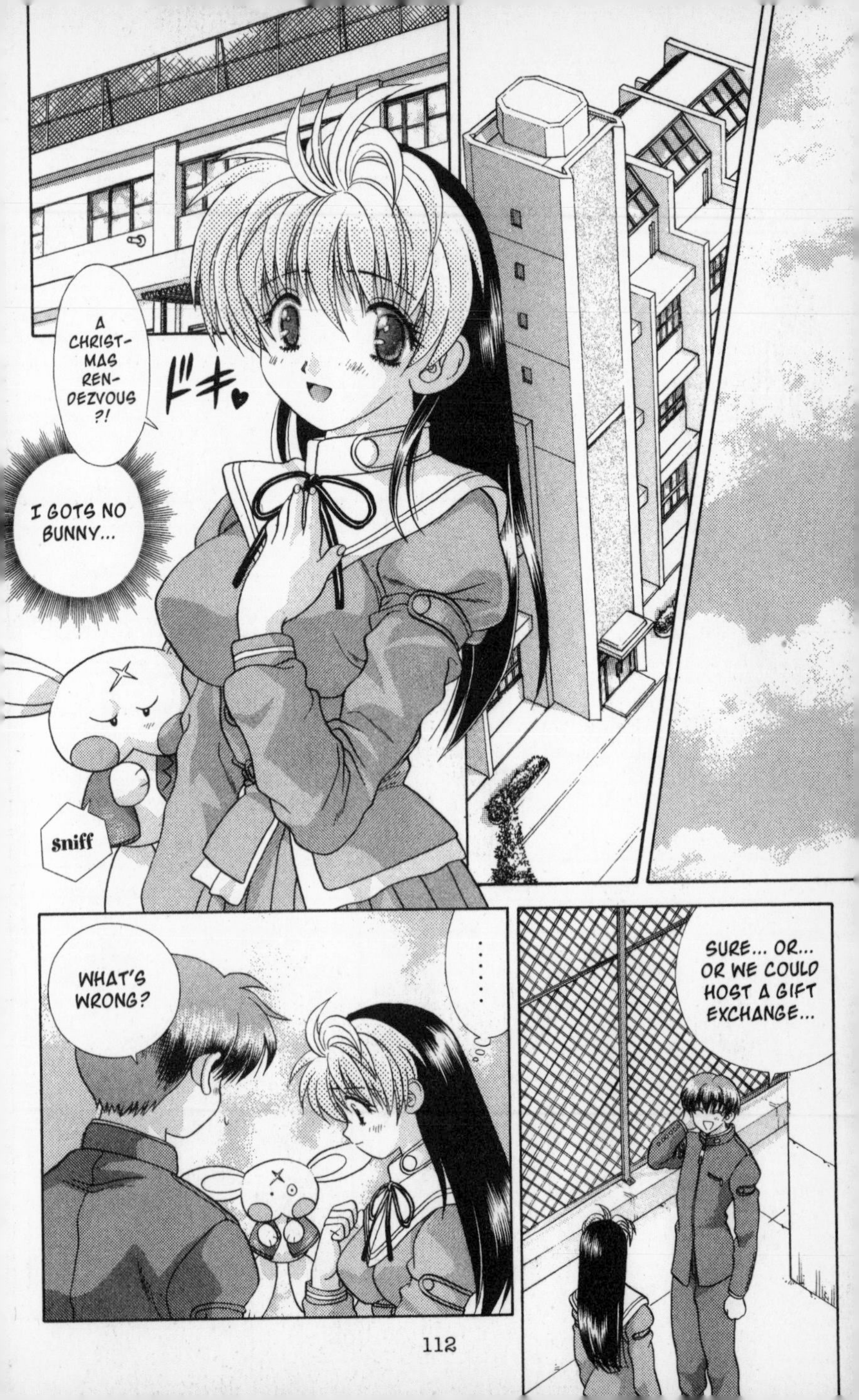
A CHRIST-MAS REN-DEZVOUS?!
ドキ♥
I GOTS NO BUNNY...
Sniff
SURE... OR... OR WE COULD HOST A GIFT EXCHANGE...
......
WHAT'S WRONG?

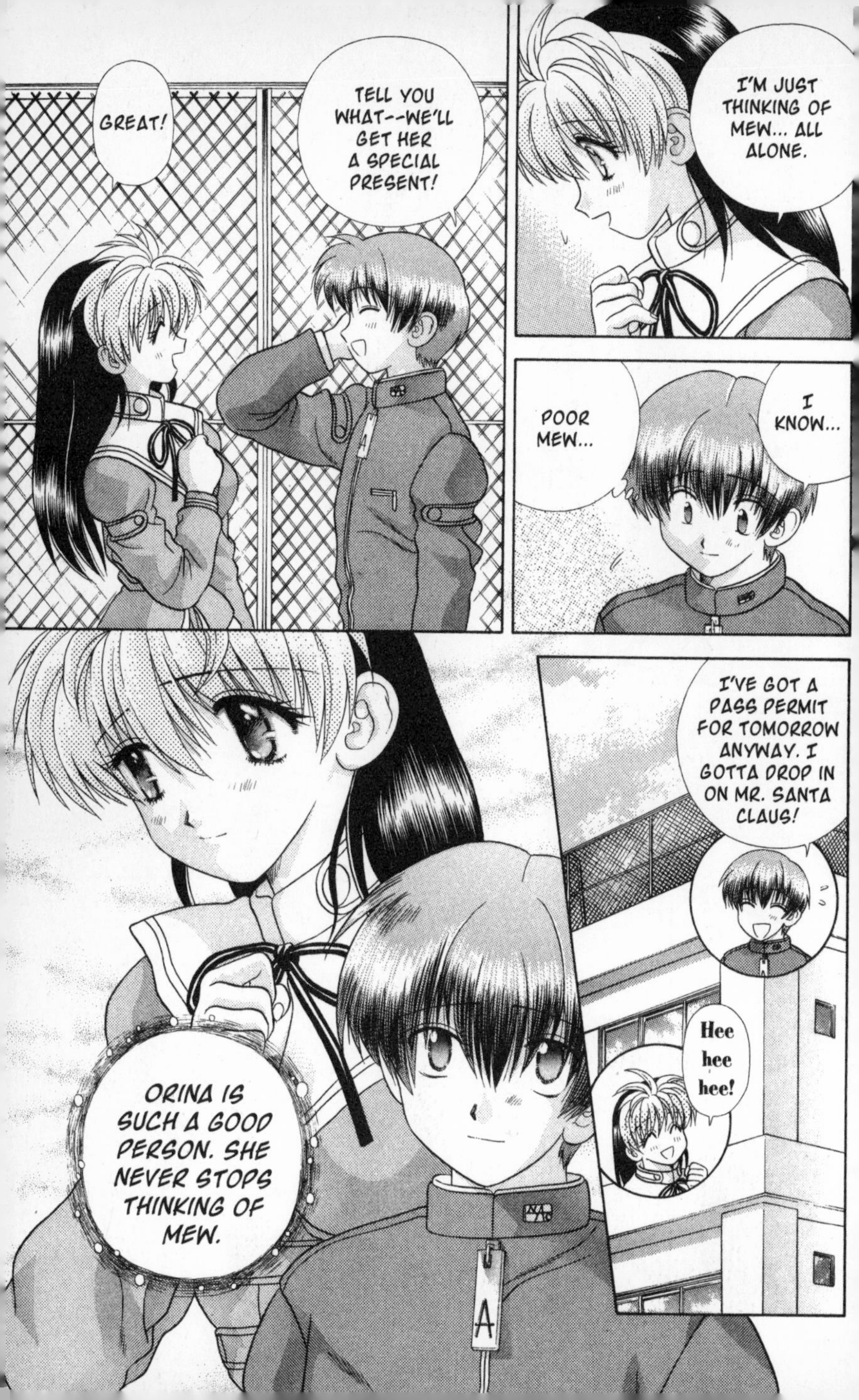

I'M JUST THINKING OF MEW... ALL ALONE.
POOR MEW...
I KNOW...
TELL YOU WHAT--WE'LL GET HER A SPECIAL PRESENT!
GREAT!
I'VE GOT A PASS PERMIT FOR TOMORROW ANYWAY. I GOTTA DROP IN ON MR. SANTA CLAUS!
Hee hee hee!
ORINA IS SUCH A GOOD PERSON. SHE NEVER STOPS THINKING OF MEW.

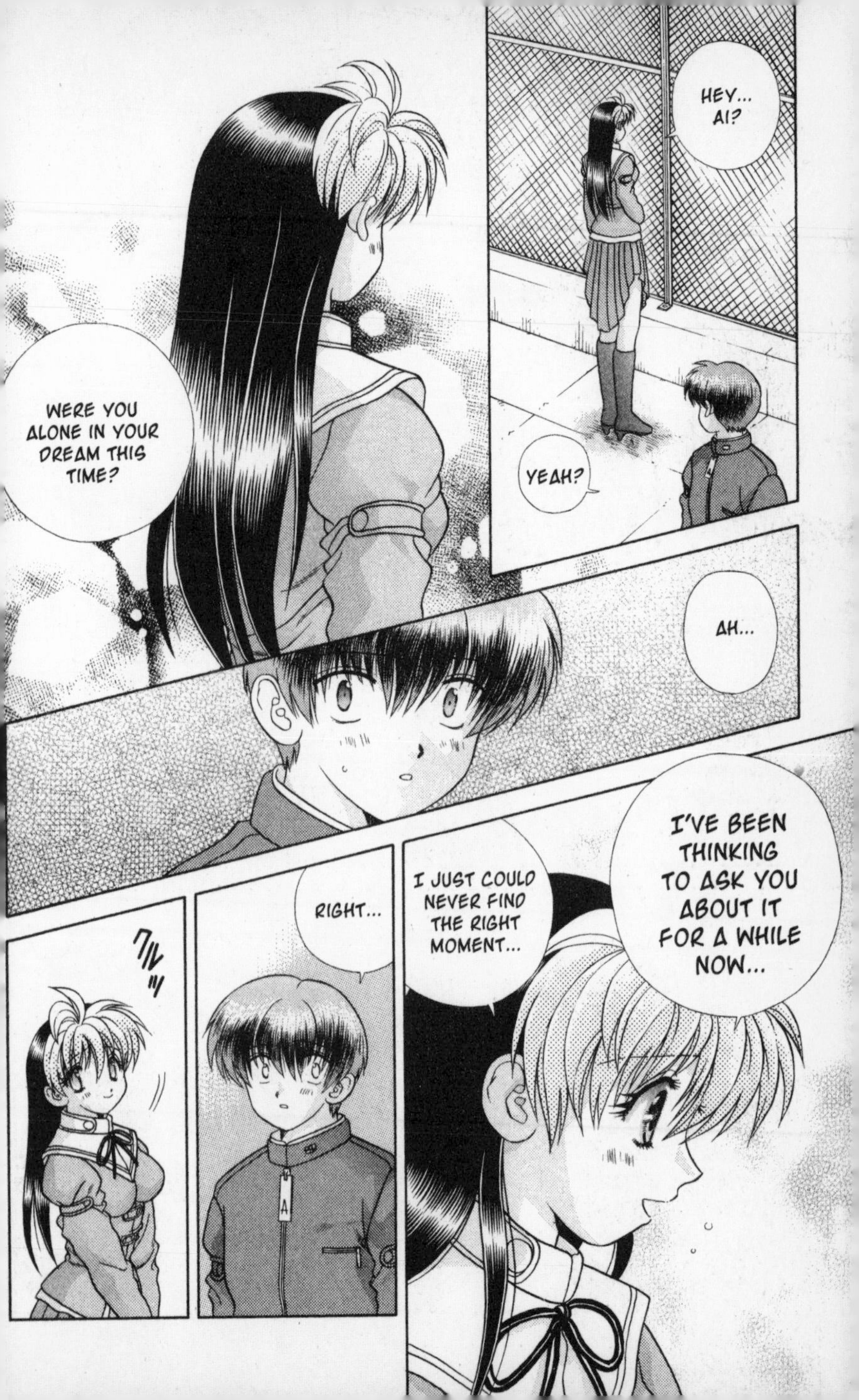
HEY... AI?
YEAH?
WERE YOU ALONE IN YOUR DREAM THIS TIME?
AH...
I'VE BEEN THINKING TO ASK YOU ABOUT IT FOR A WHILE NOW...
I JUST COULD NEVER FIND THE RIGHT MOMENT...
RIGHT...

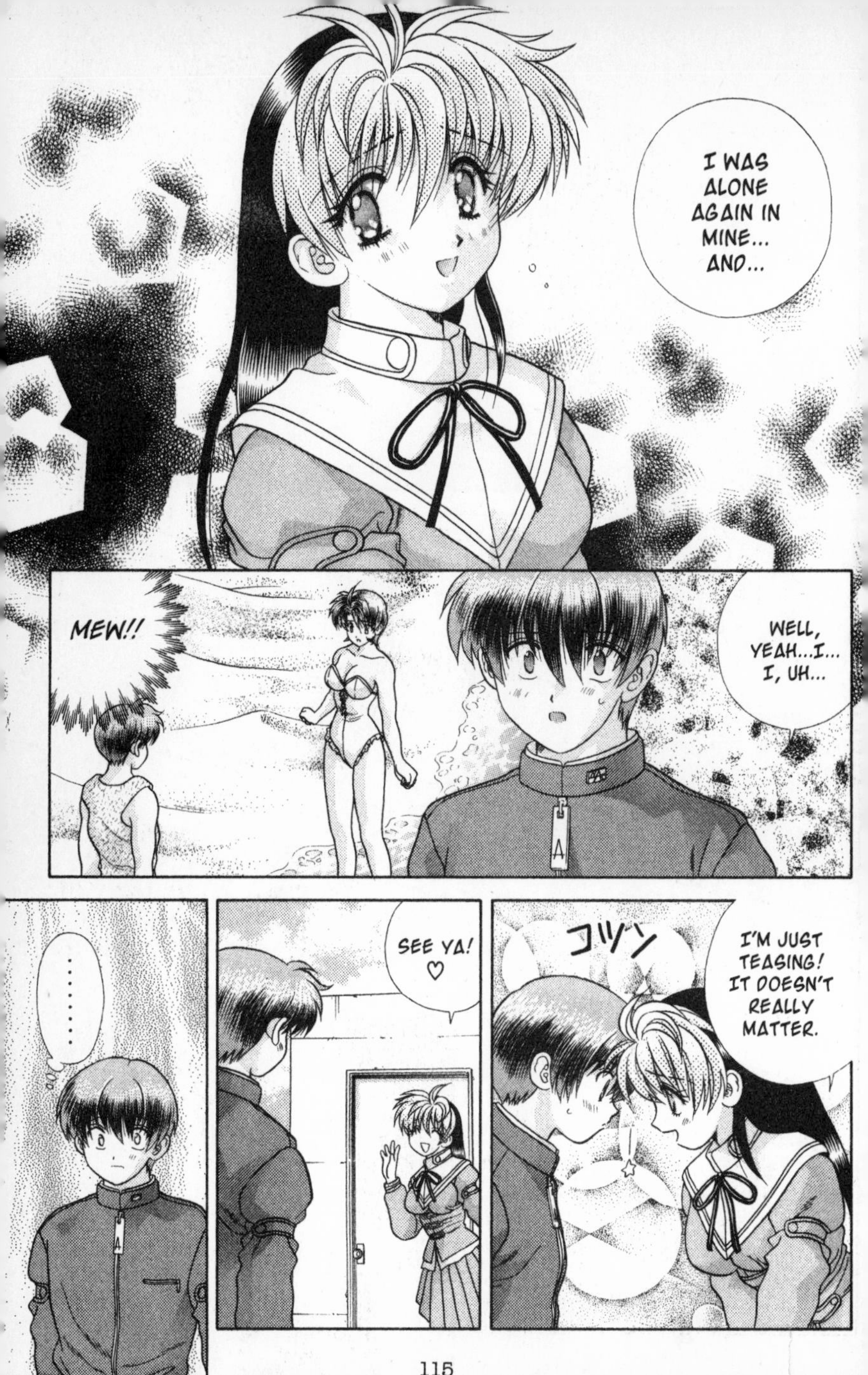
I WAS ALONE AGAIN IN MINE... AND...
WELL, YEAH...I... I, UH...
MEW!!
コツン
I'M JUST TEASING! IT DOESN'T REALLY MATTER.
SEE YA! ♡
......

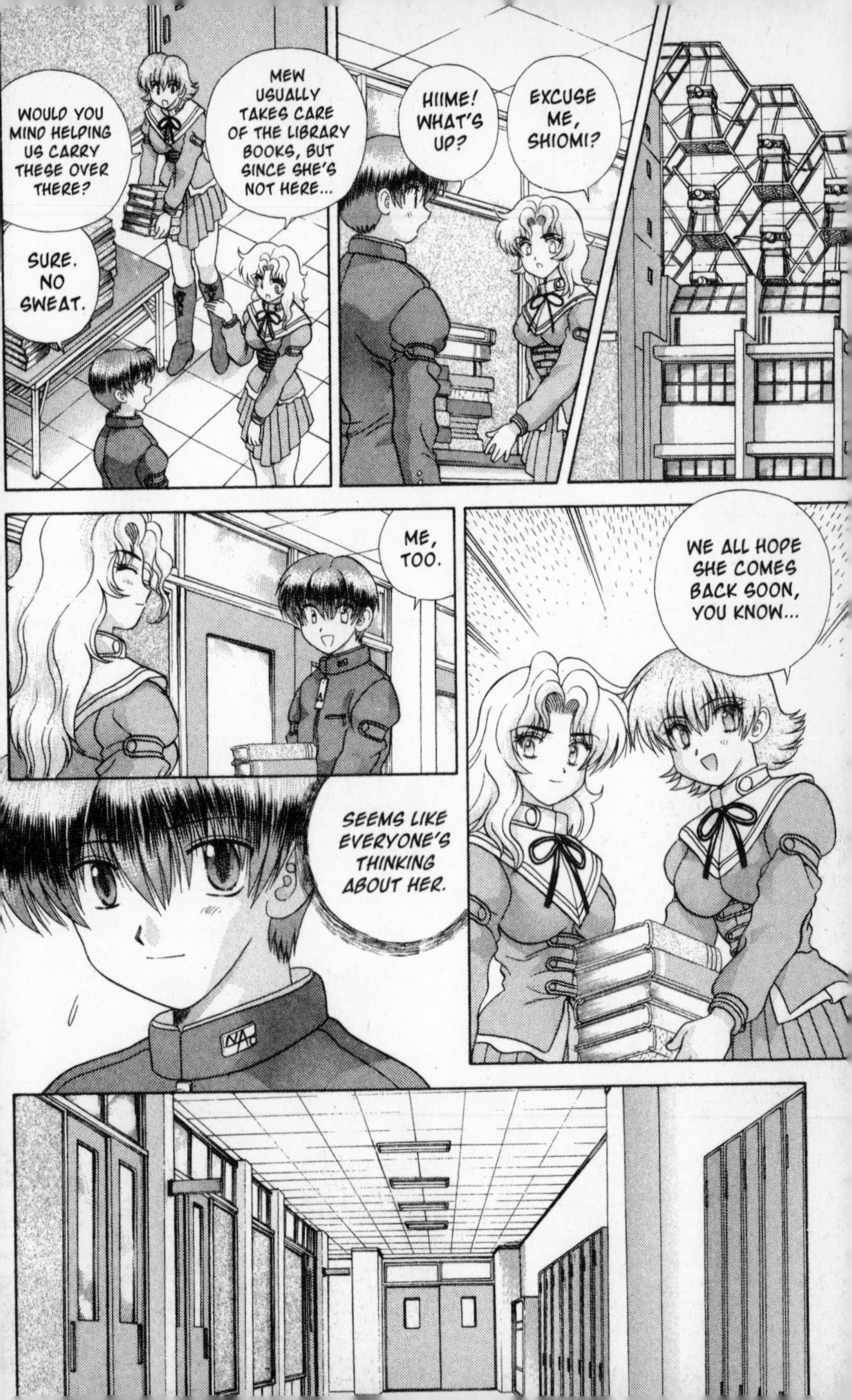
EXCUSE ME, SHIOMI?
HIIME! WHAT'S UP?
MEW USUALLY TAKES CARE OF THE LIBRARY BOOKS, BUT SINCE SHE'S NOT HERE...
WOULD YOU MIND HELPING US CARRY THESE OVER THERE?
SURE. NO SWEAT.
WE ALL HOPE SHE COMES BACK SOON, YOU KNOW...
ME, TOO.
SEEMS LIKE EVERYONE'S THINKING ABOUT HER.

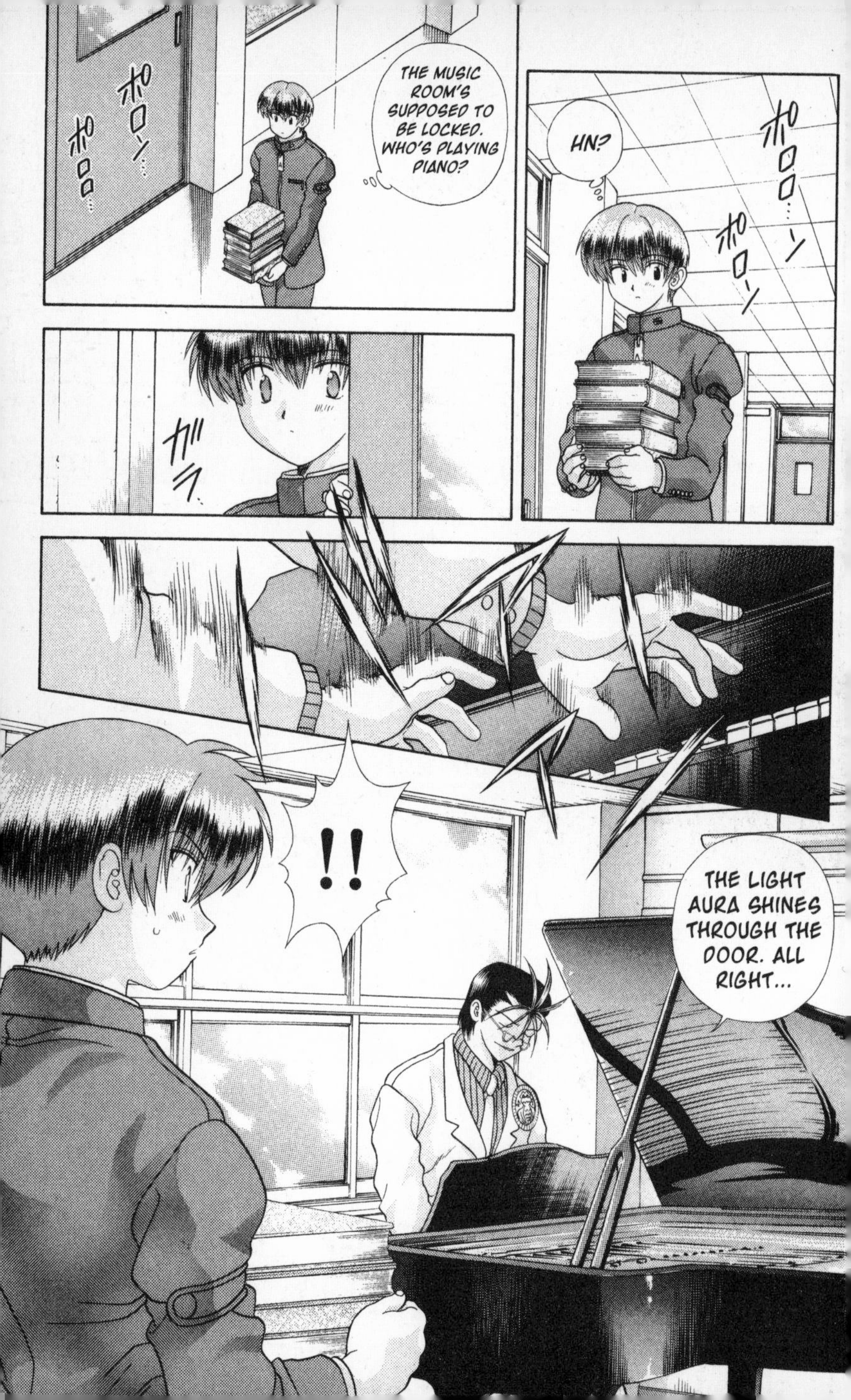

HN?
ポロロ…ン
ポローン
THE MUSIC ROOM'S SUPPOSED TO BE LOCKED. WHO'S PLAYING PIANO?
ポローン…
ポロロ…
ガラ
!!
THE LIGHT AURA SHINES THROUGH THE DOOR. ALL RIGHT...

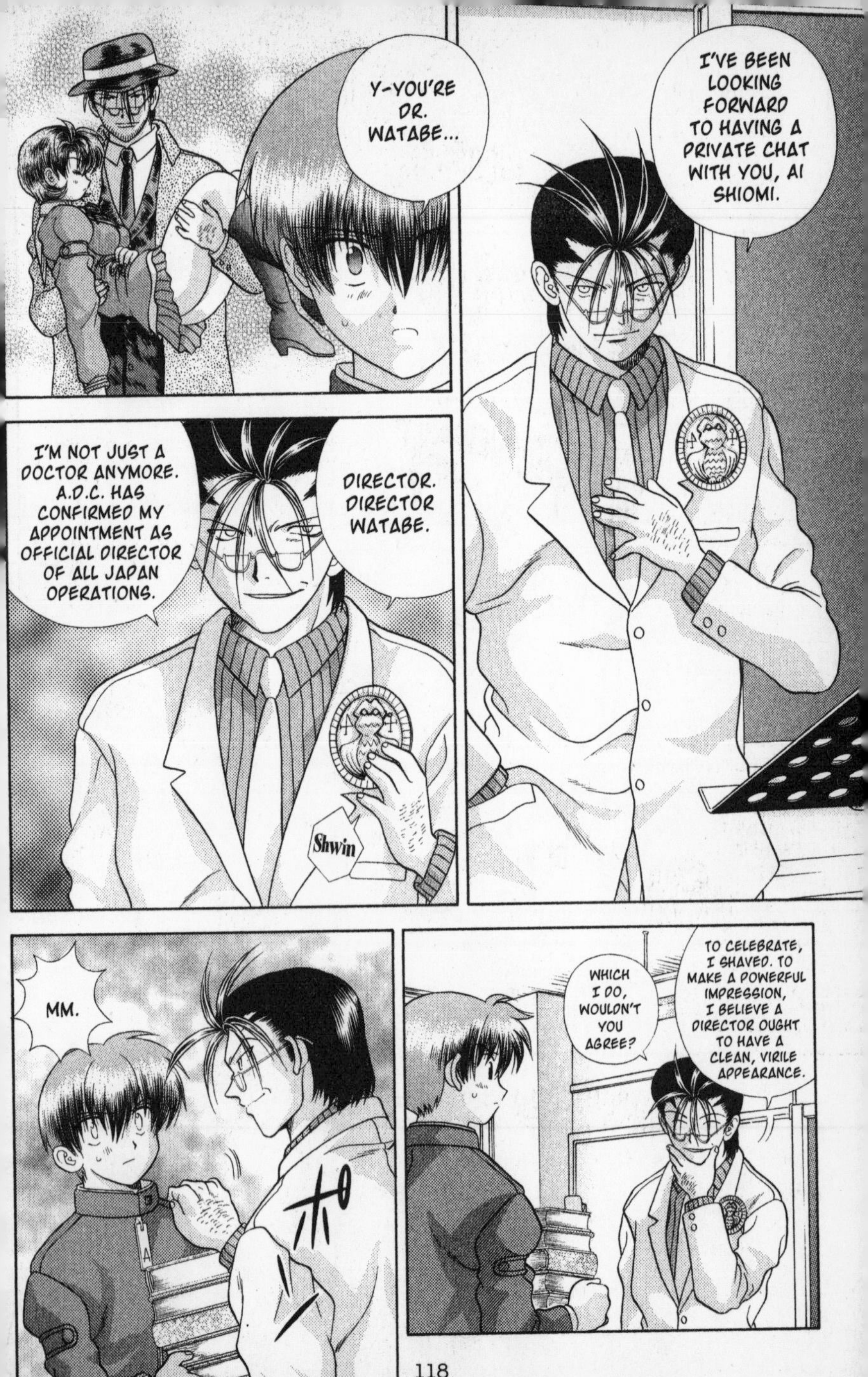

I'VE BEEN LOOKING FORWARD TO HAVING A PRIVATE CHAT WITH YOU, AI SHIOMI.
Y-YOU'RE DR. WATABE...
DIRECTOR. DIRECTOR WATABE.
I'M NOT JUST A DOCTOR ANYMORE. A.D.C. HAS CONFIRMED MY APPOINTMENT AS OFFICIAL DIRECTOR OF ALL JAPAN OPERATIONS.
Shwin
TO CELEBRATE, I SHAVED. TO MAKE A POWERFUL IMPRESSION, I BELIEVE A DIRECTOR OUGHT TO HAVE A CLEAN, VIRILE APPEARANCE.
WHICH I DO, WOULDN'T YOU AGREE?
MM.

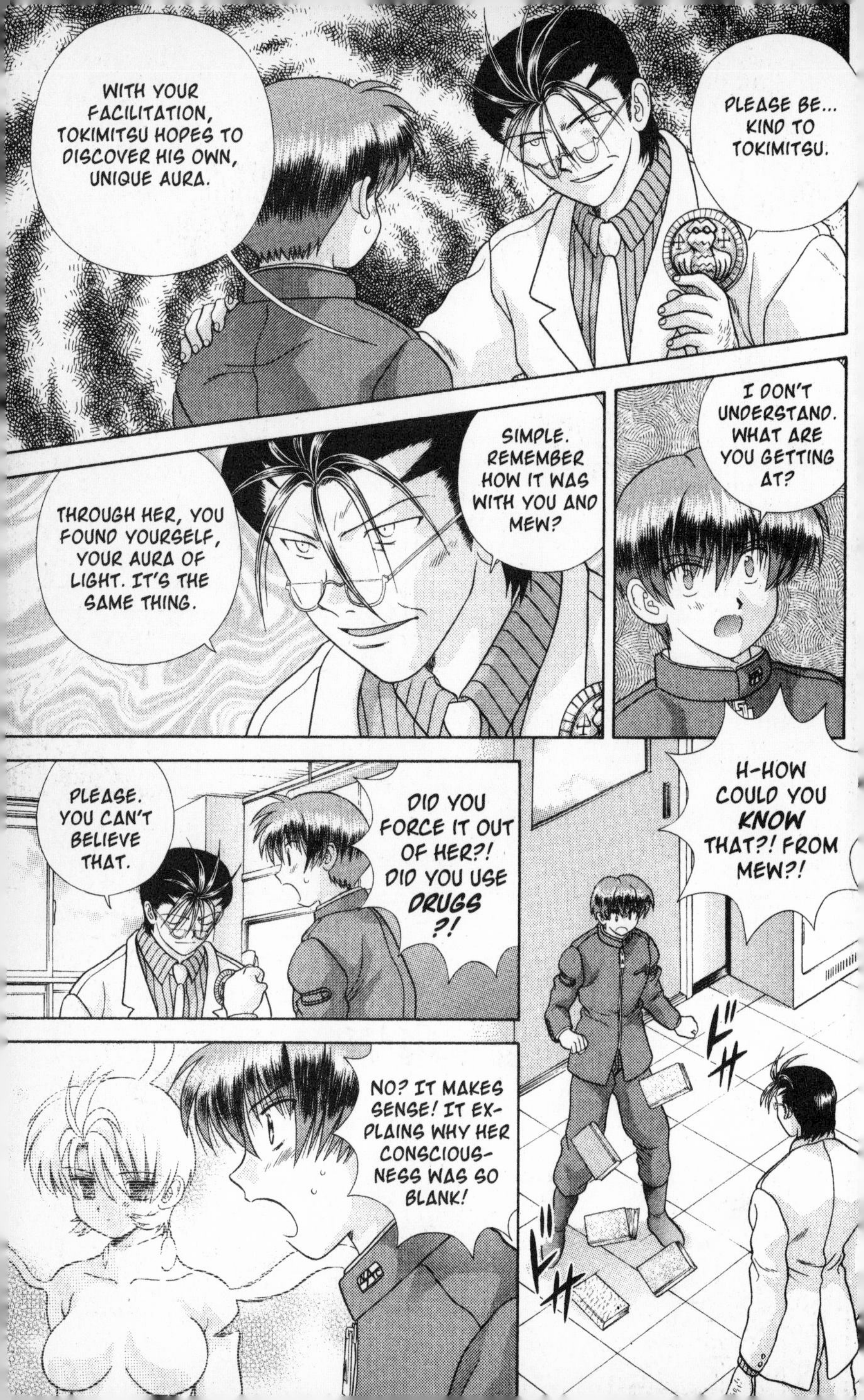

PLEASE BE... KIND TO TOKIMITSU.
WITH YOUR FACILITATION, TOKIMITSU HOPES TO DISCOVER HIS OWN, UNIQUE AURA.
I DON'T UNDERSTAND. WHAT ARE YOU GETTING AT?
SIMPLE. REMEMBER HOW IT WAS WITH YOU AND MEW?
THROUGH HER, YOU FOUND YOURSELF, YOUR AURA OF LIGHT. IT'S THE SAME THING.
H-HOW COULD YOU KNOW THAT?! FROM MEW?!
DID YOU FORCE IT OUT OF HER?! DID YOU USE DRUGS ?!
PLEASE. YOU CAN'T BELIEVE THAT.
NO? IT MAKES SENSE! IT EXPLAINS WHY HER CONSCIOUSNESS WAS SO BLANK!

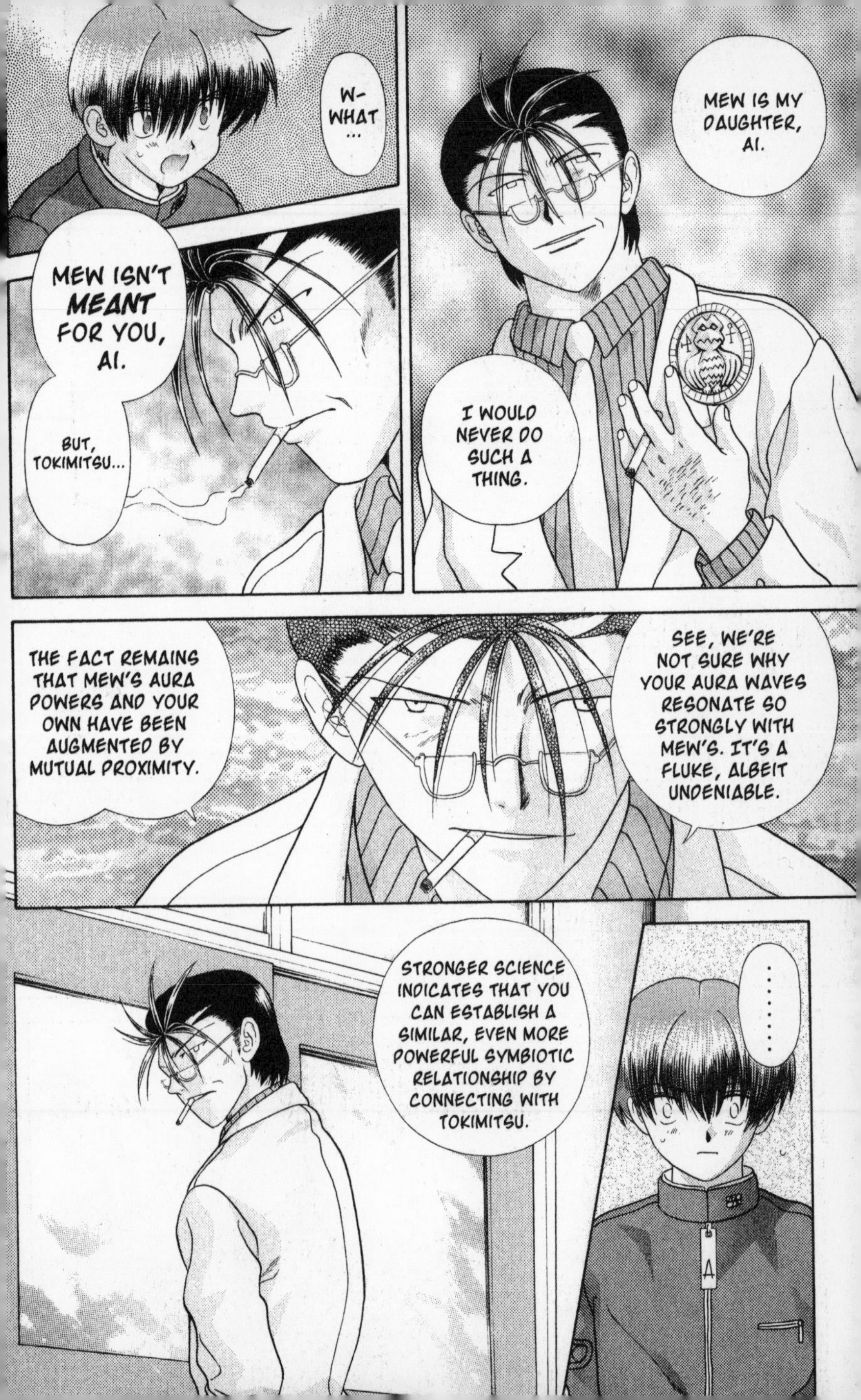
MEW IS MY DAUGHTER, AI.
I WOULD NEVER DO SUCH A THING.
W-WHAT...
MEW ISN'T *MEANT* FOR YOU, AI.
BUT, TOKIMITSU...
SEE, WE'RE NOT SURE WHY YOUR AURA WAVES RESONATE SO STRONGLY WITH MEW'S. IT'S A FLUKE, ALBEIT UNDENIABLE.
THE FACT REMAINS THAT MEW'S AURA POWERS AND YOUR OWN HAVE BEEN AUGMENTED BY MUTUAL PROXIMITY.
......
STRONGER SCIENCE INDICATES THAT YOU CAN ESTABLISH A SIMILAR, EVEN MORE POWERFUL SYMBIOTIC RELATIONSHIP BY CONNECTING WITH TOKIMITSU.

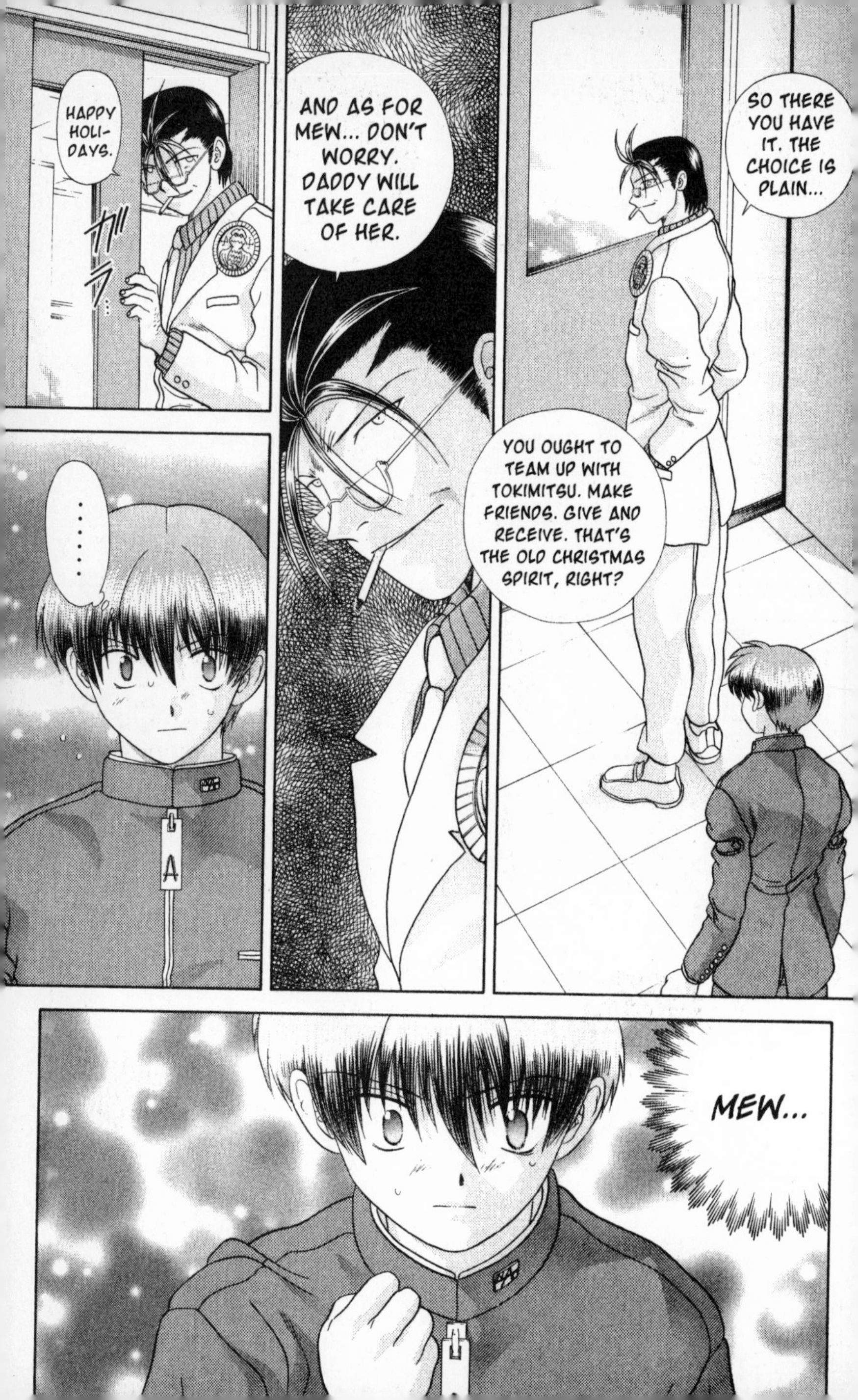
SO THERE YOU HAVE IT. THE CHOICE IS PLAIN...
YOU OUGHT TO TEAM UP WITH TOKIMITSU. MAKE FRIENDS. GIVE AND RECEIVE. THAT'S THE OLD CHRISTMAS SPIRIT, RIGHT?
AND AS FOR MEW... DON'T WORRY. DADDY WILL TAKE CARE OF HER.
HAPPY HOLI-DAYS.
......
MEW...

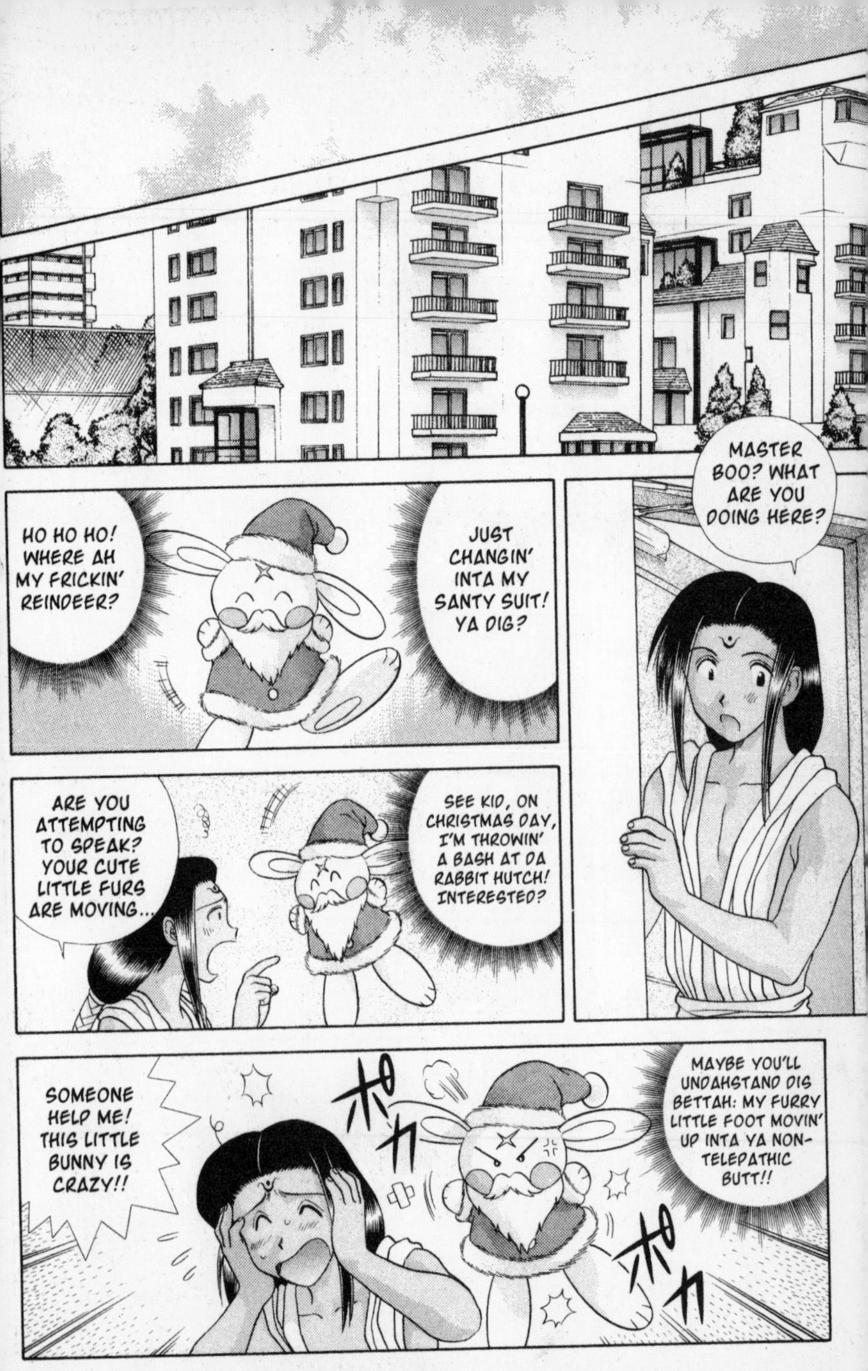
MASTER BOO? WHAT ARE YOU DOING HERE?
JUST CHANGIN' INTA MY SANTY SUIT! YA DIG?
HO HO HO! WHERE AH MY FRICKIN' REINDEER?
SEE KID, ON CHRISTMAS DAY, I'M THROWIN' A BASH AT DA RABBIT HUTCH! INTERESTED?
ARE YOU ATTEMPTING TO SPEAK? YOUR CUTE LITTLE FURS ARE MOVING...
MAYBE YOU'LL UNDAHSTAND DIS BETTAH: MY FURRY LITTLE FOOT MOVIN' UP INTA YA NON-TELEPATHIC BUTT!!
ポカ
ポカ
SOMEONE HELP ME! THIS LITTLE BUNNY IS CRAZY!!

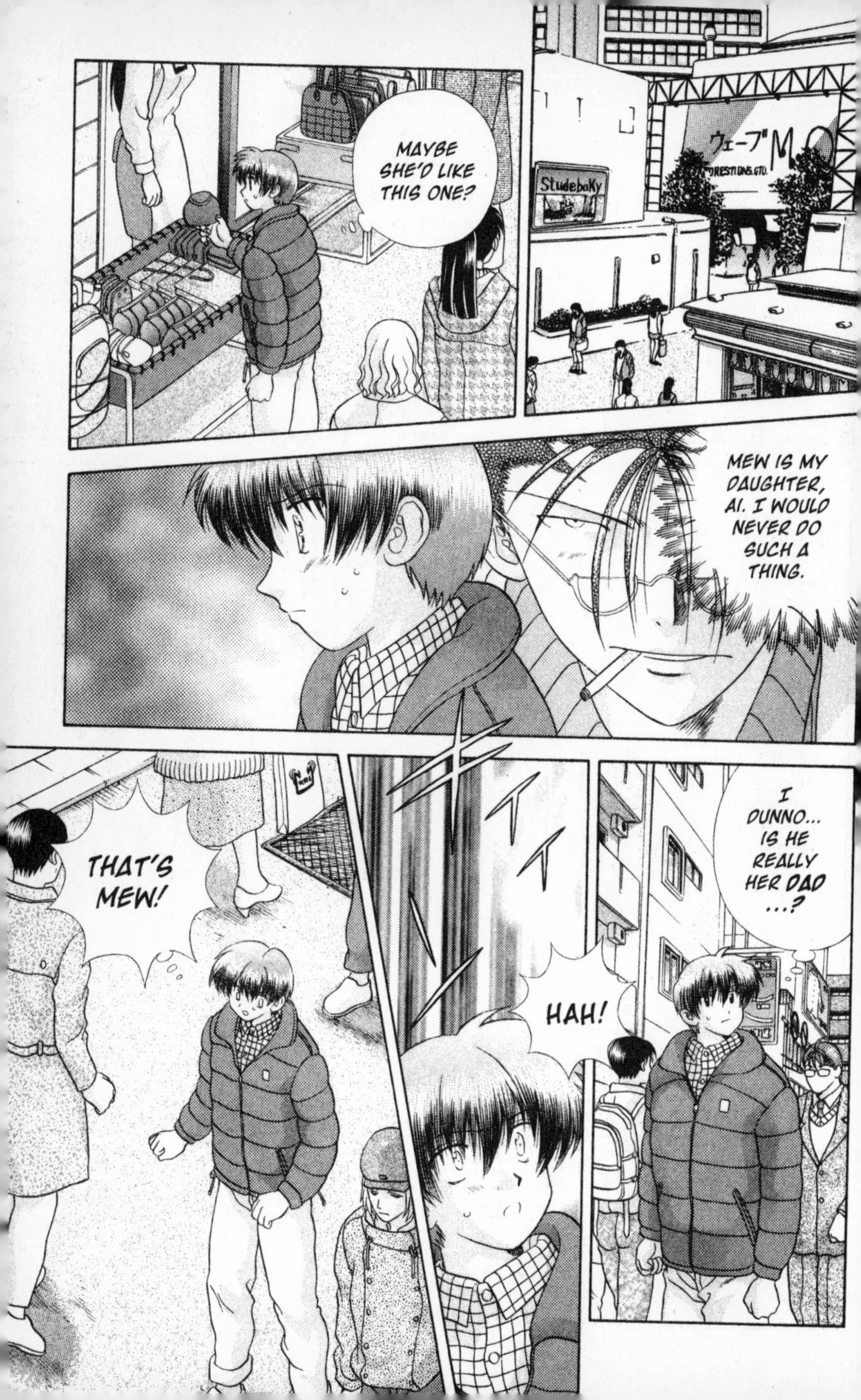
Studebaky
MAYBE SHE'D LIKE THIS ONE?
MEW IS MY DAUGHTER, AI. I WOULD NEVER DO SUCH A THING.
I DUNNO... IS HE REALLY HER DAD ...?
HAH!
THAT'S MEW!

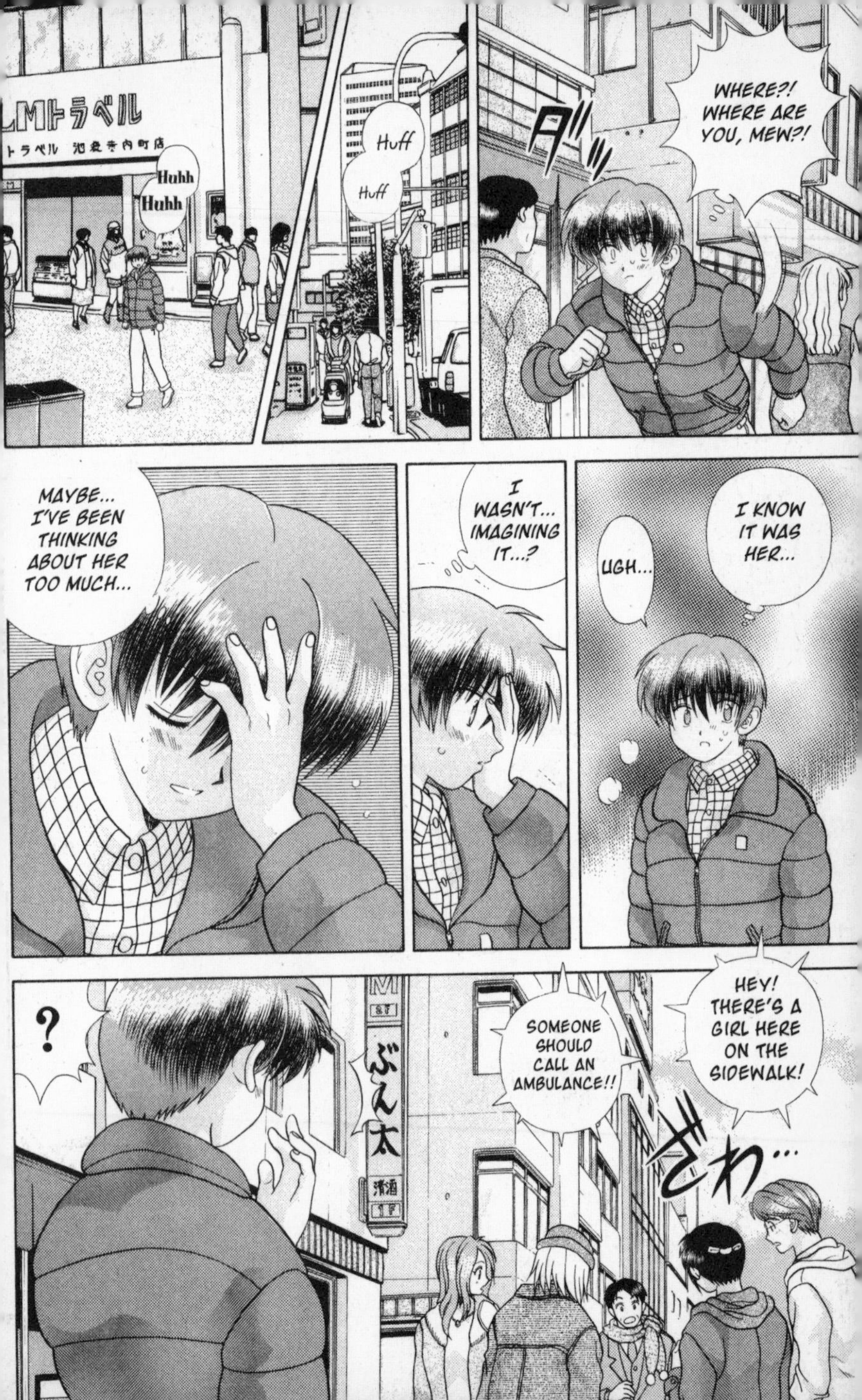

ダッ
WHERE?! WHERE ARE YOU, MEW?!
Huff
Huff
Huhh
Huhh
LMトラベル
I KNOW IT WAS HER...
UGH...
I WASN'T... IMAGINING IT...?
MAYBE... I'VE BEEN THINKING ABOUT HER TOO MUCH...
HEY! THERE'S A GIRL HERE ON THE SIDEWALK!
ざわ...
SOMEONE SHOULD CALL AN AMBULANCE!!
ぶん太
?

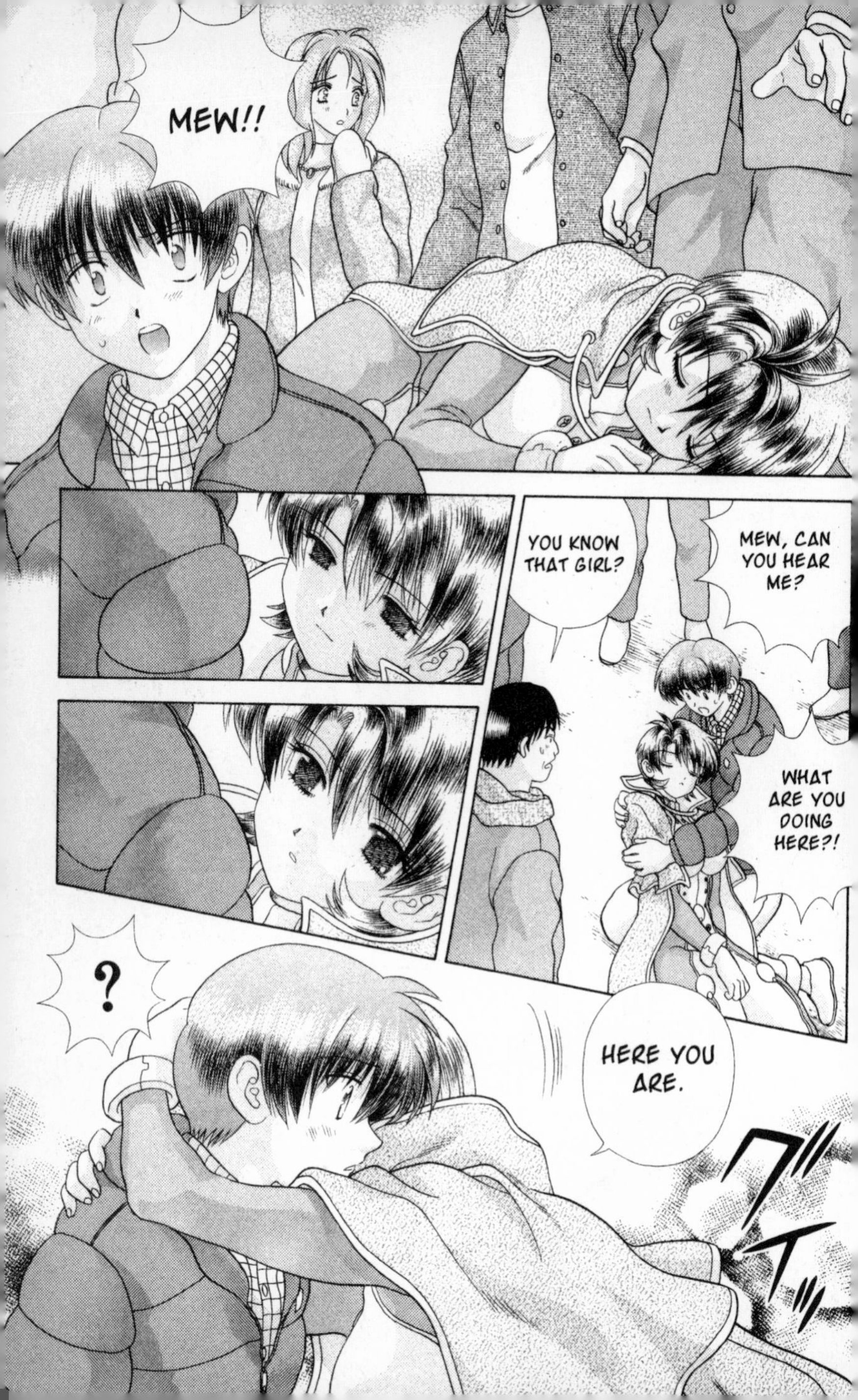
MEW!!
MEW, CAN YOU HEAR ME?
WHAT ARE YOU DOING HERE?!
YOU KNOW THAT GIRL?
HERE YOU ARE.
?
グイッ

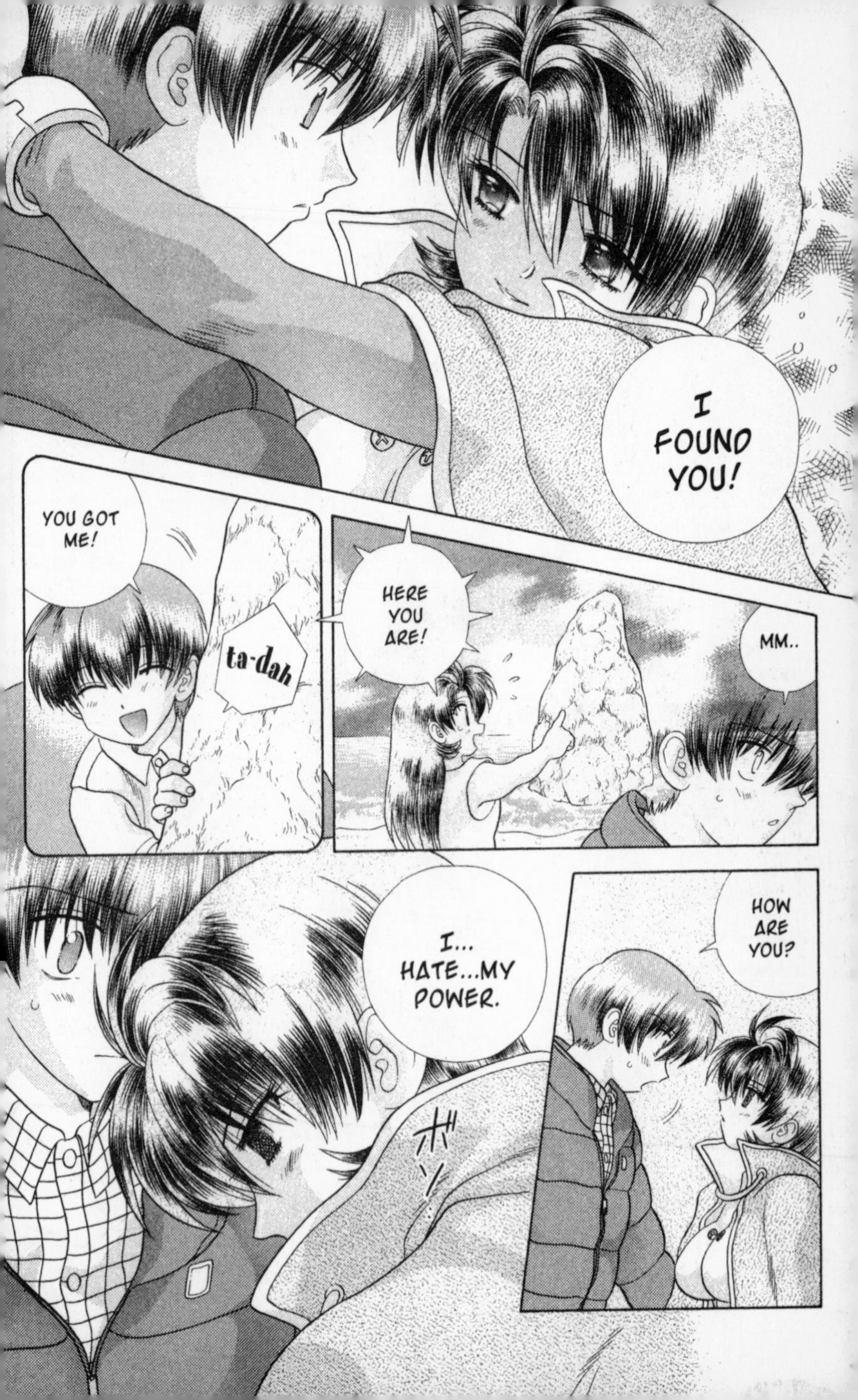
I FOUND YOU!
MM..
HERE YOU ARE!
ta-dah
YOU GOT ME!
HOW ARE YOU?
I... HATE...MY POWER.

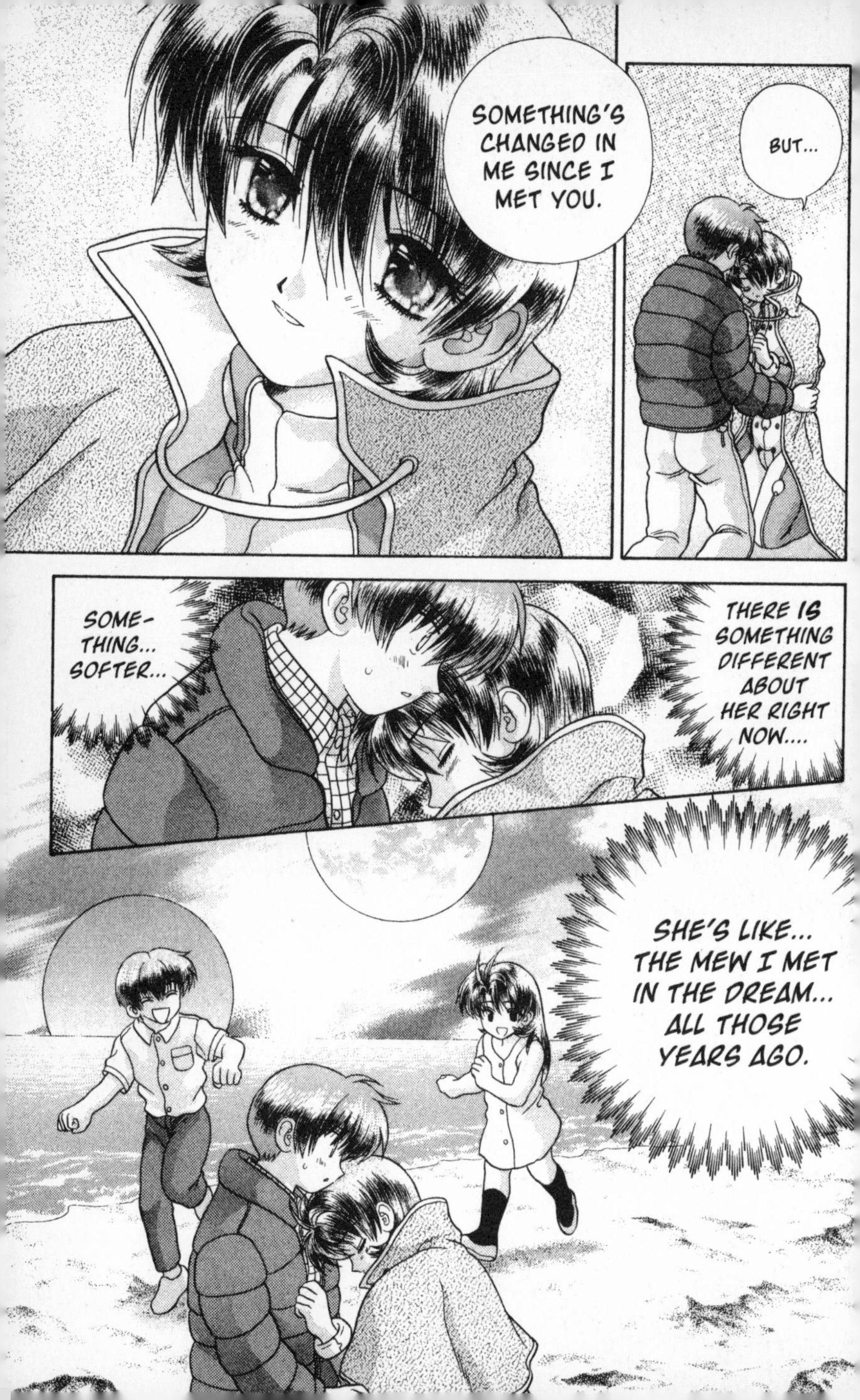
BUT...
SOMETHING'S CHANGED IN ME SINCE I MET YOU.
THERE IS SOMETHING DIFFERENT ABOUT HER RIGHT NOW....
SOME-THING... SOFTER...
SHE'S LIKE... THE MEW I MET IN THE DREAM... ALL THOSE YEARS AGO.

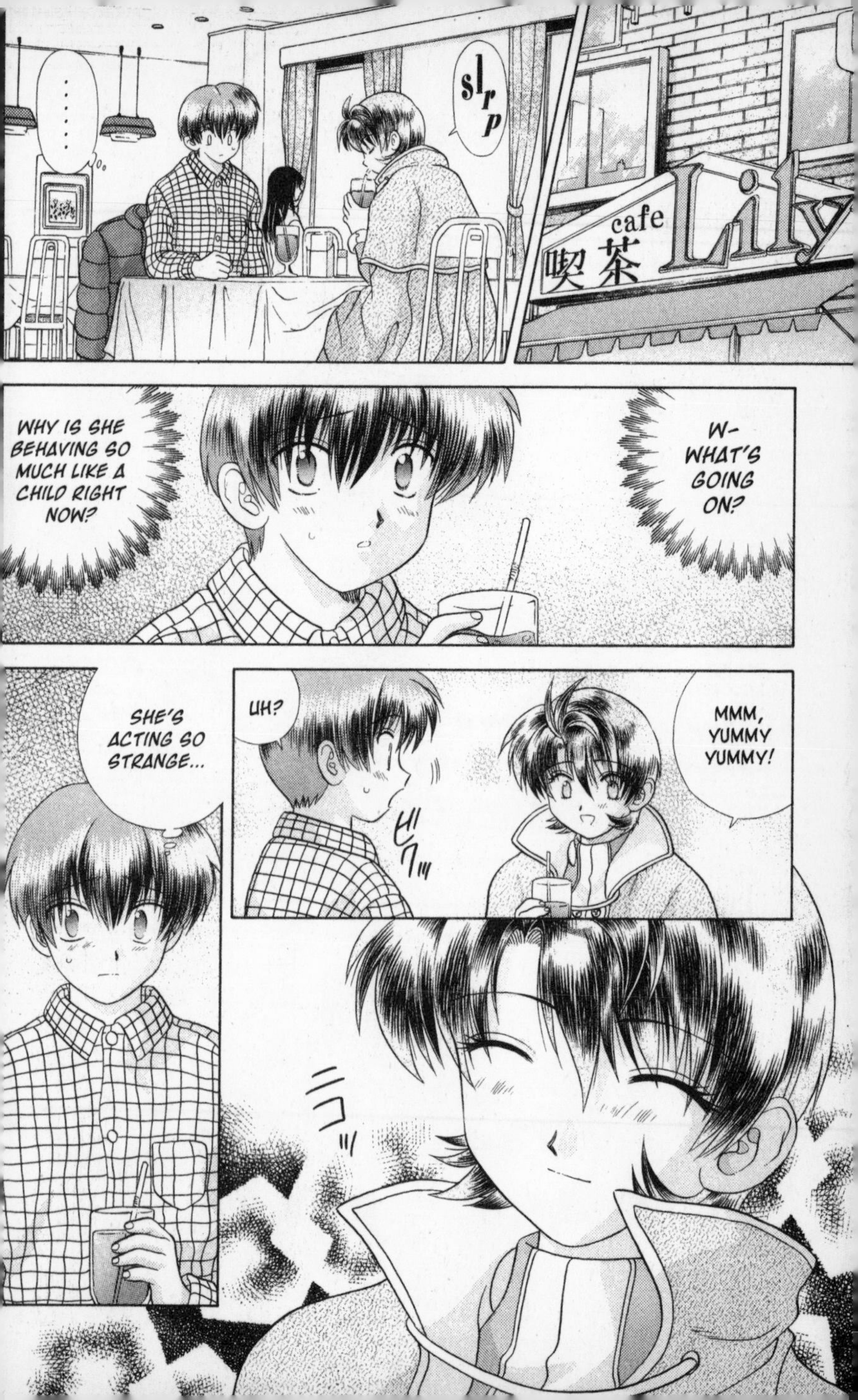
喫茶 cafe Lily
slrp
......
W-WHAT'S GOING ON?
WHY IS SHE BEHAVING SO MUCH LIKE A CHILD RIGHT NOW?
MMM, YUMMY YUMMY!
UH?
SHE'S ACTING SO STRANGE...

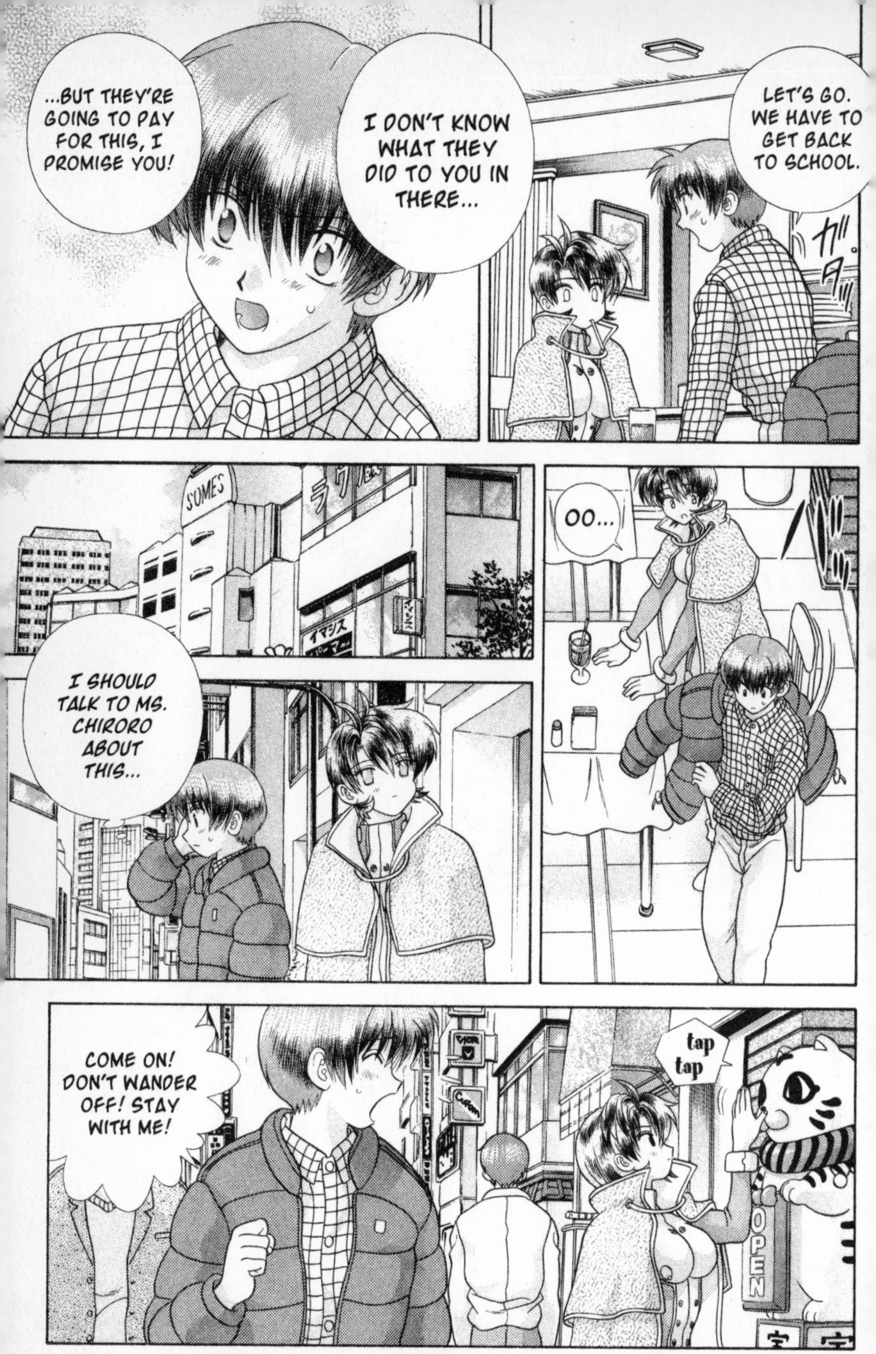
LET'S GO. WE HAVE TO GET BACK TO SCHOOL.
I DON'T KNOW WHAT THEY DID TO YOU IN THERE...
...BUT THEY'RE GOING TO PAY FOR THIS, I PROMISE YOU!
OO...
SOMES
I SHOULD TALK TO MS. CHIRORO ABOUT THIS...
tap tap
COME ON! DON'T WANDER OFF! STAY WITH ME!
OPEN

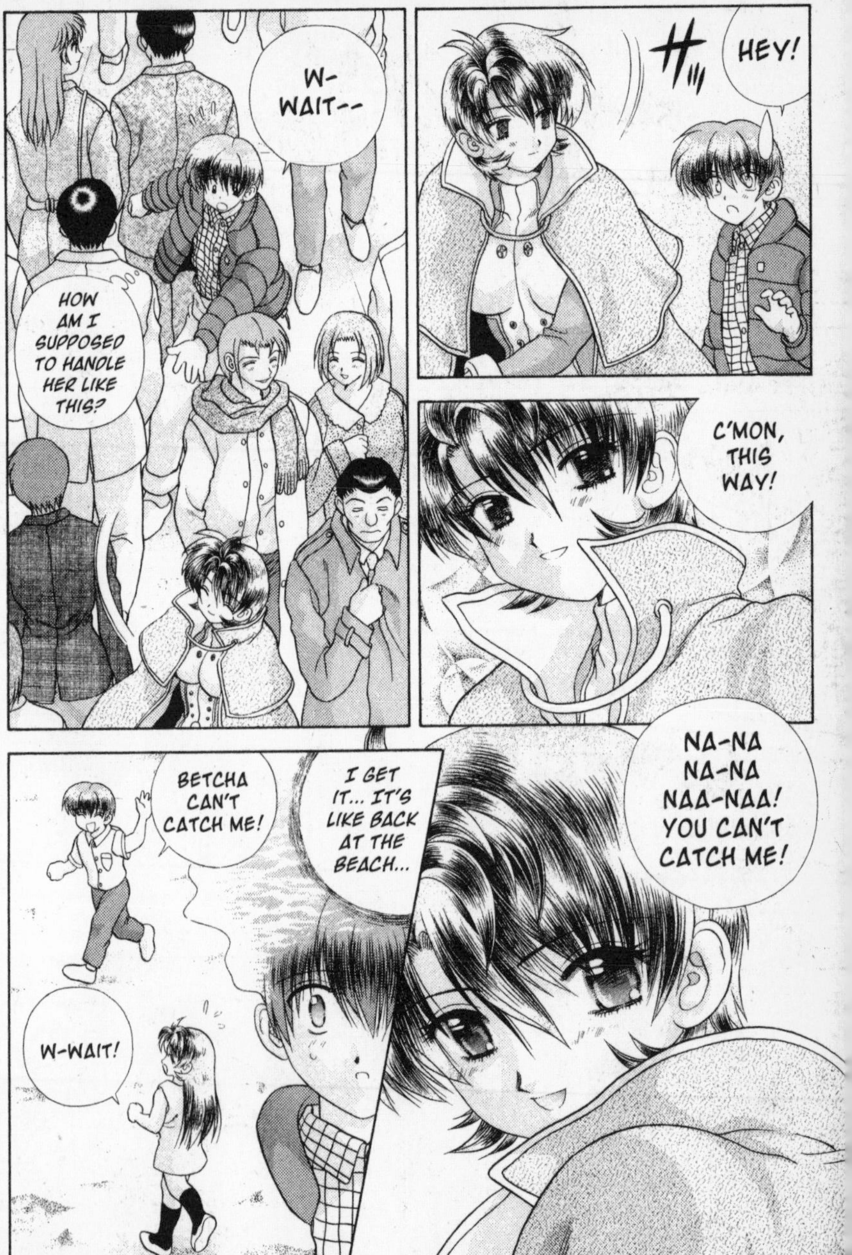
HEY!
C'MON, THIS WAY!
W- WAIT--
HOW AM I SUPPOSED TO HANDLE HER LIKE THIS?
NA-NA NA-NA NAA-NAA! YOU CAN'T CATCH ME!
I GET IT... IT'S LIKE BACK AT THE BEACH...
BETCHA CAN'T CATCH ME!
W-WAIT!

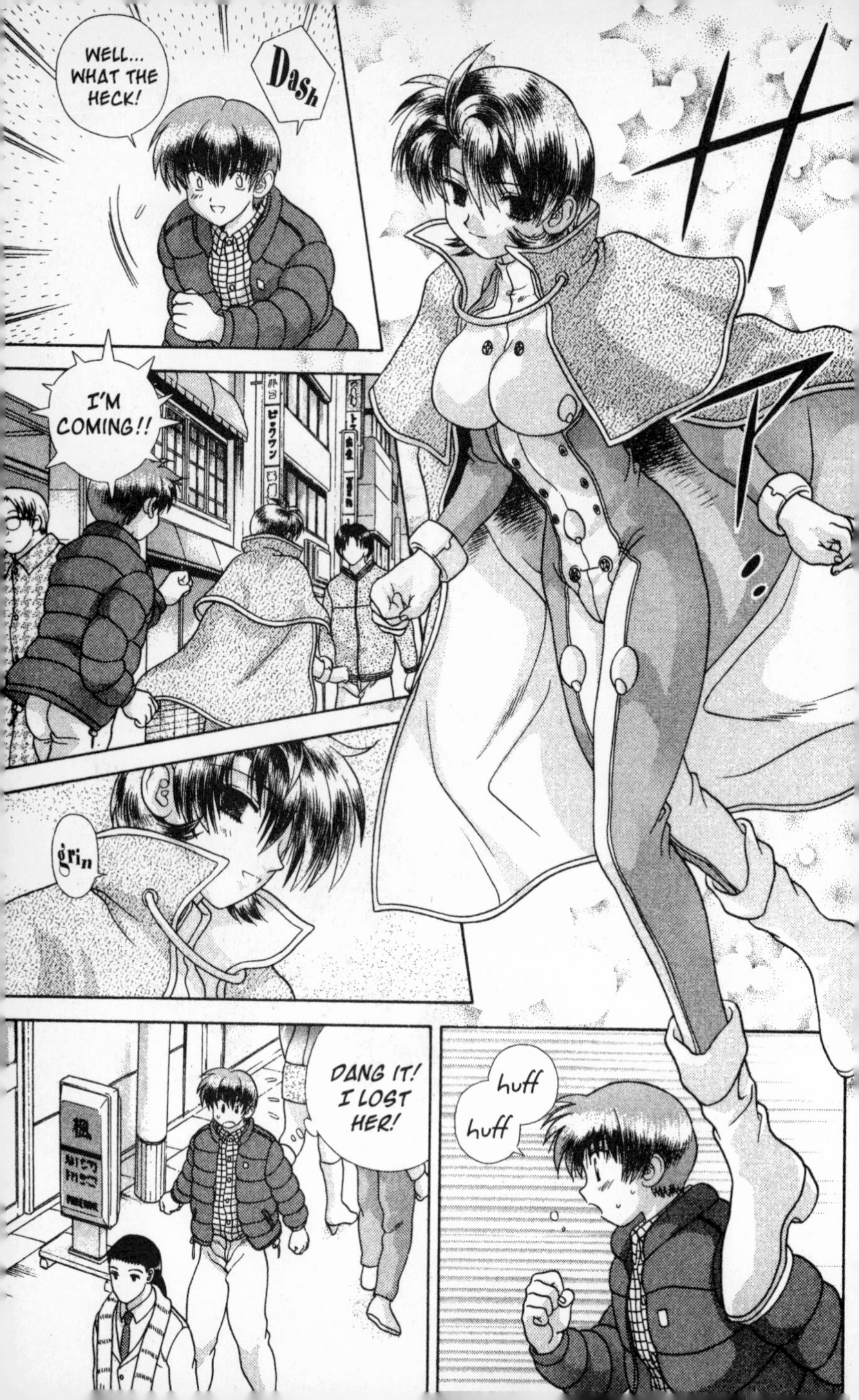
WELL... WHAT THE HECK!
Dash
I'M COMING!!
grin
DANG IT! I LOST HER!
huff
huff

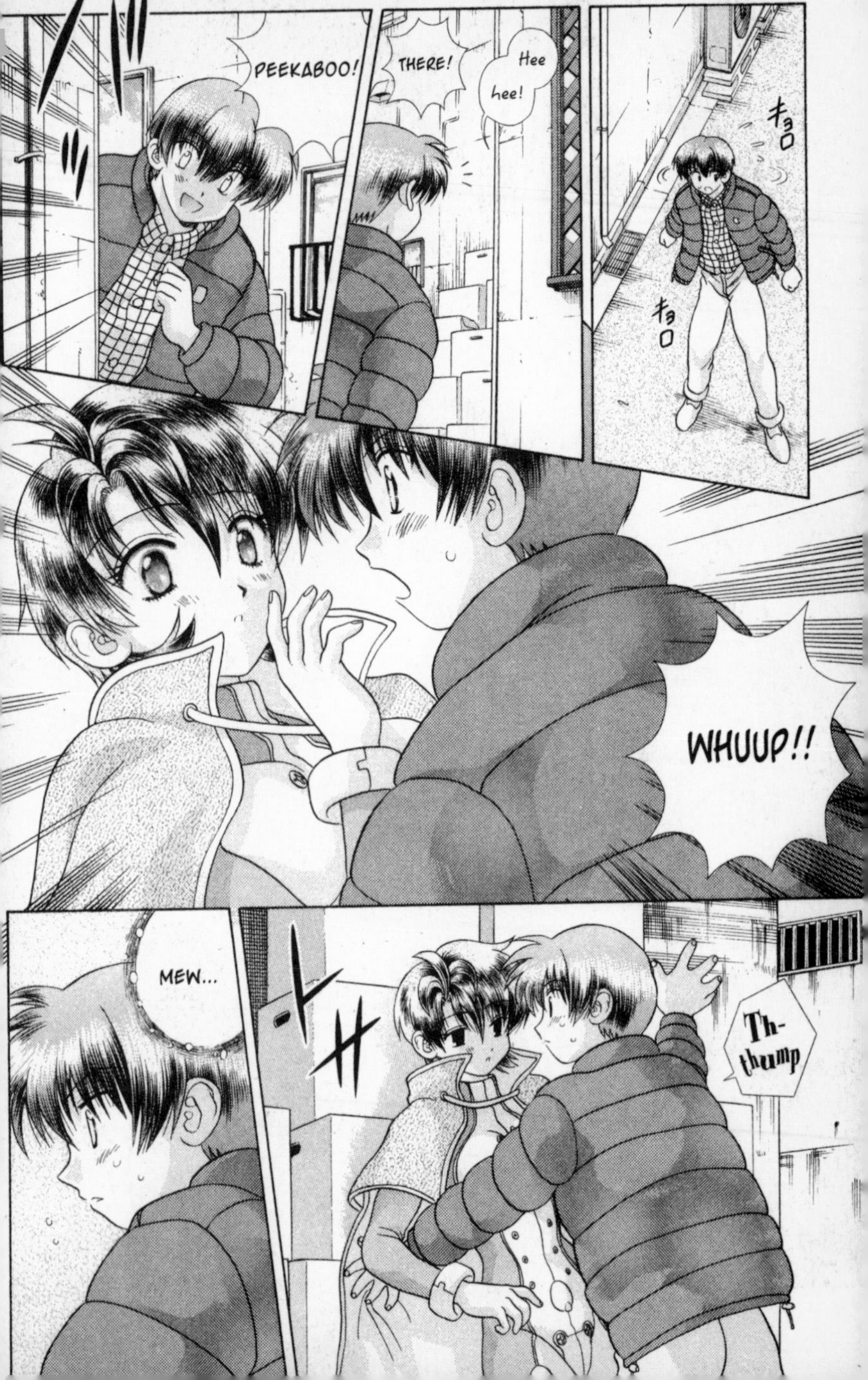
キョロ
キョロ
THERE!
Hee hee!
PEEKABOO!
WHUUP!!
Th-thump
MEW...

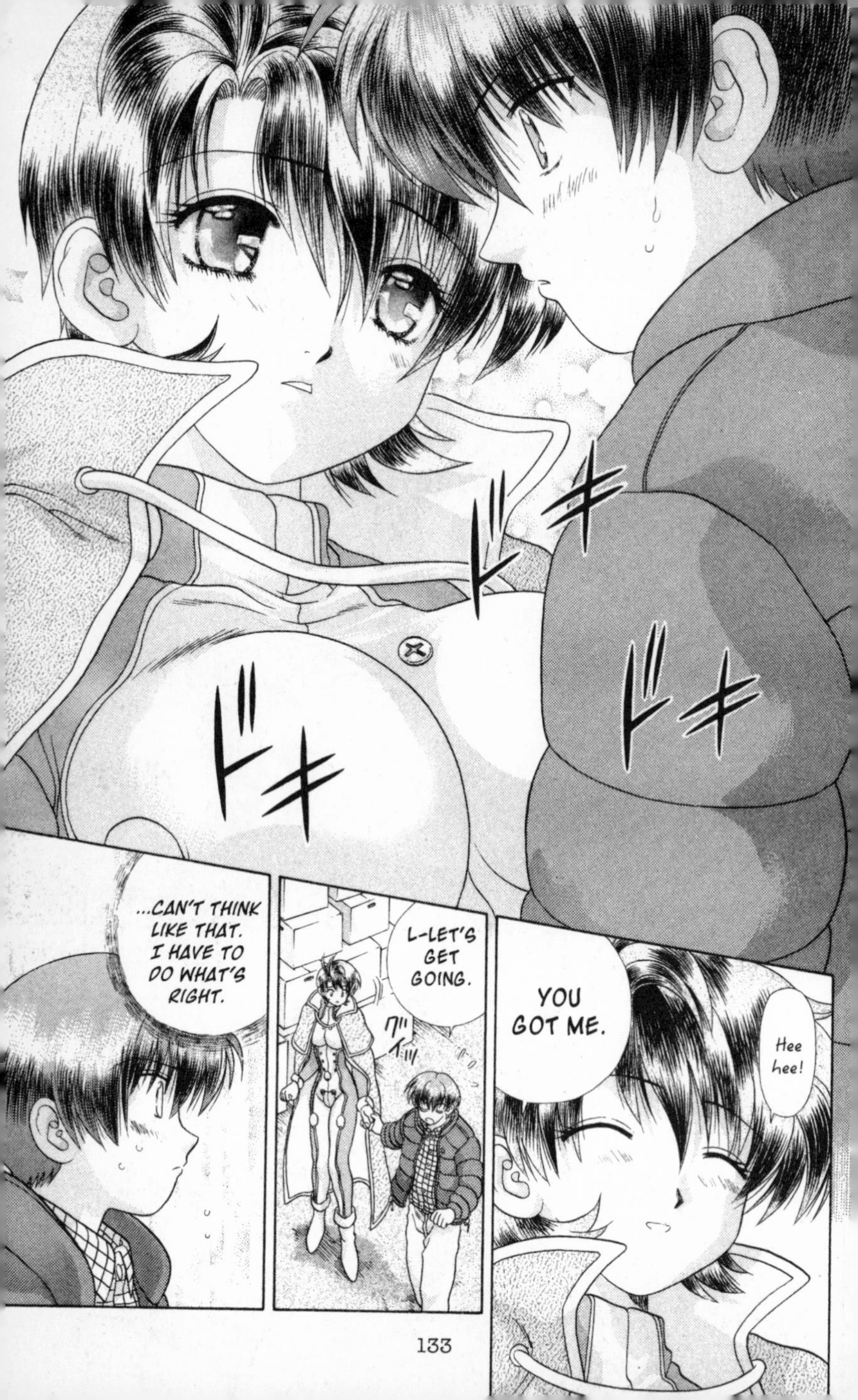
ドキ
ドキ
ドキ
YOU GOT ME.
Hee hee!
L-LET'S GET GOING.
グイッ
...CAN'T THINK LIKE THAT. I HAVE TO DO WHAT'S RIGHT.

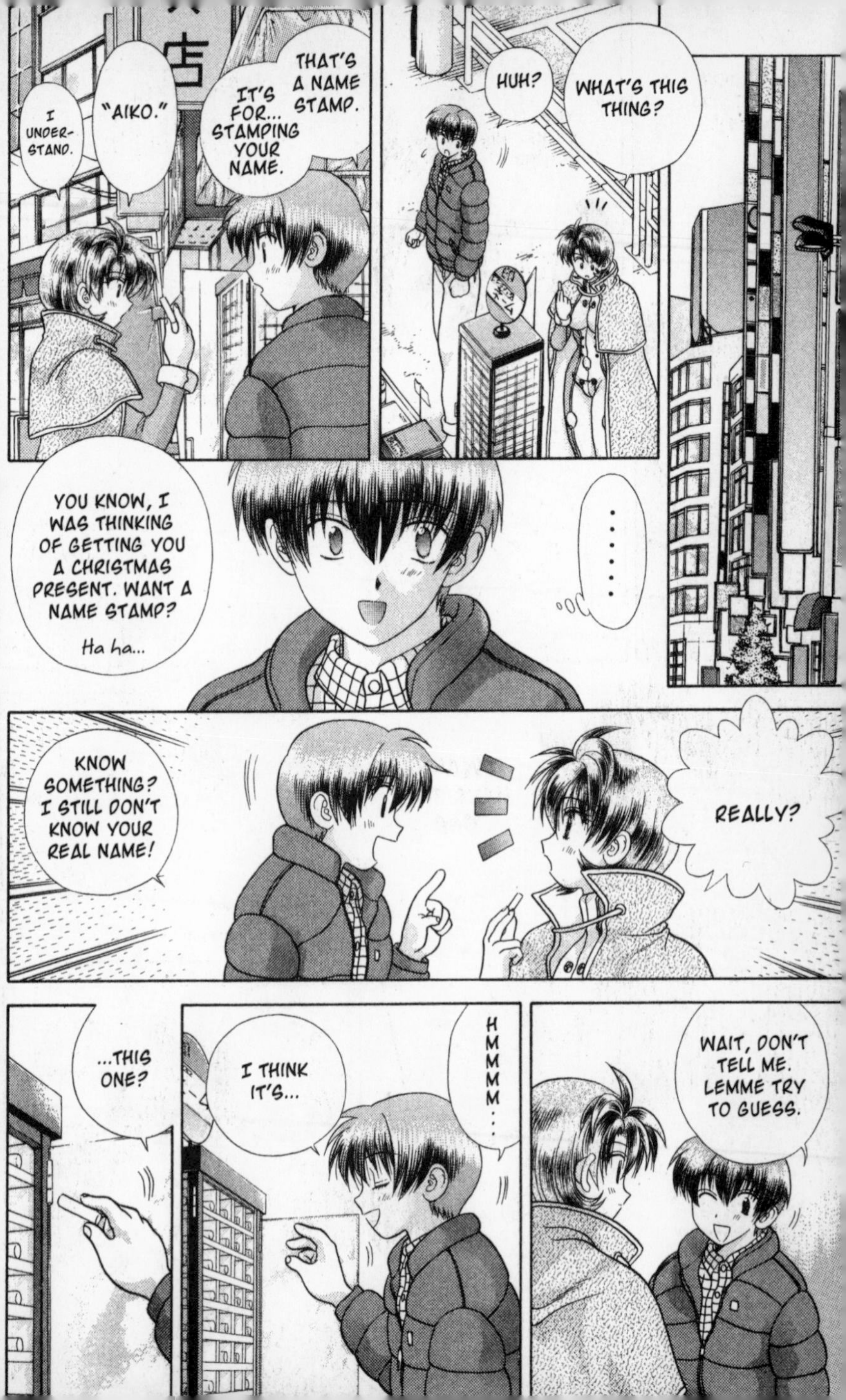
WHAT'S THIS THING?
HUH?
THAT'S A NAME STAMP.
IT'S FOR... STAMPING YOUR NAME.
"AIKO."
I UNDER-STAND.
......
YOU KNOW, I WAS THINKING OF GETTING YOU A CHRISTMAS PRESENT. WANT A NAME STAMP?
Ha ha...
REALLY?
KNOW SOMETHING? I STILL DON'T KNOW YOUR REAL NAME!
WAIT, DON'T TELL ME. LEMME TRY TO GUESS.
HMMMM...
I THINK IT'S...
...THIS ONE?

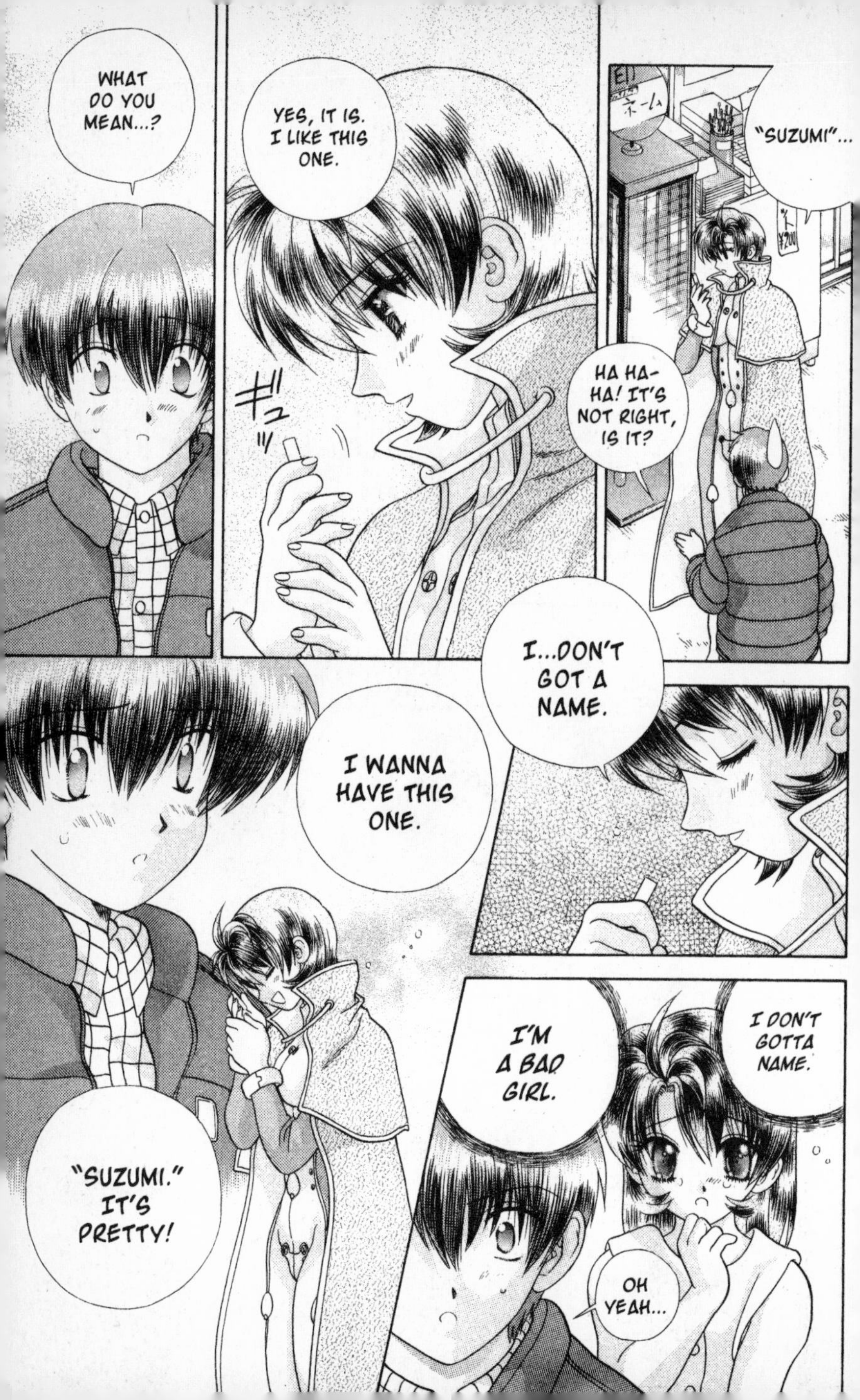
"SUZUMI"...
HA HA-HA! IT'S NOT RIGHT, IS IT?
YES, IT IS. I LIKE THIS ONE.
WHAT DO YOU MEAN...?
I...DON'T GOT A NAME.
I WANNA HAVE THIS ONE.
I DON'T GOTTA NAME.
I'M A BAD GIRL.
OH YEAH...
"SUZUMI." IT'S PRETTY!

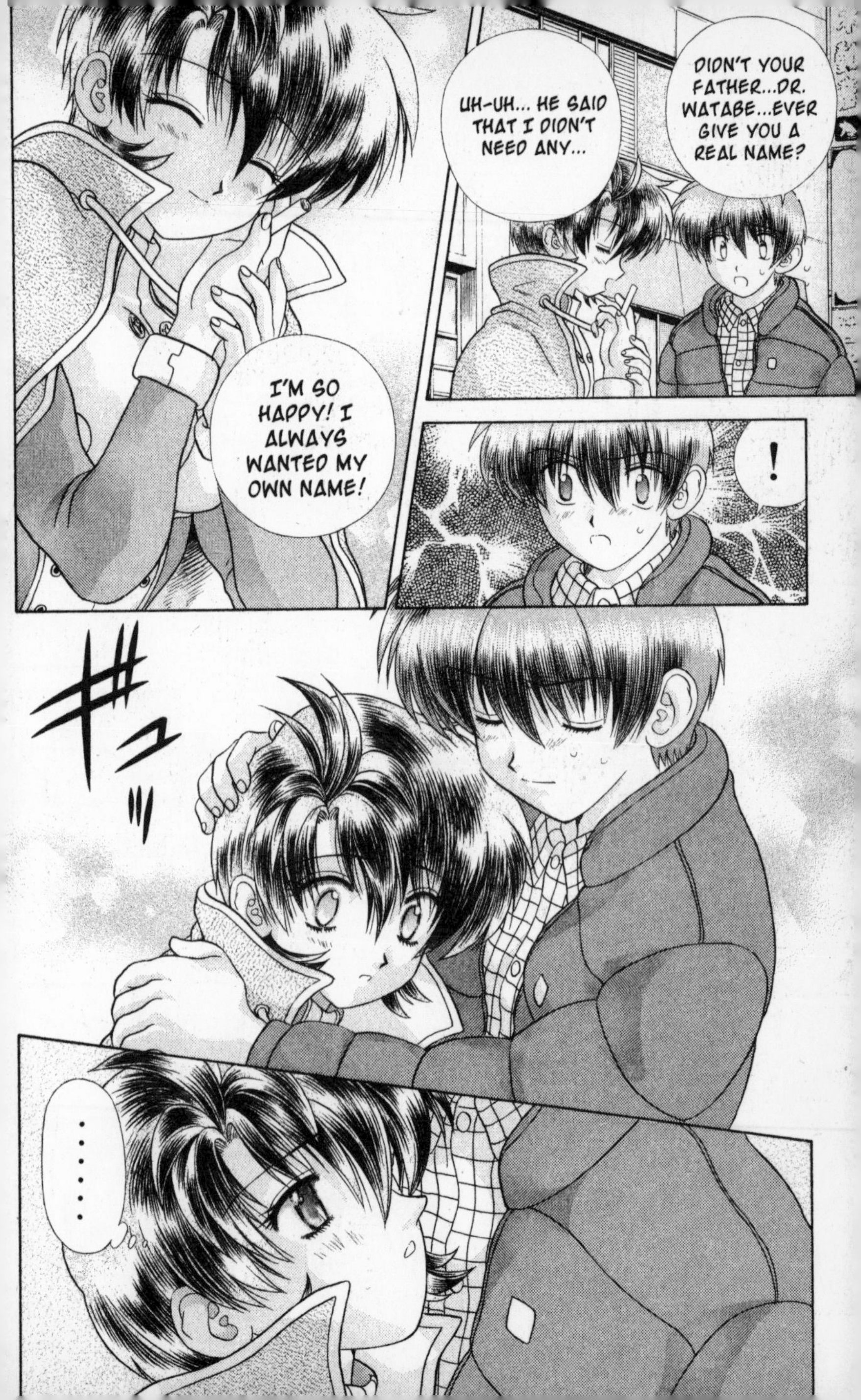
DIDN'T YOUR FATHER...DR. WATABE...EVER GIVE YOU A REAL NAME?
UH-UH... HE SAID THAT I DIDN'T NEED ANY...
I'M SO HAPPY! I ALWAYS WANTED MY OWN NAME!
!
ギュッ
......

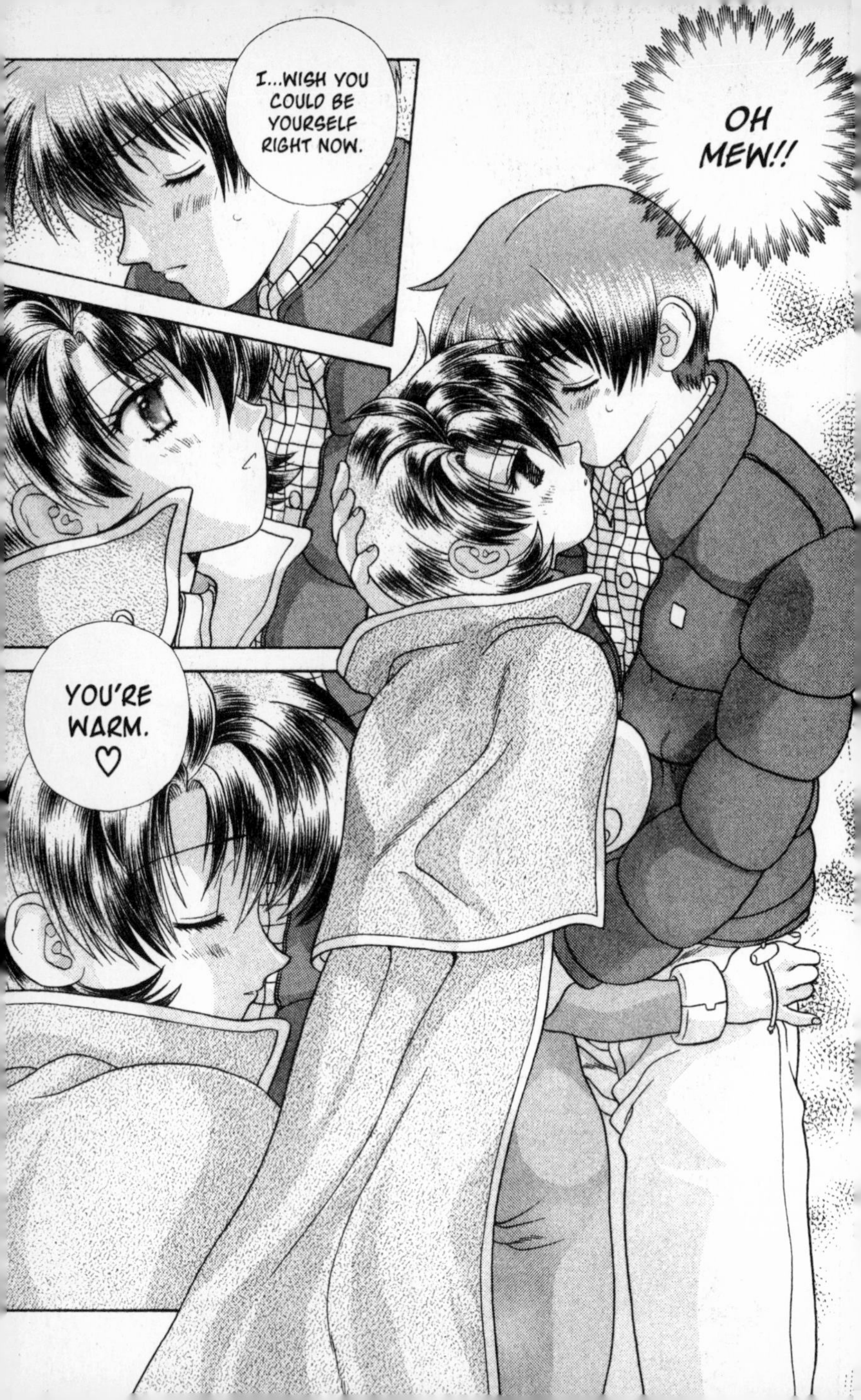
OH MEW!!
I...WISH YOU COULD BE YOURSELF RIGHT NOW.
YOU'RE WARM. ♡

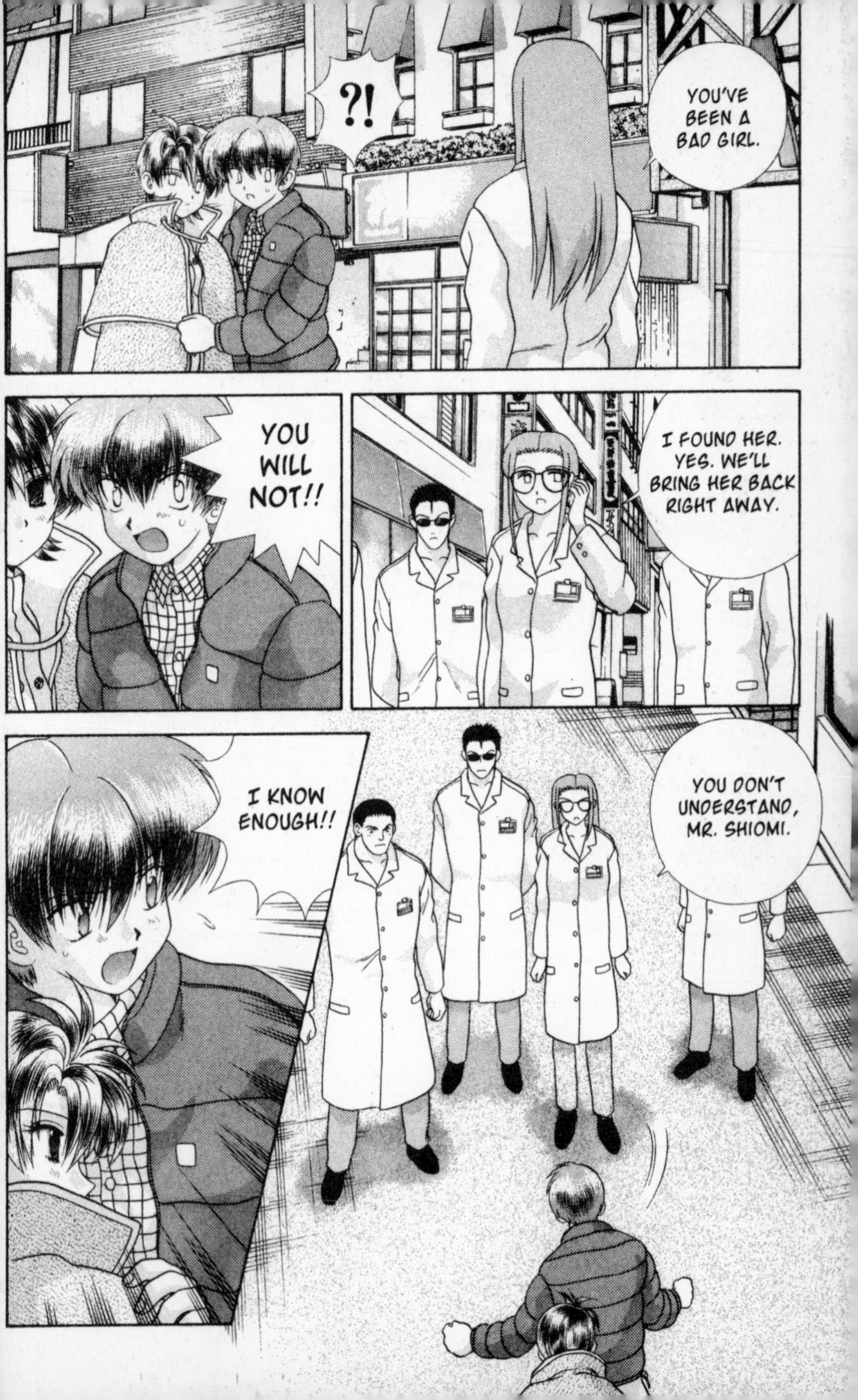
YOU'VE BEEN A BAD GIRL.
?!
I FOUND HER. YES. WE'LL BRING HER BACK RIGHT AWAY.
YOU WILL NOT!!
YOU DON'T UNDERSTAND, MR. SHIOMI.
I KNOW ENOUGH!!

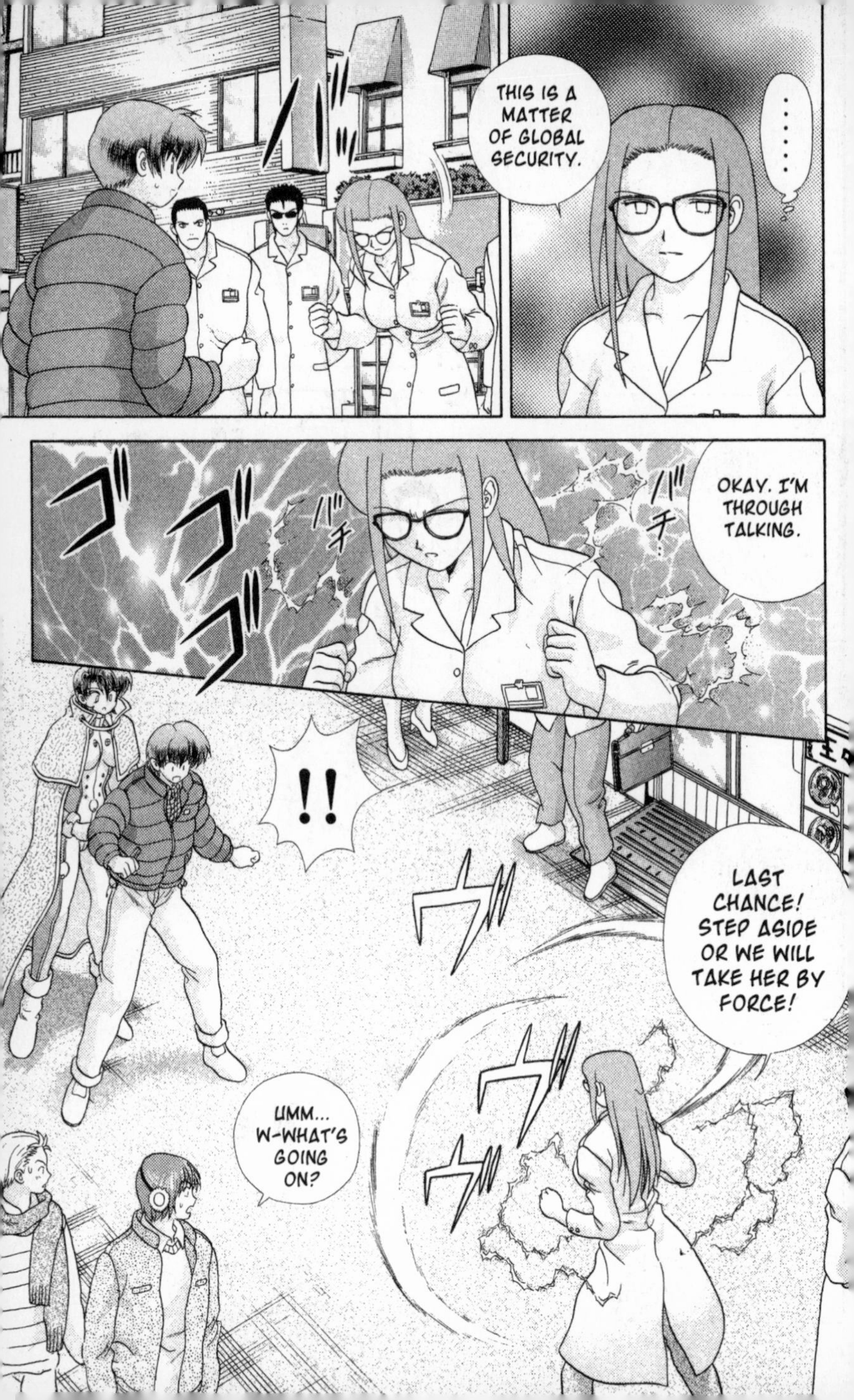
......
THIS IS A MATTER OF GLOBAL SECURITY.
OKAY. I'M THROUGH TALKING.
バチ
バチ
ゴゴゴ
LAST CHANCE! STEP ASIDE OR WE WILL TAKE HER BY FORCE!
!!
ヴヴヴヴ
UMM... W-WHAT'S GOING ON?

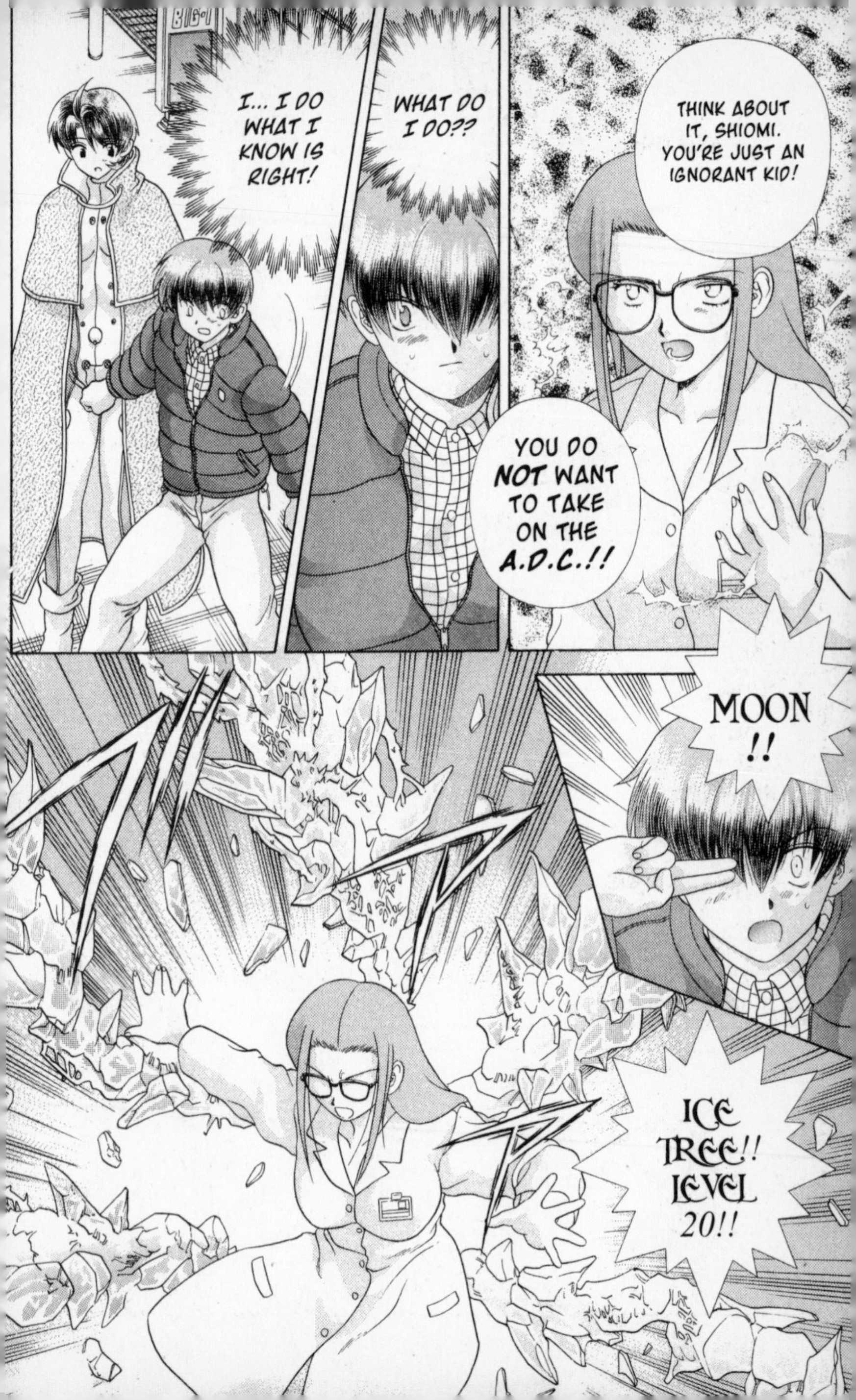
THINK ABOUT IT, SHIOMI. YOU'RE JUST AN IGNORANT KID!
YOU DO NOT WANT TO TAKE ON THE A.D.C.!!
WHAT DO I DO??
I... I DO WHAT I KNOW IS RIGHT!
MOON!!
ICE TREE!! LEVEL 20!!

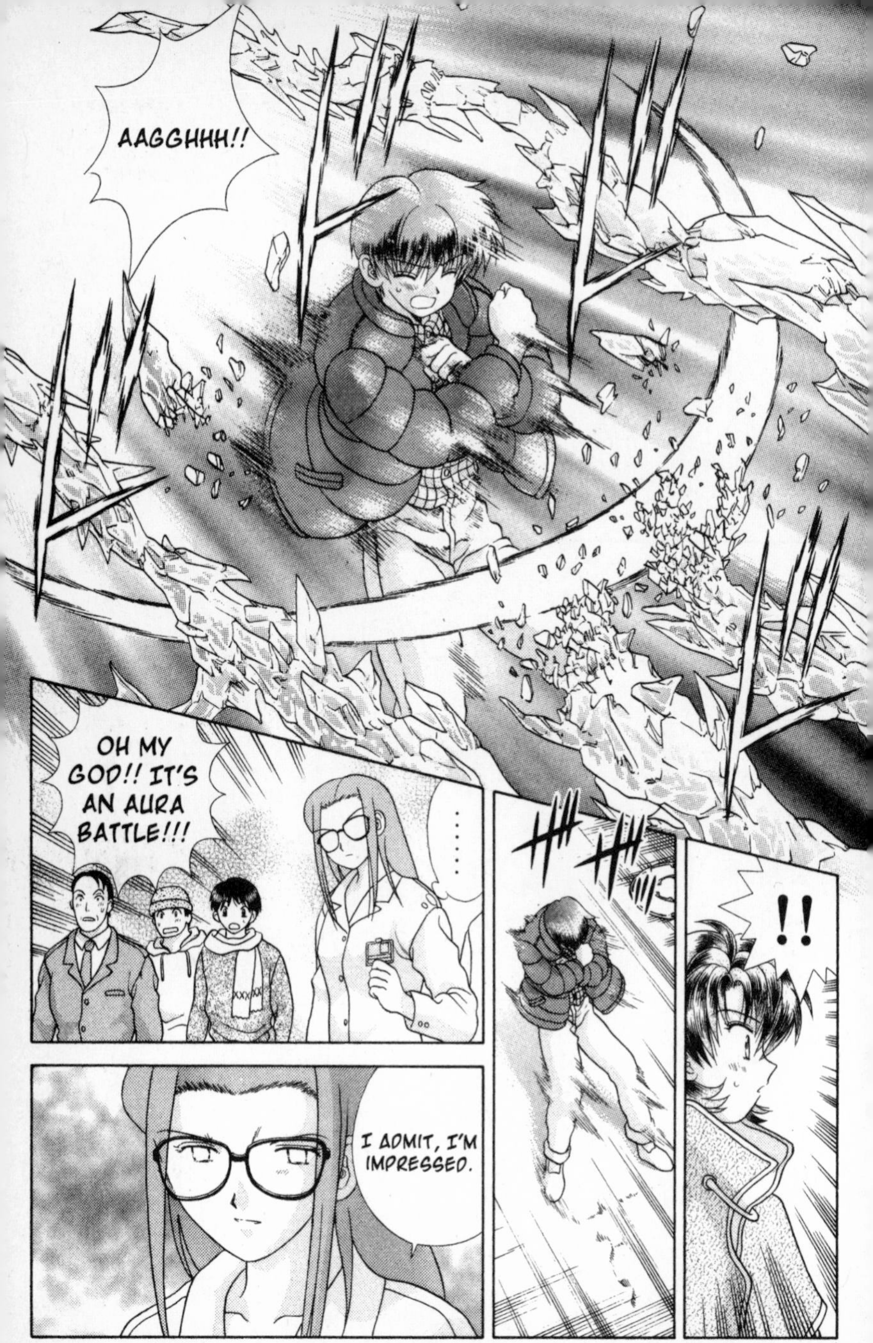
AAGGHHH!!
OH MY GOD!! IT'S AN AURA BATTLE!!!
......
!!
I ADMIT, I'M IMPRESSED.

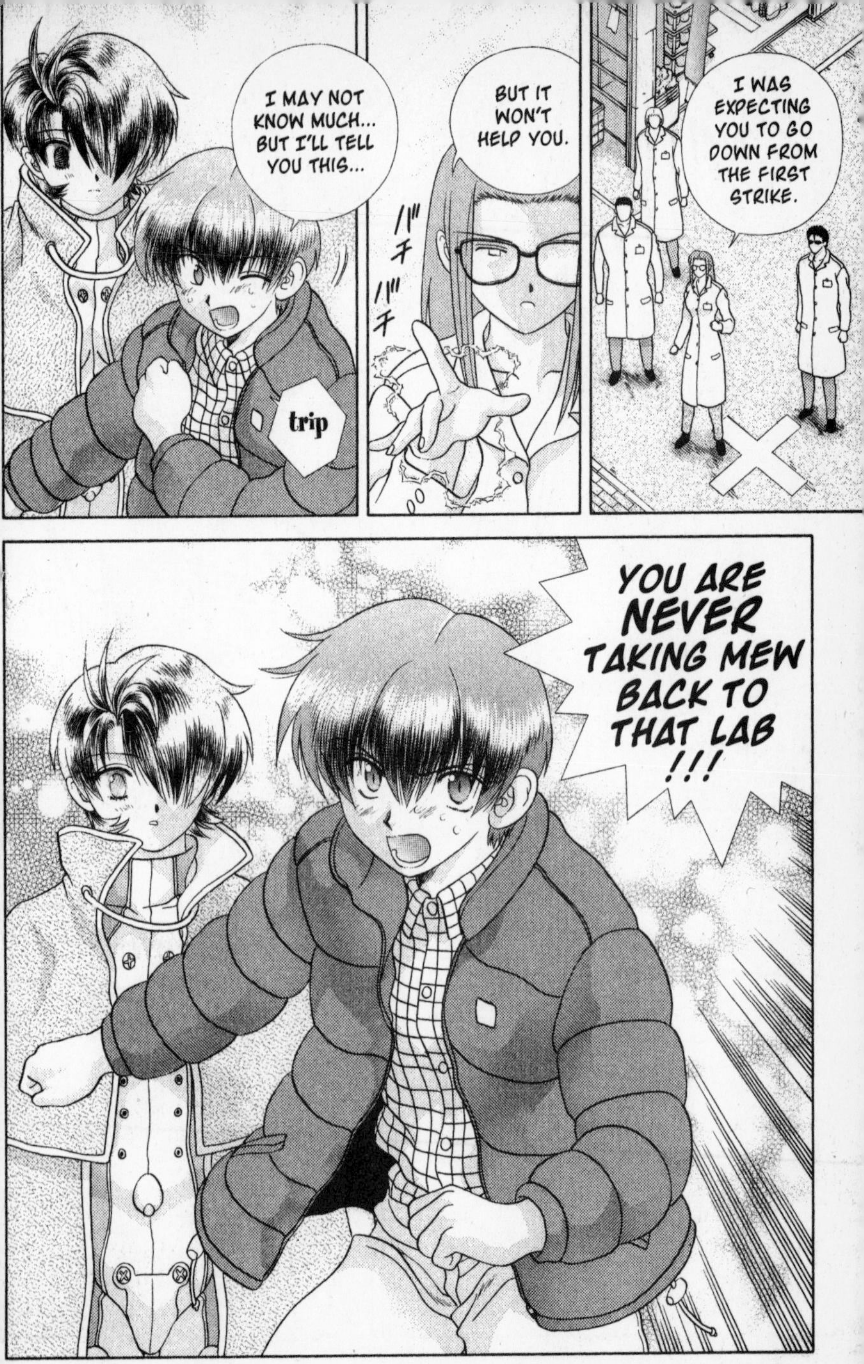
I WAS EXPECTING YOU TO GO DOWN FROM THE FIRST STRIKE.
BUT IT WON'T HELP YOU.
バチ
バチ
I MAY NOT KNOW MUCH... BUT I'LL TELL YOU THIS...
trip
YOU ARE **NEVER** TAKING MEW BACK TO THAT LAB !!!

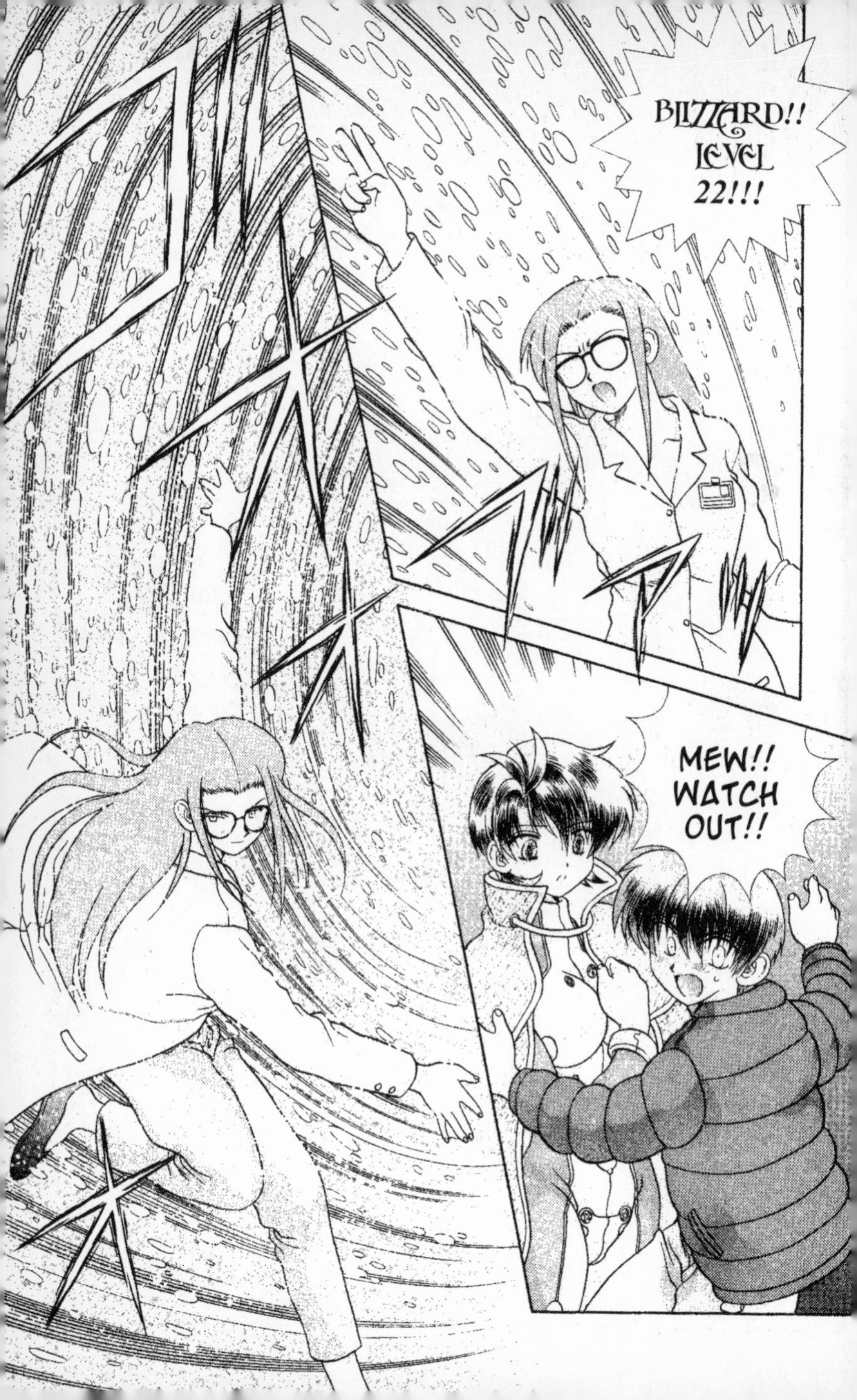
BLIZZARD!! LEVEL 22!!!
MEW!! WATCH OUT!!

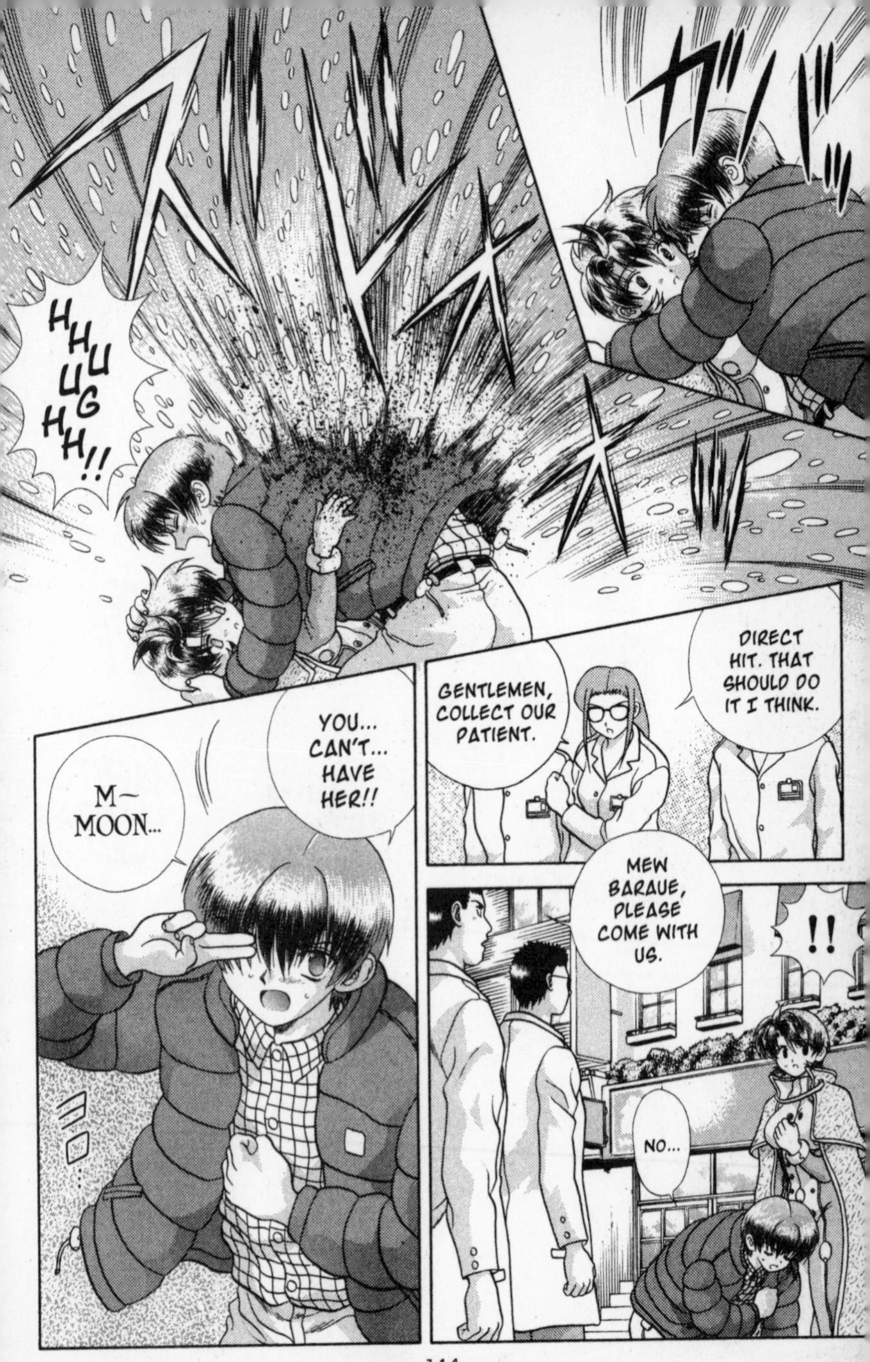
HHUUGHHH!!
DIRECT HIT. THAT SHOULD DO IT I THINK.
GENTLEMEN, COLLECT OUR PATIENT.
MEW BARAUE, PLEASE COME WITH US.
!!
NO...
YOU... CAN'T... HAVE HER!!
M-MOON...

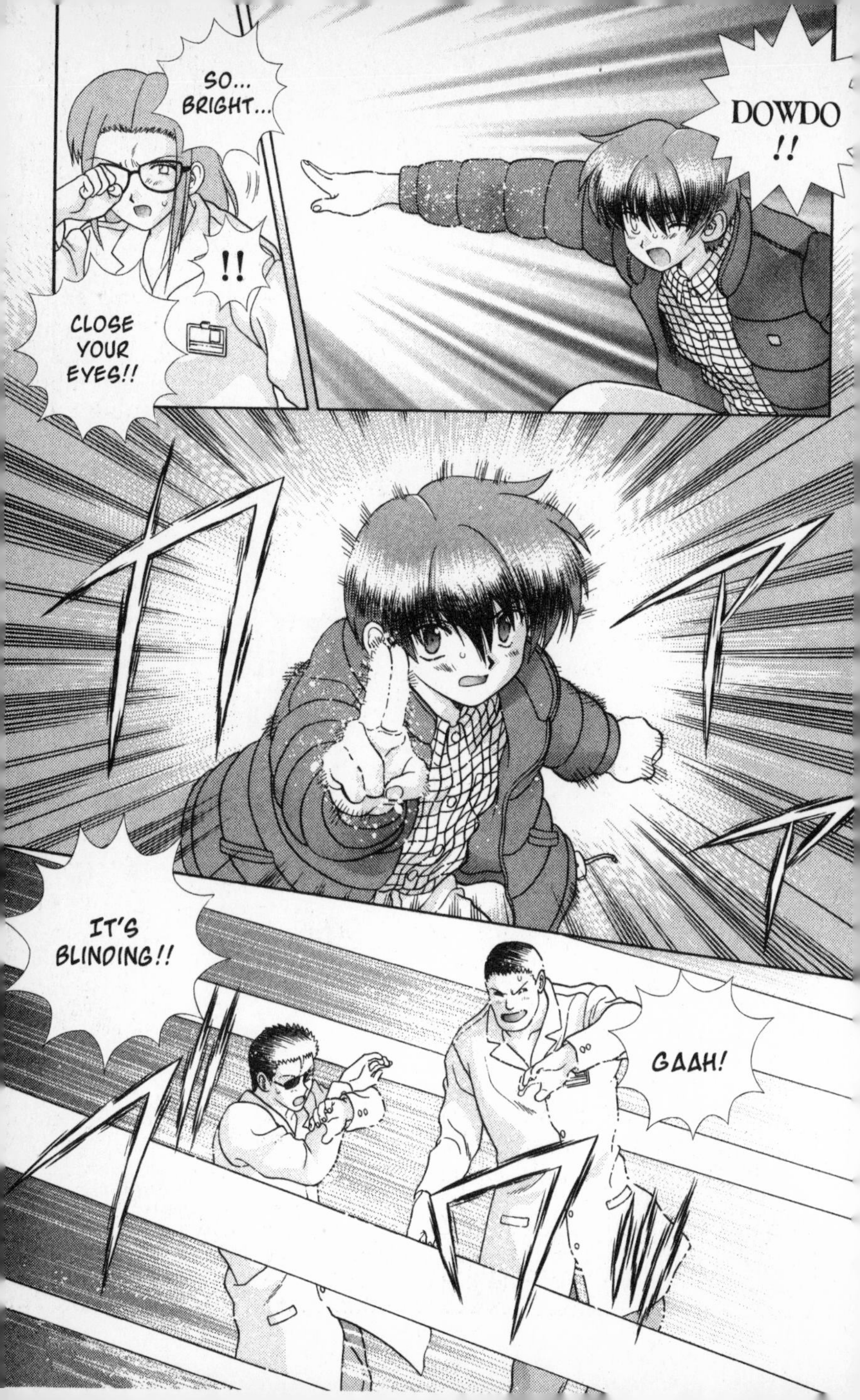
DOWDO !!
SO... BRIGHT...
!!
CLOSE YOUR EYES!!
IT'S BLINDING!!
GAAH!

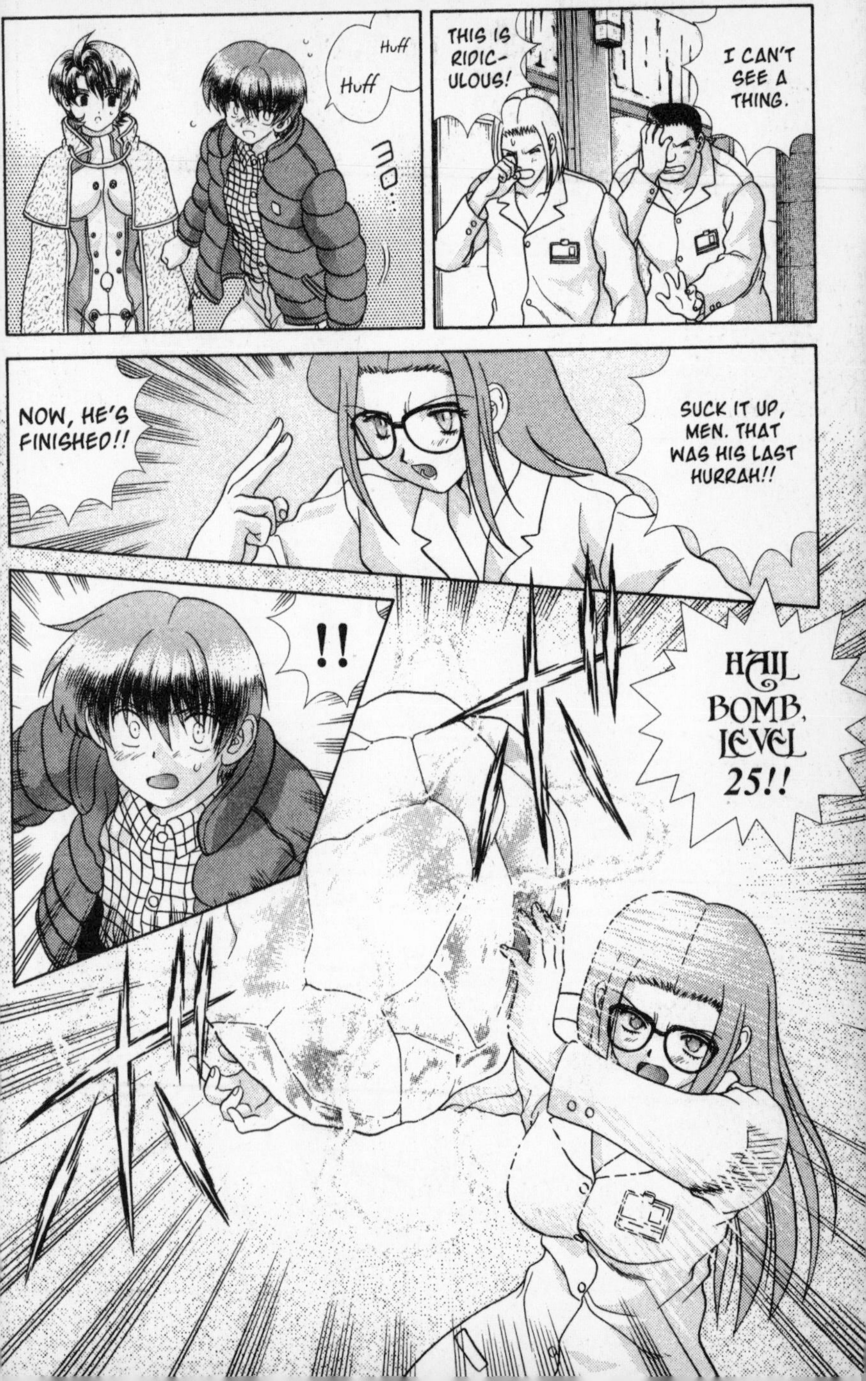
I CAN'T SEE A THING.
THIS IS RIDIC-ULOUS!
Huff
Huff
SUCK IT UP, MEN. THAT WAS HIS LAST HURRAH!!
NOW, HE'S FINISHED!!
HAIL BOMB, LEVEL 25!!
!!

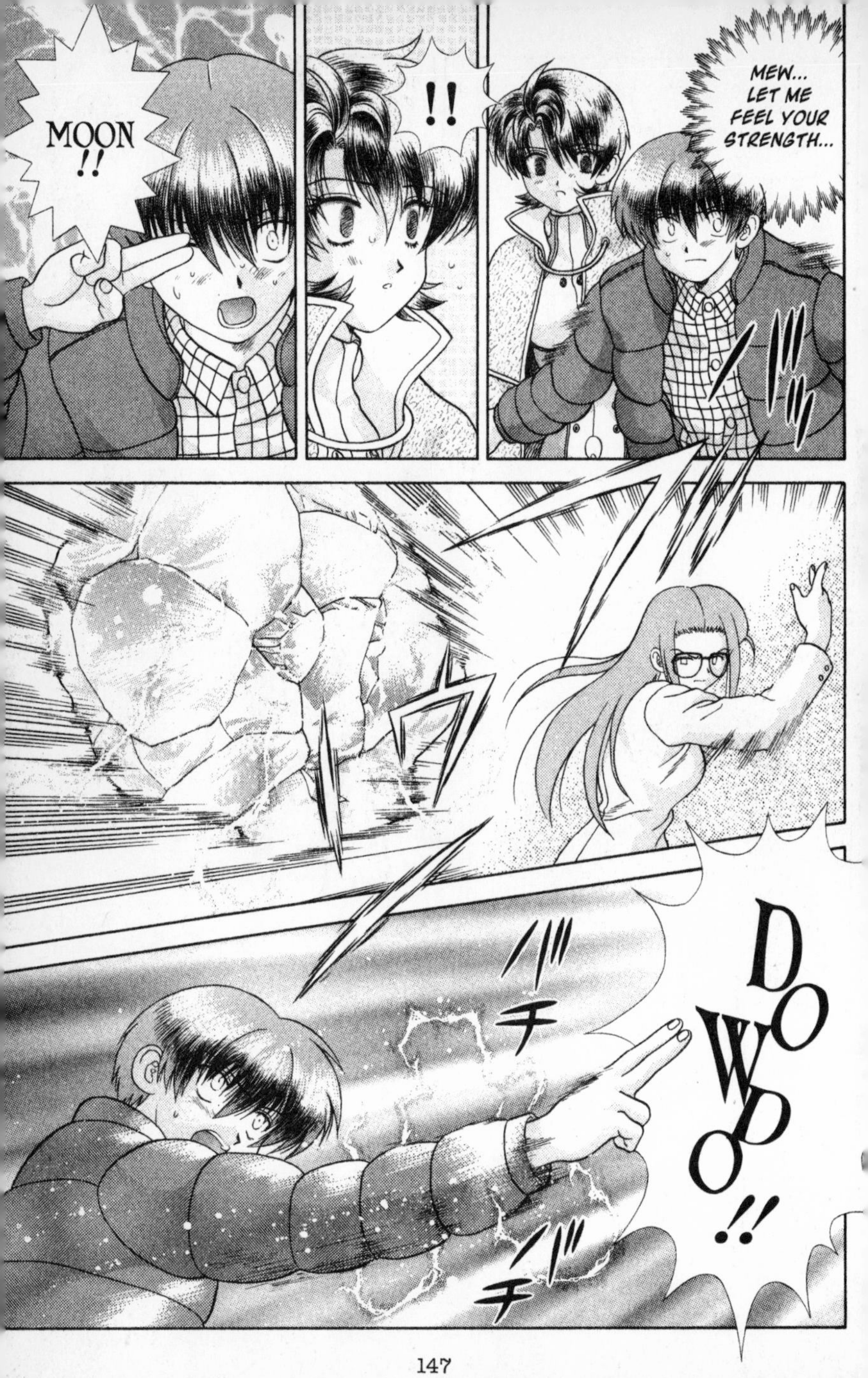
MEW... LET ME FEEL YOUR STRENGTH...
!!
MOON !!
DOWDO!!

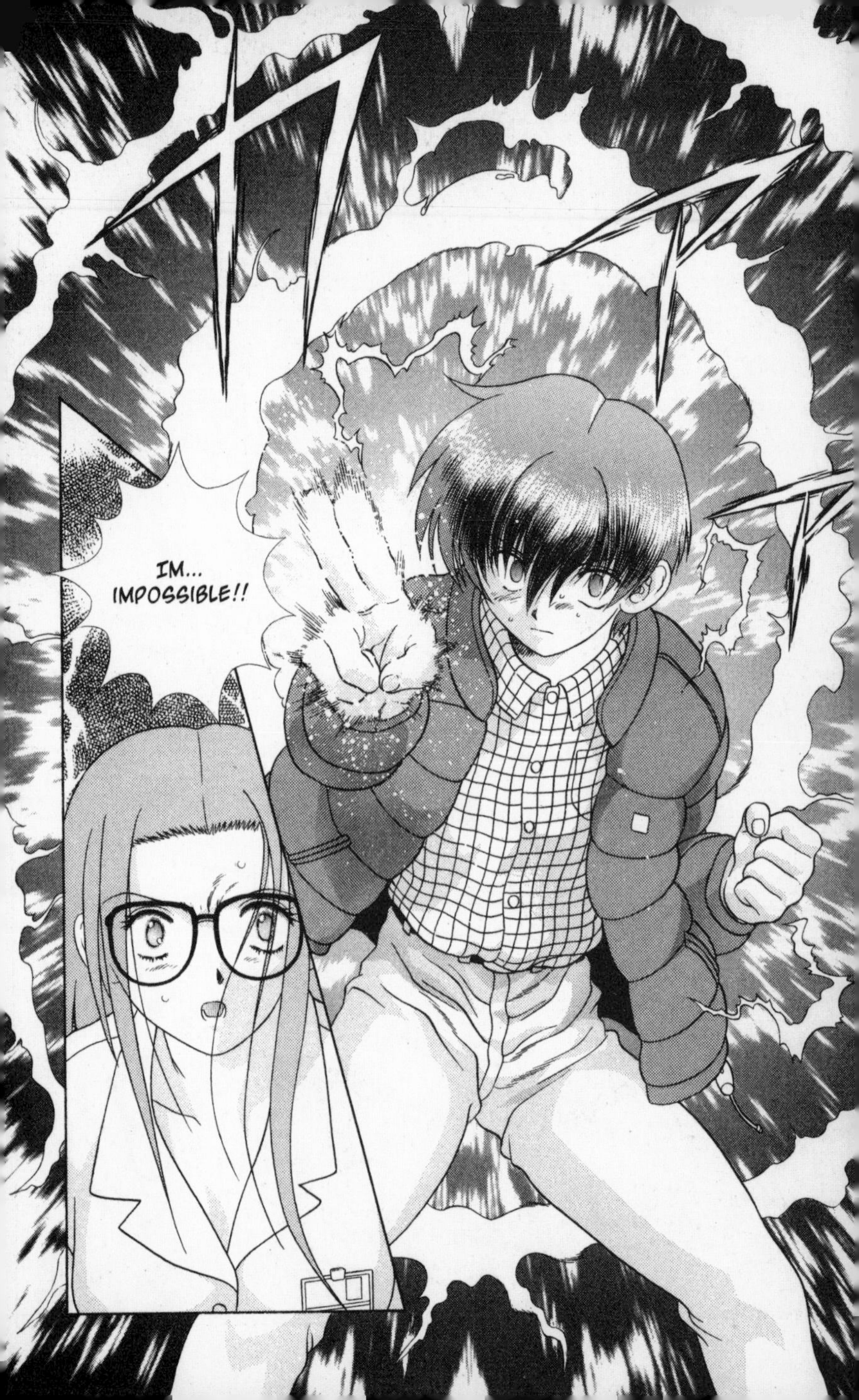
IM... IMPOSSIBLE!!

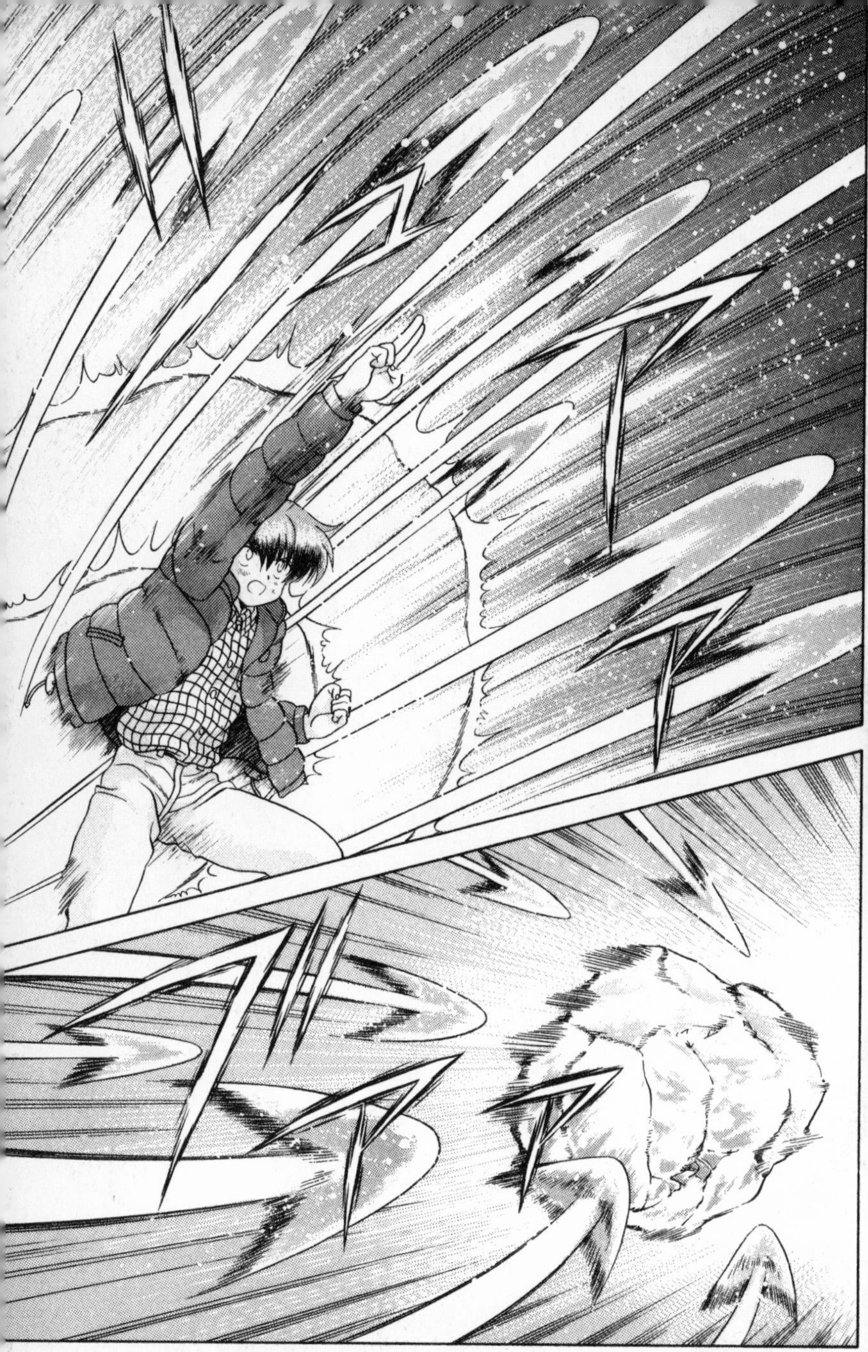

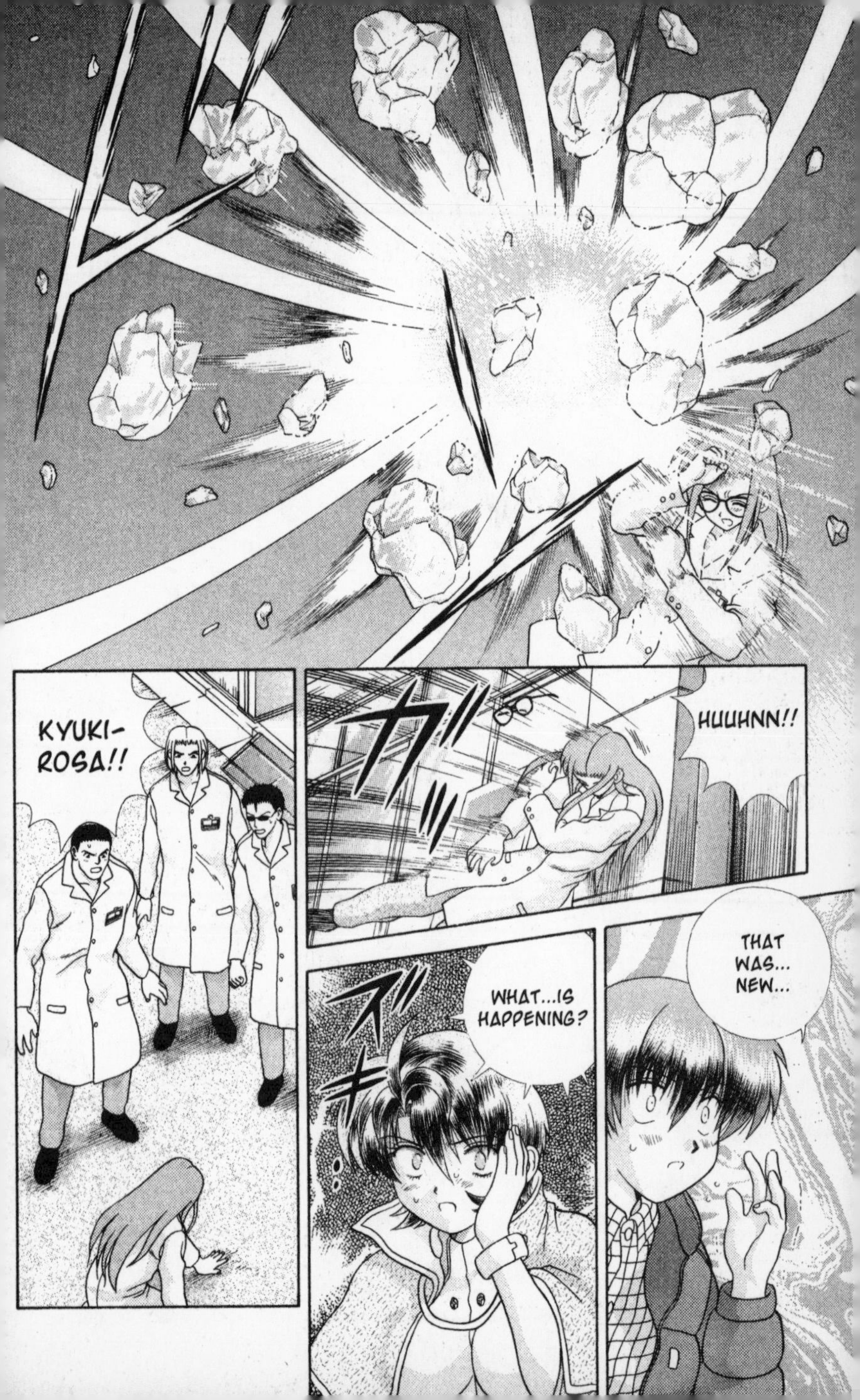
HUUHNN!!
KYUKI-ROSA!!
THAT WAS... NEW...
WHAT...IS HAPPENING?

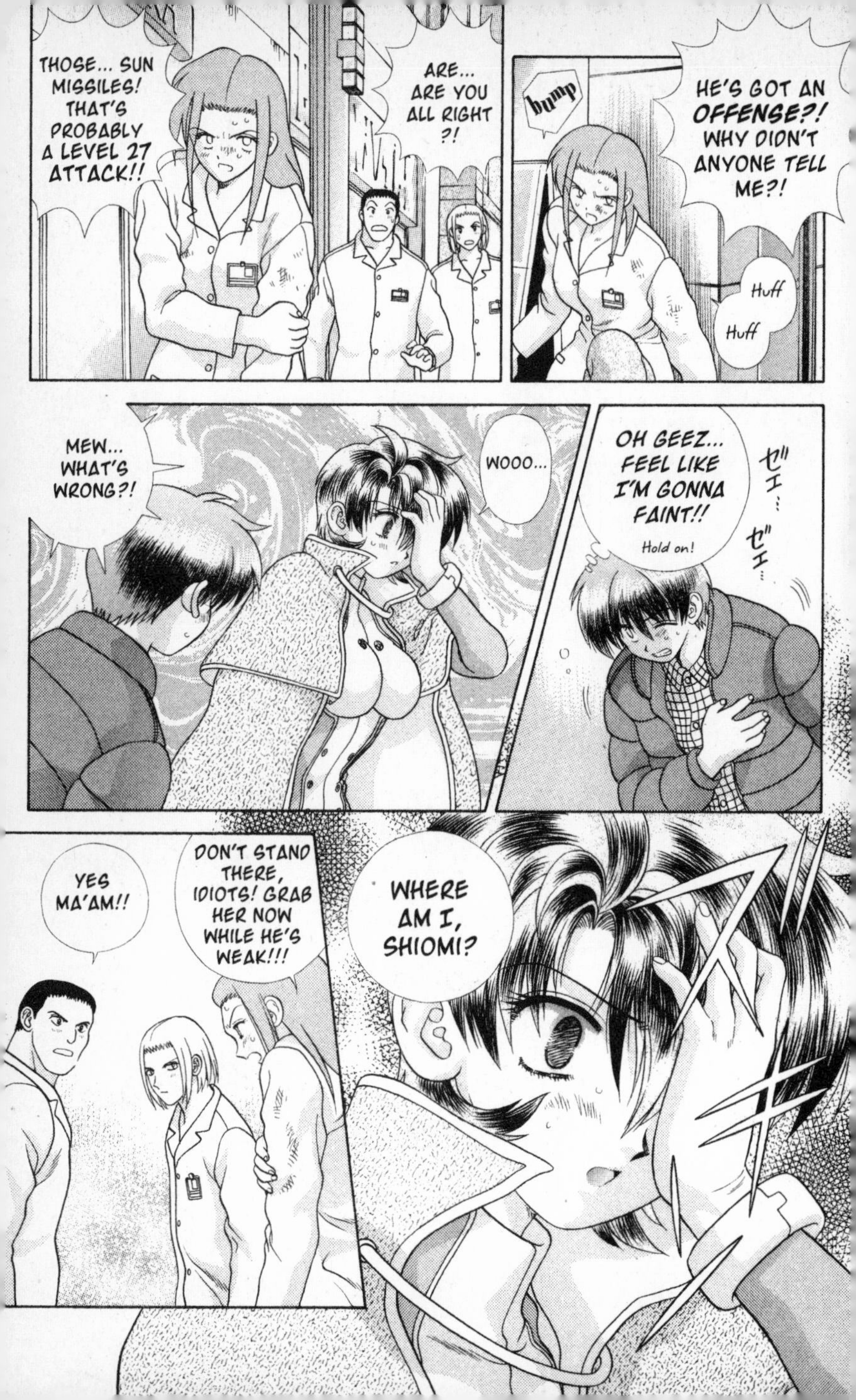
HE'S GOT AN OFFENSE?! WHY DIDN'T ANYONE TELL ME?!
bump
Huff
Huff
ARE... ARE YOU ALL RIGHT ?!
THOSE... SUN MISSILES! THAT'S PROBABLY A LEVEL 27 ATTACK!!
OH GEEZ... FEEL LIKE I'M GONNA FAINT!!
Hold on!
ゼェ…ゼェ…
WOOO...
MEW... WHAT'S WRONG?!
WHERE AM I, SHIOMI?
DON'T STAND THERE, IDIOTS! GRAB HER NOW WHILE HE'S WEAK!!!
YES MA'AM!!

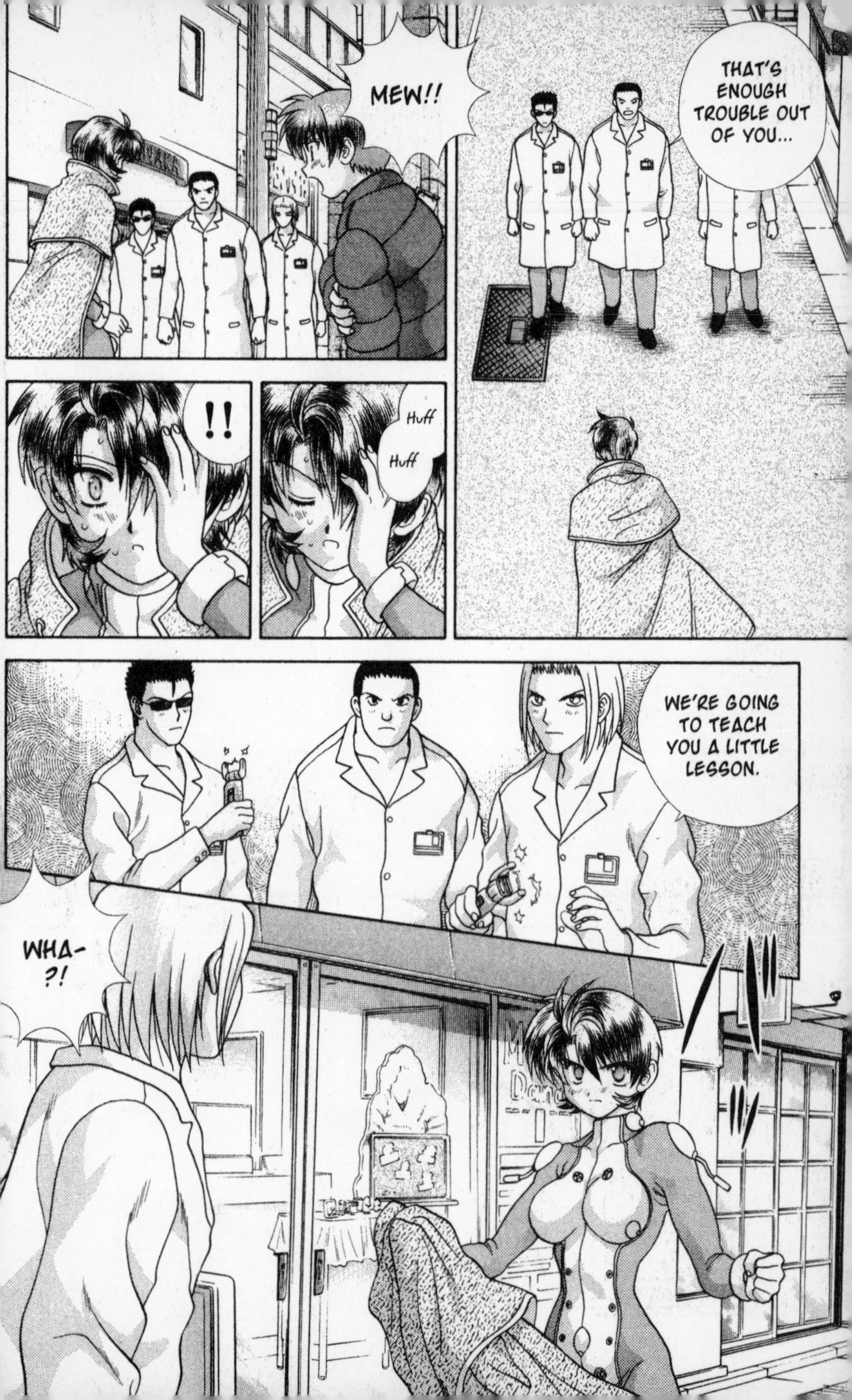

THAT'S ENOUGH TROUBLE OUT OF YOU...
MEW!!
Huff
Huff
!!
WE'RE GOING TO TEACH YOU A LITTLE LESSON.
WHA-?!

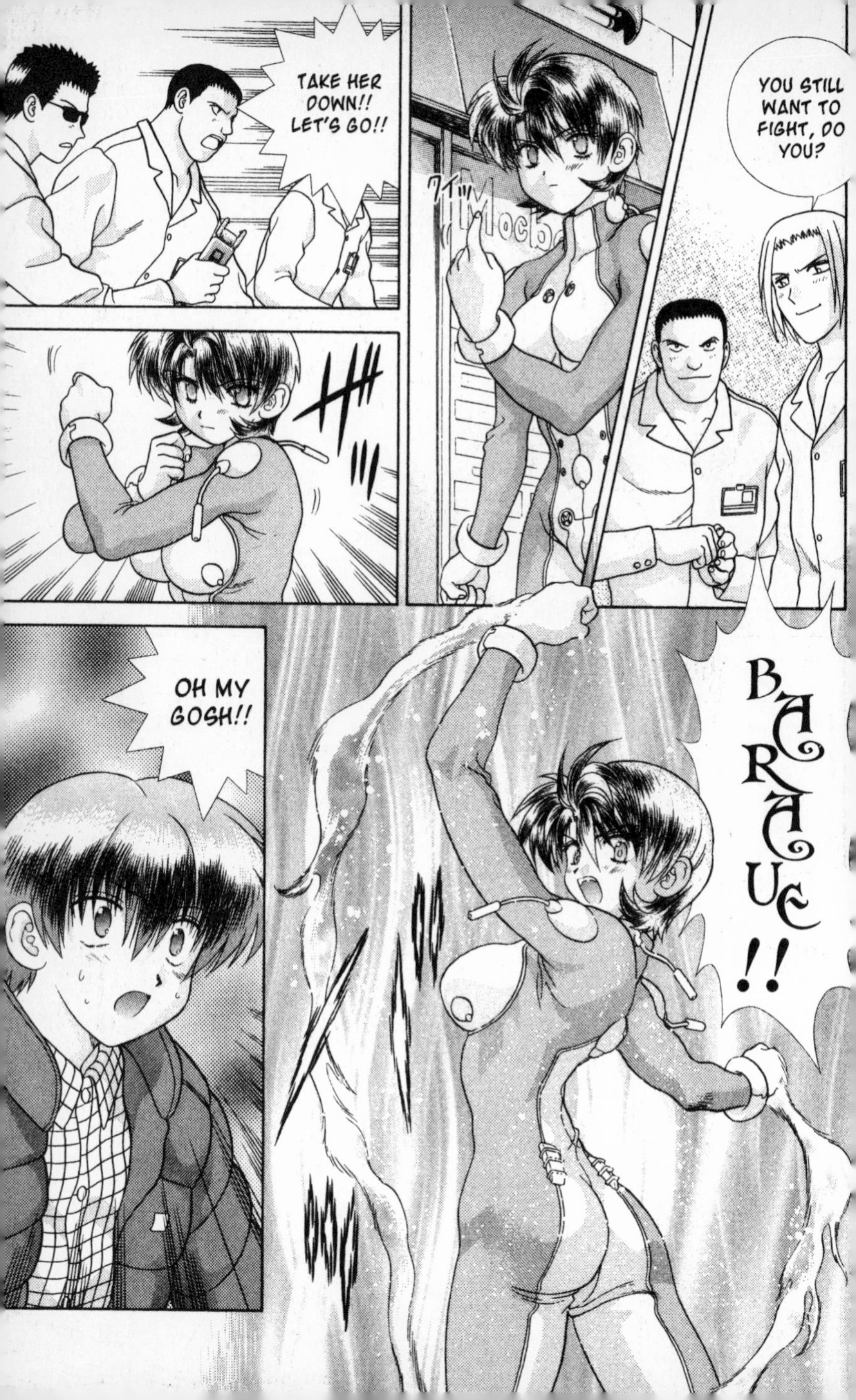
YOU STILL WANT TO FIGHT, DO YOU?
TAKE HER DOWN!! LET'S GO!!
BARAUC!!
OH MY GOSH!!

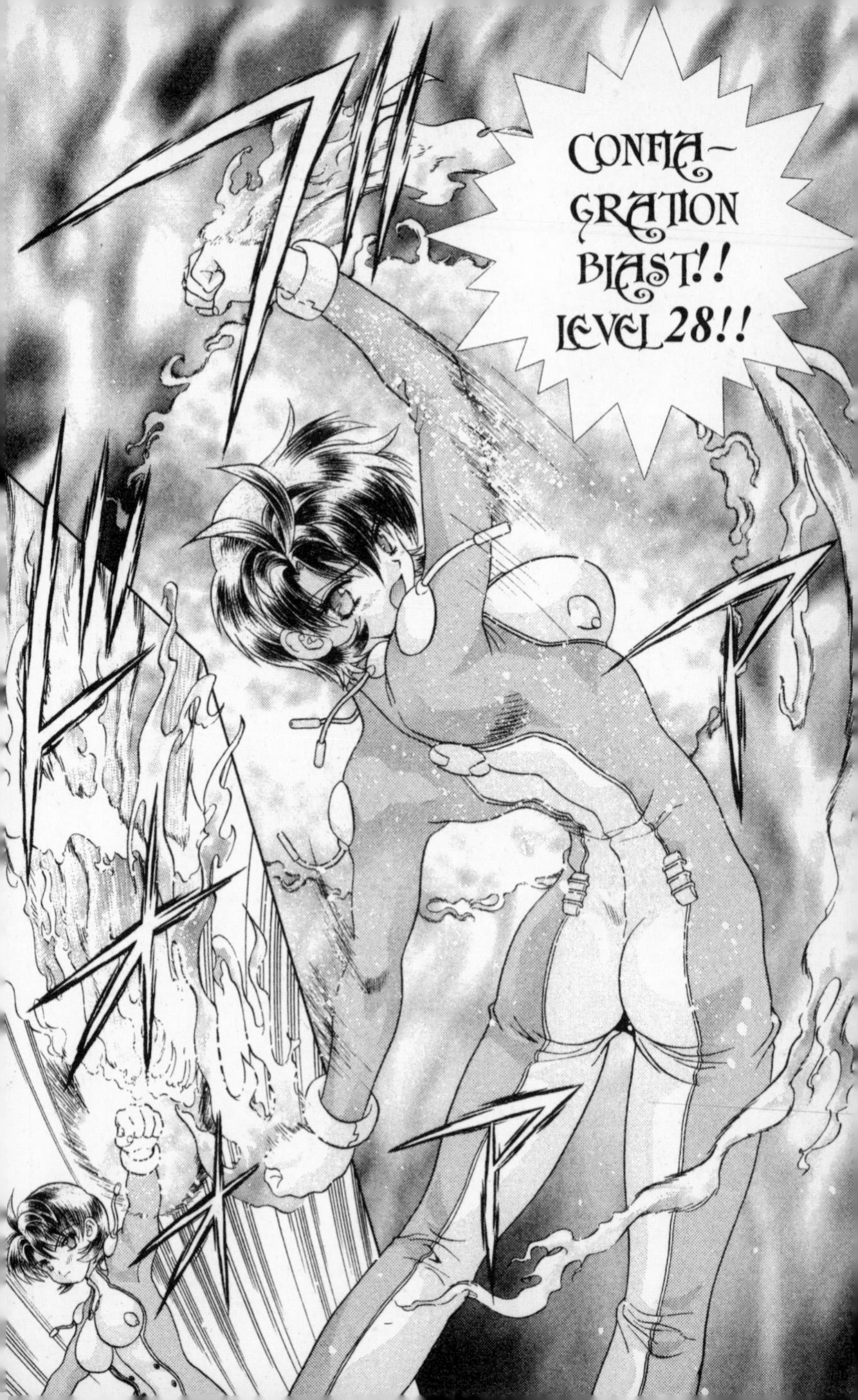
CONFLA-
GRATION
BLAST!!
LEVEL 28!!

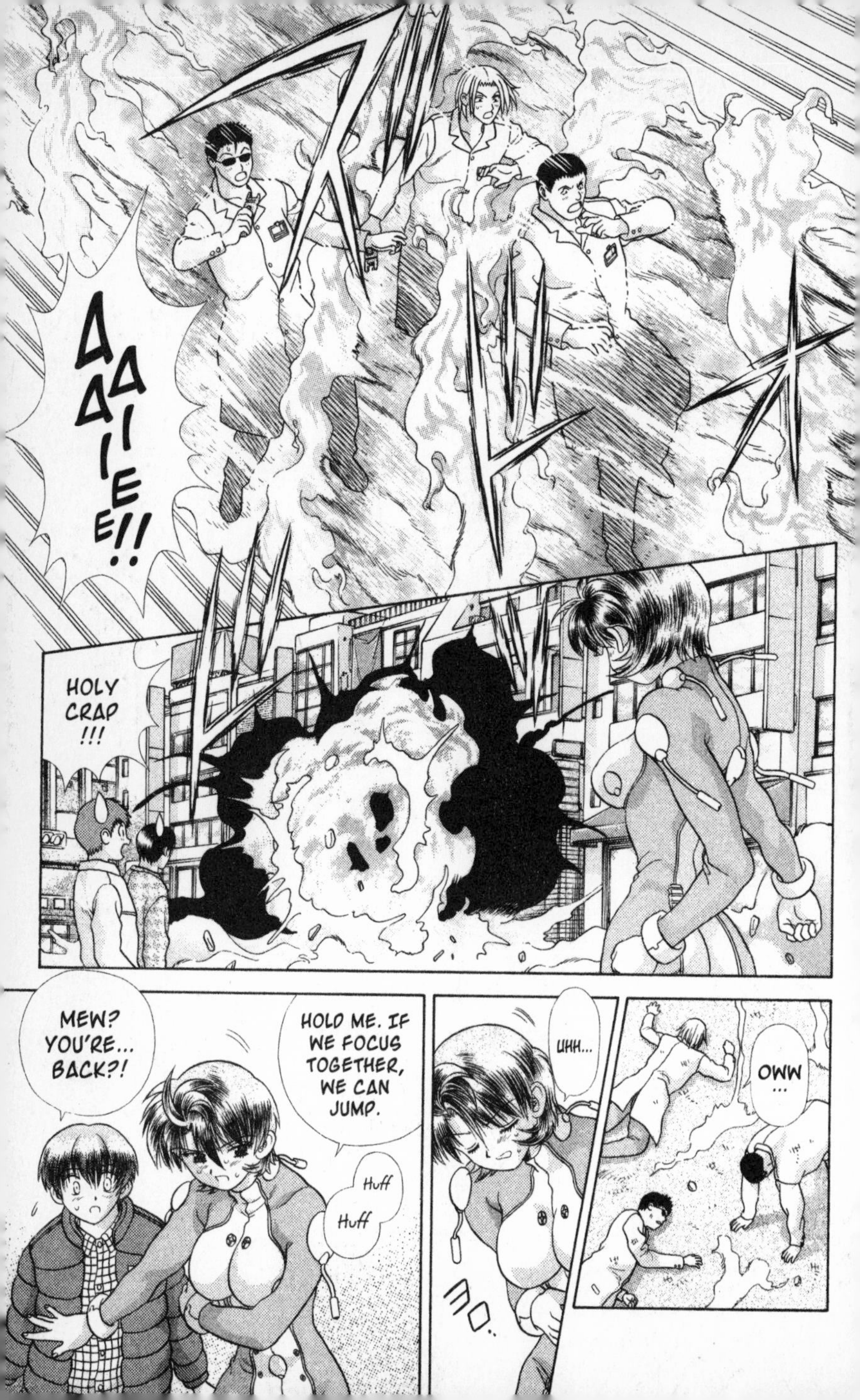
AAAIIEEE!!
HOLY CRAP!!!
OWW...
UHH...
HOLD ME. IF WE FOCUS TOGETHER, WE CAN JUMP.
Huff
Huff
MEW? YOU'RE... BACK?!

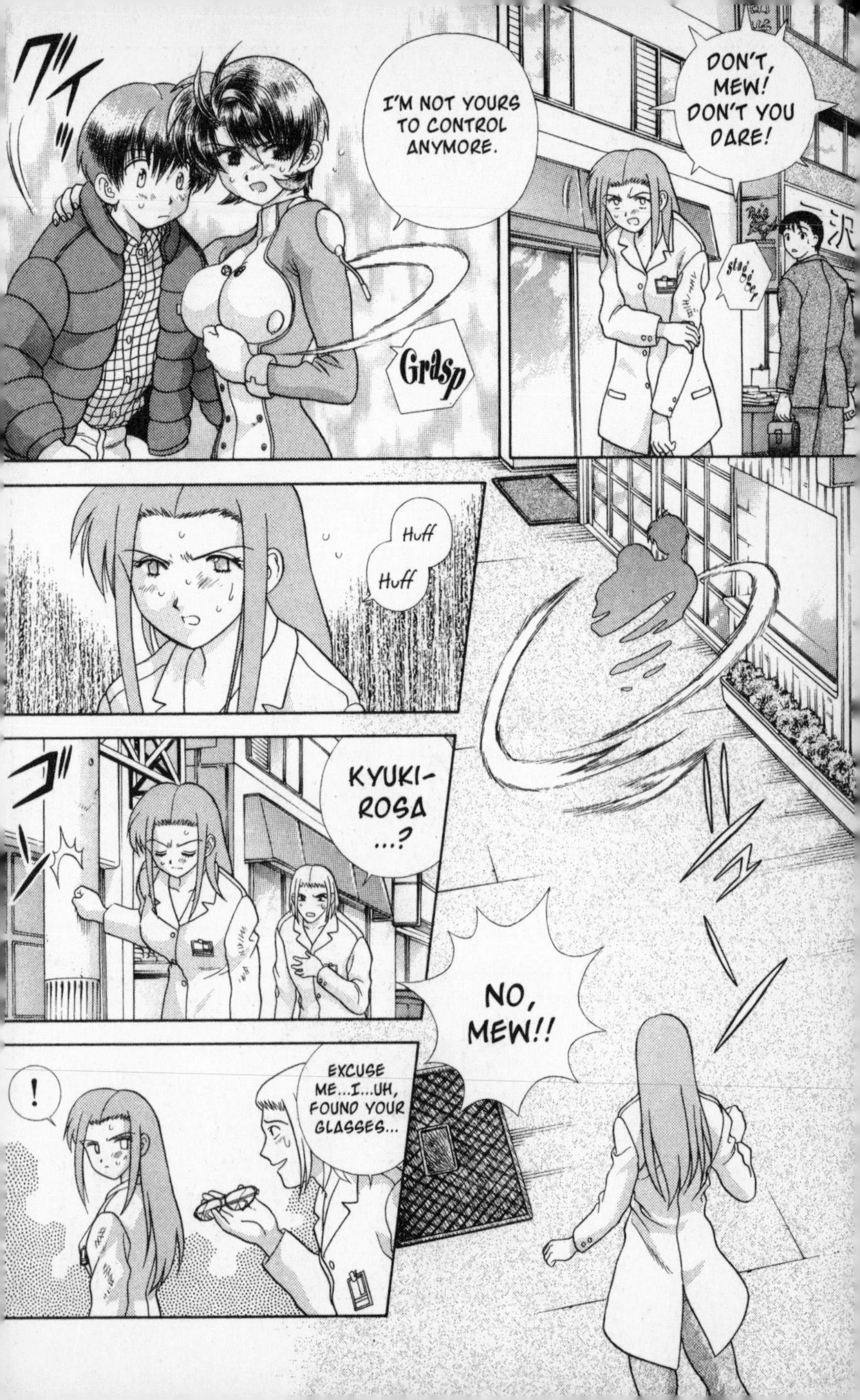
DON'T, MEW! DON'T YOU DARE!
stagger
I'M NOT YOURS TO CONTROL ANYMORE.
Grasp
NO, MEW!!
Huff
Huff
KYUKI-ROSA ...?
!
EXCUSE ME...I...UH, FOUND YOUR GLASSES...

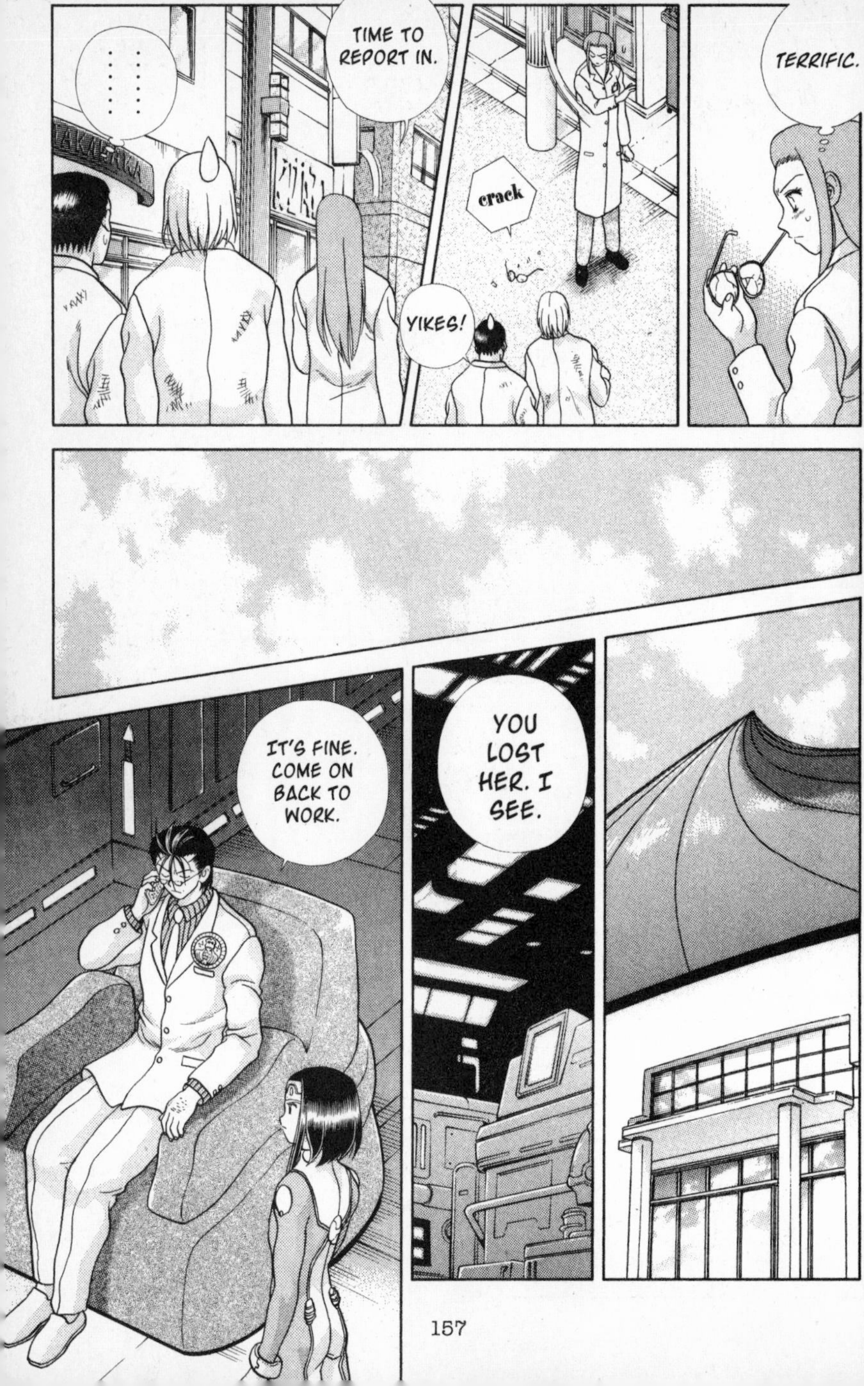
......
TIME TO REPORT IN.
crack
YIKES!
TERRIFIC.
YOU LOST HER. I SEE.
IT'S FINE. COME ON BACK TO WORK.

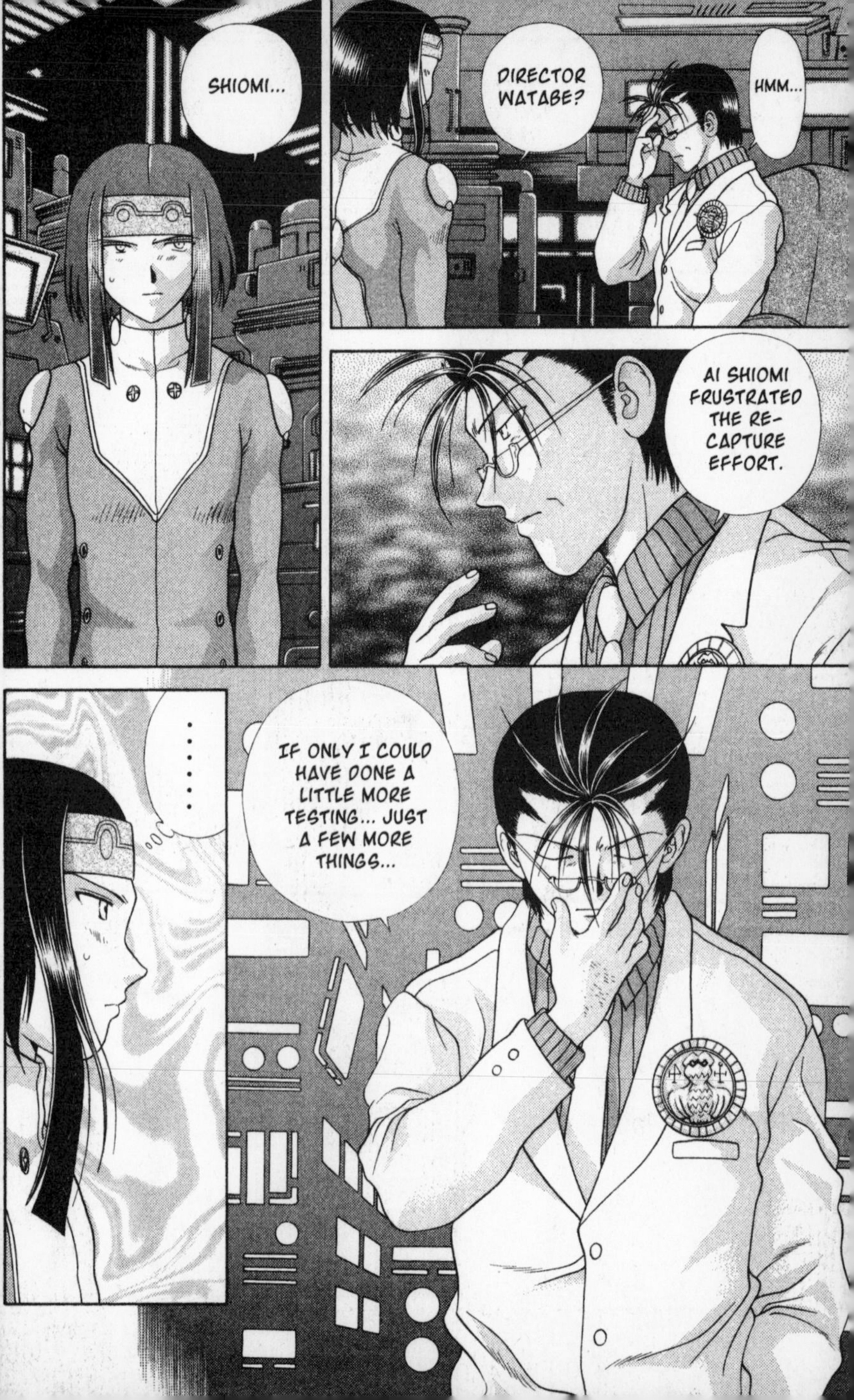
SHIOMI...
DIRECTOR WATABE?
HMM...
AI SHIOMI FRUSTRATED THE RE-CAPTURE EFFORT.
......
IF ONLY I COULD HAVE DONE A LITTLE MORE TESTING... JUST A FEW MORE THINGS...

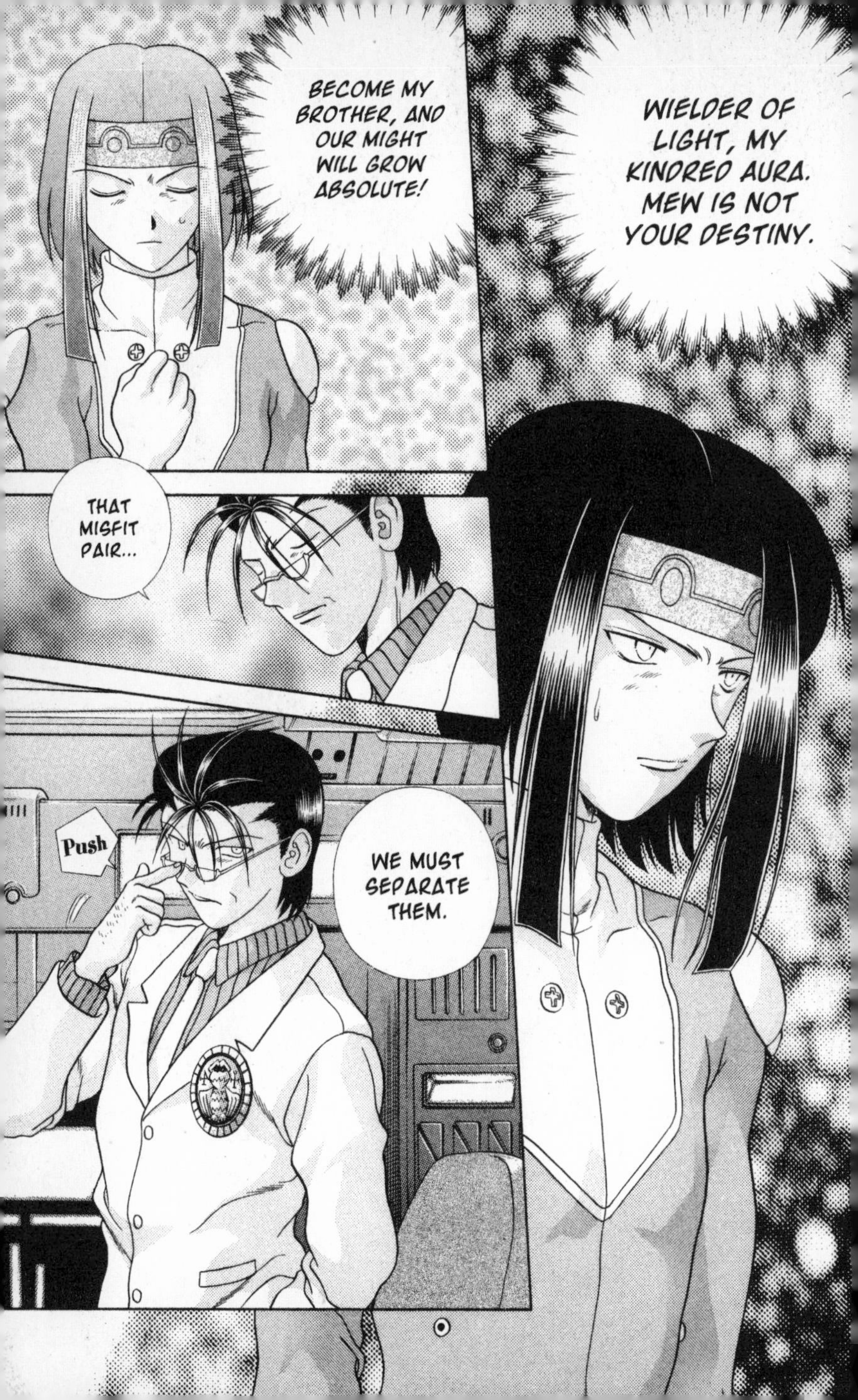
WIELDER OF LIGHT, MY KINDRED AURA. MEW IS NOT YOUR DESTINY.
BECOME MY BROTHER, AND OUR MIGHT WILL GROW ABSOLUTE!
THAT MISFIT PAIR...
Push
WE MUST SEPARATE THEM.

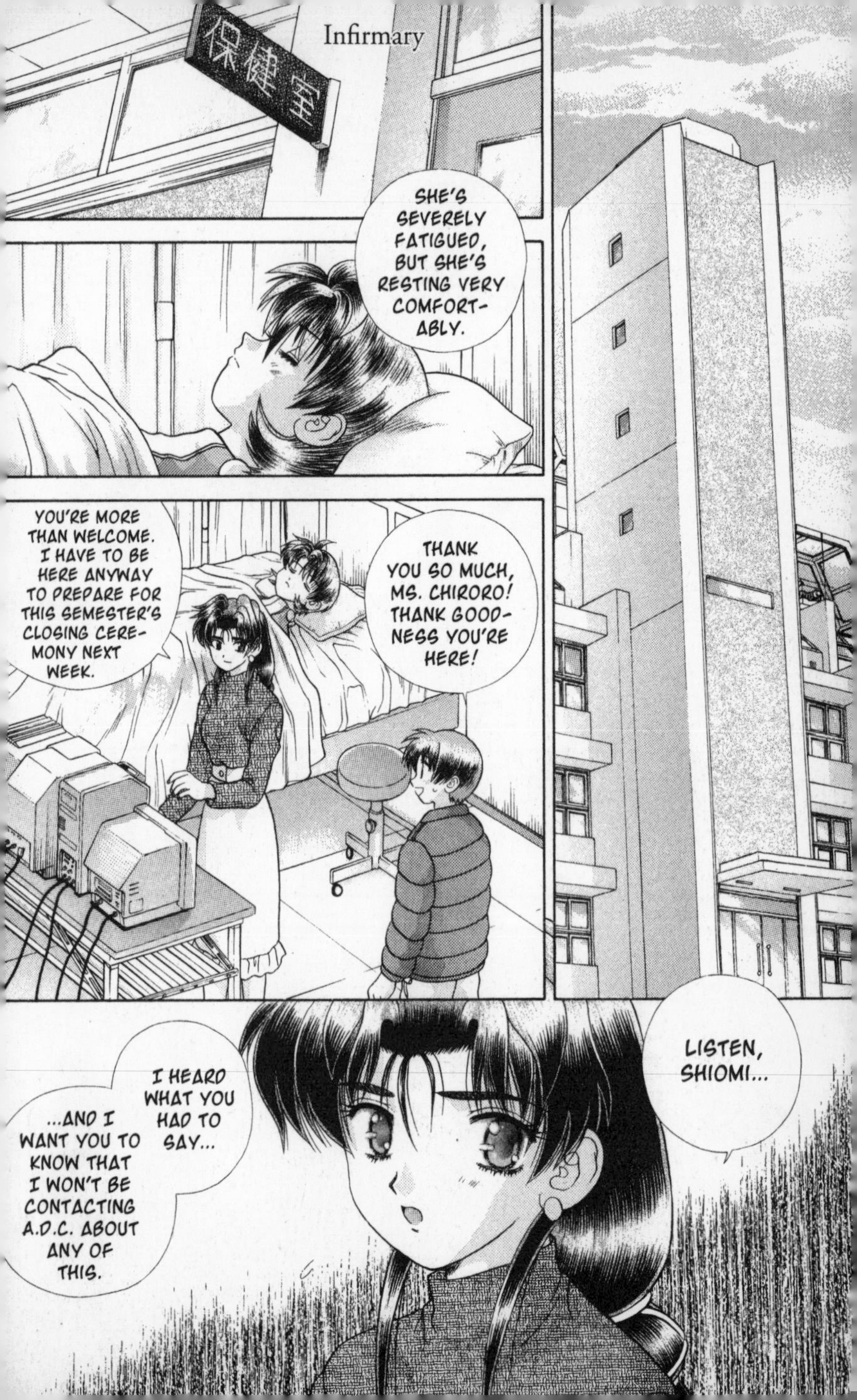

Infirmary
保健室
SHE'S SEVERELY FATIGUED, BUT SHE'S RESTING VERY COMFORT-ABLY.
THANK YOU SO MUCH, MS. CHIRORO! THANK GOOD-NESS YOU'RE HERE!
YOU'RE MORE THAN WELCOME. I HAVE TO BE HERE ANYWAY TO PREPARE FOR THIS SEMESTER'S CLOSING CERE-MONY NEXT WEEK.
LISTEN, SHIOMI...
I HEARD WHAT YOU HAD TO SAY...
...AND I WANT YOU TO KNOW THAT I WON'T BE CONTACTING A.D.C. ABOUT ANY OF THIS.

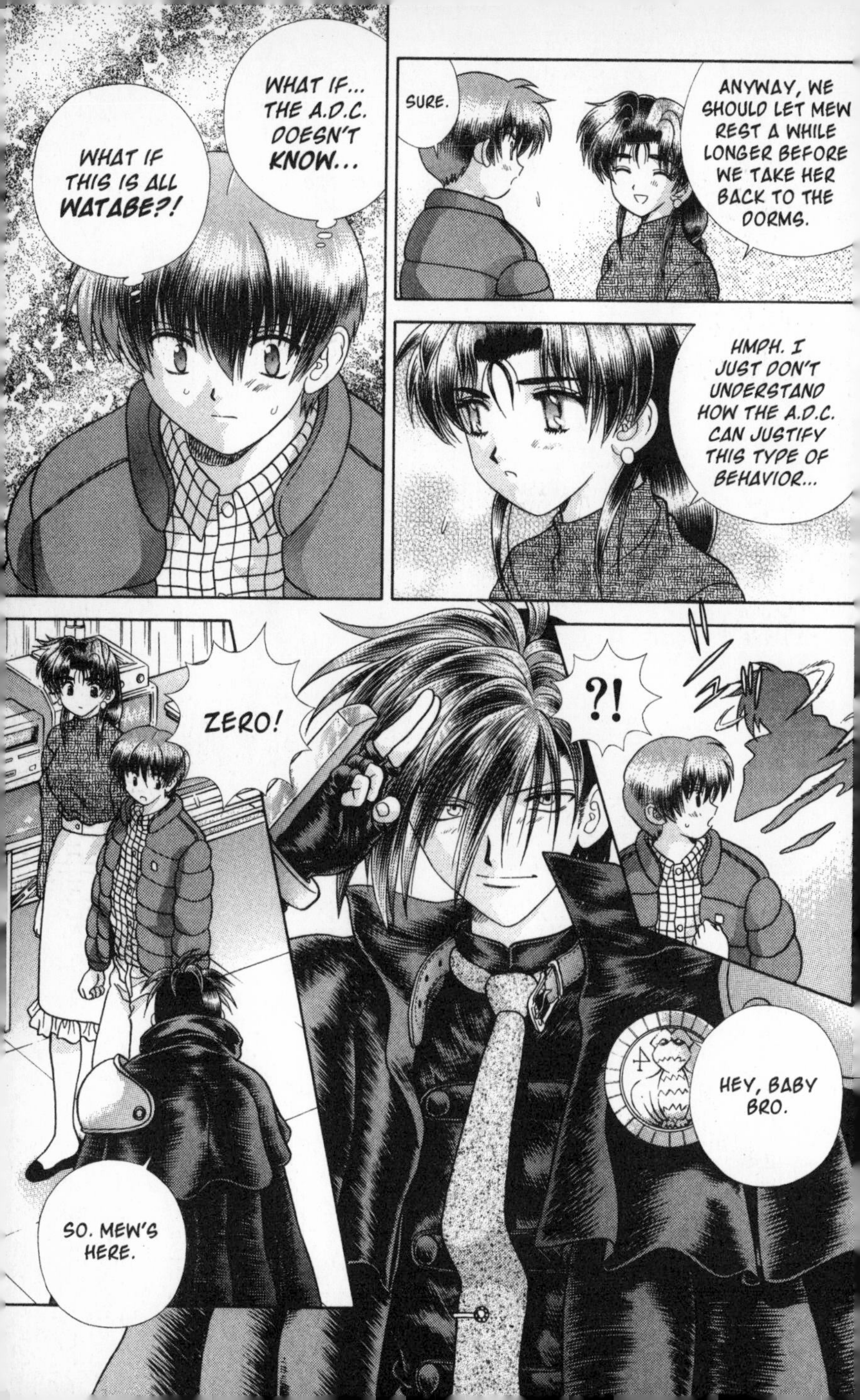
ANYWAY, WE SHOULD LET MEW REST A WHILE LONGER BEFORE WE TAKE HER BACK TO THE DORMS.
SURE.
HMPH. I JUST DON'T UNDERSTAND HOW THE A.D.C. CAN JUSTIFY THIS TYPE OF BEHAVIOR...
WHAT IF... THE A.D.C. DOESN'T KNOW...
WHAT IF THIS IS ALL WATABE?!
?!
ZERO!
HEY, BABY BRO.
SO. MEW'S HERE.

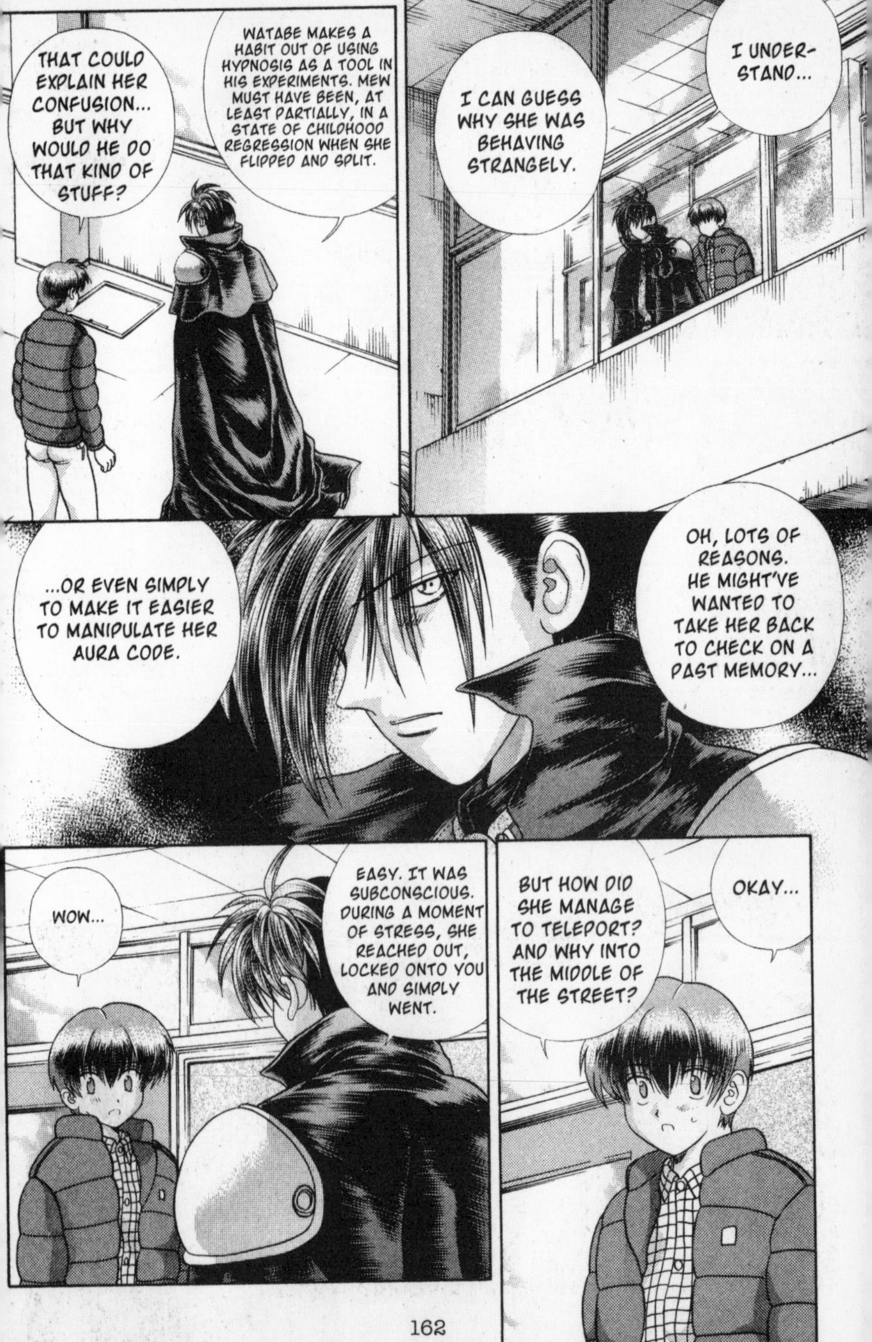
I UNDER-STAND...
I CAN GUESS WHY SHE WAS BEHAVING STRANGELY.
WATABE MAKES A HABIT OUT OF USING HYPNOSIS AS A TOOL IN HIS EXPERIMENTS. MEW MUST HAVE BEEN, AT LEAST PARTIALLY, IN A STATE OF CHILDHOOD REGRESSION WHEN SHE FLIPPED AND SPLIT.
THAT COULD EXPLAIN HER CONFUSION... BUT WHY WOULD HE DO THAT KIND OF STUFF?
OH, LOTS OF REASONS. HE MIGHT'VE WANTED TO TAKE HER BACK TO CHECK ON A PAST MEMORY...
...OR EVEN SIMPLY TO MAKE IT EASIER TO MANIPULATE HER AURA CODE.
OKAY...
BUT HOW DID SHE MANAGE TO TELEPORT? AND WHY INTO THE MIDDLE OF THE STREET?
EASY. IT WAS SUBCONSCIOUS. DURING A MOMENT OF STRESS, SHE REACHED OUT, LOCKED ONTO YOU AND SIMPLY WENT.
WOW...

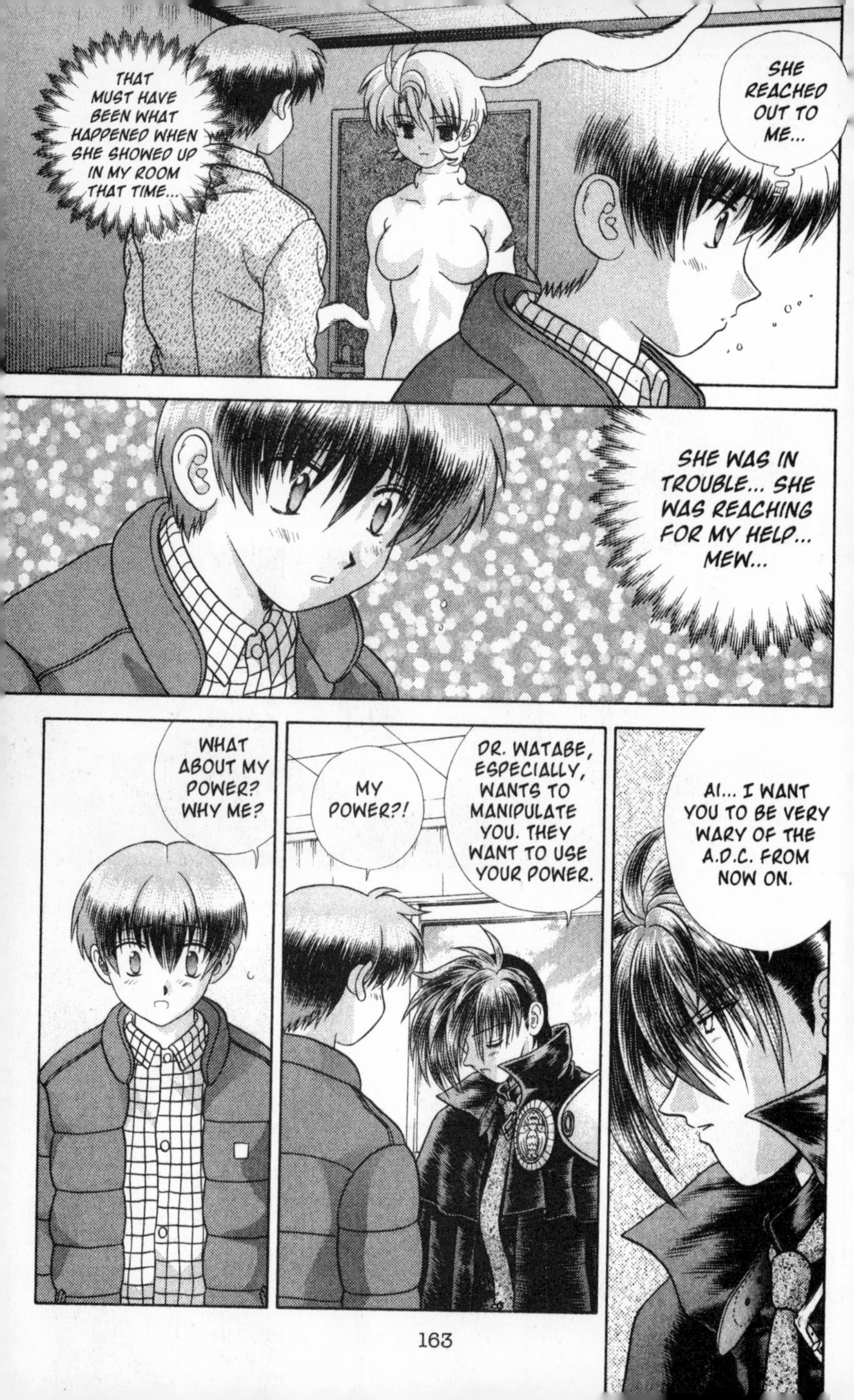
SHE REACHED OUT TO ME...
THAT MUST HAVE BEEN WHAT HAPPENED WHEN SHE SHOWED UP IN MY ROOM THAT TIME...
SHE WAS IN TROUBLE... SHE WAS REACHING FOR MY HELP... MEW...
AI... I WANT YOU TO BE VERY WARY OF THE A.D.C. FROM NOW ON.
DR. WATABE, ESPECIALLY, WANTS TO MANIPULATE YOU. THEY WANT TO USE YOUR POWER.
MY POWER?!
WHAT ABOUT MY POWER? WHY ME?

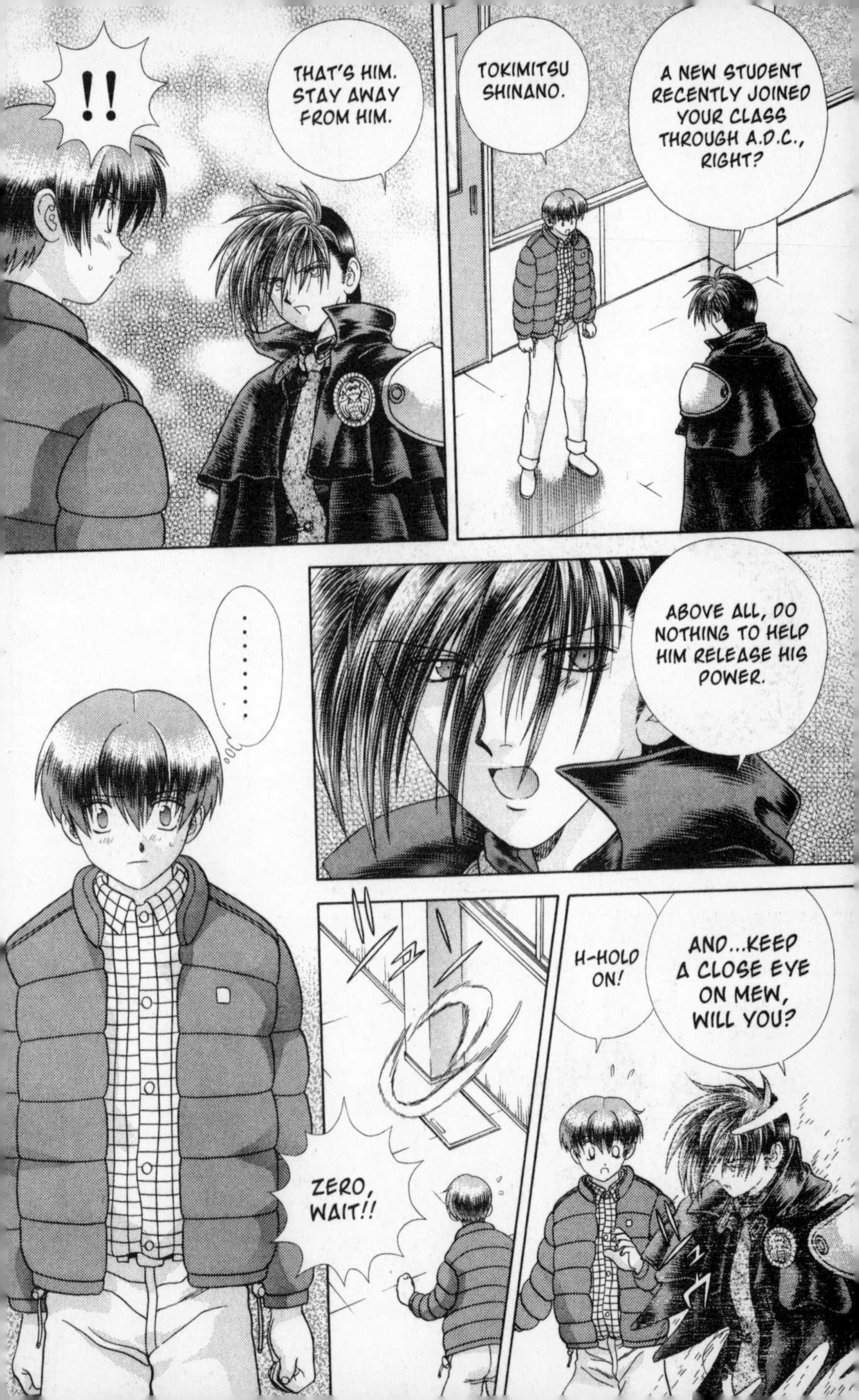
A NEW STUDENT RECENTLY JOINED YOUR CLASS THROUGH A.D.C., RIGHT?
TOKIMITSU SHINANO.
THAT'S HIM. STAY AWAY FROM HIM.
!!
ABOVE ALL, DO NOTHING TO HELP HIM RELEASE HIS POWER.
......
AND...KEEP A CLOSE EYE ON MEW, WILL YOU?
H-HOLD ON!
ZERO, WAIT!!

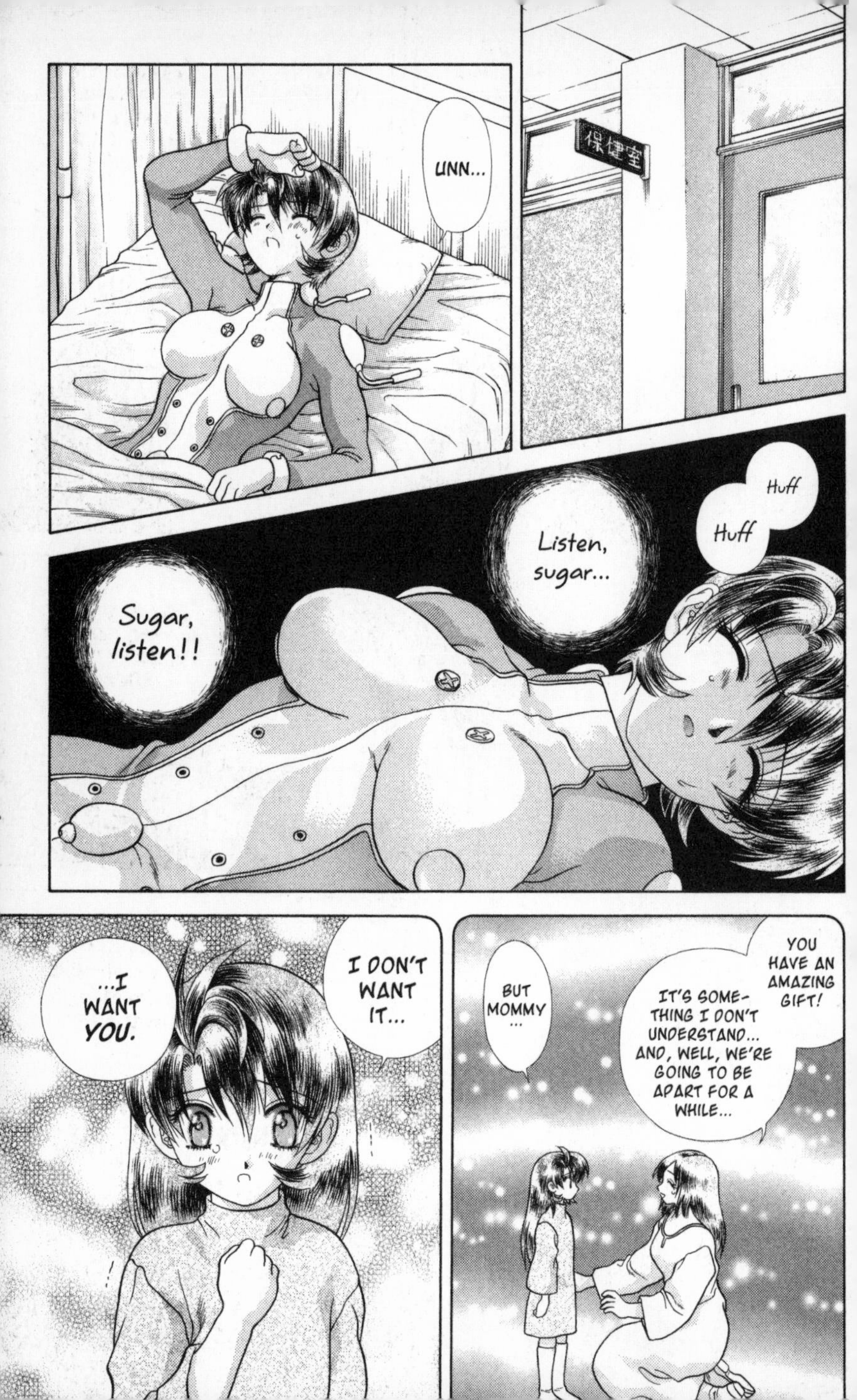
保健室
UNN...
Huff
Huff
Listen, sugar...
Sugar, listen!!
YOU HAVE AN AMAZING GIFT!
IT'S SOME-THING I DON'T UNDERSTAND... AND, WELL, WE'RE GOING TO BE APART FOR A WHILE...
BUT MOMMY ...
I DON'T WANT IT...
...I WANT YOU.

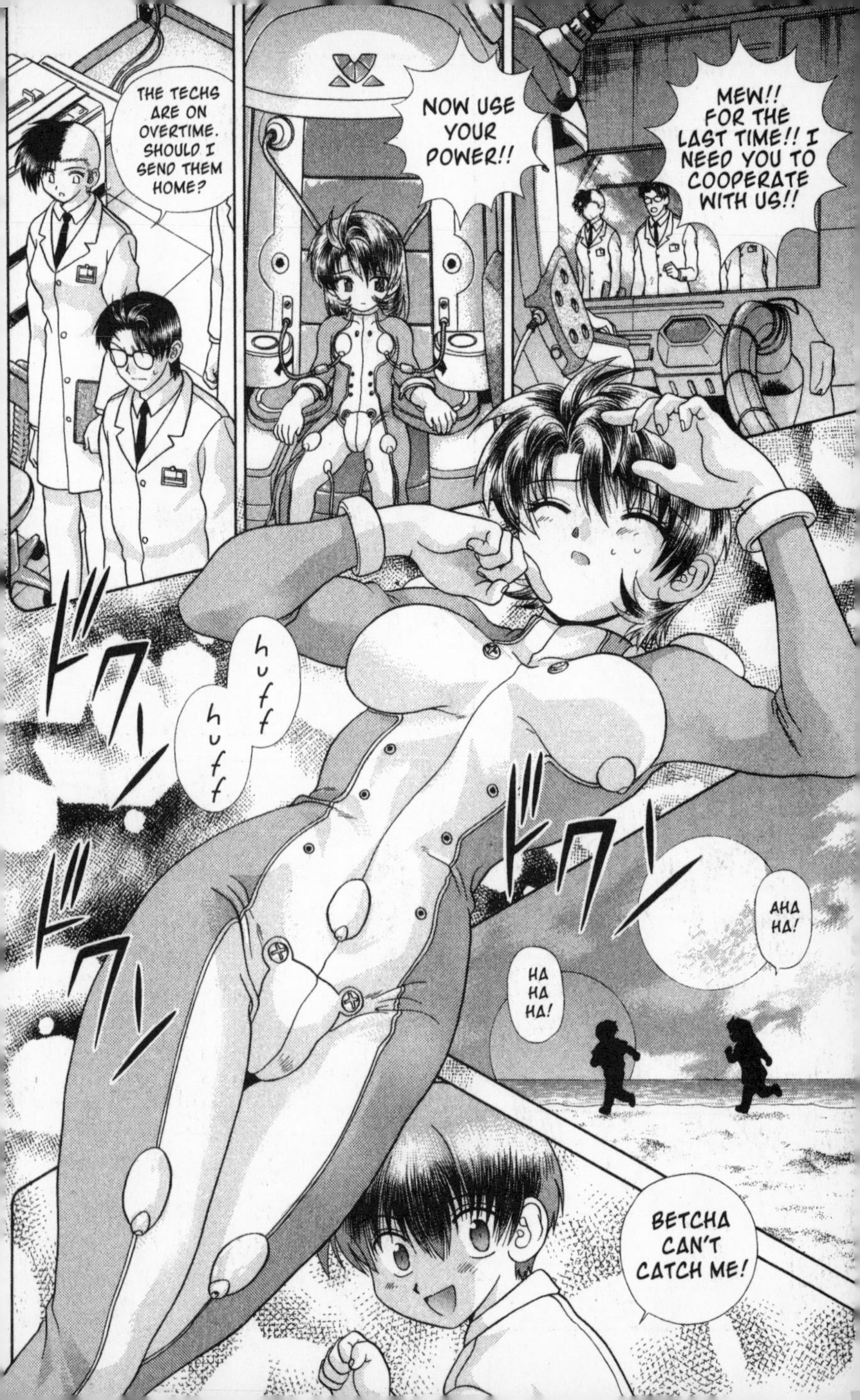

MEW!! FOR THE LAST TIME!! I NEED YOU TO COOPERATE WITH US!!
NOW USE YOUR POWER!!
THE TECHS ARE ON OVERTIME. SHOULD I SEND THEM HOME?
huff huff
ドクン
ドクン
ドクン
AHA HA!
HA HA HA!
BETCHA CAN'T CATCH ME!

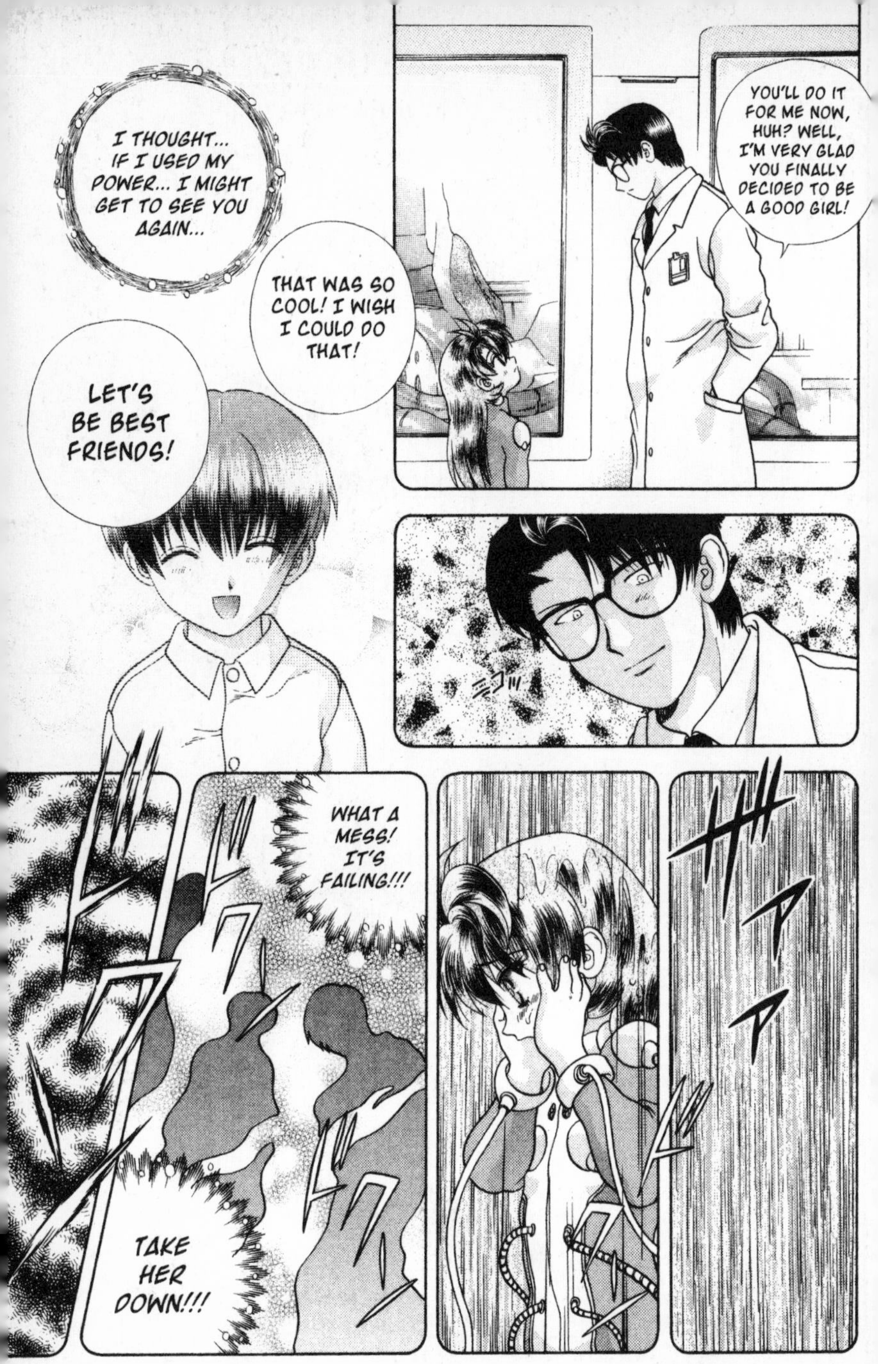
I THOUGHT... IF I USED MY POWER... I MIGHT GET TO SEE YOU AGAIN...
THAT WAS SO COOL! I WISH I COULD DO THAT!
LET'S BE BEST FRIENDS!
YOU'LL DO IT FOR ME NOW, HUH? WELL, I'M VERY GLAD YOU FINALLY DECIDED TO BE A GOOD GIRL!
WHAT A MESS! IT'S FAILING!!!
TAKE HER DOWN!!!

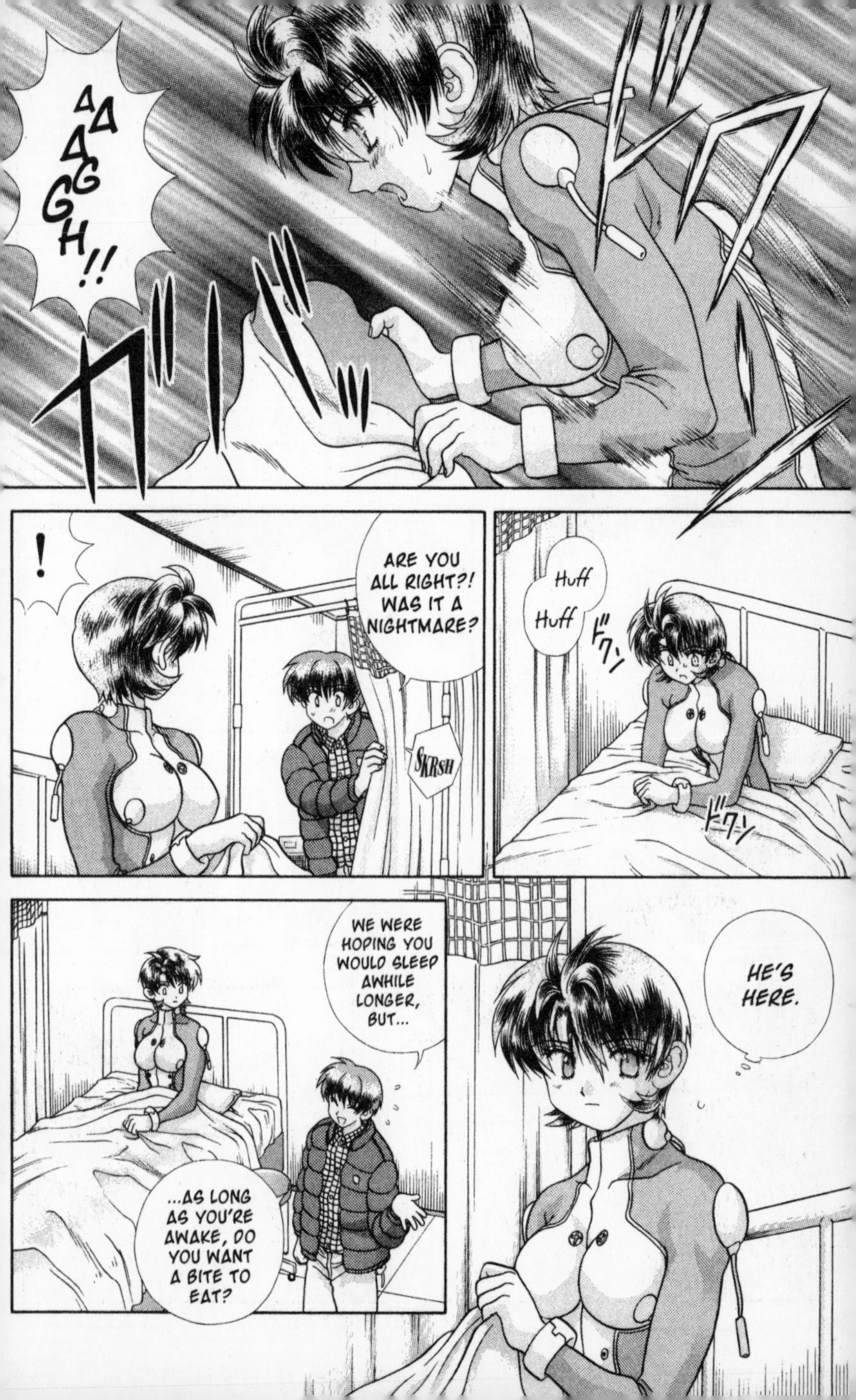

AAAGGH!!
Huff
Huff
ドクン
ドクン
!
ARE YOU ALL RIGHT?! WAS IT A NIGHTMARE?
SKRSH
HE'S HERE.
WE WERE HOPING YOU WOULD SLEEP AWHILE LONGER, BUT...
...AS LONG AS YOU'RE AWAKE, DO YOU WANT A BITE TO EAT?

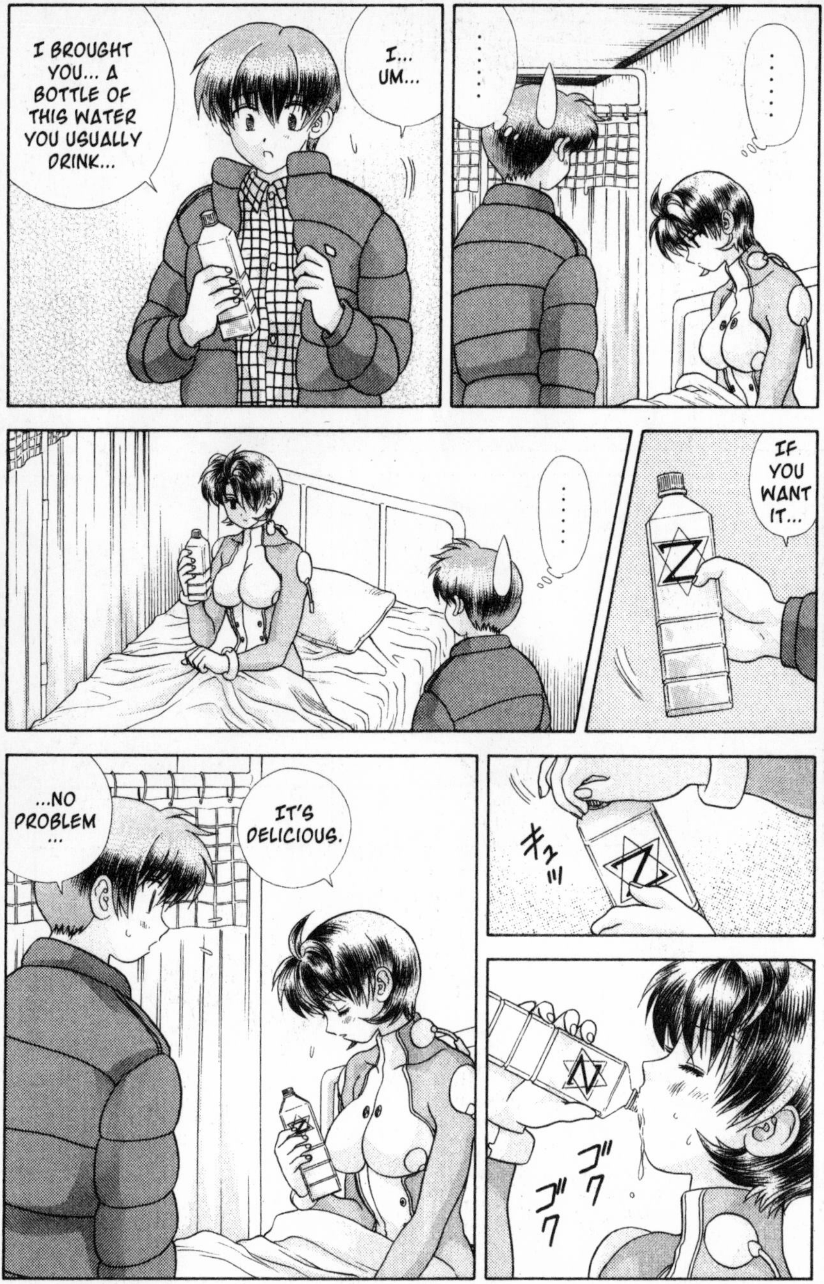
......
......
I... UM...
I BROUGHT YOU... A BOTTLE OF THIS WATER YOU USUALLY DRINK...
IF YOU WANT IT...
......
キュッ
ゴク
ゴク
IT'S DELICIOUS.
...NO PROBLEM ...

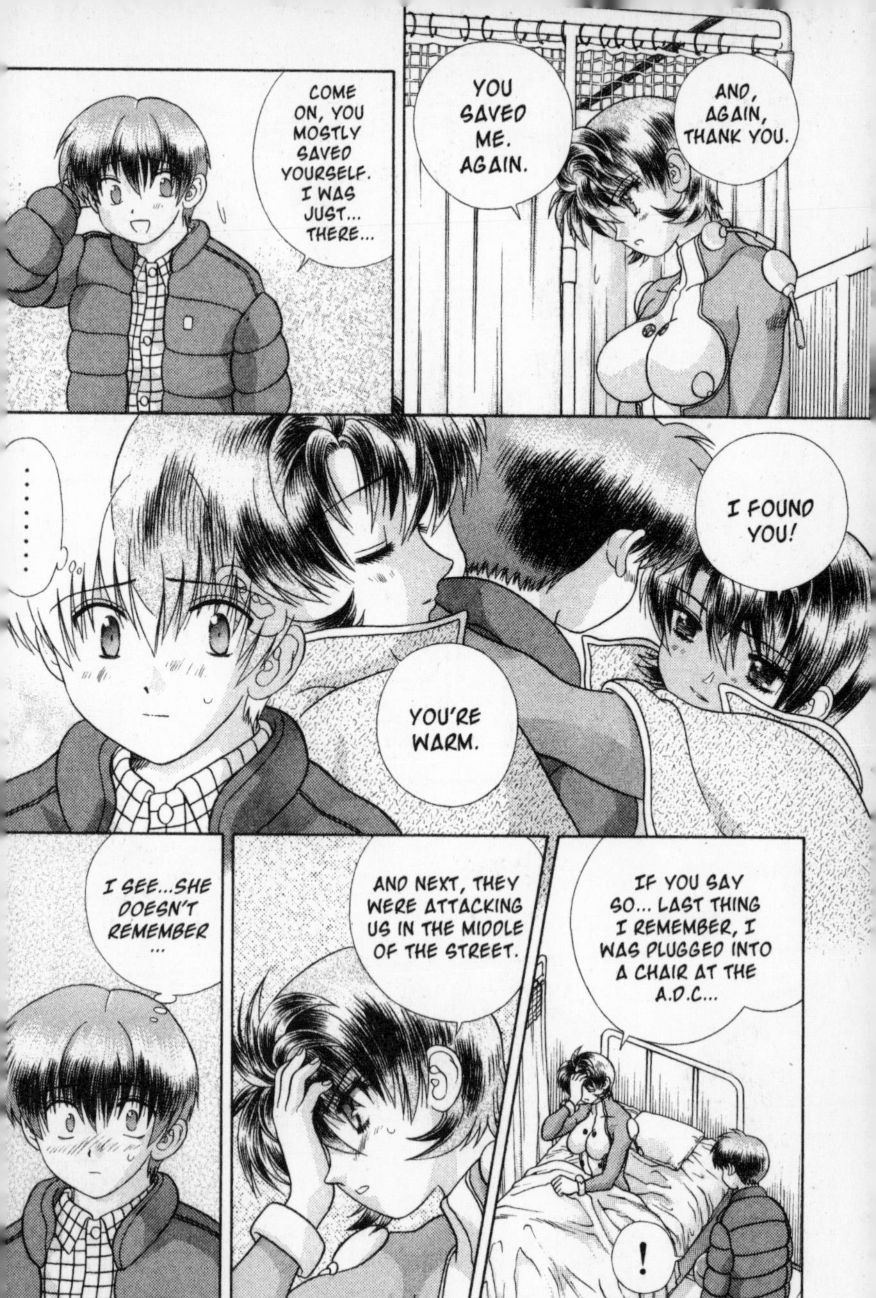
YOU SAVED ME. AGAIN.
AND, AGAIN, THANK YOU.
COME ON, YOU MOSTLY SAVED YOURSELF. I WAS JUST... THERE...
I FOUND YOU!
YOU'RE WARM.
......
IF YOU SAY SO... LAST THING I REMEMBER, I WAS PLUGGED INTO A CHAIR AT THE A.D.C...
!
AND NEXT, THEY WERE ATTACKING US IN THE MIDDLE OF THE STREET.
I SEE...SHE DOESN'T REMEMBER ...

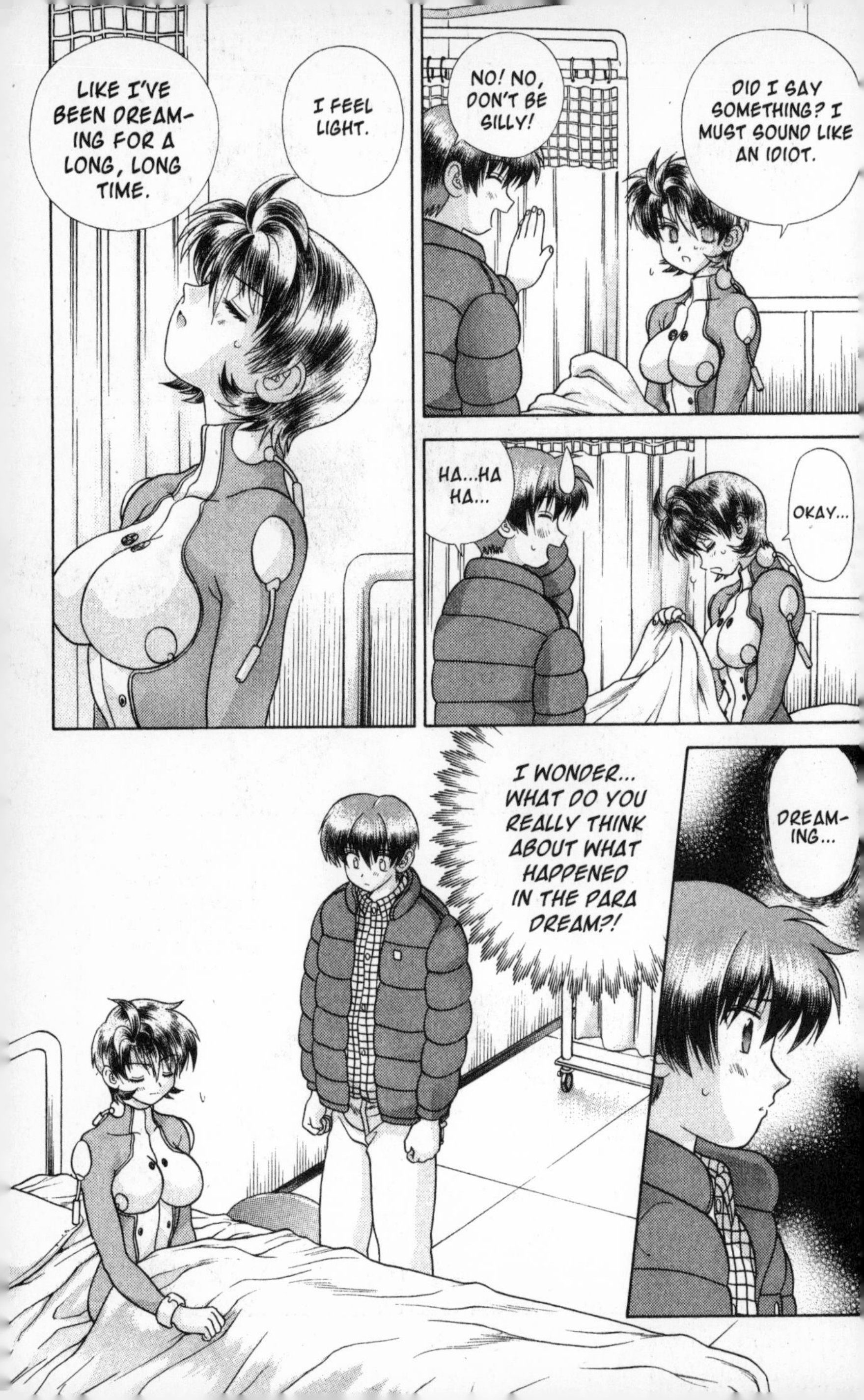
I FEEL LIGHT.
LIKE I'VE BEEN DREAMING FOR A LONG, LONG TIME.
DID I SAY SOMETHING? I MUST SOUND LIKE AN IDIOT.
NO! NO, DON'T BE SILLY!
OKAY...
HA...HA HA...
DREAMING...
I WONDER... WHAT DO YOU REALLY THINK ABOUT WHAT HAPPENED IN THE PARA DREAM?!

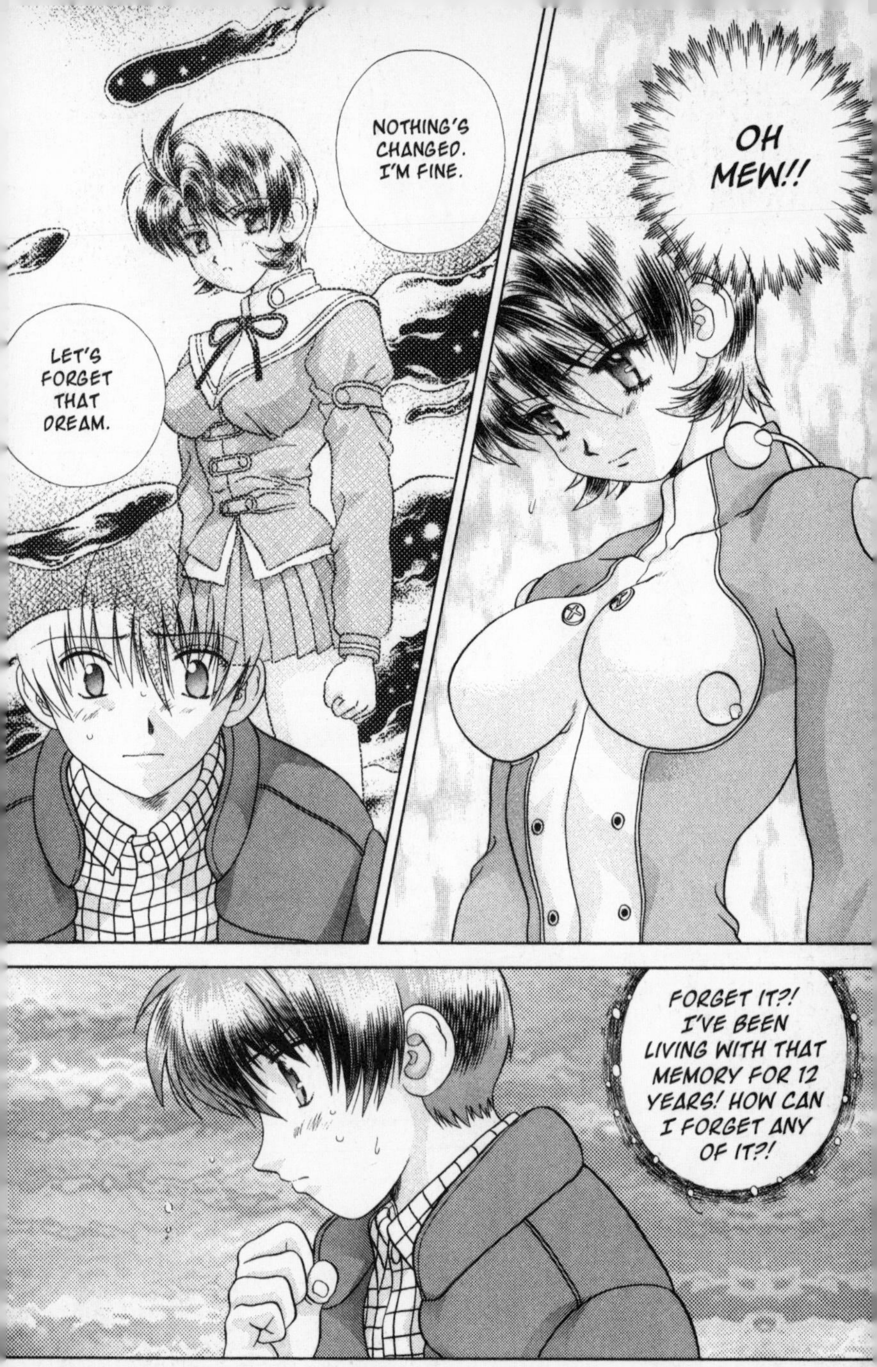
NOTHING'S CHANGED. I'M FINE.
LET'S FORGET THAT DREAM.
OH MEW!!
FORGET IT?! I'VE BEEN LIVING WITH THAT MEMORY FOR 12 YEARS! HOW CAN I FORGET ANY OF IT?!

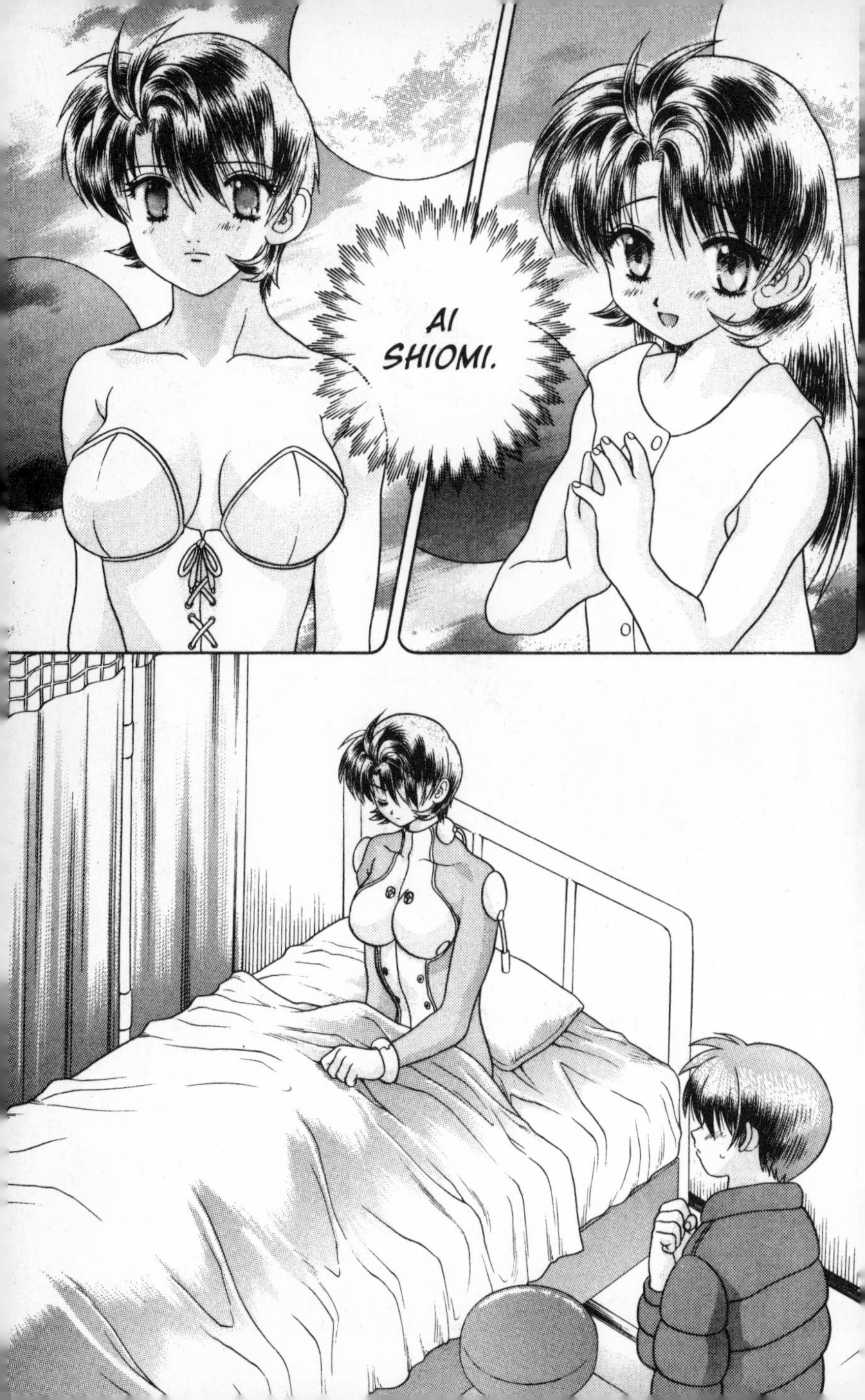
AI
SHIOMI.

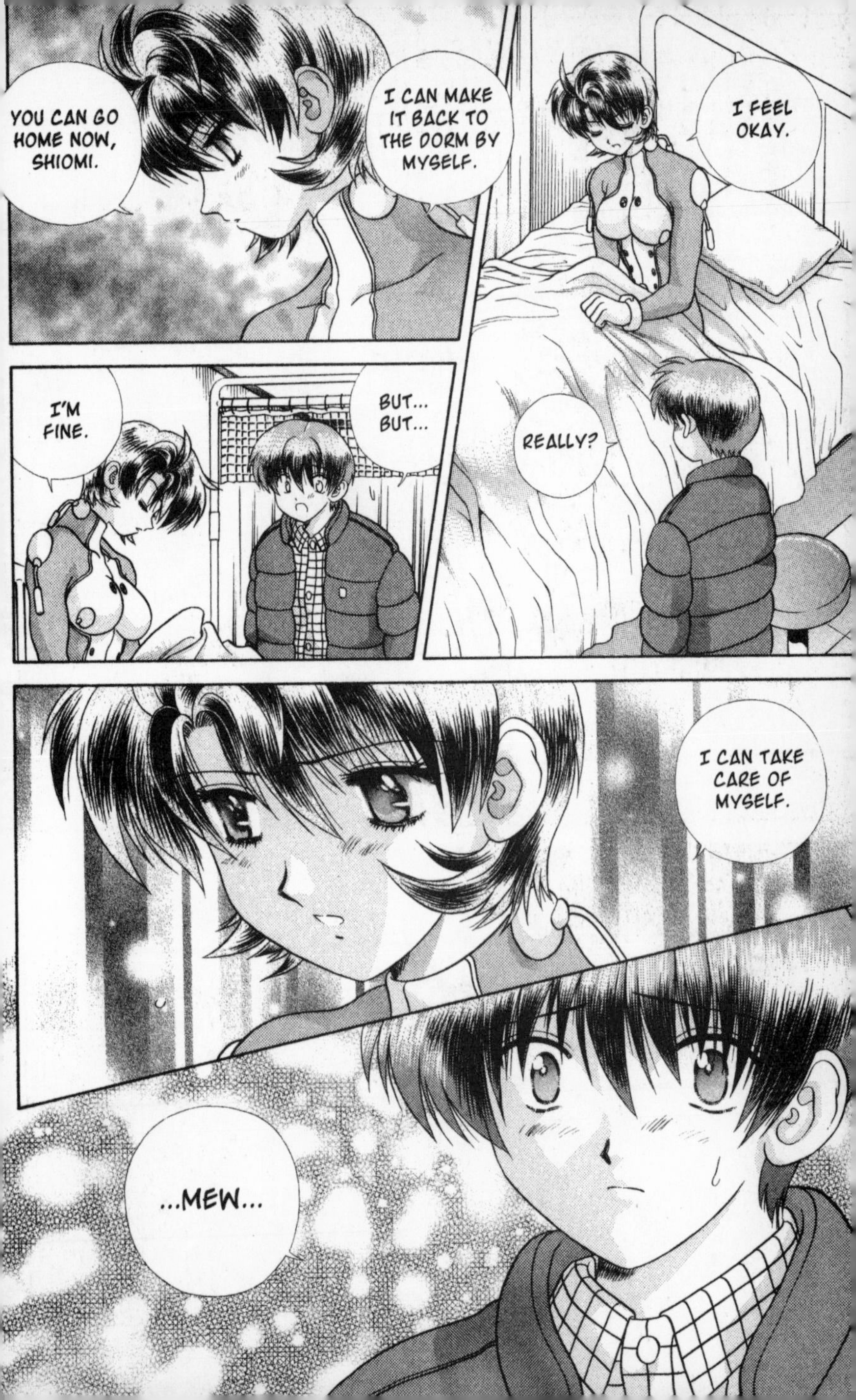
I FEEL OKAY.
REALLY?
I CAN MAKE IT BACK TO THE DORM BY MYSELF.
YOU CAN GO HOME NOW, SHIOMI.
BUT... BUT...
I'M FINE.
I CAN TAKE CARE OF MYSELF.
...MEW...

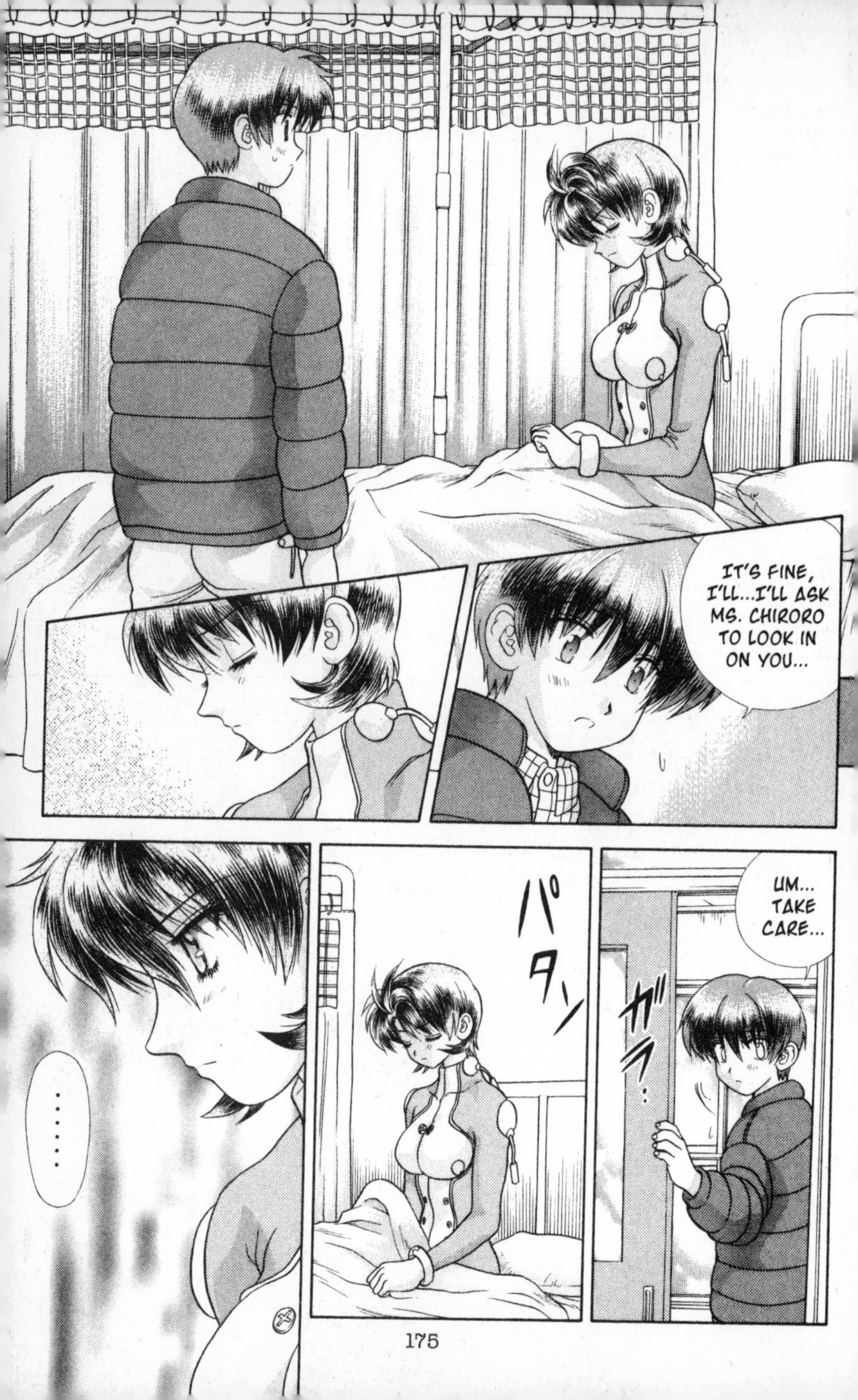
IT'S FINE, I'LL...I'LL ASK MS. CHIRORO TO LOOK IN ON YOU...
UM... TAKE CARE...
ガラ
パタン
......

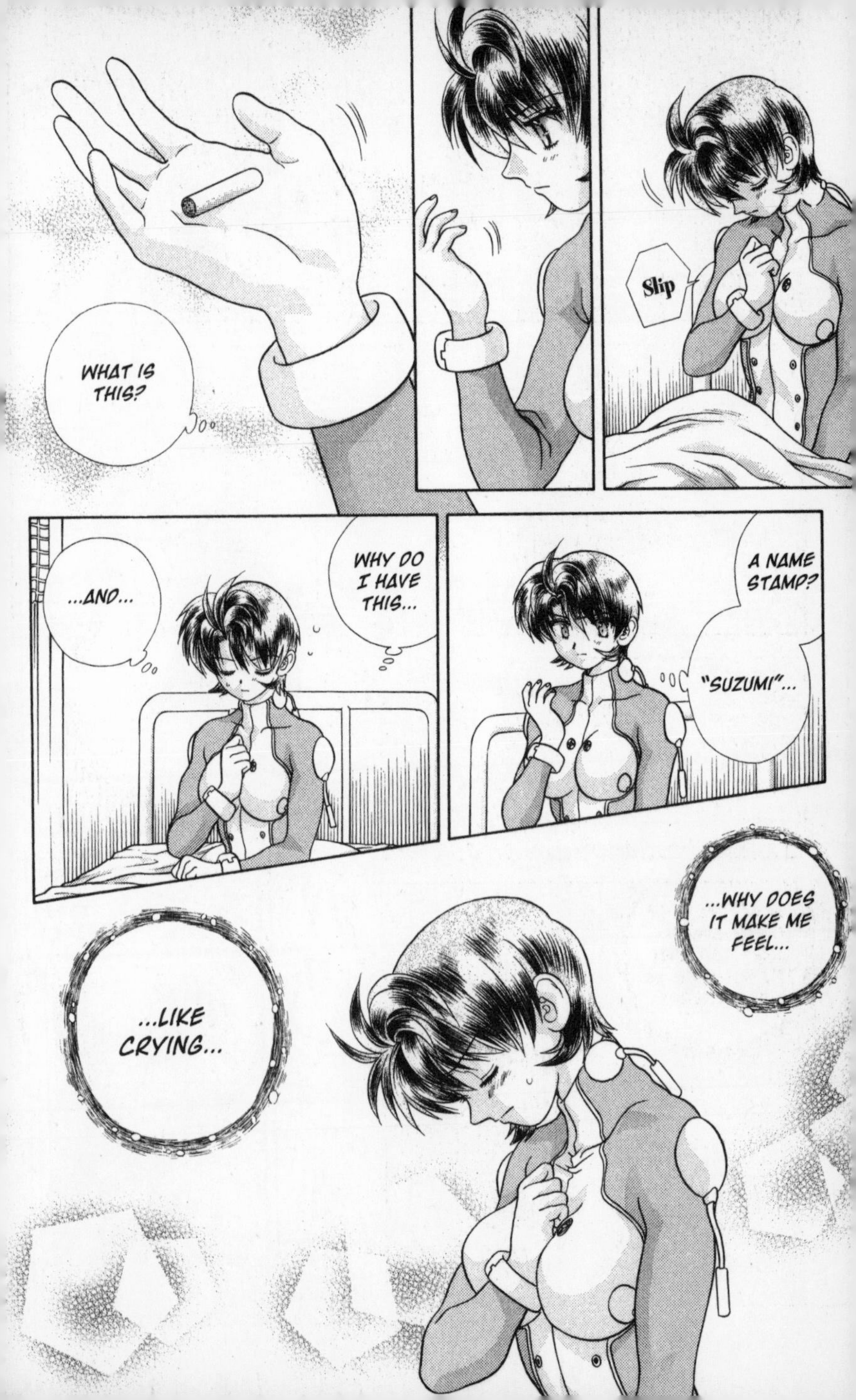
Slip
WHAT IS THIS?
A NAME STAMP?
"SUZUMI"...
WHY DO I HAVE THIS...
...AND...
...WHY DOES IT MAKE ME FEEL...
...LIKE CRYING...

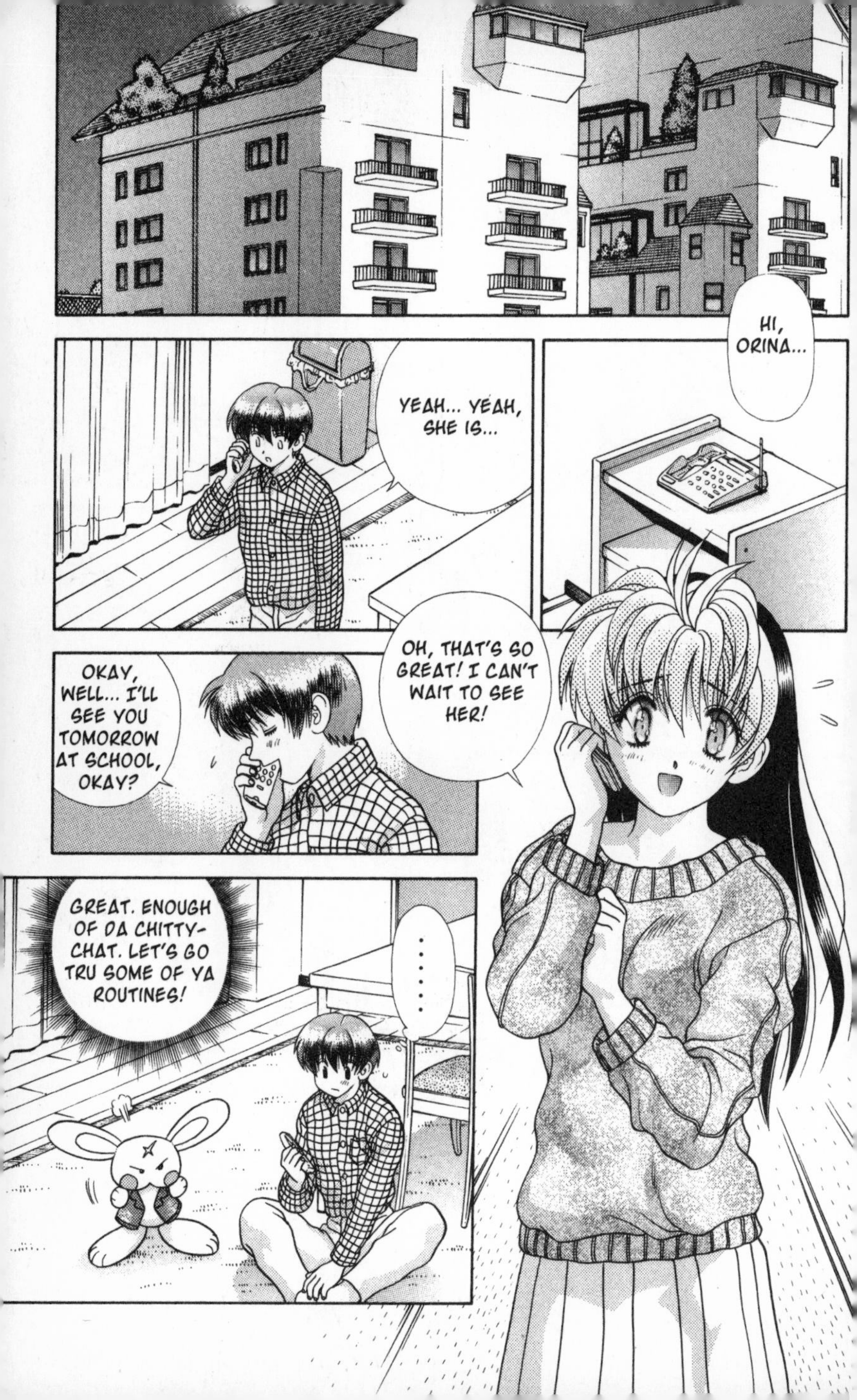
HI, ORINA...
YEAH... YEAH, SHE IS...
OH, THAT'S SO GREAT! I CAN'T WAIT TO SEE HER!
OKAY, WELL... I'LL SEE YOU TOMORROW AT SCHOOL, OKAY?
......
GREAT. ENOUGH OF DA CHITTY-CHAT. LET'S GO TRU SOME OF YA ROUTINES!

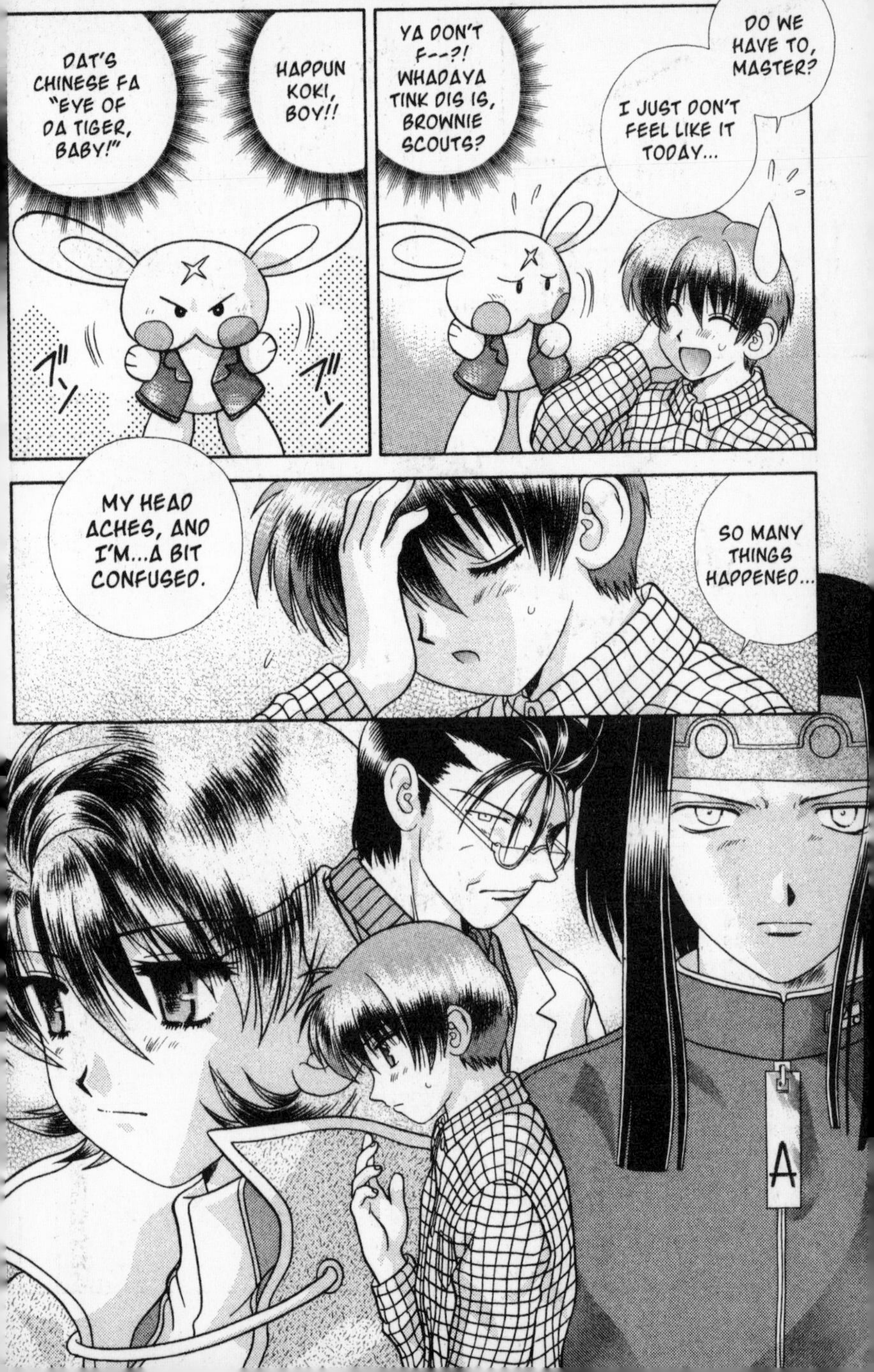

DO WE HAVE TO, MASTER?
I JUST DON'T FEEL LIKE IT TODAY...
YA DON'T F--?! WHADAYA TINK DIS IS, BROWNIE SCOUTS?
HAPPUN KOKI, BOY!!
DAT'S CHINESE FA "EYE OF DA TIGER, BABY!"
ブン
ブン
SO MANY THINGS HAPPENED...
MY HEAD ACHES, AND I'M...A BIT CONFUSED.
A

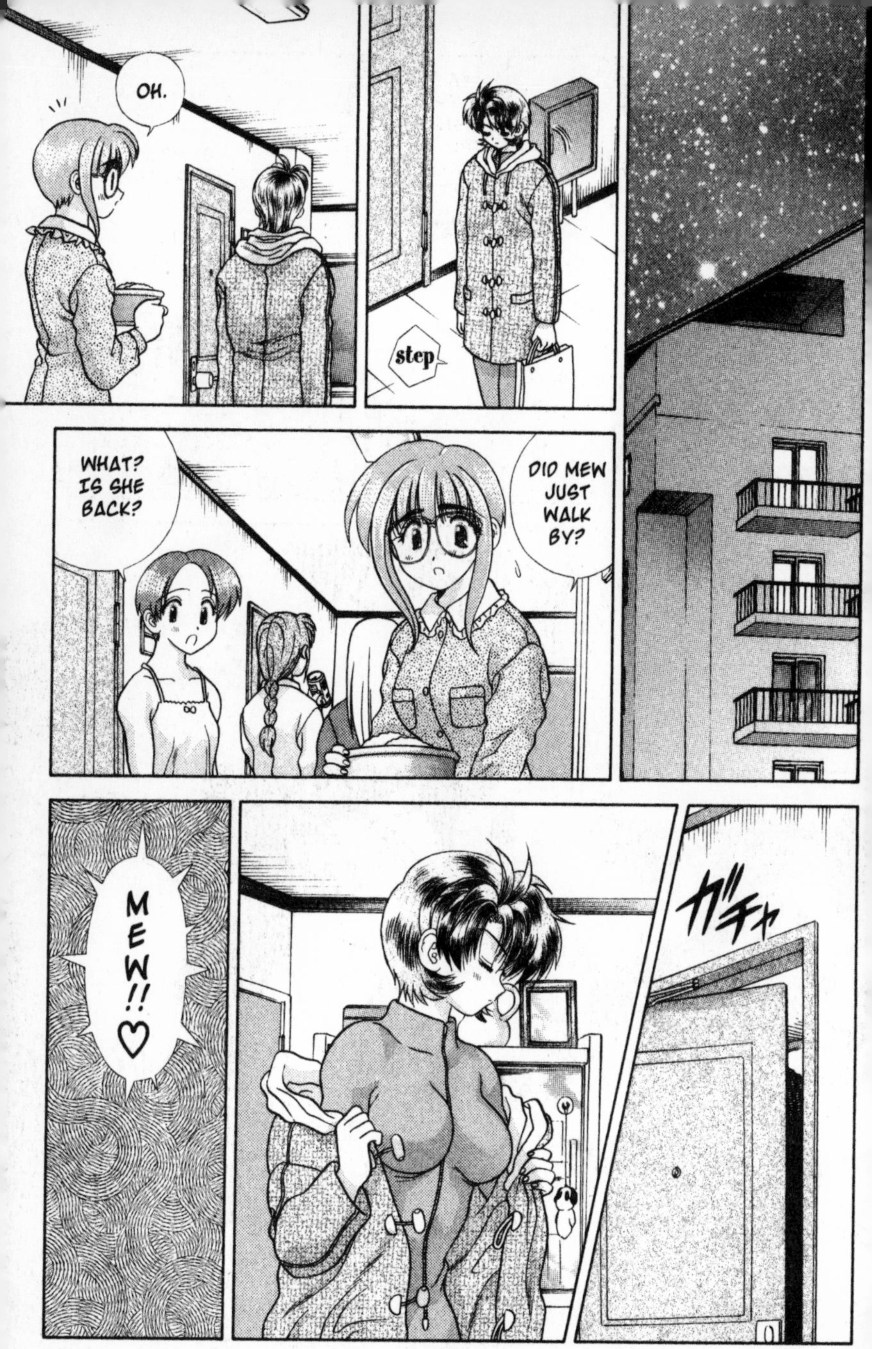
step
OH.
DID MEW JUST WALK BY?
WHAT? IS SHE BACK?
ガチャ
MEW!! ♡

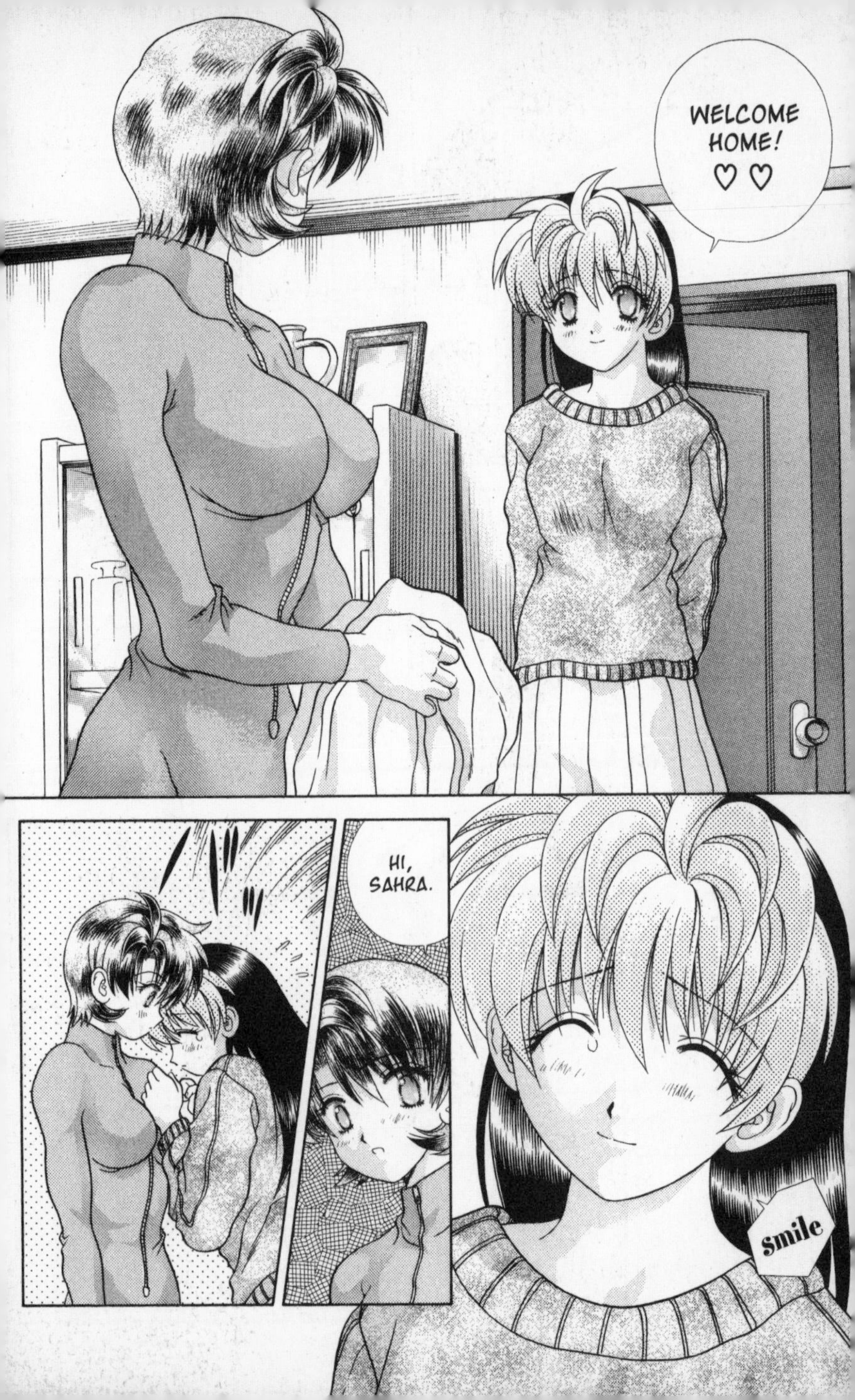
WELCOME HOME! ♡ ♡
HI, SAHRA.
smile

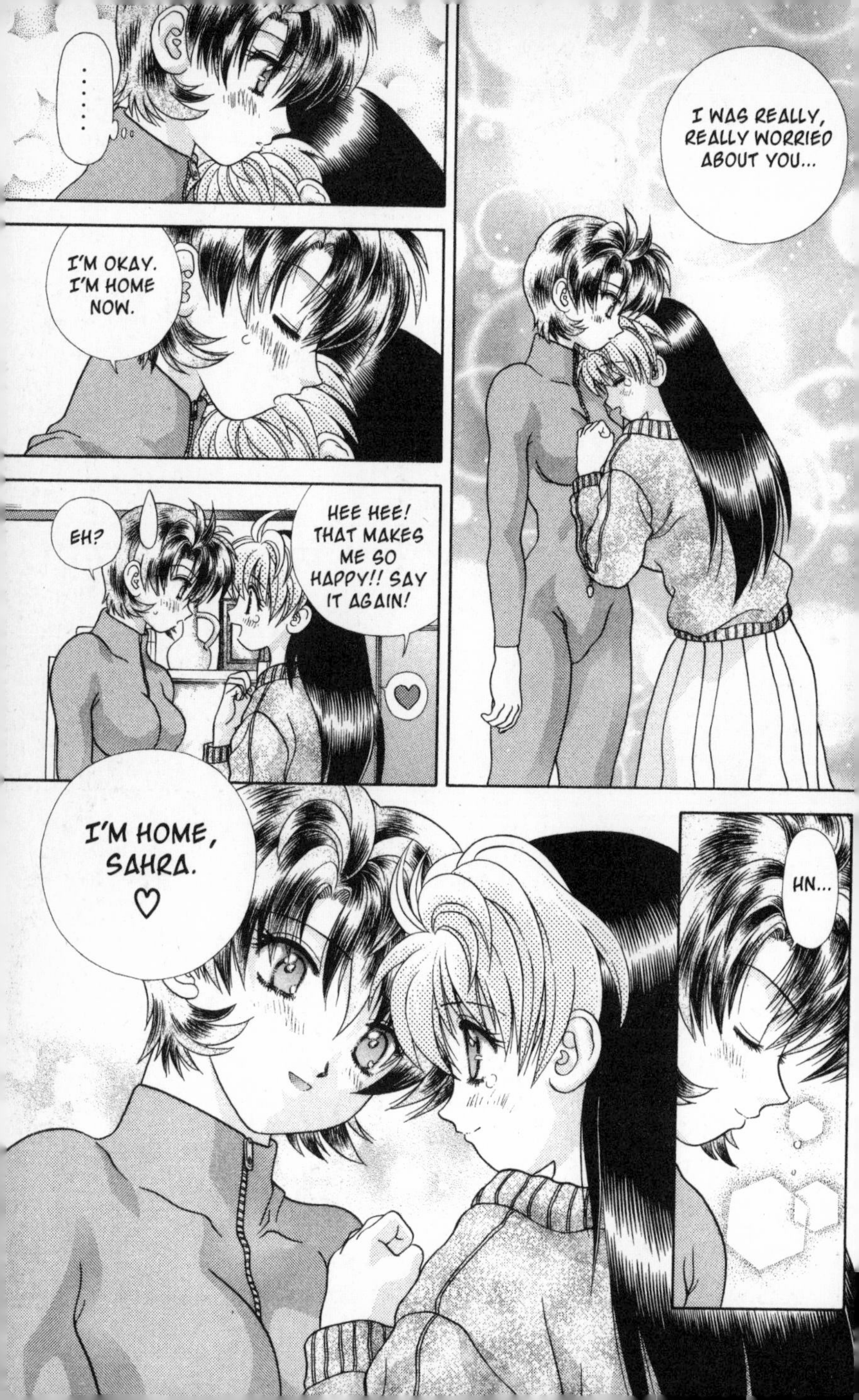
I WAS REALLY, REALLY WORRIED ABOUT YOU...
......
I'M OKAY. I'M HOME NOW.
HEE HEE! THAT MAKES ME SO HAPPY!! SAY IT AGAIN!
♥
EH?
HN...
I'M HOME, SAHRA. ♡

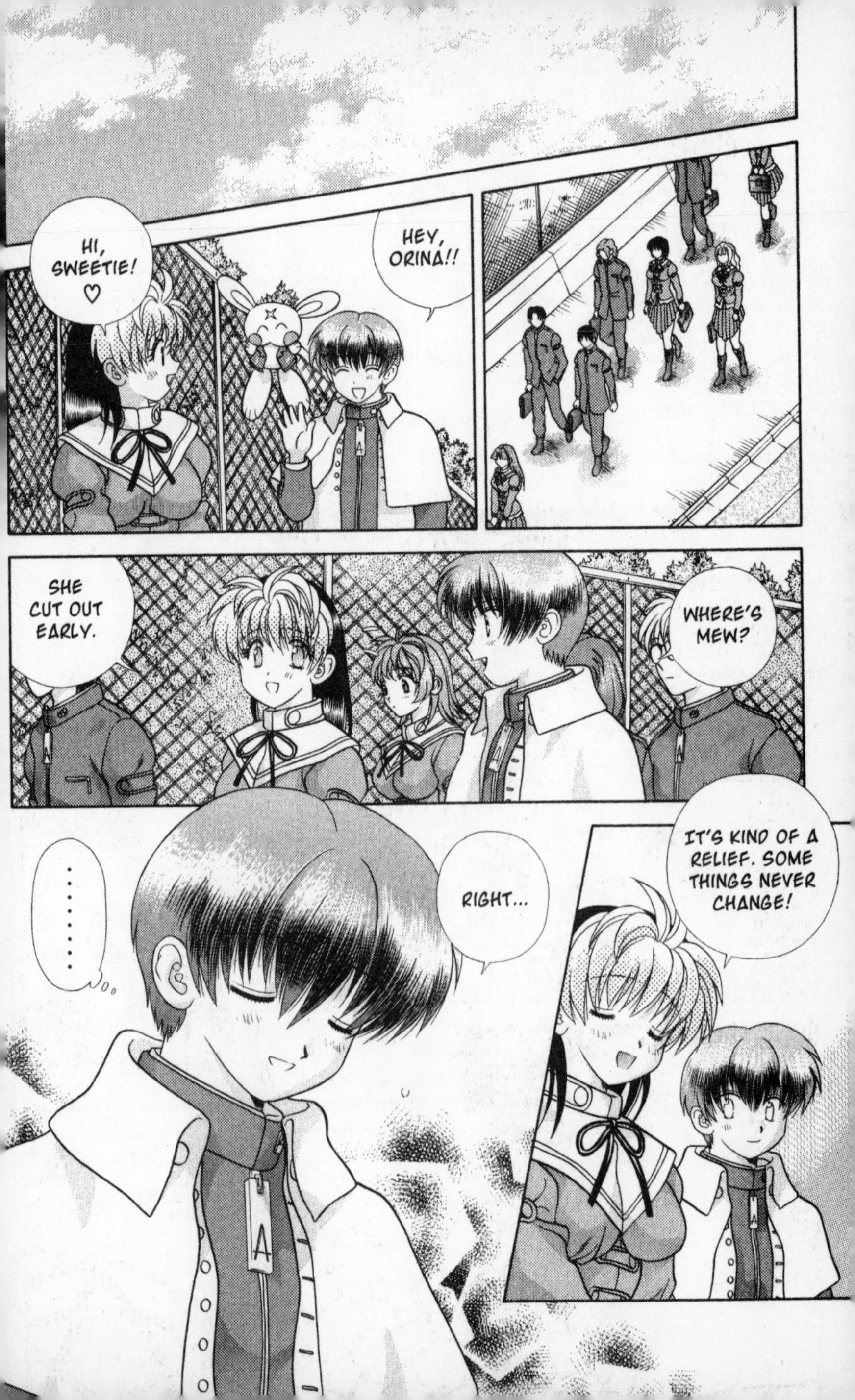
HEY, ORINA!!
HI, SWEETIE! ♡
WHERE'S MEW?
SHE CUT OUT EARLY.
IT'S KIND OF A RELIEF. SOME THINGS NEVER CHANGE!
RIGHT...
......

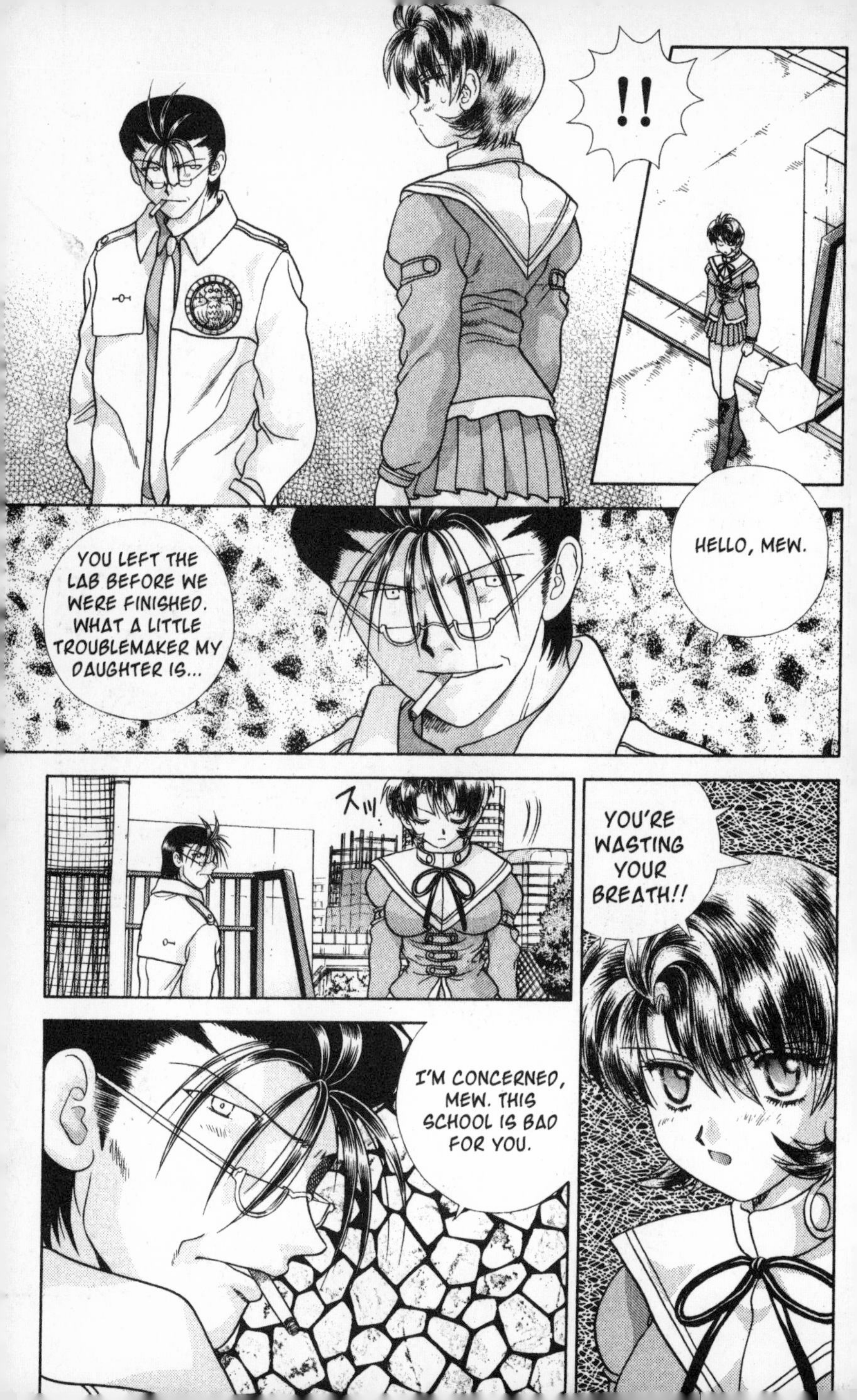
!!
HELLO, MEW.
YOU LEFT THE LAB BEFORE WE WERE FINISHED. WHAT A LITTLE TROUBLEMAKER MY DAUGHTER IS...
YOU'RE WASTING YOUR BREATH!!
スッ
I'M CONCERNED, MEW. THIS SCHOOL IS BAD FOR YOU.

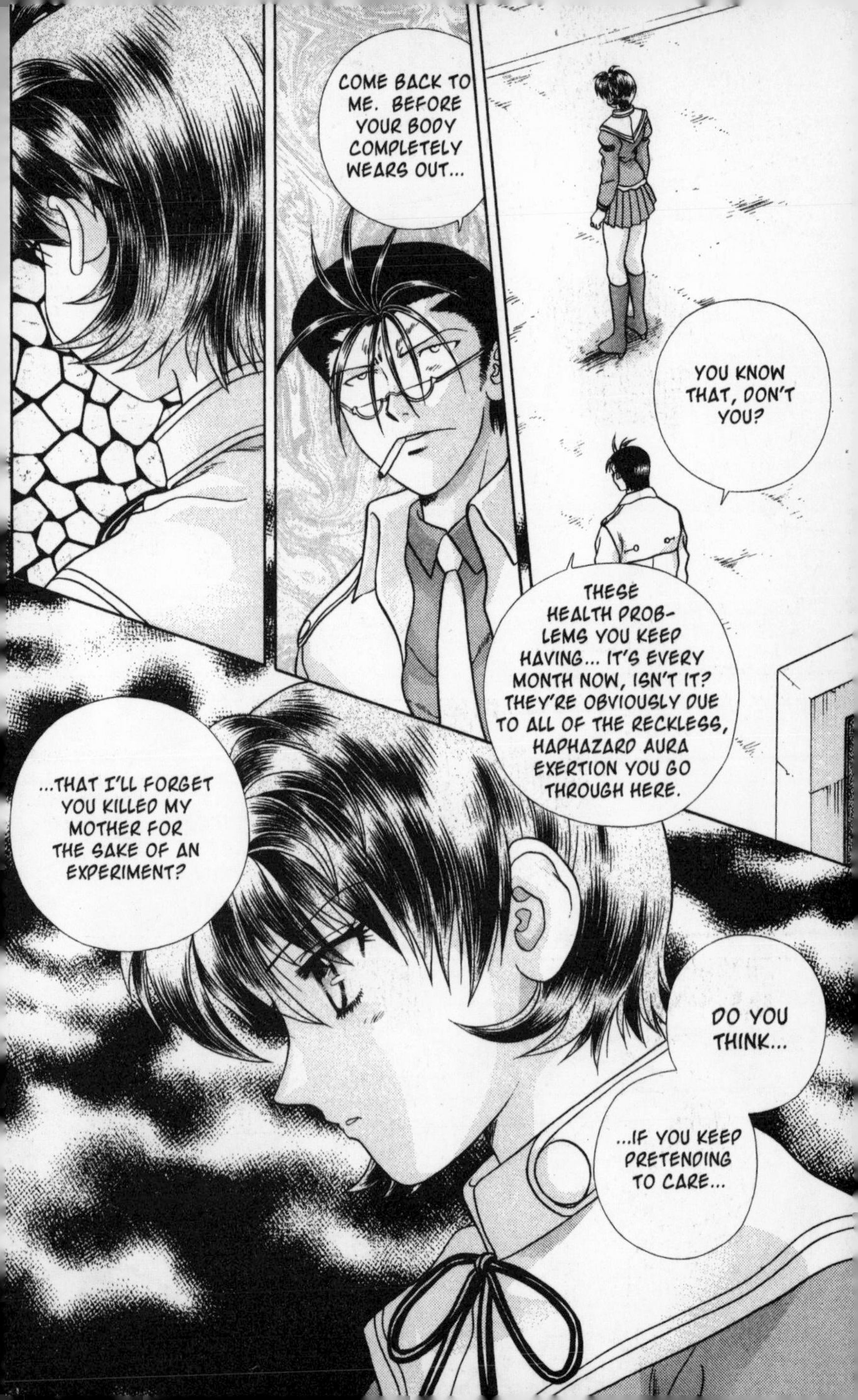
THESE HEALTH PROB-LEMS YOU KEEP HAVING... IT'S EVERY MONTH NOW, ISN'T IT? THEY'RE OBVIOUSLY DUE TO ALL OF THE RECKLESS, HAPHAZARD AURA EXERTION YOU GO THROUGH HERE.
COME BACK TO ME. BEFORE YOUR BODY COMPLETELY WEARS OUT...
YOU KNOW THAT, DON'T YOU?
DO YOU THINK...
...IF YOU KEEP PRETENDING TO CARE...
...THAT I'LL FORGET YOU KILLED MY MOTHER FOR THE SAKE OF AN EXPERIMENT?

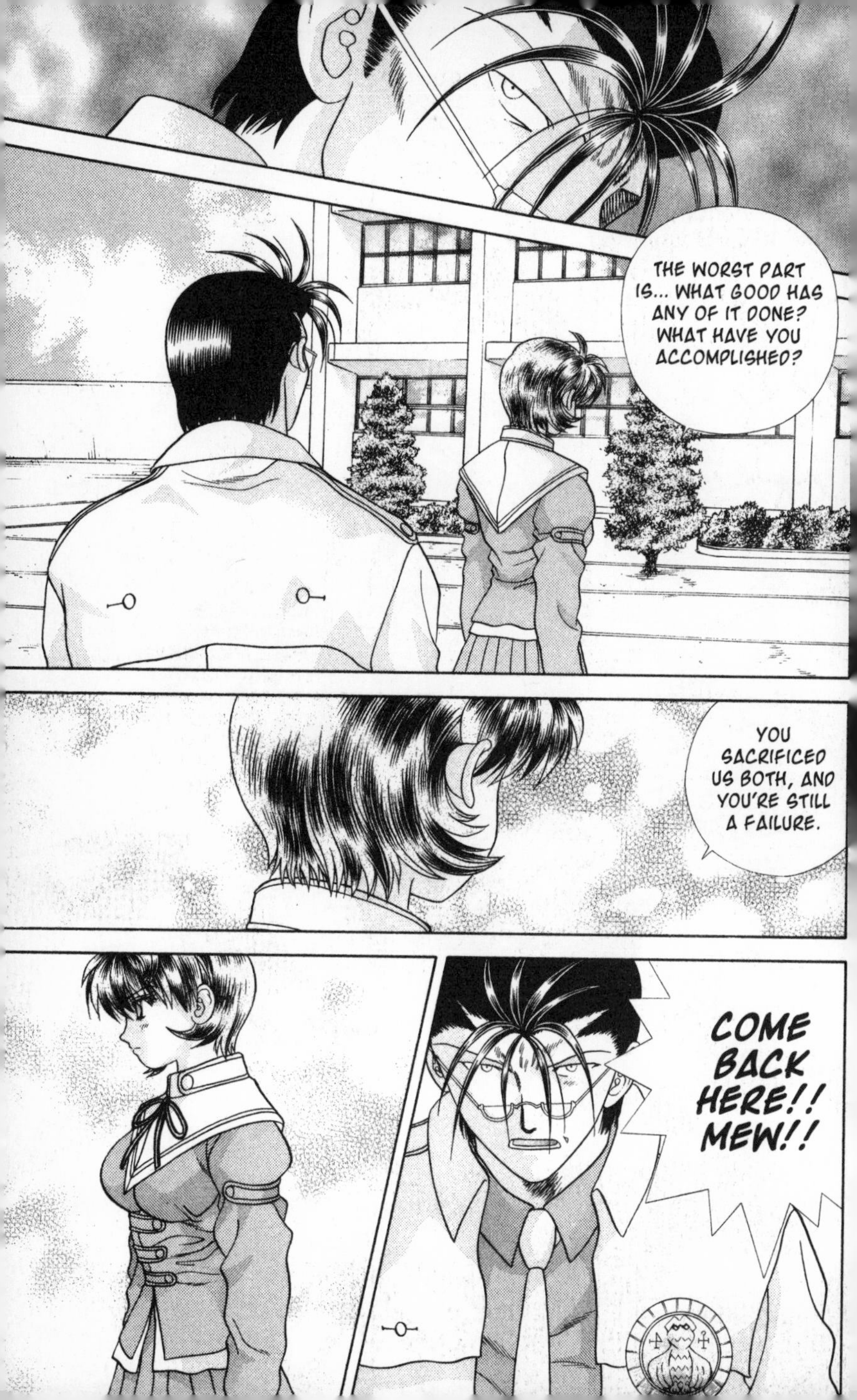
THE WORST PART IS... WHAT GOOD HAS ANY OF IT DONE? WHAT HAVE YOU ACCOMPLISHED?
YOU SACRIFICED US BOTH, AND YOU'RE STILL A FAILURE.
COME BACK HERE!! MEW!!

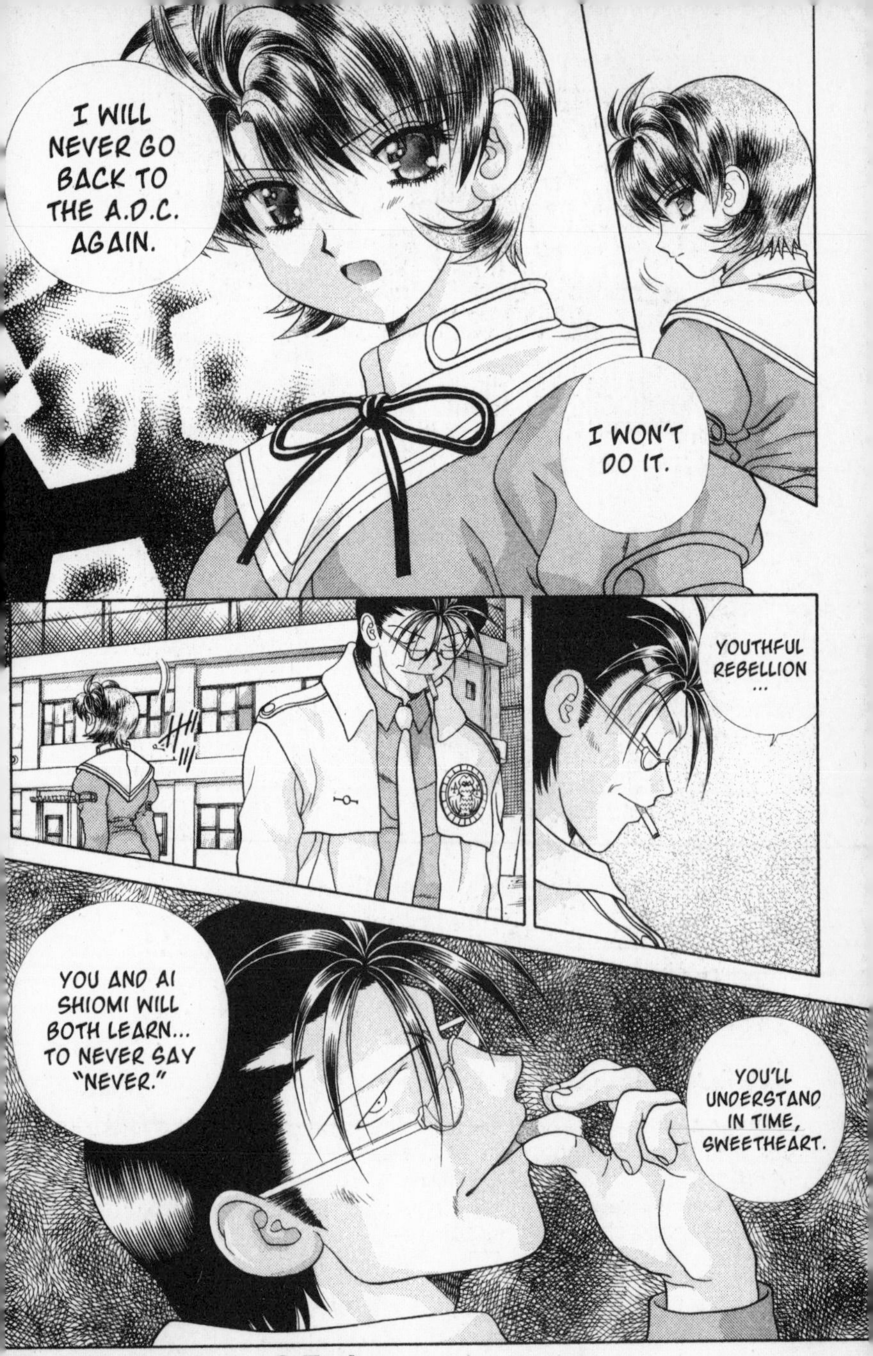
I WON'T DO IT.
I WILL NEVER GO BACK TO THE A.D.C. AGAIN.
YOUTHFUL REBELLION ...
YOU'LL UNDERSTAND IN TIME, SWEETHEART.
YOU AND AI SHIOMI WILL BOTH LEARN... TO NEVER SAY "NEVER."

Psychic Academy 8 End

PSYCHIC ACADEMY
TOKYOPOP
9
KATSU AKI

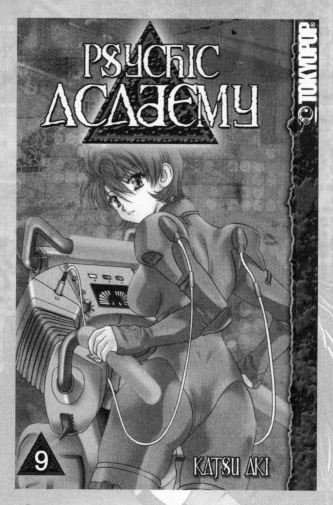

In the next volume...

Aura and "Aura" are different? Most people think of an aura as a sort of life energy emitted from humans and animals. That's different from the "Aura" in Psychic Academy. Our story has passed the turning point of the Para-dream and now heads toward the exciting climax!!

TOKYOPOP SHOP

WWW.TOKYOPOP.COM/SHOP

HOT NEWS!
Check out the **TOKYOPOP SHOP!** The world's best collection of manga in English is now available online in one place!

ARCANA

TOKYO MEW MEW A LA MODE

WWW.TOKYOPOP.COM/SHOP

MBQ and other hot titles are available at the store that never closes!

MBQ

- **LOOK FOR SPECIAL OFFERS**
- **PRE-ORDER UPCOMING RELEASES!**
- **COMPLETE YOUR COLLECTIONS**

SPOTLIGHT TOKYOPOP MANGA SUPPLEMENT

BECK: MONGOLIAN CHOP SQUAD

OT
OLDER TEEN
AGE 16+

ROCK IN MANGA!

BECK
MONGOLIAN CHOP SQUAD™
TOKYOPOP
1
Harold Sakuishi

Yukio Tanaka is one boring guy with no hobbies, a weak taste in music and only a small vestige of a personality. But his life is forever changed when he meets Ryusuke Minami, an unpredictable rocker with a cool dog named Beck. Recently returned to Japan from America, Ryusuke inspires Yukio to get into music, and the two begin a journey through the world of rock 'n' roll dreams! With cameos of music's greatest stars—from John Lennon to David Bowie—and homages to supergroups such as Led Zeppelin and Nirvana, anyone who's anyone can make an appearance in *Beck*...even Beck himself! With action, music and gobs of comedy, *Beck* puts the rock in manga!

HAROLD SAKUISHI'S HIGHLY ADDICTIVE MANGA SERIES THAT SPAWNED A HIT ANIME HAS FINALLY REACHED THE STATES!

FOR MORE INFORMATION VISIT: WWW.TOKYOPOP.COM

EDITORS' PICKS

TOKYOPOP MANGA SUPPLEMENT

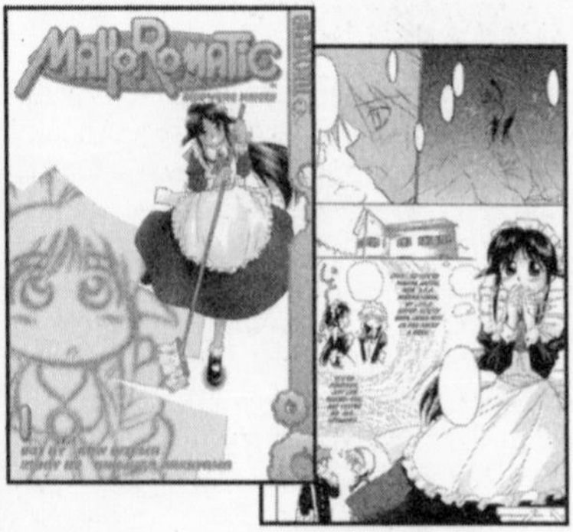

BY BUNJURO NAKAYAMA
AND BOW DITAMA

MAHOROMATIC: AUTOMATIC MAIDEN

Mahoro is a sweet, cute, female battle android who decides to go from mopping up alien invaders to mopping up after Suguru Misato, a teenaged orphan boy... and hilarity most definitely ensues. This series has great art and a slick story that easily switches from truly funny to downright heartwarming...but always with a large shadow looming over it. You see, only Mahoro knows that her days are quite literally numbered, and the end of each chapter lets you know exactly how much—or how little—time she has left!

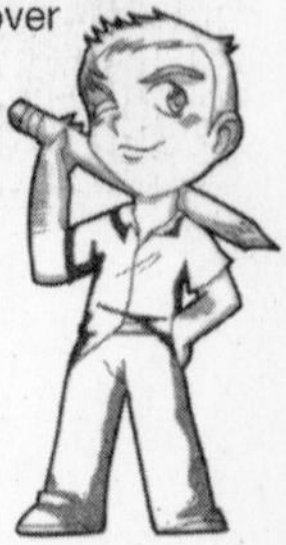

~Rob Tokar, Sr. Editor

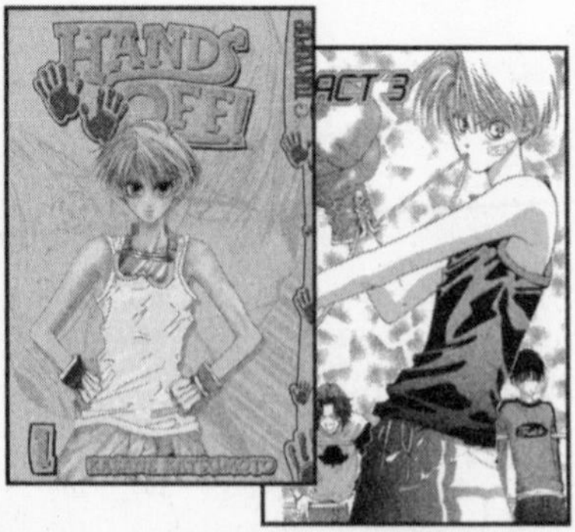
HANDS OFF!
ACT 3

BY KASANE KATSUMOTO

HANDS OFF!

Cute boys with ESP who share a special bond... If you think this is familiar (e.g. *Legal Drug*), well, you're wrong. *Hands Off!* totally stands alone as a unique and thoroughly enjoyable series. Kotarou and Tatsuki's (platonic!) relationship is complex, fascinating and heart-wrenching. Throw in Yuuto, the playboy who can read auras, and you've got a fantastic setup for drama and comedy, with incredible themes of friendship running throughout. Don't be put off by Kotarou's danger-magnet status, either. The episodic stuff gradually changes, and the full arc of the characters' development is well worth waiting for.

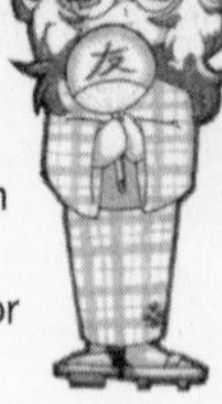

~Lillian Diaz-Przybyl, Jr. Editor